OF THE
BHĀGAVATA PURĀNA
OR
ESOTERIC HINDUISM

PURNENDU NARAYANA SINHA, M. A.,
B. L.

BENARES:
PRINTED BY FREEMAN & Co., LTD.,
AT THE TARA PRINTING WORKS.
1901.

To

ANNIE BESANT

THE BHĀGAVATA OF BHĀGAVATAS

THESE PAGES ARE RESPECTFULLY

DEDICATED

BY

HER MOST DEVOTED BROTHER.

"Let him kiss me with the kisses of his mouth: for thy love is better than wine.

"Because of the savour of thy good ointments thy name is as ointment poured forth, therefore do the virgins love thee.

"Tell me, O thou whom my soul loveth, where thou feedest, where thou makest thy flock to rest at noon; for why should I be as one that turneth aside by the flocks of thy companions?

"If thou know not, O thou fairest among women, go thy way forth by the footsteps of the flock, and feed thy kids beside the shepherds' tents."

THE SONG OF SOLOMON.

SPECIAL INTRODUCTION – BHAKTA JIM'S BHAGAVATAM CLASS

The *Srimad Bhagavatam* (AKA *Bhagavata Purana*) and I have a bit of a history. Back in 1978 I first came in contact with the Hare Krishna movement. The improbable story of how that happened and what it led to will be found in my book *The Life And Times Of Bhakta Jim.*

I was quite familiar with the *Bhagavata Purana* before I became seriously involved with the Hare Krishnas. My college library had a complete set of the books of the Hare Krishna movement, plus it had many other books on the subject of Indian religion and philosophy. I spent a lot of my free time in college reading these books. I found them compelling reading even though I couldn't fully believe in them. My first exposure to the *Bhagavata Purana* was through what we in the movement called *Krishna Book*, which was a summary of the tenth canto of the *Srimad Bhagavatam*. This book was all about the life of Krishna.

Back then *Krishna Book* came in three volumes and was lavishly illustrated. It had an introduction by George Harrison which promised that if you chanted the Hare Krishna mantra you would one day not only see God but would get to play with Him.

I also remember being surprised reading one of the chapter titles in the first volume, "Stealing the Garments of the Unmarried Gopi Girls". This turned out to be more of a childish prank by Krishna than anything else, but it did indicate that Krishna was a different concept of God than anything I had encountered before.

A Study Of The Bhagavata Purana Or Esoteric Hinduism is a translation of most of the *Bhagavata Purana*. It was published in 1901, apparently for the Theosophical Society, and was dedicated to one of its leaders, Annie Besant. I know very little about Annie Besant, but the idea that a woman could be a leader of a spiritual movement and be praised as the "Bhagavata of Bhagavatas" *back in 1901*, when Srila Prabhupada was only five years old, is quite remarkable. Women do not have leadership positions in the

Hare Krishna movement and are not generally praised for their spiritual advancement.

I dedicated *The Life And Times Of Bhakta Jim* in part to the women I knew at the Evanston Hare Krishna temple. That honor, such as it is, is more than any they are likely to get from the movement.

This translation by Purnendu Narayana Sinha is a worthy alternative to reading the complete one published by the Hare Krishna movement. That version is very expensive, has more volumes than an encyclopedia, and has elaborate (and frankly, repetitive) commentary on every verse. On the other hand this book benefits from commentary by Sridhara Swami and the thoughts of its translator, which for most readers should be more than enough. If after reading this you feel that he left out anything important you can check out the online version of the full translation that the Hare Krishna movement provides.

The Hare Krishna movement considers the *Bhagavata Purana* to be five thousand years old and infallible. I consider it a work of literature that is not nearly that old. (Scholars think it was written between the fifth and ninth centuries C.E.) While I think this book does as good a job of justifying God's ways to man as anything human minds have created, I know that it is absolutely wrong on many points, and might be wrong on many more.

I remember my reaction on reading the Fifth Canto of *Srimad Bhagavatam* in the college library. It describes the universe in a way that cannot be reconciled with reality. The Earth is flat, the Sun goes behind an enormous mountain at night, the Moon is farther away from the Earth than the Sun is, the Sun is the only source of light in the universe (the stars being planets that glow with reflected light), etc. It disturbed me that Srila Prabhupada believed the moon landings to be a hoax because the Fifth Canto described the Moon as a heavenly place where demigods lived, not the barren place the astronauts landed on.

The *Bhagavata Purana* is the book that introduces the character of Srimati Radharani. An earlier book, the *Harivamsa* describes most of the same events in Krishna's life that occur in the *Bhagavata Purana*, but while Krishna is described dancing with the Gopis no single Gopi is given special attention.

It is impossible to overstate the importance of the Gopis in the mythology of Krishna, and among the Gopis Srimati Radharani is supreme. She is worshiped alongside Krishna in every Vaishnava temple.

Having said that, there is reason for me to believe that the authors of the *Bhagavata Purana* never intended for her to be such an important character. Why do I say this? It is because she is *never named in the story.*

I cannot emphasize the importance of this detail enough. I am in a good position to recognize just how significant not giving her a name is.

I transcribed this book from page images from the Internet Archive. My donation to Project Gutenberg consisted of a plain text document and a web page, both automatically generated from a common source file. There are many, many family tree tables in this book. For the plain text version of the file I had to convert these diagrams into what is known as "ASCII art" and it was *not* fun.

When I prepared my submission to CreateSpace I wanted to add an index to the book, something the original book never had. To make an index you need to first make a list of all the words you want to index. I used a series of Linux commands to scan the plain text document looking for words that were not in the English spell checking dictionary. Another command counted how many times each of these words was used in the text and a third command sorted the list so the most used words came first. When I was finished I had a list of over four thousand words, the majority of them names. I got this list down to 435 names and technical terms that were used enough to be worth indexing. There is no shortage of names in the *Bhagavata Purana*. Even women's names are well represented. We can only assume that the authors of this book deliberately avoided naming Krishna's most favored Gopi.

To put this in Biblical terms, imagine that the part of the Bible that my mother refers to as "The Begats" ran on for hundreds of pages and the Blessed Mother was not referred to as Mary but only as "Jesus' Mom." That may give you some idea.

For an example of how strange it is that the Gopis are never named, imagine a New Testament where none of the twelve disciples is named.

Many of the Gopis would eventually be given names: in other Puranas, in the poetry of Jayadeva and Vidyapati, and in the plays of Rupa Goswami.

The Chaitanya movement (which the Hare Krishna movement is based on) considers the Gopis the most exalted worshipers of Krishna. They abandoned their husbands, their families, and their worldly duties to be with Krishna.

There is a story in the Gospel of Luke where a man wants to follow Jesus, but only after he buries his father. Jesus tells him that he must abandon such worldly duties and follow him immediately. The Gopis did not need to be told. When they heard Krishna's flute they came running, no matter what they might have been doing.

The *Bhagavata Purana* contains more than the life of Krishna. You will read of the origins of the Universe, the spiritual evolution of all living beings, the other avataras of Vishnu that incarnated themselves before Krishna, and much much more. There is plenty to interest the student of mythology, of philosophy, or anyone who enjoys high fantasy or just a good story.

This book is not simply a transcription of the original book. The original was very badly proofread and inadequately typeset. Names were not always spelled consistently either: Hiranyakasipu was spelled three different ways, sometimes on the same page. Five types of *mukti* were listed, but only four were defined in the footnotes. As for the typesetting, the author clearly wanted to use the macron to indicate a longer than usual vowel sound but was forced to settle for a combination of circumflexes for lower case characters and accents for upper case characters. This combination made an already error-filled book look even worse.

I have spent many hours correcting these errors and consider it a labor of love, even if the love fell short of actual *bhakti*.

While I am at best a lapsed Vaishnava I do have the desire to make the *Bhagavata Purana* more widely read. My donation to Project Gutenberg has been downloaded for free 703 times as I write this. That's a lot more transcendental literature than I ever distributed in the movement!

I cannot promise you that reading this book will make it possible for you to one day play with God. I left that path thirty years ago and can't imagine returning to it. But I *can* promise you some very interesting reading!

Bhakta Jim

PREFACE.

The Bhāgavata is the most popular of all Purānas and it is held in the highest esteem by Vaishnavas in all parts of India. It was the most authoritative book with such religious teachers as Shri Chaitanya. Several commentaries have been written on this great work. It is however strange that there has been so much discussion about the authoritative character of the work. The readers are all familiar with that discussion and I need not refer to it further than to say that the discussion does not in any way affect the intrinsic merit of the book, and the verdict of the public is so certain in this respect that the book will continue to be the most popular of all Purānas, despite any thing that may be said as to its authorship or the period of its appearance.

The Padma Purāna devotes a chapter to the worship of this Purāna and calls it the most exalted of all the Purānas and the book is actually worshipped in many Hindu houses. The Purāna is recited all over India by learned Pandits and Sādhus and its subject matter is familiar to every Hindu.

PROFESSOR WILSON SAYS: — "Bhāgavata is a work of great celebrity in India and exercises a more direct and powerful influence upon the opinions and feelings of the people than perhaps any other of the Purānas. It is placed fifth in all the lists but the Padma Purāna ranks it as the eighteenth, as the extracted substance of all the rest. According to the usual specification it consists of eighteen thousand slokas, distributed amongst three hundred and thirty-two chapters divided into twelve Skandhas or books. It is named Bhāgavata from its being dedicated to the glorification of Bhagavat or Vishnu."

Referring to the Tenth Skandha, Professor Wilson says "The tenth book is the characteristic part of the Purāna, and the portion upon which its popularity is founded. It has been translated into, perhaps, all the languages in India, and is a favourite work with all descriptions of people."

Much as the book commands the respect of the Hindus, it has brought upon itself the ridicule and sarcasm of those that attack Hinduism. It is the Tenth Skandha which has given the greatest handle to all adverse criticism and it is the one Skandha in the whole book which is so little understood by foreigners, unacquainted with the genius of the Hindu religion, particularly with its love aspect which is the peculium of all real devotees in every great religion. But the modern professors of great religions, being lost in their material surroundings, have entirely lost sight of that aspect. The songs of Solomon will stand out in all ages as an expression of enthusiastic and rapturous love of the human soul for the Divine Lord, whether the Christians of the modern day understand them or not. The Divvans and Sufis bore the highest love to their divine Lover, whether or not the Mohammedans of the present day follow the outpourings of their heart.

Love in religion is a Science. It is the natural outcome of the human soul, when it is freed from impurities and cured of distractions.

All religions speak of the purity of the mind, and they speak also of devotion to God or Īshvara. But no religion other than Hinduism treats of the gradual development of the mind as a Science, treats of its purification and then of its natural attraction for Īshvara and the final assimilation of human life to Isvaric life as the law of the Universe. And no book in Hinduism deals with the subject so systematically specially with reference to the history of the Universe, as the Bhāgavata Purāna does. I have tried to understand the book myself as an earnest student, with the light afforded by the book itself. I have been greatly helped in the understanding of of the book by the commentary of Śridhara Svāmi which is by common consent the most authoritative of all the commentaries on the Bhāgavata Purāna. Once a Pandita prided himself before Sri Chaitanya on his having put an interpretation upon a certain sloka of the Purāna different from that of Śridhara Svāmi. Now "Svāmi" is the designation of a learned Sanyassi, such as Śridhara Svāmi was and it also means a husband. Sri Chaitanya remarked "one that does not follow the Svāmi is unchaste." Such was the high opinion which the great Teacher held regarding Śridhara's commentary.

I have purposely avoided making any reference to the commentaries made by the followers of Srī Chaitanya as I intend to study them separately along with the teachings of his school.

The method of treatment followed in this study will speak for itself. I have separated the text from my own observations except in the introductory chapter and in the reference to Sukadeva in the chapter on Virāt Purusha, and one can follow the text itself, without accepting any of my own views. I believe I have faithfully reproduced the text in its essential features, I have omitted unimportant details, poetical descriptions, prayers and adorations, some of them most beautiful and sublime — and I have also omitted the introduction by Suta and his concluding words. Suta related the Purāna to Rishi Sounaka and others as he heard it from Sukadeva.

The proofs have passed through different hands and the transliteration of Sanskrit words has been differently made. For instance [Sanskrit Letter] has been rendered as s, ś, s and sh. Though I would prefer ś, the dash has been generally omitted, for the convenience of the printer. There have been also several mistakes in names.

My best thanks are due to the several gentlemen, who have gone through the proofs and specially to my friend Mr. Bertram Keightley M. A., who has gone through nearly the whole of the manuscripts.

Table of Contents

A Study Of The Bhagavata Purana Or Esoteric Hinduism

SKANDHA I.

THE IDEAL OF BHĀGAVATA PURĀNA: A DISCOURSE BETWEEN VYĀSA AND NĀRADA.

"I have duly respected the Vedas, the teachers and the sacrificial fire, I have put the sense of all the Vedas into the Mahābhārata and have made their sacred lore accessible to all classes of men. I have done all this, nay, much more. Still I think my work is not fully done." So thought Veda Vyāsa, the adept author of the Kali Yuga, while meditating on the sacred banks of the Sarasvati, and his heart became heavy with something, he knew not what. At this time Nārada appeared before him — Nārada, who knew all that transpired in the Trilokī and who could enter into the hearts of all beings. "Thou hast fully known," said Nārada, "all that is knowable, for thou hast written the excellent Mahābhārata, which leaves nothing unsaid. How is it then thou feelest dispirited as if thy object were not gained?" What could Vyāsa say in reply; he only inquired from the seer Nārada the cause of his uneasiness.

Nārada entered into a free criticism of the Bhagavat Gitā, the philosophical portion of the Mahābhārata, pointed out its shortcomings and suggested to

Vyāsa what next to do. A few remarks will be necessary to understand all this.

There are seven planes Bhūr, Bhuvar, Svar, Mahar, Jana, Tapas and Satya.

Bhūr is the terrestrial plane.

Bhuvar is the astral plane.

Svar is the plane of Kāma and desires.

These three planes, collectively known as Trilokī, are the planes of personality. Kāma is the guiding principle of existence in Trilokī, and a recurrence of births and re-births its main characteristic. With every Night of Brahmā, this triple plane comes to an end, transferring its energies to the next higher plane, and is re-born with every Day of Brahmā. Mahar is intermediate between Trilokī and the three higher Lokas of Universality.

The Vedic school laid great stress on communion with the Devas of Svar Loka or Svarga or Indra Loka, and this was pre-eminently known as Vedic Yajna. The performance of Vedic Yajna led only to a prolonged gratification of kāma in Svar Loka. But however long the period might be, it was limited by the magnitude of the force (Apūrva) which buoyed up the individuality in the Svar Loka. As the Gitā says, when the merits are exhausted the observer of Vedic Dharma enters again into the transitory plane. The course of births and re-births is then set up anew, with constant transformations and with all the miseries of existence conditioned by personality.

This was not Mukti or liberation. The followers of the post-vedic or Upanishad school contended that liberation lay in crossing the triple plane of individuality to the higher cosmic planes of universality. When an individual reaches the higher planes, he does not again become subject to transformations, and to the constant recurrence of births and re-births. There is one continued life, one continued existence in the higher planes, till the end of cosmos or the Life of Brahmā. This life is not measured by personalities but is the cosmical life, and the individuality becomes a cosmical entity. Further there is life also beyond the cosmos, in the highest plane, the abode of the Supreme.

The Gitā only incidentally describes the highest plane in the following sloka:

"That is my supreme abode, by reaching which (Jivas) do not recur (to fresh births). Not the Sun, not the Moon, not even fire illumines that." — XV. 6.

Krishna also refers to that plane in VIII. 20 and XV. 4. 5.

The Gitā lays down Nishkāma Karma, or the unselfish performance of the duties of life (Sva-dharma) as the first step towards reaching the higher planes. The sense of separateness is killed by Nishkāma Karma. Then the Gitā takes the disciple to Upāsanā or communion with the Purusha of the highest plane, but scarcely a glimpse is given of that plane and its surroundings. The Mahābhārata does not throw any light on the dwellers of the higher planes, nor does it give any details of those planes. Without any distinct prospect of trans-Trilokī life, one is asked to adhere to the duties appertaining to one's own sphere of life (Sva-dharma) and to perform those duties unselfishly. However transitory the things of Trilokī may be, there are attractions enough for the frail sons of Manu, abounding in passions and desires. What can then bind a man to the higher planes and the highest Purūsha of those planes or Bhagavān? It is only a description of the grandeur and the glory of those planes and of Bhagavān. Such description begets Bhakti or holy attachment, and it is this Bhakti which sets up a real communion with Bhagavān. Frail as man is, the mere performance of duties makes him attached to them, unless he is bound to the higher planes by the tie of holy attachment. The Gitā is however silent as to the attractions of the higher planes and of Bhagavān. This was the defect pointed out by Nārada.

"O thou great Muni, as thou hast treated of Dharma and of other things, so thou hast not recited the glory of Vāsudeva". — I. 5. 9.

"This universe is also an aspect of Bhagavān, for its creation, preservation and end proceed from Him. Thou knowest all this thyself. But thou hast shown to others only a portion of this truth." — I. 5. 20.

"Salutations to Thee, Bhagavān, let me meditate on Vāsudeva. Salutations to Pradyumna, Aniruddha and to Sankarshana. He who, by naming these *mūrtis* in the *mūrtiless*, whose only *mūrti* is mantra, makes offerings to Yajna Purusha, is the complete seer." — I. 5. 37-38. A mystery lies veiled in this Śloka.

But who is this Nārada? Why should we accept his authority? Nārada was therefore careful to give his own account, elaborated by the enquiries of Vyāsa. All students of occultism will do well to read carefully this account which forms a fitting preliminary to the Bhāgavata.

ACCOUNT OF NARADA.

SKANDHA I. CHAP. 5 & 6.

"In the previous Kalpa, in my former birth, I was born of a certain maid-servant of Vedic Rishis. Certain Yogis had collected at a place to pass the rainy season and I was engaged as a boy to serve them. Seeing me void of all fickleness as a boy and self-controlled, the Munis, who looked on all with equal eyes, were kind to me, especially as I gave up play, followed them, served them and talked little. With the permission of the regenerated I at one time partook of the remnants of their meal and the impurities of my mind were all removed. When thus my mind became pure, my inclination grew towards their Dharma. By their favor I heard them sing the beautiful stories of Krishna. Hearing those stories every day with faith, I gained holy love for Krishna. Through that love my mind became fixed in Him and I came to perceive my Sthūla and Sūkshma bodies as only false reflections of the real Self or Brahmā. The Bhakti that grew up in me destroyed my Rajas and Tamas. Then when the kind Rishis were about to leave the place, they imparted to me the most occult knowledge which had been given to them by Bhagavān himself. Through that knowledge I have known the Māyā of Bhagavān. It is by that knowledge that one reaches the plane of Bhagavān. As I cultivated this occult knowledge, Bhagavān appeared Himself and gave me knowledge and powers direct."

4

[Śridhara Svāmi, the commentator of Bhāgavata Purāna notes the following points in the above story (1) Sevā, *i.e.*, service of and attendance on Mahātmās, (2) their kripā or favor, (3) trust in their Dharma, (4) hearing the stories of Bhagavān, (5) attachment to Bhagavān, (6) knowledge of Self by the discrimination of the Sthūla and the Sūkshma body, (7) firm Bhakti, (8) knowledge of the reality of Bhagavān, (9) at the last the appearance of omniscience and other powers through the favor of Bhagavān.]

What followed then, inquired Vyāsa? Nārada continued:

"Sometime after my teachers, the Bhikshus, had gone away, my mother died of snake-bite. I deemed that an act of God and went towards the North. After crossing several forests, rivers and mountains, I at last reached a solitary forest and there sat under a pipal tree. As directed by my teachers, I meditated on self in self through self. My mind had been completely conquered by Bhakti. As I was devotedly meditating on the lotus feet of Bhagavān with tear-drops in my eyes, Hari gradually appeared in my heart. O Muni, the hairs of my body stood on end through exuberance of holy love, I was completely lost in joy and knew not either self or any other. The indescribable Īshvara spoke thus in solemn words:

"O thou that dost not deserve to see me in this life, I am difficult to be seen by imperfect Yogis, whose likes and dislikes have not been completely burnt up. I have shown myself to thee that thy Kāma may all be centred in me. When I am the object of Kāma, the Sādhu gives up all other desires. By prolonged service of Mahātmās, thy mind is firmly fixed in me. Therefore shalt thou give up this faulty body and acquire my companionship. The mind fixed in me is never destroyed in creation or in pralaya, nor does the memory fail.'"

"So saying Īshvara disappeared. In time, when I was drawn towards the pure body with which I was favored by Bhagavān, the body of my five Bhūtas fell down on the extinction of my Prārabdha Karma. When the Kalpa came to an end my new body was indrawn by the breath of Brahmā who was going to sleep. After one thousand Yuga Cycles, when Brahmā awoke and desired to create, I, Marichi, and other Rishis came out. Since then I have invariably observed Brahmācharya and through the favor of

Vishnu have been travelling all over Trilokī, both inside and outside, my passage being wholly unobstructed. The Devas gave me this Vinā which is adorned with Svara-Brahmā. By playing upon this Vinā I send forth songs of Hari all round. These songs are the only means of crossing the ocean of recurring lives."

[This is the mystery of Nārada as related in the Purānas. Nārada is the repository of occult knowledge from the previous Kalpa. The first and foremost adept of this Kalpa, his mission is to spread occult knowledge, by unceasingly playing on the seven musical notes. He is ever watchful and always bides his time in all cyclic changes. He is the only Rishi of whom the Vina is a constant accompaniment, as it is of the goddess Sarasvati. His sphere of action is Trilokī, and the dwellers of Bhūr, Bhuvar, and Svar alike respect him. He is the universal counsellor, even of the highest Devas and of the highest Rishis. His constant mission is the good of the Universe. One thing is said of him, that he sometimes serves his purpose by setting one against another and amongst the ignorant his name is a bye-word for quarrel. However that be, the greatest good of the Universe in this Kalpa has been always done by him. It is under his inspiration, that Valmiki and Vyāsa wrote their most occult works, and his benign influence is observed in all universal changes for good. The Bhāgavata recites his constant endeavours to do good and we shall consider them in detail hereafter.]

VIRAT PURUSHA.

SK. I. CH. 18 & SK. II. CH. I.

Vyāsa drew upon his inspiration and wrote the Bhāgavata. He taught this Purāna to his son, the wonderful Suka. Suka did not marry, as Rishis in his time did. He left his home and roamed about the world at large, stark naked. The separation was painful to Vyāsa and he went out in search of his son. While he passed near a tank, the Apsarasas, who were freely indulging in play, hastily drew up their clothes, feeling ashamed. "Strange!" exclaimed Vyāsa, "I am old and covered. But when my young son, wholly uncovered, went this way, you remained unmoved." And the Deva-ladies replied, "Thy son knows not man and woman, but thou knowest." This exalted Suka was the worthy propounder of the Bhāgavata Purāna.

Rājā Parikshit, son of Abhimanyu and grandson of Arjuna, the successor of Rājā Yudisthira on the throne of Hastināpura, forgot himself in a fit of anger and placed a dead serpent round the neck of a Rishi. For this he was cursed by the Rishi's son to meet with untimely death at the end of a week. The Rājā became penitent and deemed the curse an act of God. He prepared himself for death and took up his abode on the sacred banks of the Ganges in company with all the Rishis. The Rājā asked what a man on the point of death should do. The Rishis present could not give any satisfactory answer. At this time Suka appeared, followed by a host of boys, who took him to be a mad man. Suka was then only sixteen with long flowing hairs and well-built body, blooming with nature's beauty. All rose up as they saw the very young Rishi, and gave him the first seat. He related the Bhāgavata Purāna to Parikshit in seven days.

The Rājā repeated his question to Suka — "What is a dying man, specially one who desires to attain Moksha, to do? What are the duties of men and what are they not to do?"

Suka replied: — "A man on the approach of death is to give up all fear of death and is to cut off all likes and dislikes by dispassion. He is to leave his house, bathe in pure water and duly make his āsana in some solitary place. He is then to meditate on the three lettered Pranava with mind concentrated by Dhārāna and Dhyāna till he attains *samādhi*. If, however, his mind gets distracted by Rajas and Tamas, he is again and again to practise Dhārāna."

"What Dhārāna is it that speedily brings on concentration and purity of mind?" was the next question.

Suka replied: — "Dhārāna of the Sthūla aspect of Bhagavāna, by a fully controlled mind." He then went on dilating on the Sthūla or Universe aspect, called Virāt Purusha or Mahāpurusha. The present, the past, the future is manifest in that aspect. The Virāta Purusha is the soul of an Egg-like body with a seven-fold cover of earth, water, fire, air, ākasa, Ahankāra, and Mahat, respectively.

Pātāla is His feet, Rasātala His heels, Mahātala His ankles, Talātala His legs, Sutala His knees, Vitala the lower portion of His thighs, and Atala the upper portion.

Bhūr Loka is His loins, Bhuvar Loka His navel, Svar Loka His breast, Mahar Loka His throat, Jana Loka His mouth, Tapas Loka His forehead, and Satya Loka is the head of the thousand-headed Virāt Purusha. Indra and other Usra Devas (the world Usra meaning, literally, a ray of light) are his hands.

The Dik or space gods are his ears. The twin gods Asvini Kumāra are his nose.

Agni is His mouth.

The firmament is His eyes and the Sun-god His sight.

Day and night are His eye-lashes.

The graceful movement of His eye-brows is the abode of the Supreme.

Water is His palate, taste His tongue.

The Vedas are known as His Brahmā-randhra.

Yāma is His tusk.

The objects of affection are His teeth.

His enchanting smile is Māyā.

The endless creation is His side-glance.

His lower lip is shame, and the upper greed.

Dharma is His breast. Adharma His back.

Prajāpati is His generative organ.

The Mitrā-Varuna gods are His sense of taste.

The seas are His belly, the mountains His bony system and the rivers His veins and arteries.

The trees are the hairs of the Universe-bodied.

The powerful wind-god is His breath.

Time is His movement.

His play is the flow of Gunas.

The clouds are His hairs.

Twilight is His clothing.

Prakriti is His heart.

His manas is the moon, which is the source of all transformations.

Mahat is His Chitta.

Rudra is His Ahankāra.

Horses, mules, camels and elephants are His nails.

All the other animals are His loins.

The birds are His wonderful art.

He is the abode of Manu, Buddhi and Man.

Gandharva, Vidyādhara, Chārana and Apsaras are His musical notes.

The Asuras are His strength.

The Brāhmana is His mouth, the Kshatriya His hands, the Vaisya His thighs, and the black Sūdra His feet.

The Devas severally and collectively are His *havis* or sacrificial ghee, and yajna is His karma.

This is Virāt Purusha. This is how the Universe-aspect of Purusha is realised in meditation, more as a means of concentration, than as the end.

When the mind is sufficiently fixed by Dhārāna or contemplation of Virāt Purusha, it has next to meditate on the Purusha in the heart.

SKANDHA II.

THE PURUSHA IN ALL HEARTS.

SKANDHA II., CHAP. 2.

Some meditate within their own body on the Purusha of the size of
prādesa (the space of the thumb and forefinger) in the space covered by
the heart, who dwells there. He has four hands containing Sankha (conch),
chakra (a sharp circular missile), Gadā (club) and Padma (lotus). His face
is smiling, His eyes are as wide as lotus petals, and His cloth is yellow as
the filament of the Kadamba flower. His armlets glitter with gems and
gold. His crown and earrings sparkle with brilliant stones. Adepts in Yoga
place His feet on the pericarp of the full blown lotus in the heart. With Him
is Srī (Lakshmī). The Kaustubha gem is on His neck. He is adorned with a
garland of ever blooming wild flowers. His hair is curling and deep blue.
His very look is full of kindness to all.

As long as the mind is not fixed by Dhārāna, meditate on this form of
Īshvara, with the help of thy imagination. Concentrate your mind on one
limb after another, beginning with the feet of Vishnu and ending with His
smiling face. Try to grasp every limb in thought and then proceed to the
next-higher. But as long as Bhakti or Devotion is not developed, do not fail
to contemplate also on the Universe aspect of Purusha.

THE DEATH OF THE YOGI AND AFTER.

SKANDHA II., CHAP. 2.

When all desires are controlled by meditation, and the Yogi is lost in the contemplation of Vishnu, he sits in proper posture, pressing his feet against the anus and perseveringly draws the vital air upwards to the six centres. He draws the air in the navel centre (Manipur) to the cardiac plexus, thence to the plexus beneath the throat (Visúddha), thence gradually by intuition to the root of the palate. (Śridhara Svāmi calls this last the higher part of Visúddha chakra, and remarks that the vital air is not displaced from that position. This may be called the pharyngeal plexus.) Thence he takes the vital air to Ajna chakra, which is situated between the two eye-brows. Then he controls the seven holes (the ears, the eyes, the nostrils and the mouth). He then looks steadily for half a Muhurta, and if he has not a trace of desire left in him gives up the body and the Indriyas, passes out through the Brahmā-randhra and attains the state of Vishnu.

[It will be noticed above that six plexuses are mentioned other than the Sacral and the prostatic.

In the death of the desireless Yogi, there is no record of thereafter, for nothing is known beyond our cosmos.]

"But, O king," said Suka, "if the Yogi seeks for the highest cosmic state or for the roamings of aerial Siddhas over the whole of cosmos, in full control of the eight Siddhis, he will then take his Manas and Indriyas with him. It is said that these Masters of Yoga can move both inside and outside Trilokī, for their Linga Sarira consists of the atoms of air. The state attained by those that acquire Samādhi by Upāsana, Tapas and Yoga cannot be reached by Vedic Karma. In space when the Yogi moves towards the Brahmā Loka or Satya Loka, he first goes by means of his Sushumnā Nādi to Vaisvānara or the fire-god for the Sushumnā by its light extends beyond the body. His impurities being all washed away, he goes upwards to the Sisumāra Chakra of Hari (*i.e.*, up to the highest point of Trilokī, as will be explained afterwards). Then crossing that Chakra of Vishnu, which is the navel of the Universe, he reaches the Mahar Loka with his pure Linga Sarira. There the dwellers of Svarga cannot go. Mahar

Loka is the abode of Brahmāvids, where Bhrigu and other adepts who live for a whole Kalpa dwell.

"The Yogi remains in Mahar Loka till the end of the Kalpa, when, seeing the Trilokī burnt up by fire from the mouth of Ananta or Sankarshana, the fires reaching even Mahar Loka's he moves towards the abode of Paramesthi (Satya Loka or Brahmā Loka). This highest Loka lasts for two Parārddhas and is adorned by the chariots of the kings of Siddhas. There is no sorrow in Brahmā Loka, no infirmity, no death, no misery, no fear of any kind. But the Yogi suffers from mental pain caused by sympathy with those that suffer for their ignorance of the supreme state in the recurrence of births with their endless miseries.

"There are three courses for those that go to Brahmā Loka. Some by the excellence of their merits get responsible cosmical positions at the next Kalpa. Others remain in the Brahmā Loka till the end of the cosmos or Brahmānda. The Upāsakas of Bhagavān however may at their will pierce through the cosmos or Brahmānda and reach the trans-cosmic plane of Vishnu. The text goes on to say how this is done. The cosmos consists of seven Pātalas and seven Lokas, together forming the fourteen-fold Bhuvana, which extends over 50 Krores of Yojanas (1 Yojana = 8 miles). Surrounding this is a covering of the earthy principle, such as was not used up in the formation of the cosmos, extending over one krore of yojanas. (According to some this covering extends over 50 krores of yojanas.) The second cover is of water, extending over ten times as much space as earth, the third of fire, the fourth of air, the fifth of ākása, the sixth of Ahankāra, the seventh of Mahat, each covering ten times as much space as the one preceding. The eighth cover is Prakriti, which is all pervading. The Linga Sarira of the Yogi in passing through the earthy cover, becomes earthy, through water becomes watery, and through fire, fiery. With the fiery body he goes to the air cover and with the airy cover to the ākása cover. He passes also through the Tanmātras and senses them. He passes through Prāna itself and becomes all action. Having thus crossed the Sthūla and Sūkshma coverings, the Yogi reaches the sixth covering that of the Transformable or Ahankāra Tatva, which is the absorber of the Tanmātras and of the Indriyas. Thence he goes to Mahat Tatva and thence to Pradhāna, where all the Gunas find their resting place. Then becoming all

Pradhāna himself full of bliss, he attains with the exhaustion of all *upādhis* the trans-cosmic Atmā, which is Peace and Bliss.

"These are the two ways to Mukti, the one prompt and the other deferred as sung in the Vedas."

The following Diagram may be of some help in understanding the above:
—

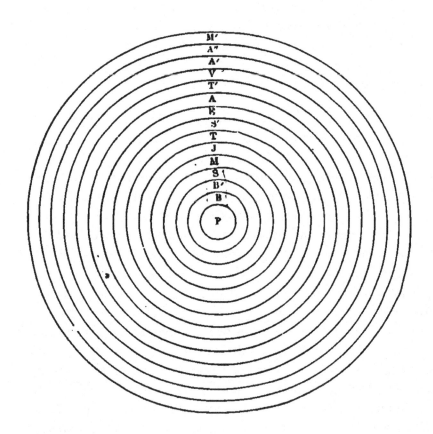

KEY TO THE CIRCLE.

M' = Mahat cover 1,000,000 Krores or 50,000,000 Krores Yojanas.

A" = Ahankāra cover 100,000 or 5,000,000 Krores Yojanas.

A' = Ākās cover 10,000 or 500,000 Krores Yojanas.

V = Vayu cover 1000 or 50.000 Krores Yojanas.

T' = Tejas cover 100 or 5000 Krores Yojanas.

A = Āpas cover 10 or 500 Krores Yojanas.

E = Earth cover 1 or 50 Krores Yojanas.

S'= Satya Loka

T = Tapas Loka

J = Jana Loka

M = Mahar Loka

S = Svar Loka

B' = Bhuvar Loka

B = Bhūr Loka

P = Seven Pātālas

S' to P = 50 Krores Yojanas.

A' to E = Includes Tanmatras, Indriyas and Prana.

Prakriti surrounds the whole circle.

WHAT MEN ARE TO DO AND WHAT THEY ARE NOT TO DO.

SKANDHA II. CHAP. 3.

This was the second part of Parikshit's question, and to this general question, the answer is also general. Those that want divine glory worship Brahmā. Those that want their Indriyas to be powerful worship Indra and so on. But those that are desirous of Moksha must practise Bhakti Yoga towards the supreme Purusha. Of all Upasakas, this is the only means of attaining supreme bliss, unswerving Bhakti or devotion to Bhagavān and the company of Bhāgavatas.

THE BHAGĀVATA PURĀNA AS RELATED BY BRAHMĀ TO NĀRADA.

SKANDHA II. CHAP. 4-6.

I. THE CREATION.

Parikshit next asked "How did Bhagavān create this Universe, how does He preserve it, how will He draw it in? What are the Śaktis by which He manifests Himself directly and indirectly? What are His actions?"

Suka replied, these were the very questions asked by Nārada of his father Brahmā.

Brahmā replied: — "Wishing to become manifold, the Lord of Māyā, influenced Kala, Karma and Svabhāva, by his own Māyā". (Kala is the flow of Time and is, according to the Bhāgavata Purāna, the Śakti of Purusha. Karma is the *adrishta* of Jiva or the Jiva record of the previous Kalpa. Svabhāva is the essence of Prakriti). Under the influence of Purusha, the first disturbance in the equilibrium of the Gunas follows from Kala, transformation follows from Svabhāva and the development of Mahat Tatva follows from Karma. When Rajas and Tamas manifest themselves in Mahat Tatva, it is transformed into Ahankāra Tatva, with predominant Tamas. Ahankāra Tatva by transformation becomes threefold.

16

— Sātvika, Rājasika and Tāmasika, i.e., Jnāna Śakti (potency to produce the Devas), Kriyā Śakti (potency to produce the Indriyas), and Dravya Śakti (potency to produce the Bhūtas), respectively.

Tāmasa Ahankāra was first transformed into Ākása, Ākása into Vayu, Vayu into Agni, Agni into Āpas, and Āpas into Prithivi, Sātvika Ahankāra was transformed into Manas and the ten Vaikārika Devas.

[The Vaikārika Devas are the Adhidevas or the Energy-giving gods of the ten Indriyas. Sensing is *in* Man or Adhi-Ātmā, it is of the object or Adhi-bhuta and is *caused by*Vaikarika Deva or Adhi-Deva. Thus the object seen is Adhi-bhūta, the sight is Adhyātma and the manifesting Energy of sight is Adhideva.]

The Vaikārika Devas are —

Dik for Hearing;

Vayu for Touch;

Sun for Sight;

Varuna for Taste;

Asvini Kumāras for Smell;

Agni for Speech;

Indra for Pani or action of the hand;

Upendra or Vishnu for Pada or action of the foot;

Mitra or Yāma for Payu or excretion;

and Prajāpati for Upastha or generation.

Rājasika Ahankāra was transformed into the ten Indriyas.

The foregoing can be shown in the following table: —

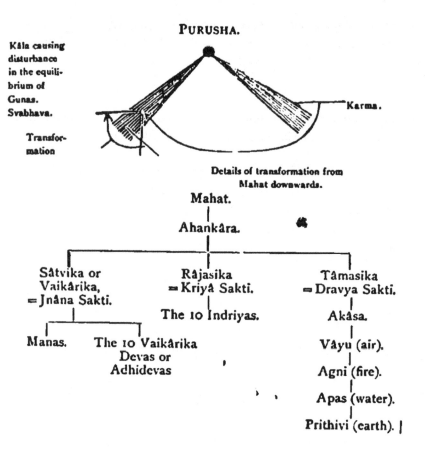

PURUSHA.

Kâla causing disturbance in the equilibrium of Gunas. Svabhava.

Transformation

Karma.

Details of transformation from Mahat downwards.

Mahat.

Ahankâra.

Sâtvika or Vaikârika, = Jnâna Sakti.

Râjasika = Kriyâ Sakti.

Tâmasika = Dravya Sakti.

The 10 Indriyas.

Akâsa.

Manas.   The 10 Vaikârika Devas or Adhidevas

Vâyu (air).

Agni (fire).

Apas (water).

Prithivi (earth). |

This is the Kârana creation or the creation of the materials of the Individual creation. They could not, however, unite and proceed further with the work of creation. The Śakti of Bhagavān then permeated them and the cosmic Egg or Brahmānda was formed. The Egg remained for a thousand years unconsciously submerged in the primal waters. Purusha then influenced Kāla, Karma and Svabhāva to send forth vitality into it. It is this Purusha that emerged from the Egg with thousands of heads and thousands of limbs and is known as Virāt Purusha. The seven Lokas and the seven Pātālas are parts of His body. This is the first Avatāra, the Ādi Purusha that creates, preserves and destroys. All the objects of creation are His Avatāras, or Śaktis or Vibhutis. The Lilā Avatārs of Virāt Purusha or special Incarnations for the preservation of the Universe are detailed below.

II. PRESERVATION BY LILĀ AVATĀRAS.

SKANDHA II. CHAP. 7.

1. *Varāha* — In order to raise the Earth from the waters, the Purusha adopted the body of Varāha or Boar and killed with His tusks the first Daitya Hiranyāksha.

2. *Yajna* — was born of Ruchi and Ākuti. The Suyama Devas were born of Yajna. He dispelled the fears of Trilokī.

3. *Kapila* — was born of Kardama Prajāpati and his wife Devahūti. He taught Brahmā Vidyā to his mother.

4. *Dattātreya* — He preached Yoga to his disciples, who acquired powers and became liberated.

5. *The Kumāras.* — Sanat Kumāra, Sanaka, Sanandana and Sanātana. They completely promulgated the Ātmā Vidyā, which had been lost in Pralaya.

6. *Nara Nārāyana.* — They were born of Dharma and his wife Murti, daughter of Daksha. Their Tapas was so great that the Deva ladies could not shake it.

7. *Dhruva.* — Though a boy, he could not bear the words of his step-mother. He went into the forests and made Tapas. He was rewarded with ascent to Dhruva Loka or the region of the polar star.

8. *Prithu.* — He milked out riches and edibles from the earth.

9. *Rishabha.* — Rishabha was the son of Nàbhi by Sudevi or Meru Devi. He roamed about as Parama Hansa.

10. *Hayagrīva.* — This horse-headed Avatāra appeared in the Vedic Yajna and promulgated the Vedas.

11. *Matsya.* — Vaivasvata Mann found out this Avatāra at the end of a cycle of Yugas. He preserved all beings and the Vedas from the waters of the Deluge.

12. *Kūrma.* — At the great churning of the Ocean, the Tortoise Avatāra supported the Mandāra mountain.

13. *Nrisinha.* — The Man-Lion Avatāra killed Hiranyakāsīpu.

14. *Hari* — saved the Elephant King of the famous story of Gajendra Moksha.

15. *Vāmana* — measured the Trilokī by His two steps.

16. *Hansa* — related Bhakti Yoga, Gnana and Bhāgavata Purāna to Nārada.

17. The presiding deity of each Manvantara.

18. *Dhanvantari* — promulgated the science of medicine.

19. *Parasu Rāma* — suppressed the Kshatriyas who became disregardful of the Brāhmanas and the Sāstras.

20. *Rāma* — destroyed Lankā and killed Rāvana.

21. *Rāma* and *Krishna.* — The tenth Canto of Bhāgavata is entirely devoted to their deeds.

22. *Vyāsa.* — He divided the trunk of the Veda tree into several branches.

23. *Buddha.* — When the Asuras came to know the Vedic mysteries and to oppress people, Buddha incarnated Himself in order to confound them by preaching a variety of by-religions.

24. *Kalki* — will appear before the end of Kali Yuga, to set things right.

Besides these Lila Avatāras, there are Māyā Guna Avatāras and Vibhūtis or Śaktis.

In *creation* these are:

Tapas, Brahmā, the Rishis, and the Nine Prajāpatis.

In *preservation* they are:

Dharma, Vishnu, Manu, Devas and Kings.

In *Pralaya* they are:

Adharma, Śiva, Serpents and Asuras.

O Nārada, this is, in brief, the Bhāgavata Purāna. You relate it to others in a much more expanded form, so that people may have Bhakti or Divine attachment to Bhagavān.

THOUGHTS ON THE ABOVE.

The above account of creation relates to Trilokī and to the dwellers of Trilokī. After creation, some come down from the higher planes and hold responsible positions as we have already seen. The Vaikārika Devas, who may be identified with the Vedic Devas, are created or rather manifested in the Trilokī before the Individual creation. They appertain to what the Purāna calls Kārana or causal Creation. The Vaikritika Devas and Deva Yonis, known as Elemental in Theosophical language, are created according to their Karma in the previous Kalpa and are subject to gradual evolution during the Kalpa. The Vaikarika Devas, however, remain as they are during the whole of the Kalpa. Similarly the Devas of the higher planes, e. g., Kumudas, Ribhus, Pratardanas, Anjanābhas and Pratitābhas of Mahar Loka, Brahma Purohitas, Brahma Kayikas, Brahma Mahā Kayikas and Amaras of Jana Loka, Ābhasvaras, Mahābhasvaras, and Satya Mahābhasvaras of Tapas Loka and Achyutas, Súddha Nibāsas, Satyābhas and Sanjnā Sanjnins of Satya Loka these are not affected by creation in Trilokī. The dwellers of those Lokas other than Devas are also similarly not affected. The story of creation is a simple one. As the Linga Purāna says, when Earth is scorched up in the summer season, it becomes fallow and the roots of vegetation remain underground. They, however, wait for the rainy season to germinate again and grow in all the varieties of the previous vegetation. Similarly when the previous creation is burnt up by the fires of Pralaya, the roots remain imbedded in Prakriti, which becomes fallow. The fallowness is removed on the approach of the creative period or Kāla. Kāla, according to Bhāgavata, is a Śakti of Purush or the Unmanifested Logos. Then transformation follows in Prakriti according to Svabhāva or the inherent nature of Prakriti and Karma, or the root-record of the previous Kalpa gives shape to the transformation.

Śridhara Svāmi quotes a sloka, which says that there are three Purusha manifestations. The first Purusha is the creator of Mahat and other elemental principles (Tatvas). The Second Purusha is the dweller of the Cosmic Egg. The Third Purusha is the pervader of all beings.

Creation is divided into two stages. First the creation of the principles themselves or Tatvas, which unite to form globes and individuals. This is called Kārana creation. Secondly the creation of individuals and of globes. This is called Kārya or resultant creation. Following the law of periodicity, the First Purusha energises the latent Karma or Jiva-record of the previous Kalpa, and prepares the ground for the development of that Karma, by setting Prakriti into active transformation. This is the First Life Wave which caused the principles to appear by themselves. The First Purusha permeated these principles as pure Ātmā.

But the principles could not unite to make the forms, and to make individuals and globes. Purusha, as pure Ātmā could not guide them further, as the gulf between Purusha and Prakriti was too wide. So Purusha had to limit Himself further, by uniting with Mūla Prakriti, as one undivided whole, and so becoming the guiding principle of all individual workings in our universe, the pervader of all individuals and globes as Ātma-Buddhi. The Universe as a whole is represented as an Egg, and the Second Purusha or Virāt Purusha is the soul of that Egg. Individuals and globes appear as germs in that Egg, and are all brought into manifestation in time by the Third Purusha Brahmā.

The Second Purusha is called the First Avatāra and the seed and resting place of all other Avatāras. An Avatāra is a highly evolved Jiva, that has attained the Logoic state and that *comes down* from his exalted position, to serve the universe. Why is the second Purusha called an Avatāra? The Brihad Āranyaka Upanishad raises the veil a little on this point.

"This was before Ātmā, bearing the shape of man (the first born from the Egg, the embodied soul, the Virāt with heads and other members of the body) Looking round, he beheld nothing, but himself. He said first: 'This am I'. Hence the name of I was produced.

"*And because he, as the first of all of them consumed by fire all the sins, therefore he is called Purusha. He verily consumes him, who strives to obtain the state of Prajāpati, prior to him.*" Sankarāchārya explains the under-lined portion as follows: — "And because he, "Prajāpati in a former birth, which is the cause, as the first of those who were desirous to obtain the state of Prajāpati by the exercise of reflection on works and knowledge, viz, "as the first of all of them," of all those desirous of obtaining the state of Prajāpati, consumed by the perfect exercise of reflection in works and knowledge all the sins of contact, which are obstacles to the acquirement of the state 'of Prajāpati' because such was the case, therefore he is called Purusha, because, he, *pur* (first) (did) *ush* (burn)

Therefore by the words: "He consumes him," it is meant, that the perfect performer obtains the highest state of Prajāpati, he, who is less perfect, does not obtain it, and by no means, that the less perfect performer is actually consumed by the perfect.

Here the word Prajāpati refers to the Second Purusha.

The state of the Second Purusha is the highest achievement of Jiva. It is the meeting ground of Jiva and the Supreme Purusha. The Second Purusha may be different for each Kalpa, it may be for each Brahmānda. He is the Īshvara, the Lord of our Universe. He holds the whole creation unto His bosom, and is the sustaining force of all. In the three aspects of Brahmā, Vishnu and Śiva, he guides the creation, the preservation and the dissolution of the Universe. Those that could not attain His state, though they strove for it equally as eminent as the Second Purusha, that are to become the Second Purusha in perhaps another Kalpa or Brahmānda, are the Lilā Avatāras. They remain merged in the Second Purusha or Īshvara and they manifest themselves in the Universe, only when a necessity arises for their manifestation. The Bhāgavata contends that of all Lila Avatāras, only Krishna is Purusha Himself the others being only partial manifestations of Purusha.

"These are the parts and aspects of Purusha. Krishna is Bhagavān Himself." — I-3-28.

Tamas is dark, opaque and heavy on the physical plane, indolent and ignorant on the mental plane, non-perceptive on the spiritual plane.

Rajas is translucent, and constantly moving on the physical plane; distracted constantly, acquiring likes and dislikes, and exercising intellection on the mental plane; and partially perceptive on the spiritual plane.

Satva is light and transparent on the physical plane, cheerful and buoyant on the mental plane, and fully perceptive on the spiritual plane. True perception and real knowledge follow from Satva. By partial understanding and semblance of knowledge, the results of Rajas, people become distracted and led astray.

Tamas keeps down all beings and enchains them to materiality in the course of evolution, and there is a point in the downfall of beings as well as of globes, beyond which there is a complete break-down. Satva counteracts Tamas and the preservation and improvement of the Universe, rather of Trilokī, there fore mean the infusion of Satva. Vishnu represents Satva and so Vishnu is the Preservative aspect of Virāta Purusha. When Rajas and Tamas predominate in Trilokī, when the lowest plane Bhūr becomes heavy with Tamas, the Lilā Avatāras appear and infuse Satva into the Lokas.

आबयत्येष सत्वेन लोकान्वैल्ओकमावनः ।
लीलअवताराजुलतो देवतिर्ब्ङमतादियु ॥

SKANDHA I., CHAP. 2-34.

This Preserver of Lokas preserves the Lokas by means of Satva, by incarnating in Deva, Animal, Human and other kingdoms as Lilā Avatāras.

The Third Purusha is Brahmā in Creation, Vishnu in Preservation and Śiva in dissolution. Vishnu as the Ātmā in each being manifests Himself in action consciousness and will. Brahmā is the propelling power in the Involution of beings, which gives them their physical body. Vishnu is the propelling force in the evolution of beings through physiological action (Prāna), sensation, intellect, and lastly the development of the spiritual faculties.

THE BHĀGAVATA PURĀNA AND ITS PARTS.

SKANDHA II., CHAP. 10.

The next question of Rājā Parikshit was most comprehensive. It related to all knowledge of the Universe in all details. In answering the question, Suka related the whole of the Purāna, from beginning to end. In doing so, the Muni gave a short introduction as to the history of the Purāna. When Brahmā regained his drowsy consciousness at the dawn of the present Kalpa, he knew not how to bring back the former state of things. He practised Tapas. Then Bhagavān appeared and related to him the Bhāgavata Purāna. Brahmā taught the Purāna to his son Nārada. Nārada gave it to Vyāsa, and Vyāsa to his son Suka.

The Purāna has ten parts: —

1. *Sarga* — the creation of the Bhūtas, Tanmātras, Indriyas, Ahankāra and Mahat, or of the materials that form individuals, and the appearance of Virāt Purusha.

2. *Visarga* — the Individual creation by Brahmā or the creation of the individual life forms.

3. *Sthāna* — the preservation of the created beings in their own states by Bhagavān.

4. *Poshana* — the divine favor to those that properly remain in their own states.

5. *Manvantara* — the duties of the Rulers of Manvantaras.

6. *Uti* — desires that bind one to Trilokī.

7. *Isānukathā* — stories of the Avatāras and of the followers of Hari.

8. *Nirodha* — the sleep of Hari and of all individual souls a Pralaya.

9. *Mukti* — the continued perception of the identity of self and of Brahmā.

10. *Asraya* — The Final Resort, Para Brahma or Paramātma from whom Creation and Dissolution both proceed.

This brings us to the end of the Second Skandha.

SKANDHA III.

BHĀGAVATA AS RELATED BY MAITREYA TO VIDURA.

The Third and Fourth Branches of the Bhāgavata are related by Maitreya to Vidura. Maitreya was the disciple of Parāsara, father of Vyāsa. Parāsara learned the Purāna from Sānkhyāyana, Sānkhyāyana from Sanat Kumāra and Sanat Kumāra from Atlanta Deva.

I. — THE CREATION

SKANDHA III., CHAP. 5-6.

At Pralaya, the Śakti of Bhagavān was asleep. That Śakti is Māyā, which is Sat-asat or Existing-nonexisting. Existing eternally as root, and not so existing as forms. Following the law of Periodicity (Kāla), Purusha fecundated Māyā. Mahat and other principles appeared by transformation. All these principles were Devas, having in them germs of consciousness, action and transformation. They could not unite to form the Universe, being divergent in character. They prayed to Īshvara for power to unite. Taking Prakriti as a part (Śakti) of Him, Īshvara entered into the 23 Tatvas or root principles. He awakened the Karma that remained latent in them. By Kriyā Śakti, He then united then. The 23 Tatvas, acting under Divine

27

Energy and the impulse of Karma that had remained latent in them, formed the Virāt body, each bearing its own share in the work. The Purusha within this body — Virāt Purusha or Hiranya Purusha — with all beings and globes included in Him, dwelt for one thousand years in the waters (like the embryo in the waters of the uterus.) This Embryonic Purusha divided self by self, onefold by Daiva Śakti, tenfold by Kriyā Śakti and threefold by Ātmā Śakti. The onefold division is in the Heart. The tenfold division is in the Prānas (Prāna, Apāna, Samāna, Udāna, Vyāna, Nāga, Kūrma, Krikara, Devadatta and Dhananjaya,) for the Prānas are not Tatvas or principles, but they form an aspect of Purusha. The threefold division is Ātmā in every being which is triune with its three sides — Adhyātma, Adhibhūta and Adhidaiva. The Purusha infused His Śakti into the Virāt body, for the development of powers in the Tatvas. The Adhyātma mouth appeared with its Adhibhūta speech and Adhidaiva Agni. Similarly the following appeared: —

Adhyātma.	Adhibhūta.	Adhidaiva.
Tongue	Rāsa (taste)	Varuna.
Nose	Gandha(smell)	Asvini Kumāras.
Eye	Rūpa(sight)	Āditya.
Skin	Sparsa (touch)	Vayu.
Ear	Sabda (sound)	Dik.
Epidermis	Sting	Gods of vegetation
Upastha		
(generative organ)	Generation	Prajāpati.
Pāyu	Secretion	Mitra
Hand	Actions of hand	Indra.
Pāda (foot)	Movements of foot	Vishnu.
Buddhi	Bodh (deliberation)	Brahmā.
Manas	Sankalpa and Vikalpa (true and false perception)	Moon.
Ahankāra	Aham perception	Rudra.
Chitta	Thought	Brahmā

The Trilokī also appeared, Svar from the head, Bhuvar from the navel and Bhūr from the feet. With these Lokas appeared the Devas and other beings, who are the transformations of the Gunas. From the predominance of Satva, the Devas went to Svar Loka. Men and the lower Kingdoms entered Bhūr Loka from the predominance of Rajas in them. By the predominance of Tamas, the different classes of Bhūtas remained in Bhuvar Loka. The Brāhmana appeared from the mouth, the Kshatriya from the hands, the Vaisya from the thighs and the Sūdra from the feet.

THOUGHTS ON THE ABOVE

We have considered the manifested Logos in the Universe. We shall now consider His manifestation in Man, the microcosm. The teachings are all collected from the Upanishads.

(i.) — *The manifestation in the heart.* — A detailed knowledge of this manifestation is called Dahara Vidyā in Chandogya. The Upanishads speaks of Ātmā in the cavity of the heart.

गुहाहितं गह्वरेष्ठं पुराणं ।

"Guhahitam Gahvarestham Purānam" is a well-known passage from the Upanishads. The Purusha in the heart is also called Prādesa or the span-sized Purusha and is the favourite object of meditation in Paurānika Upāsanā. The Upanishads call Him thumb-sized and there is an interesting discussion as to the size in Sāriraka Sutras I-3-24 to 26 and the Bhāshya thereupon.

(ii.) — *The Manifestation in the Prānas.* — The Upanishads say: —

सएव प्राण एव प्रज्ञात्मानन्दो ऽजरो ऽमृतः ।

"It is this Prana that is consciousness itself, Bliss, without infirmities and death."

तेषा एते पञ्चब्रह्म पुरुषाः ।

"They are these five Brahmā Purushas."

Again —

Again— हृदय स्खषिषु ब्रह्म पुरुषः ।

"Brahmā Purusha in the openings of the heart." The heart is called the abode of Brahmā. There are five openings of this abode of Brahmā and there are five gate-keepers. These gate-keepers or *dvāra-pālas* are the five Prānas. They are called Brahmā Purushas as they pertain to Brahmā. As long as the king is in the heart, the doorkeepers remain in the body. These door-keepers being inevitable accompaniments of Brahmā in the heart, are also themselves the outer aspects of Brahmā.

(iii.) — *The manifestation as Ātmā which is triune.* What is a man but a bundle of experiences on the planes of Jāgrat, Svapna and Sushupti. Each of these experiences has a threefold aspect or in Vedāntic expression is a Triputi. These aspects are:

1. the object experienced or Adhibhūta,

2. the experience itself or Adhyātma,

3. and the Deva which gives the consciousness of that experience or Adhidaiva.

In material expression, the object outside is Adhibhūta. The reception of its image is Adhyātma. The light that shews the image to be what it is, is Adhidaiva. As we have said, each experience is a three-sided triangle. All the triangles in the Jagrat state, analysed by the Vedāntins into fourteen, are represented by the first letter *a* in Pranava. All the triangles or Triputis in the dream state are represented by the second letter *u*. In Tāraka Brahmā Yoga, *a* is merged in contemplation into *u*, and *u* is merged into *ma*. In *ma* there is only one triangle, which is the primary triangle to which all other triangles in *a* and *u* may be reduced. The Adhibhūta side of this triangle is *ānanda* by the *vritti* of Avidyā. The Adhyātma side is the *vritti* of Avidyā. The Adhidaiva side is Īshvara. Life in Trilokī is conditioned by this triangle. The object of Tāraka Brahmā Yoga is to cross the Triptiti, to cross the three letters of Pranava. It is only in the fourth *pāda* of Pranava that he finds his resting place, that pāda being situated beyond the Trilokī.

The three manifestations of the Third Purusha in Jivas or individuals, may be said to relate to their different stages of evolution. Thus Prāna manifests itself only in the lower life kingdoms, the minerals and vegetables. The Prāna or life process is more elaborate in the vegetables than in the minerals. Purusha then manifests itself in the senses and emotions in the Animal kingdom and in intellect in the lower human kingdom the manifestation being three fold.

The last manifestation of Purusha, the one-fold manifestation in the heart, is in higher man.

II. — VASUDEVA AND SANKARSHANA.

SKANDHA III., CHAP. 8.

When this universe remained submerged in the waters of Pralaya, the eyes of Vāsudeva remained closed in sleep. He opened His eyes, lying down on the Serpent King Ananta or Sankarshana. He indulged in self and was without action. Inside His body was Bhuta-Sūkshma or all beings in a subtle state of latency. Only Kāla-Śakti manifested itself and He dwelt in those waters in self, as fire remains in wood, with powers controlled. Having slept for one thousand Yuga cycles in the waters, with only Kāla-Śakti manifesting His work, He found the lotuses of the Lokas in His body. He then looked at the Sūkshma, that was within Him. That Sūkshma became pierced with Kāla — propelled Rajas, and small as it was, it came out of his navel region. By the action of Kala, which awakens Karma, it suddenly grew up into a lotus bud. Vishnu entered this Loka Padma or the Lotus of Lokas. Brahmā then appeared in that Lotus. He looked on all sides and became four-faced, but he could not find out the Lokas. Though he was in the Lotus himself, confused as he was, he knew not the whole Lotus. Whence am I? Whence is this Lotus? So thought Brahmā. And he searched below to feel the lotus-stalk. The search was vain for one hundred years.

For another hundred years he meditated within self, and lo! there appeared within his heart one *Purusha* lying down on the body of Sesha (the serpent king). (The description of the Purusha is much the same as we have read of the *Prādesa Purusha*. So it is not given here.) Brahmā prayed to that Purusha and was told to practise Tapas for acquiring the power of creation.

III. — THE CREATION BY BRAHMA.

SKANDHA III., CHAP. 10.

When Bhagavān disappeared, Brahmā, as directed, practised meditation for one hundred Deva-years. He found his lotus abode moved by air. With all the power acquired by *Ātmā Vidyā* and *Tapas,* he drank up all the waters and the air. He found the *Lokas* attached to the overspreading Lotus and he had only to divide them. He entered into the Lotus bud and divided it into three parts — the *Trilokī.* This is the creation of the *Trilokī.* The higher Lokas (Mahar, Jana, Tapas and Satya) are the transformations of *Nishkama Karma* or unselfish action. So they are not destroyed in each Kalpa, but they last for two Parardhas.

"What is Kāla", asked Vidura, "that has been described as a *Śakti of Hari?*"

"*Kāla* is the disturber of *Gunas*", replied Maitreya, "causing transformations. In itself it is without any particularity and is without beginning or end.

"With Kāla as the Nimitta or efficient cause, Bhagavān only manifested Himself. The Universe has no separate existence from that of Brahmā. It is only Kāla that makes the Universe manifest."

The Creation of Brahmā is ninefold, Prākrita and Vaikrita, Prākrita-Vaikrita being the tenth. The Pralaya is of three kinds:

1. By Kāla or Nitya. Flow of time is the only cause of this Pralaya.

2. By Dravya or Naimittika. Dravya is the fire from the mouth of Sankarshana, at the end of one Kalpa.

3. By Guna or Prākritika, the Gunas devouring their own actions. The forms of Pralaya will be considered in the study of the Twelfth Branch.

    A. — Prākrita Creation, i.e. the Creation of Principles or Tatvas.

        I. Mahat — Which is the out-come of the first disturbance of the equilibrium of the Gunas.

        II. Ahankāra — Dravya + Jnāna + Kriyā.

        III. Tanmātra — Result of Dravya Śakti.

        IV. Indriyas — Result of Jnāna and Kriyā Śakti.

        V. Vaikārika — Devas and Manas.

        VI. The five-fold Tāmasika creation.

    B. — Vaikrita or Individual Creation.

        VII. Urdha Srotas — or with upward current of the food taken, the Sthāvara or Immobile kingdom with six divisions.

            1. Vānaspati — Plants that fructify without flowers.

            2. Oshadhi — Creepers that last till the ripening of fruits.

            3. Latā — Ascending creepers.

            4. Tvaksāra — Those of which the growth is not in the centre, but in the dermal regions, as bamboos.

            5. Virudh — Non-ascending woody creepers.

            6. Druma — Flowering plants.

The consciousness of all the six classes is almost obscured by Tamas. They are sensitive only to internal touch. They have many peculiarities.

VIII. Tiryak-Srotas. — With slanting food current. The position of the animal stomach as regards the animal mouth is such that food is not taken in vertically, but either horizontally or slantingly. The animal kingdom has 28 divisions. The animals are ignorant, with predominating Tamas, with the sense of smell largely developed in them so much that they mostly perceive by that sense, and with the faculties of the heart entirely undeveloped. The 28 classes are:

1. Living on the ground.

i. — The cloven-footed.

(1) Cow, (2) goat, (3) buffalo (4) krishnasara, the spotted antelope, (5) hog, (6) gavaya, a species of ox, (7) ruru, a kind of deer, (8) sheep, (9) camel.

ii. — The whole hoofed.

(10) Ass, (11) horse, (12) mule, (13) goura, a kind of deer, (14) sarabha, a kind of deer, (15) chamari, a kind of deer.

iii. — The five-nailed.

(16) Dog, (17) jackal, (18) wolf, (19) tiger, (20) cat, (21) hare, rabbit, (22) porcupine, (23) lion, (24) monkey, (25) elephant, (26) tortoise, (27) alligator.

2. (28) Aquatic animals and birds.

IX. Arvāk-Srotas or with downward food current, the Human kingdom with predominant Rajas, given to Karma, mistaking misery for happiness.

C. — Prākrita- Vaikrita.

> X. The Kumāras. The Kumāra creation is partly Prākrita and partly Vaikrita.

Besides these, there is

D. — Vaikrita Dev Creation.

There are eight divisions of Vaikrita Devas:

1. Vivudha,

2. Pitri,

3. Asura,

4. Gandharva and Apsarā,

5. Siddha, Charana and Vidyādhara,

6. Yaksha and Raksha,

7. Bhuta, Preta and Pisācha,

8. Kinnara, Kimpurusha, Asvamukha and others.

The Vaikarika and Vaikrita Devas form one class.

THOUGHTS ON THE ABOVE.

Prākrita creation is that which gives rise to and is connected with all individuals. Excepting the Tāmasic or Avidyā creation, which we shall consider later on, the other divisions of this creation were caused by the first life impulse, given by the First Purusha. The Tāmasic creation was brought into manifestation by the Third Purusha Brahmā.

The division of the life-kingdoms according to the movements of the food taken is peculiar to the Pauranic system. It will be interesting to know from the physiological stand-point whether it is necessary for the development of the brain that the spinal column should be erect, whether it is necessary for the formation of the spinal column, that the stomach should retain a certain position, and to know also how far the fixture of the plants is an impediment to the development of any nervous system in them.

It is remarkable that the mineral kingdom is not mentioned as a distinct life-kingdom. The reason appears to be that the creative process is divided into two periods. In the first period formless Jivas take form after form, till the lowest material form is reached. This is elemental creation or the creation of Devas, as described in detail in Ch. XXI. Sk. IV. The Purāna goes on to say: — "Then Brahmā created the Manus." III.-24-49. The Manu creation shews, how mind was gradually developed through Vegetable, Animal and Human creations, out of the Mineral Kingdom, represented by the Mountain Chief Himālaya. The giving up by Sāti, of the body acquired from Daksha and her rebirth as the daughter of the Mountain King show how the elemental creation gave way to a fresh creative process, which took its start from the Mineral Kingdom.

The Kumāras form a peculiar creation. "They are Prakrita in as much as they partake of the character of Devas and they are Vaikrita, as they partake of the character of men." *Śridhara.* — The great commentator also says: — "Sanaka and other Kumāras are not created in every kalpa. The account of their creation is only given in the first Kalpa, called Brahmā. In reality, the Vegetable and other life kingdoms are created in every Kalpa. Sanaka and others being created in Brahmā Kalpa only follow the creations in other Kalpas."

Upon death, men go to Bhuvar Loka, where they become Bhūtas, Pretas and Pisāchas. Then they go to Svar Loka, where they become Devas, not the Devas of Deva creations but only temporary Devas. When their merits are exhausted, they come down upon earth, to begin life as men again. But if by unselfish Karma and devotion, men pass across the limits of the triple plane, they go first to Mahar Loka. Here they are called Prajāpatis. Bhrigu and other Prajāpatis who are the ordinary dwellers of Mahar Loka, are described in one sloka of Bhāgavata, as bearing the life period of one Kalpa. (II. 2. 25). In the next sloka it is said that the Yogins who go to

Mahar Loka, remain there till the end of the Kalpa, when at last they go to Satya Loka.

But in another sloka, the Purāna says: — "When the night of Pralaya follows, the three Lokas, Bhūr, Bhuvar and Svar, are burnt by the fire from the mouth of Sankarshana. Troubled by the excessive heat of that fire, Bhrigu and others proceed from Mahar Loka to Jana Loka." III-11-3O.

This shews that the dwellers of Mahar Loka live for the life time of Brahmā or two Parārdhas.

This is also made clear by the following commentary of Śridhara on III-10-9: —

"Why did Brahmā make the three Lokas into one division? This Trilokī consisting of Bhūr, Bhuvar and Svar — is the place that is to be made in every Kalpa or day of Brahmā for the enjoyment of Jivas (or individuals). But Jivas dwell in the higher Lokas as well. Why are not those Lokas created then in every Kalpa? This is because they are the transformations of unselfish (Nishkāma) action or Dharma — the Lokas themselves and the dwellers thereof. The Trilokī and the dwellers thereof are the transformations of selfish (Kāmya) action. Therefore they have birth and death in every Kalpa. But Mahar and other Lokas are begotten by unselfish action heightened by Upāsanā (or devotion), and they last for two Parārdhas, which is the life time of Brahmā. And the dwellers of those Lokas generally attain mukti (or liberation) after that period."

The ordinary dwellers of Jana Loka are the Kumāras. When men in course of evolution reach Jana Loka, they become Kumāras.

We have already seen that the essence of life in the higher Lokas is unselfishness. It is for this reason that the Gitā speaks of unselfish action in the first instance as an essential requisite of spiritual life. But it is not unselfish action alone which enables us to get rid of our personal desires and to assimilate ourselves with that one life which pervades all. Devotional love is another equally essential requisite.

It is impossible for us to realise the different experiences in the four higher Lokas.

The famous Brahma Sūkta has the following line: — "The three feet of Īshvara, bearing eternal happiness in the higher Lokas." The eighteenth Śloka in Chapter VI. of the Second Skandha is an exposition of this line. Śrīdhara has the following commentary on that line:

"Happiness in Trilokī is fleeting and temporary. Though Mahar Loka is on the path of liberation, the dwellers of that Loka have to leave it at the end of every Kalpa. The happiness there is therefore not ever-lasting. In Jana Loka, the happiness is ever-lasting, as long as the dwellers do not leave the place. But they have to witness the miseries of the dwellers of Mahar Loka, when they come to Jana Loka, at the end of the Kalpa. In Tapas, there is absolute want of evil. In Satya, there is freedom from fear or liberation."

We have left the Devas (not the elementals that pass through the life kingdoms of this earth) out of consideration. Their evolution is worked out in all the seven Lokas. Their names and characteristics in each Loka are given by Vyāsa in his commentaries on Patanjali's Sutras. Those who are ordinarily known as Devas are the dwellers of Svar Loka. The Deva Yonis or lower Devas are dwellers of Bhuvar Loka and Bhūr Loka. Men have nothing to do with the Devas of the higher Lokas. The Devas of Trilokī are indifferent, friendly or inimical to men. Left alone, they do not interfere with men. But when men try to gain superiority over them, by the acquisition of Brahma Vidyā, they try to throw obstacles in their way.

The Brihad Āranyak Upanishad says: — "Even the gods verily are not able to prevent him from the possession of the state of all." I.-4-10

Again, "As verily many beasts maintain a man, so every man maintains the gods. It is not pleasant, even if one beast is taken away, how then, if many? Therefore it is not pleasant to them, that men should know this *i.e.* the truth of the nature of Brahmā." Commenting on this, Śankarāchāryya quotes a Śloka from Anugrta: "The world of the gods is surrounded by performers of works. But the gods do not wish that mortals should abide above."

38

Śankarāchāryya goes on to say: — "Therefore the gods try to exclude, like cattle from tigers, men from the knowledge of Brahmā, as it is their desire, that they should not be elevated above the sphere of their use. Whom they wish to liberate, to him they impart belief &c., and unbelief to him whom they wish not to liberate."

Ānanda Giri, the commentator of Śankarāchāryya, quotes the following Śloka: —

"Devas do not protect men, rod in hand, like cattle-keepers. When they wish to protect a man, they impart the necessary intelligence to him."

Nothing is said in the Purānas, as to Devas of the higher Lokas.

The Prākrita Devas are intimately connected with our senses and intellect. It is through their direct help, that we are able to perceive and to conceive. Hence they are called Adhi-devas or Vaikāric Devas. They are not individuals and the remarks made above as to Devas, do not apply to them.

IV. DIVISIONS OF KĀLA.

SKANDHA III. CHAP. 11.

The unit of Kala at the Sūkshma pole is Paramānu, which is the minutest part of the created thing, not united to form a body. At the Sthula pole is the whole Sthula creation known in its entirety as Parama Mahān. The time during which the Sun crosses in his orbit one paramānu is the Kāla unit paramānu. The time during which he crosses the whole system in his orbit, *i.e.*, crosses all the twelve signs of the Zodiac, is Parama Mahān or one Samvatsara. The units of time and space are thus the same.

1 Dvyanuka = 2 Paramānus.

1 Trasarenu = 3 Paramānus.

1 Truti = 3 Trasarenus.

1 Vedha = 100 Trutis.

1 Lava = 3 Vedhas.

1 Nimesha or wink = 3 Lavas.

1 Kshana = 3 Nimesha.

1 Kāsthā = 5 Kshanas.

1 Laghu = 15 Kāsthās.

1 Nādikā = 15 Laghus.

1 Muhurta = 2 Nādikās.

1 Yāma or Prahara = 6 or 7 Nādikās.

1 Ahorātra (of the Mortals) = 8 Yāmas.

1 Paksha (Sukla or Krishna) = 15 Ahorātras.

1 Māsa (Month) = 1 Sukla + 1 Krishna Paksha.

1 Ritu = 2 Māsas.

1 Ayana = 6 Māsas (Uttara or Dakshinā.)

1 Vatsara = 2 Ayanas.

1 Vatsara = 12 Masas

1 Vatsara = 1 Ahorātra of Devas.

1 Samvatsara = 1 year of Solar months.

1 Parivatsara = 1 year of Jupiter months.

1 Idāvatsara = 1 year of Savana months.

1 Svanuvatsara = 1 year of Lunar months.

1 Vatsara = 1 year of Stellar months.

One hundred Samvatsaras is the maximum age of men.

Satya, Tretā, Dvāpara and Kali a cycle of these 4 Yugas and their Sandhyās and Sandhyānsas consist of 12 thousand divine years.

The beginning of a Yuga is its Sandhyā. The end of a Yuga is its Sandhyānsa. Sandhyā and Sandhyānsa are not included in a Yuga and Yuga Dharma is not to be performed while they last.

```
Sandhyā of Satya Yuga =              400 Deva years.
    Satya Yuga       =            4,000    "      "
Sandhyānsa of Satya Yuga            400    "      "
Sandhyā of Treta Yuga               300    "      "
    Treta Yuga                    3,000    "      "
Sandhyānsa of Treta Yuga            300    "      "
Sandhyā of Dvāpara Yuga             200    "      "
    Dvāpara Yuga                  2,000    "      "
Sandhyānsa of Dvāpara Yuga          200    "      "
Sandhyā of Kali Yuga                100    "      "
Kali Yuga                         1,000    "      "
Sandhyānsa of Kali Yuga             100    "      "
                                 12,000 Deva years.
```

Dharma is enjoined for the period between Sandhyā and Sandhyānsa, which is called Yuga.

```
Dharma has all the 4 pādas or feet in Satya,
  "     "    only 3 pādas in Treta,
  "     "    only 2 pādas in Dvapara,
  "     "    only 1 pāda in Kali.
```

1,000 Yuga cycles is one Day of Brahmā or one Kalpa,

i.e., 1 Day of Brahmā = 1,000 x 12,000 Deva years,

$$= 1,20,00,000 \text{ Deva years.}$$

An equal period of time is also reckoned as one Night of Brahmā. 14 Manus reign during the Day of Brahmā, each Manu reigning for:

$$\frac{1,000}{14} = 71 \ 3/4$$

i.e., a little over 71 Yuga Cycles. Converted into Deva years: —

1 Manvantara = $\dfrac{12,000 \times 1,000}{14}$ = 8,57,142 6/7 Deva years.

1 Deva year = 360 Lunar years.

1 Manvantara = $\dfrac{12,000,000 \times 360}{14}$ = 3,37,142,657 1/2 Lunar years.

The Manvantaras have their Manus, successors of Manus, Rishis and Devas.

The Rishis, Indras, and Devas appear together.

In the daily creation of Brahmā, Animals, Men, Pitris and Devas are born according to their own Karma.

During the Manvantara, Bhagavān preserves this universe by His own Satva, directly as Manvantara Avatāras and indirectly as Manus and others. When Pralaya approaches, Bhagavān withdraws His Śaktis (or powers). Trilokī is then burnt up by fires from the mouth of Sankarshana. Bhrigu and other dwellers of Mahar Loka proceed to Jana Loka. The waters of Pralaya sweep away everything before them. In that watery expanse, Hari remains seated upon the coils of Ananta, with His eyes closed.

With every Day and Night, the age of Brahmā declines. He lives for one hundred years only. Half of Brahmā's age is called Parārddha. The first Parārddha has expired, the second has commenced with our Kalpa. Every day of Brahmā is called one Kalpa.

At the beginning of the first Parārddha was Brahmā Kalpa, when Brahmā or the present Kosmos was born.

At the end of the first Parārddha was Padma Kalpa, when the Loka-Padma (the lotus of Lokas) appeared at the navel of Hari.

The first Kalpa of the second Parārddha, which is the present Kalpa, is called Varāha Kalpa. Hari incarnated as Varāha or Boar during this Kalpa.

The two Parārddhas are but a wink of Bhagavān. Kāla cannot measure him.

```
[1 Day of Brahmā    =           12,000,000   Deva years,
 1 Night of Brahmā  =           12,000,000   Do.
                                24,000,000   Do.


 Multiplying by                        360
 1 year of Brahmā   =        8,640,000,000   Deva years.
 Multiplying by                        100
  Age of Brahmā     =      864,000,000,000   Deva years.
 Multiplying by                        360
                       311,040,000,000,000   Lunar years.
```

```
1 Kali Yuga, including Twilight (Sandhyā and Sandhyānsa)
    = 1,200 X 360 = 4,32,000 Lunar years.


Varāha Kalpa = 50 X 360 + 1 = 180001st Kalpa.


The present is the seventh Manvantara of that Kalpa.
```

The present Kali Yuga is the 28th Yuga of that Manvantara and 4,994 years of that Yuga have expired in the present year of Christ 1894.

THEOSOPHICAL CORRESPONDENCES. The words Kalpa and Manvantara are carelessly used in Theosophical literature. But I shall use those terms, specially with reference to page 309 of the second volume of the *Secret Doctrine* (first edition.)

1 Kalpa = 7 Rounds.

1 Round = 2 Manvantaras.

The Pralaya at the end of seven Rounds therefore means the Pralaya of Trilokī.

The last Globe Chain of which the Moon formed a living planet belonged to Pādma Kalpa. Our Globe D is the 18,001st since the birth of the Kosmos. There will be 17,999 more such Globes, one after each Pralaya of Globe Chains. There will be 18,000 more Pralayas of the Globe Chain. Then there will be a general dissolution or Prākritika Pralaya, not only of the Globe Chain, but of the whole Kosmic system.

V.-THE CREATION BY BRAHMA (*Continued*) III. 12.

The first creation of Brahmā was the five-fold Avidyā, *viz*: —

1. Tamas or ignorance of Self (Avidyā in Patanjali.)

2. Moha or egoism (Asmitā.)

3. Mahā Moha or desire for enjoyment (Rāga).

4. Tāmisra or mental disturbance on the non-fulfilment of desires (Dvesha).

5. Andha Tāmisra or false perception of death (Abhiniveśa).

Brahmā was not pleased with this dark creation. He purified his soul by meditation on Bhagavān and created Sanaka, Sananda, Sanātana and

Sanatkumara. These Munis had no performances (for their own evolution). They were Urdha-retas. Brahmā, addressing them, said — "Sons, go and multiply yourselves." But they sought Moksha, and heeded him not. Brahmā got enraged at the disobedience of his sons, and, though he tried to put down his anger, it burst forth from between his eye-brows and appeared as Kumāra Nila-Lohita or Blue-Red. The boy, the first born of Devas, wept and cried out to Brahmā — "Give me names and give me abodes." "That shall be done," replied Brahmā, "and, as thou wept like a boy, thou shalt be called Rudra or the Weeper. The heart, the Indriyas, Prāna, Ākāsa, Vāyu, Agni, Apas, Prithvi, the Sun, the Moon and Tapas are your abodes. Manyu, Manu, Mahinasa, Mahān, Śiva, Ritadhvaja, Ugra-retas, Bhava, Kāla, Bāmadeva and Dhrita-vrata these are thy eleven names; Dhi, Dhriti, Rāsaloma, Nijut, Sarpi, Ilā, Ambikā, Irāvati, Svadhā, Dikshā and Rudrāni, these are thy wives. Beget sons, as thou art Prajāpati." Thus ordered, Nila-Lohita begot sons like unto himself in might, form and habits. The Rudras became numerous, and they spread all round the Universe ready almost to devour it. Brahmā became afraid of his creation, and, addressing himself to Rudra, said — "O Chief of Devas, desist from such creation. Thy progeny with their fiery eyes are consuming all and even consuming me. Take to Tapas for the joy of all beings. By Tapas thou shalt create the Universe as it was of yore. By Tapas thou shalt gain that Bhagavān who dwells in all hearts." "Amen," said Rudra, and he went into the forests to make Tapas.

Brahmā then begot ten sons: — Marichi, Atri, Angirasa, Pulastya, Pulaha, Kratu, Bhrigu, Vasishtha, Daksha and Nārada. Nārada came from Brahmā's bosom, Daksha from his thumb, Vasishtha from his Prāna, Bhrigu from his skin, Kratu from his hands, Pulaha from his navel, Pulastya from his ears, Angirasa from his mouth, Atri from his eyes and Marichi from his Manas.

Dharma came from Brahmā's right breast, where Nārāyana himself dwells. Adharma, the parent of Mrityu (or Death) came from his back. Kāma came from his heart, Anger from his eye-brows, Greed from the lower lip. Vāk or speech came from his mouth, the Seas from his generative organ and Death from his anus.

Kardama, the husband of Devahūti, was born of Brahmā's Chhāya or shadow. So there was creation out of the body and the mind of Brahmā. Brahmā took a fancy to his daughter Vāk (or speech). Marichi and his other sons dissuaded him from the incestuous connection. And the Creator in shame gave up his body which was taken up by Space and which is known as dewy darkness. "How shall I bring back all the previous Creation?" So thought Brahmā at one time, and the four Vedas appeared from his four mouths. The Yajnas, the Upavedas, the Philosophies, the four parts of Dharma, and the duties of Āsramas also appeared.

Brahmā had another body void of incestuous impulses and he thought of enlarging the Creation. But he found himself and the Rishis, powerful though they were, unsuccessful in this respect. He thought there was some unforeseen impediment, so he divided his body into two. A pair was formed by that division. The male was Svāyambhuva Manu and the female was his wife Śatarūpā. Since then creation multiplied by sexual intercourse. Svāyambhuva Manu begot five children in Śatarūpā — two sons, Priyavrata and Uttānapāda, and three daughters, Ākūti, Devahūti and Prasūti. He gave Akuti in marriage to Ruchi, Devahūti to Kardama and Prasūti to Daksha. This changing universe is filled with their progeny.

PRE-MANVANTARIC CREATION.

The descent of Spirit into Matter is indicated by the overshadowing Tamas creation, The individuals reach the spiritual plane at the time of Pralaya and lose all sense of I-ness. Their memory becomes perfectly dead to all previous connections and experiences and even as to self as a distinct unit. The child starts with a body of his own, and faculties limited to that body. The Jiva children that came into existence at the beginning of the Universe had however nothing peculiar to themselves, and they had even to acquire the sense of I-ness.

First, the Jiva identifies himself with his body and mind, his own phenomenal basis. For, if he identifies himself with the universal spirit, there is no action for him, no working out of his own Karma. Though from the standpoint of the highest wisdom individuality is a delusion, for the one unchangeable ever-lasting element in Jiva is Ātmā, and at the final stage of development man has to separate himself from his phenomenal basis and to identify himself with Ātmā, which is the real self, still the sense of separateness is necessary for the process of creation and for the gaining of experiences. This sense is two-fold, —

1. The non-perception of Ātmā as Self, called Avidyā by Patanjali and Tamas in the Purānas, and

2. The perception of the *upādhi* as self, called Asmitā by Patanjali and Moha in the Purānas.

Attachment and aversion, likes and dislikes, are equally necessary for continued individual action. The Jiva eats what he likes and does not eat what he dislikes. He associates himself with certain objects, ideas and thoughts and shuns others. His likes and dislikes form the guiding principle of his actions. These affinities are called Rāga and Dvesha by Patanjali and Mahā Moha and Tamisra in the Purānas.

The tenacious desire to live in the present body is called Abhinivesha by Patanjali. This desire becomes an instinct in the Jiva, so necessary is it for his preservation. The Purānas call it Andha-Tāmisra. Śridhara explains it as the shock we receive from a separation from all our present enjoyments. For, according to him, the idea of death is nothing but a sense of separation from our present enjoyments.

These forms of Avidyā were called into being that the forms of the previous Kalpa might be brought into existence, or that the work of creation might be undertaken. These faculties are the very essence of life manifestation. But the process has now been reversed. The work of creation is over. We have acquired the experiences of earth-life, and we are now destined to take a journey back to our home, the bosom of Īshvara, from which we all came. We have now to undo our sense of separateness. The five forms of Avidyā are therefore called miseries (klesha) by Patanjali and he lays down rules for getting rid of them.

After invoking Avidyā, Brahmā created the Kumāras, who were the most spiritual of the beings to be created. They were so spiritual, that they could not take any part in the work of creation. They had to bide their time, till there was spiritual ascent in the Universe.

The Rudras, called the Blue-Red Kumāras, come next. Though highly spiritual themselves they did not object to take part in the work of creation. But as real factors in the work of dissolution, they were entirely out of place in the work of creation. We owe our idea of separateness or individuality to the Rudras. In the scale of universal life the agencies of dissolution carve out individual lives and their mission ends there.

The ten Rishis form the next Creation. Further descent of life in the Universe brought forth ten distinct types of Intelligence. We shall consider these types later on. Then comes the story of Brahmā's incest. Brahmā could not directly take part in the Creation. His task was simply to bring back the former state of things through a graduated series of intermediaries. First appeared those that had to hold cosmic positions of responsibility, some throughout the Kalpa and others throughout the Manvantara. With the powers invoked, the temptation to evolve an independent Creation with the help of Vāch, the potency of Mantras had to be got over. This done, Brahmā thought of the Monads of the previous Kalpa, and the first Manu appeared with his wife Sata-rūpā or Hundred-formed. All forms of Creation existed in Idea before further manifestation, and Sata-rūpā was the collective aspect of all such Ideas.

THE FIRST OR THE SVAYAMBHUVA MANVANTARA.

VI. BHŪR AND VARAHA

SKANDHA III., CHAP. 13.

Said Manu to Brahmā — "I shall do thy behests, O Lord. But tell me where my Prajā (progeny) and myself are to be located. The Bhūr of the previous Kalpa where all beings found shelter is lost in the great ocean of Pralaya. Bestir thyself and raise it up, O Deva."

Brahmā thought within Himself what was to be done, when lo! out from His nostril came a Boar, no bigger than a thumb. In a moment the Boar assumed gigantic proportions and all space resounded with his roar. The dwellers of the Jana, Tapas and Satya Lokas worshipped Him by chanting the Mantras of the three Vedas. He roared once more for the good of the Devas and instantly plunged into the waters. Though an incarnation of Yajna, He tried to discover the Bhūr by smelling like an ordinary animal. He dived down as far as Rasātala and there found the Bhūr Loka. He then raised it up on His tusks. The Daitya King Hiranyāksha resisted and in rage the Boar killed him. The Rishis then worshipped Him knowing His true form to be Yajna.

THOUGHTS ON THE ABOVE.

[Bhūr is the main system of Trilokī. The Varāha Avatāra restored the system after the Kalpa Pralaya. Bhūr being the lowest of the Seven Lokas corresponds to Prithvi Tatva and hence to the sense of smell. The boar is pre-eminently the animal of smell. The materialisation of the Prithvi principle for the purpose of globe formation was an effort of the energy of the Logos and the *smelling* out of Bhūr by the Varaha is suggestive. The Globe evolution is preparatory to Monadic evolution. The pent up Karma of the previous Kalpa develops itself on the Globes. All beings are mutually interdependent for their evolution. They help one another in the work of evolution, and one makes sacrifices that the others may grow. Some have to wait, till others come forward. Then they become united in the further race for progress. This great cosmic process, this mutual sacrifice is Yajna itself, which is typified in the Boar Incarnation. The Vedic Yajna gives prominence to the Communion of men with Devas, as at the early stages this is an all important fact of evolution. The Varāha is called the first Yajna Avatāra and all the parts of His body are named with reference to Vedic Yajna, as He by raising Bhūr prepared the field for Karma.]

VII. THE STORY OF HIRANYĀKSHA.

SKANDHA III., CHAP. 14.

Diti, the daughter of Daksha, approached one evening her husband
Kasyapa, son of Marichi. She was overpowered with the passion of love
and became importunate. Kasyapa asked her to wait. Rudra was presiding
over sunset. His astral attendants, the Bhūtas and Pishachas, were roaming
over the Universe. With His three eyes representing the Sun, Moon and fire
he could see every thing. His hesitation to yield to Diti was of no avail, and
the Muni had to yield. There Diti became ashamed of her weakness. She
was afraid she had offended Rudra and she helplessly prostrated herself at
the feet of Kasyapa praying for his forgiveness. "Thou hast disobeyed me,"
said Kasyapa, "and hast shown disrespect to the companions of Rudra, thy
mind is impure and so is the time of Evening (Sandhyā). These four evils
will cause the birth of two wicked sons from thee. They will oppress the
Trilokī and the Lokapālas (Preservers of the three Lokas). When their
inequities exceed all bounds, Vishnu will Himself incarnate to kill them."

For one hundred years Diti conceived her twin sons. Even from within the
womb they shed lustre all round, which even overpowered the Lokapālas.
The Devas went to Brahmā to ascertain the cause of this disaster. He
related to them the following story.

"My Mānasa-putras, Sanaka and others were once in Vaikuntha, the abode
of Bhagavān. Impatient to see Bhagavān the Kumāras hurriedly passed
through the six portals (Kaksha). At the seventh portal, they found two
doorkeepers of equal age with clubs in their hands, richly adorned with
golden crowns and other ornaments. They had four hands and looked
beautiful in their blue colour. The Kumāras heeded them not, but opened
the gate with their own hands as they had opened the other gates. The door
keepers stopped them with their clubs. The Kumāras were put out by this
unforeseen obstruction and addressing the doorkeepers gave vent to their
feelings thus: — 'What mean you by making this distinction? In Him the
Lord of Vaikuntha, there is no difference whatsoever. The whole of this
Universe is in Him. Do you dread any danger to Him, as to a common
being, and why will you admit some and not others? But you are His

servants. So we do not intend to be very hard on you. But you must descend from this elevated plane and take your birth where passion, anger and greed prevail'."

"The door-keepers became terrified at this curse and fell at the feet of the Kumāras. All that they prayed for was that while passing through the lowest births, they might not have Môha, beclouding their recollection of Bhagavān. Bhagavān knew what had transpired outside. He hastened on foot with Lakshmī by His side to where the Munis stood. The Kumāras prostrated themselves before Him Whom they had so long meditated upon in their hearts. With intent eyes they looked steadily on Him and longed to see Him again and again. The Kumāras lauded Him with words full of import. Bhagavān addressing them said: — 'These my door-keepers are by name Jaya and Vijaya. They have slighted you, and it is right that you have cursed them. I sanction that curse. For they are my servants, and I am indirectly responsible for their deeds. I always respect Brāhmanas, as my glory is derived from them. These door-keepers did not know my regard for you, and they therefore unintentionally slighted you. But they shall instantly reap the fruit of their evil deeds and come back to Me when their punishment is over. Please therefore decide where they are to go.' The Kumāras knew not what to say. They thought they had not done right and they asked to be excused. 'It is all right for Thee to extol the Brāhmanas in this way, for Thou art the Preserver of Dharma and Thou teachest others what to do. But if, really, we have done wrong, let us be punished and let not our curse visit these innocent door-keepers.' Bhagavān replied: — 'It is I who have uttered the curse through your mouths. My will shall be done. These door-keepers shall be born as Asuras, but they shall come back to Me speedily.' These two door-keepers, O Devas, have now appeared in Diti's womb. I have no power to overcome them. But when the time comes for the prevalence of Satva, Bhagavān Himself will do what is needed."

The Devas went away and waited for events. The two Daityas Hiranyāksha and Hiranyakasipu were born of Diti, after a conception of one hundred years. Hiranyāksha though elder by birth was younger by conception.

THOUGHTS ON HIRANYĀKSHA.

[Diti is literally 'Cutting,' 'Splitting,' or 'dividing.' Jaya and Vijaya mean victory. Hiranya is gold. Hiranyāksha means gold-eyed. Hiranyakasipu means gold-bedded. The key to the mystery lies in the fact that Jaya and Vijaya were the door-keepers of Vishnu and their external form was that of Vishnu. The Purusha in the Heart is the Counterpart in microcosm of the Purusha in the Universe. And we have found above that the five or ten door-keepers or Brahmā-Purushas in the Heart are the five or ten Prānas in man. By analogy, therefore, which is a potent factor in the solution of mysteries, we find that Jaya and Vijaya are the two-fold manifestations of Prana in Vaikuntha, the in-going and out-going energies of Purusha. The life principle is an aspect of Bhagavān and stands at His very gate. It is this outer aspect of Purusha that is the mainspring of all material activities, of all life-manifestations and of the material development of the universe. The duality represents Tāmasic inaction and Rājasic activity. Hiranyāksha would have no life-manifestation, no appearance of globes, he would continue a state of things verging on Prālayic sleep. Hiranyakasipu was the very ideal of material greatness and material grandeur. Kumbhakarna slept and Rāvana worked. The brothers Jaya and Vijaya passed through the dividing energy of Diti, to cause the material manifoldness of the Universe. The Varāha as representing the awakened Jivic Karma fought with the Asura that opposed the development of that Karma, which could only fructify on the Bhūr system.]

VIII. DEVA AND DEVA-YONI CREATION.

SKANDHA III., CHAP. 20.

Vidura asked Maitreya: How did Marichi and other Rishis and also Svāyambhuva Manu carry out Brahmā's orders to create.

Maitreya continued the story of Creation in reply to Vidura.

We have heard of the primal dark creation of Brahmā, consisting of five-fold Avidyā. Referring to that, Maitreya said, it was a creation of shadows. Brahmā was not pleased with this shadowy creation. He gave up the dark body and it became night, At that time Yakshas and Rākshasas were born and they took it up. The body was not only dark, but it was the seat of hunger and thirst. The new-born therefore in their hunger and thirst ran after Brahmā to devour Him. Some of them said: "Have no mercy on Him as father." Others said "Devour him." Brahmā became afraid of them and said — "Save me. You are my sons. You should not devour me." Those that said "Devour" are Yakshas and those that said "Do not save him" are Rākshasas. Brahmā then created the Devas, with His radiant Sātvika body.

This body when given up became day and the playing Devas took it up. Brahmā then created the Asuras out of His thigh. They became extremely passionate and ran after Brahmā void of all shame. In great distress Brahmā prayed to Vishnu and the Creator was told to give up His body of passion. The body was given up and it became Sandhyā, or evening. The Asuras accepted Sandhyā as their wife. Evening is the time for lust and passion. Brahmā then created the Gandharvas and Apsaras with His body of beauty, which when given up became Moon-light. With his indolence, Brahmā created the Bhūtas and Pisāchas. They were stark naked and had long loose hair. Brahmā closed his eyes on seeing them. After a time he gave up his yawning body and the Bhūtas and Pishāchas took it up. The body that causes secretion is called "Sleep."

That which causes delusion is "Madness." Indolence, yawning, sleep and madness all these four were taken up by Bhūtas and Pisāchas for their body. Brahmā knew His powers and He created with His invisible body the Sādhyas and Pitris. By His power of becoming invisible, He created Siddhas and Vidhyādharas and gave them His body with that power. By His reflected image He created the Kinnaras and Kimpurushas, who took up that image for their body. At dawn, they sing in pairs the praise of Brahmā. Brahmā did not find any progress in creation with all these Bhoga (expansive) bodies. He threw away His body and from His hair the elemental serpents or Nāgas were born. After all, Brahmā created the Manūs and Rishis.

IX. THE PROGENY OF KARDAMA.

SKANDHA III. CHAP. 21-24.

Kardama Rishi was ordered by Brahmā to create. This led him to pray to
Vishnu on the sacred banks of the Sarasvati, near Vindu Sarovara. Vishnu
appeared before him with Lakshmī by His side. He revealed to Kardama a
happy future. The Rishi was to marry Manu's daughter, to have by her nine
daughters and one son, an Incarnation of Vishnu Himself, who was to
promulgate the Tatva Vidyā. Shortly after, Svāyambhuva Manu came to
Kardama's hermitage, with his wife Sata-rupā and offered to the Rishi his
daughter Devahūti in marriage. Kardama accepted her as his wife. He had
by her nine daughters and the Avatāra Kapila. Brahmā with his sons the
Rishis came to Kardama and congratulated him and his wife Devahūti
upon having Bhagavān Vishnu for their son. He then asked Kardama to
give his daughters in marriage to the Rishis. Kardama followed his father's
behests and gave his daughters duly in marriage to the Rishis. Kalā, he
gave to Marichi, Anasuyā to Atri, Sraddhā to Angirasa, Havirbhu to
Pulastya, Gati to Pulaha, Kriyā to Kratu, Khyāti to Bhrigu, Arundhati to
Vasishtha and Sānti to Atharvan. The Rishi then went to the forest for yoga
and left his wife in charge of Kapila.

THOUGHTS ON KARDAMA.

[Devahūti means offering to Devas, which is universal service. She is the
progenitor of those forms of life which have a spiritual influence over the
whole Trailokya.

"Kalā" is part, a digit of the Moon.

"Anasuyā" means absence of envy. From the proverbial chastity of Atri's
wife the word also means the highest type of chastity and wifely devotion.

"Sraddhā" means faith.

"Havirbhu" means born of sacrificial oblation.

"Gati" means course, path.

"Kriyā" means performance (of Yajna) and action.

"Khyāti" means fame, praise and also proper discrimination.

"Arundhati" would perhaps mean one that does not stop or hinder. Probably the word means a wife who helps her husband in the performance of duties and does not stop or prevent him.

It is for this reason that the Star Arundhati is pointed out to the bride at the nuptial ceremony.

"Sānti" is peace, the well known invocation of the Vedas at the end of a Mantra.

"Kardama" means clay. He was born of Brahmā's Chhāyā or shadow.

Devahūti, being wedded to the materialised shadow of the whole Universe, gave rise to certain female types which in their turn on being wedded to the Rishis, the highest Planetary Intelligences, became the progenitors of all the life forms of the Universe. Kapila was one of the earliest Rishis. The word — Kapila means tawny or brown coloured.]

X. KAPILA'S INSTRUCTION TO HIS MOTHER DEVAHŪTI.

SKANDHA III., CHAP. 25-33.

We now come to an important part of the Bhāgavata Purāna, the teachings of Kapila to his mother in the Yoga philosophy of the Bhagavat Purāna. They adapt the Sānkhya and the Yoga systems to Bhakti or devotion. For a full knowledge of the teachings I refer my readers to the Purāna itself, I shall only give the salient points and avoid details as much as possible, without breaking the continuity of the discourses. "Yoga directed towards Ātmā brings about Mukti. Chitta attached to the transformations of Gunas causes Bondage; attached to Purūsha, it causes Mukti. When the mind is pure and free from distractions, man perceives Ātmā in himself, by Wisdom, Dispassion and Devotion. There is no path so friendly to the Yogins as constant devotion to Bhagavān. Company of Sādhus opens wide the door to Mukti. They are Sādhus who have forbearance and compassion, who are friendly to all beings, who have no enemies, who are free from passions, and above all who have firm and undivided Bhakti in Me. They give up all for My sake and they hear and speak no words that do not relate to Me. Their company removes the impurities of worldliness. Men first hear about Me from the Sādhus. By faith their heart is drawn towards Me, and they have devotion for Me. Devotion causes Dispassion and makes easy the path of Yoga. By indifference to the Guna transformations of Prakriti, by wisdom fostered by Dispassion, by Yoga and by Bhakti (devotion) offered to Me, the Jiva attains Me even while in this body."

"When the Indriyas (the senses and the mind), that manifest the objects of external and internal perception, become trained by the performance of Vedic Karma, their spontaneous Vritti (or function) in a man of concentrated mind is in Satva which is the same as Vishnu. This Vritti which is void of all selfishness is Bhakti in Bhagavān. It is superior to Mukti. It instantly destroys the Kosha (Astral body) as the digestive fire consumes food. The devoted have no yearning for that Mukti (Sāyujya or Nirvāna) which makes the Jiva one with Me. But they prefer ever to talk with each other about Me, to exert themselves for My sake and ever to meditate on Me. Mukti comes to them unasked. My Vibhutis, the eight Siddhis (*anima &c.*) and all the glory of the highest Lokas are theirs, though they want them not. I am their Teacher, their Friend, their Companion, their all. So even Kāla cannot destroy them."

"Purusha is Ātmā. He is eternal, void of Gunas, beyond Prakriti, all pervading, self luminous and all manifestating."

"Prakriti is Pradhāna, one in itself, but is also the source of all differences (*visesha*), possessed of three Gunas, unmanifested (*avyakta*) and eternal."

"The twenty four transformations of Prakriti called Prādhānika or Saguna Brahma are: —

"5 Mahā Bhūtas — Earth, Water, Fire, Air and Akāsa.

"5 Tanmātras — Smell, Taste, Rūpa, Touch and Sound.

"10 Indriyas — Ear, Skin, Eye, Tongue, Nose, Speech, Hand, Foot, Upastha and Pāyu.

"4 Divisions of Antahkarana — Manas, Buddhi, Chitta and Ahankāra."

"Kāla is the twenty-fifth. But according to some, Kāla is Prabhāva or Śakti of Purusha. Those who identify themselves with Prakriti are afraid of Kāla. Kāla as the outer aspect of Purusha disturbs the equilibrium of Gunas in Prakriti."

"Purusha energised Prakriti and the Gunas led to transformations following the action of Daiva or Karma, (Jivic record of the previous Kalpa). Prakriti brought forth the refulgent Mahat Tatva. The seed of the Universe was in the bosom of Mahat, and it manifested the Universe and destroyed the darkness of Pralaya by its own light."

"Chitta which is Vāsudeva and Mahat, is Satva, transparent and pure, and the perception of Bhagavān is achieved by this division of Antahkarana."

"Transparence (fitness for the full reflection of Brahmā) immutability and tranquility are the characteristics of Chitta, as of water in its primal state."

"Mahat Tatva was transformed into Ahankāra Tatva, with its Kriyā Śakti. Ahankāra became three-fold — Sātvika (Manas), Rājasika (Indriyas) and Tamasika (Bhūtas) i.e.Kartri or Cause, Karana or Instrument and Kāryya or effect."

"Sankarshana is the Purusha of Ahankāra. He is the Thousand-Headed and Ananta (endless.)"

"Manas is Sankalpa and Vikalpa. It is the generator of Kāma (or desire.) So Aniruddha, the king of Indriyas, blue as the blue-lotus of autumn, the Purūsha of Manas, has with patience to be got over by yogins."

"Buddhi is Rājasa transformation of Ahankāra. The perception of objects, dependence on the Indriyas, doubt, wrong-knowledge, right-knowledge, memory and sleep these are the functions of Buddhi. (Pradyumna is the Purūsha of Buddhi.)"

[The terminology here adopted will appear strange to the Vedantin scholar. The divisions of Antahkarana are here adopted to the sacred Tetractys or Chatur-vyuha, consisting of Vāsudeva, Sankarshana, Aniruddha and Pradyumna. In Devotional practice, Antahkarana should be made the channel for higher communion and its divisions are the divisions of spiritual perception.

Chitta is the highest aspect of Antahkarana corresponding to Mahat Tatva in the Universe, with the Purusha always reflected in it. This aspect corresponds to Vāsudeva, the highest Purusha in the Tetraktys.

Ahankāra is the bare individuality, transformable into peculiarities, but not so transformed. Sankarshana is the corresponding Purusha.

Manas is Kāma or desire brought on by likes and dislikes. It consists of the mental tendencies of attachment, repulsion and indifference. Aniruddha is the corresponding Purusha.

Buddhi is in one word the Chitta of Patanjali, — that which functions through the physical brain.

Pradyumna is the corresponding Purusha.]

"The Indriyas are also the Rajasika transformations of Ahankāra."

Prana through its Kriyā Śakti gave rise to the Karma Indriyas. Buddhi through its Jnāna Śakti gave rise to the Jnāna Indriyas. The Tanmatras and the Maha Bhūtas then came out in order of transformation. All these principles could not, however, unite to bring forth the creation. Purusha then permeated them, and the Cosmic Egg with its covers was formed. Details are given as to how the Indriyas and Antahkarana with their Adhyātma, Adhibhūta and Adhidaiva appearing in the Virāta Purusha, rose up from sleep as it were only when Chitta finally appeared.

Kapila then dilated on the relations between Purusha and Prakriti, using the illustration of the sun reflected on water and re-reflected on the wall. He showed how Mukti could be attained by discrimination of Prakriti and Purusha — the seer and the seen.

Devahūti asked how Mukti was possible when Prakriti and Purusha were eternally co-existent, and inter-dependent in manifestation. A man might for a time realize that the Purusha was free from the fears of relativity, but his Karma had connected him with the Gunas and the fears would recur as the ultimate cause could not be removed. Kapila replied, "By unselfish performance of duties, by purification of mind, by intense Bhakti in Bhagavān fostered by the recital of His glory, by wisdom based on the knowledge of the Tatvas, by strong dispassion, by austere yoga, by intense concentration on Ātmā, Prakriti becomes daily subdued and it is finally consumed, even as the wood is consumed by its own fire, caused by constant friction. Given up as already enjoyed and constantly found fault with, Prakriti does no harm to the Purusha centred in Self. Dreams do harm in sleep. But when a man wakes up, they lose all power to injure, as they are then found to be dreams only."

Kapila then explained the Ashtānga Yoga of Patanjali, as adapted to Bhakti and gave a graphic description of Vishnu as the object of meditation.

He then explained Bhakti Yoga. Bhakti Yoga is either Saguna or Nirguna. As Saguna it is either Satvika, Rājasika or Tamasika.

Nirguna Bhakti Yoga is that in which the mind runs towards Bhagavān, even as the Ganges runs towards the Sea, with a constant spontaneous flow. The Devoted spurn Sālokya, Sārshti, Sāmipya, Sārūpya and Sāyujya union[1] even when offered to them and they prefer to serve Bhagavān ever and ever. Compassion and friendliness to all beings are the essential qualifications of the Devoted. They must be humble, respectful and self controlled. They must pass their days in hearing and reciting the glory of Bhagavān.

Kapila then described in vivid terms the life and death of a man of the world and his passage after death to Yāma Loka. He described the rebirth and went through every detail of foetal existence. The foetus acquires

---

1These are the five kinds of Mukti.

Sālokya is residence in the same Loka with the Supreme Being.

Sārshti is equality with the Supreme Being in all the divine attributes.

Sāmipya is assimilation to the deity.

Sāynjya is absorption into the Supreme Being.

(The definition of Sārūpya is missing from the original text. It means having the same bodily features as the Supreme Being).

consciousness in the seventh month and gets a recollection of previous births. This recollection is lost on being born.

Those who selfishly perform their Dharma and worship Devas and Pitris go to Sōma Loka, and after partaking of Sōma, they are again re-born. And even their Lokas are destroyed with the daily Pralaya of Brahmā.

Those who unselfishly perform their duties and give themselves up entirely to the Supreme Purusha go through Sūrya (Sun) to the transcosmic Loka of Parama Purusha. The worshippers of Hiranyagarbha (Brahmā) reach Brahmā Loka or Satya Loka and there wait for two Parārddhas *i.e.* for the life time of Brahmā and upon the final dissolution of the Brahmānda go to the trans-cosmic plane of Parama Purusha.

Brahmā, Marichi and other Rishis, the Kumāras and Siddhas do their assigned work unselfishly, but their Upāsanā admits of distinction. So they are absorbed in the Second or the First Manifested Purusha at Pralaya and become re-born at creation.

Devahūti heard all this from Kapila. Her doubts were all removed and she found the light within herself. She remained fixed in meditation as long as her Prārabdha was not exhausted. She then attained Mukti.

Kapila first went towards the North. The sea then gave Him place, where He still lies in deep Samādhi, for the peace of Trilokī. (Gangā Sāgar or Saugor is said to be the seat of Kapila).

SKANDHA IV.

THE GENEALOGY OF MANU AND THE RISHIS.

SKANDHA IV. CHAP. 1.

In every Manvantarā, there are one Manu, sons of Manu, Devas, Indra or king of the Devas, seven Rishis and one Avatāra of Vishnu. The Avatāras of Purusha propel Manu and others to their work. At the end of every cycle of 4 Yugas, the Rishis by their Tapas find out the lost Srutis and revive the old Dharma. The Manus propound the Dharma. The sons of Manu including their descendants and others preserve the Dharma, in their respective times, to the end of the Manvantara. The Devas help them in their work. Indra preserves the Trilokī and sends down rains. VIII. — 14.

In the Svāyambhuva Manvantara, Svāyambhuva was Manu, the Tushita Devas were the Devatās, Marichi and others were the seven Rishis, Yajna was both Avatāra and Indra. Priyavrata and Uttānpada were the two sons of Manu.

A number of genealogical tables are given below:

(N. B. The female names are given in italics)

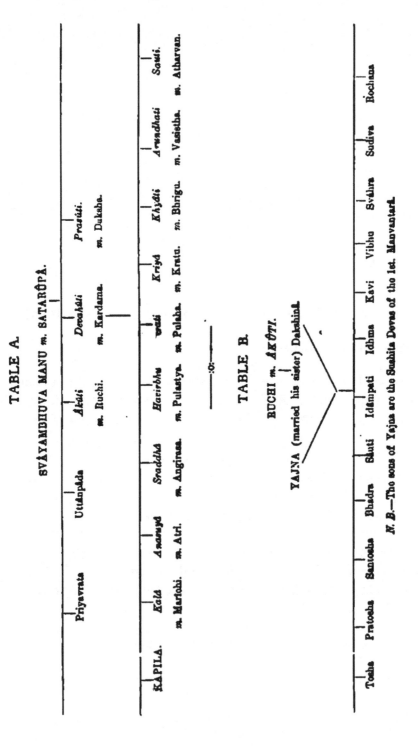

TABLE A.

SVÁYAMBHUVA MANU m. SATARÛPÁ.

Priyavrata	Uttánpáda			
		Ákúti	Devahúti	Prasúti
		m. Ruchi.	m. Kardama.	m. Daksha.

KAPILA.	Kalá	Anasuyá	Sraddhá	Havirbhu	...vati	Kriyá	Khyáti	Arundhati	Santi
	m. Marichi.	m. Atri.	m. Anginas.	m. Pulastya.	m. Pulaha.	m. Kratu.	m. Bhrigu.	m. Vasishtha.	m. Atharvan.

:o:

TABLE B.

BUCHI m. ÁKÛTI.

YAJNA (married his sister) Dakshiná

Tosha	Pratosha	Santosha	Bhadra	Shuti	Idaspati	Idhma	Kavi	Vibhu	Svahna	Sudiva	Rochana

N. B.—The sons of Yajna are the Sanhita Devas of the 1st. Manvantara.

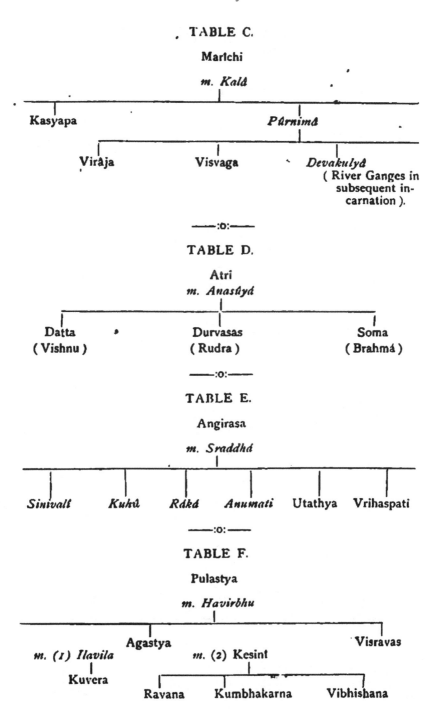

TABLE C.

Marïchi

m. Kalā

- Kasyapa
- *Pûrnimā*
  - Virāja
  - Visvaga
  - *Devakulyā*
    (River Ganges in subsequent incarnation).

——:o:——

TABLE D.

Atri

m. Anasûyā

- Datta (Vishnu)
- Durvasas (Rudra)
- Soma (Brahmā)

——:o:——

TABLE E.

Angirasa

m. Sraddhā

- *Sinivalï*
- *Kuhû*
- *Rākā*
- *Anumati*
- Utathya
- Vrihaspati

——:o:——

TABLE F.

Pulastya

m. Havirbhu

- Agastya
  - *m. (1) Ilavila*
    - Kuvera
  - *m. (2) Kesinï*
    - Ravana
    - Kumbhakarna
    - Vibhishana
- Visravas

63

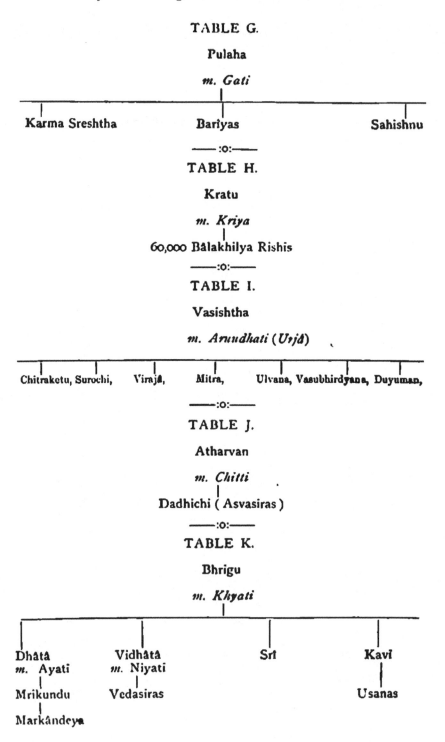

TABLE G.

Pulaha

m. Gati

| Karma Sreshtha | Bariyas | Sahishnu |

——:o:——

TABLE H.

Kratu

m. Kriya

60,000 Bâlakhilya Rishis

——:o:——

TABLE I.

Vasishtha

m. Arundhati (Urjâ)

| Chitraketu, Surochi, | Virajâ, | Mitra, | Ulvana, Vasubhirdyana, Duyuman, |

——:o:——

TABLE J.

Atharvan

m. Chitti

Dadhichi (Asvasiras)

——:o:——

TABLE K.

Bhrigu

m. Khyati

Dhâtâ *m. Ayati* — Vidhâtâ *m. Niyati* — Srî — Kavi

Mrikundu — Vedasiras — — Usanas

Markândeya

TABLE L.

Daksha *m.* Prasûti.

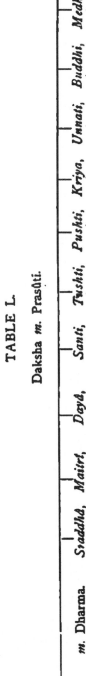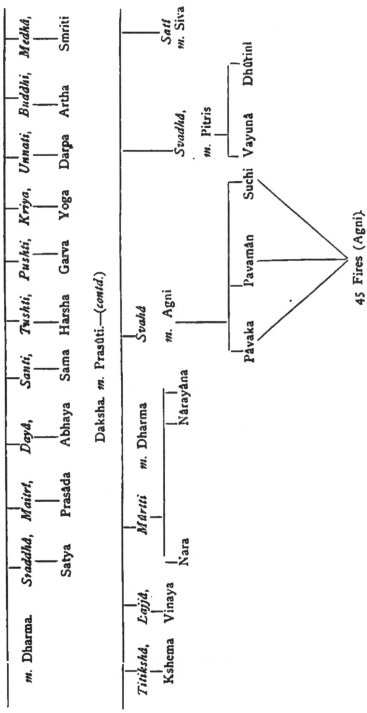

Daksha *m.* Prasûti.—(*contd.*)

TABLE M.

——:o:——

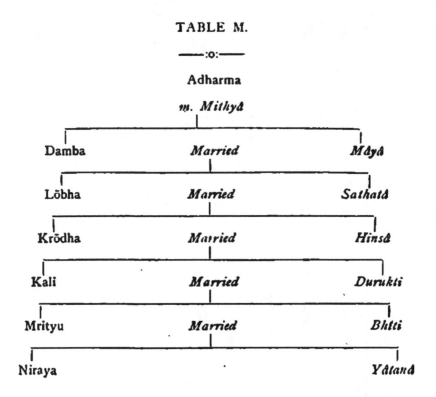

Adharma

m. Mithyá

Damba	*Married*	*Máyá*
Löbha	*Married*	*Sathatá*
Krödha	*Married*	*Hinsá*
Kali	*Married*	*Durukti*
Mrityu	*Married*	*Bhíti*
Niraya		*Yátaná*

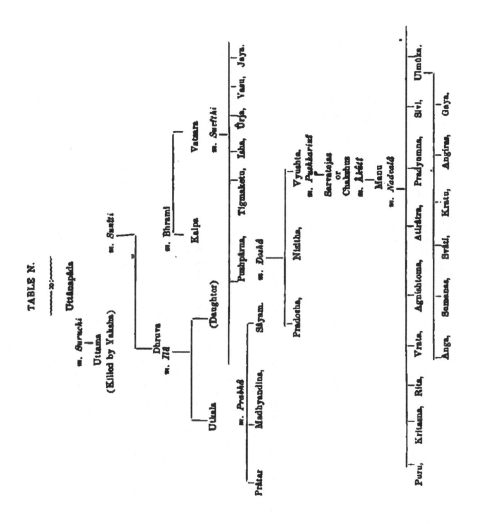

TABLE N.

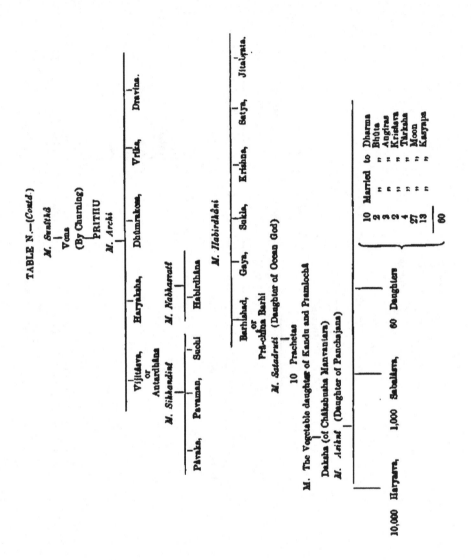

TABLE N.—(Contd.)

TABLE O.

Dharma

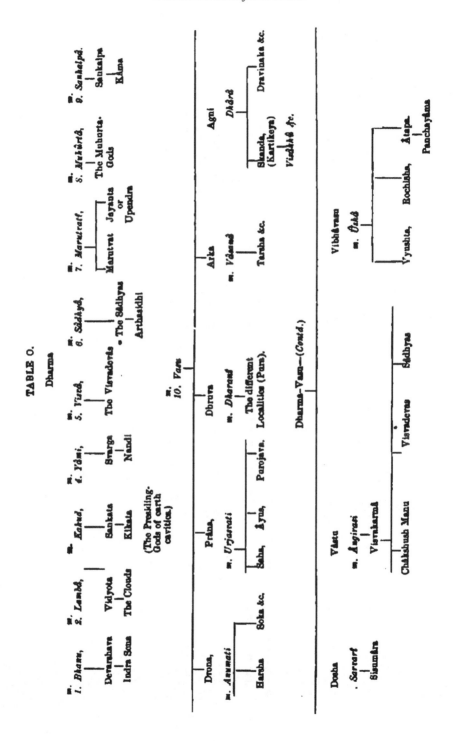

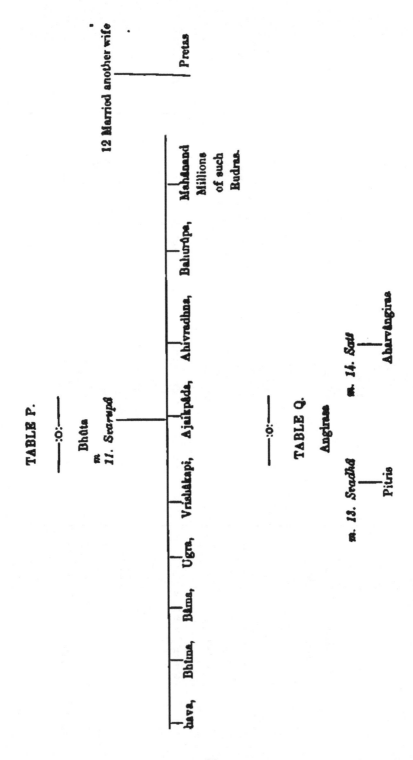

TABLE R.

Krisâsva

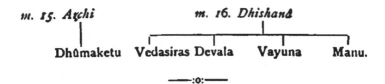

m. 15. Aŗchi   *m. 16. Dhishanâ*

Dhûmaketu   Vedasiras Devala   Vayuna   Manu.

——:o:——

TABLE S.

Târksha

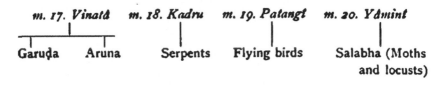

m. 17. Vinatâ   *m. 18. Kadru*   *m. 19. Patangî*   *m. 20. Yâminî*

Garuḍa   Aruna   Serpents   Flying birds   Salabha (Moths
and locusts)

——:o:——

TABLE T.

Chandra (Moon)

m. 21 to 47. Krittikâ &c (Stars in the lunar path on the Ecliptic.)

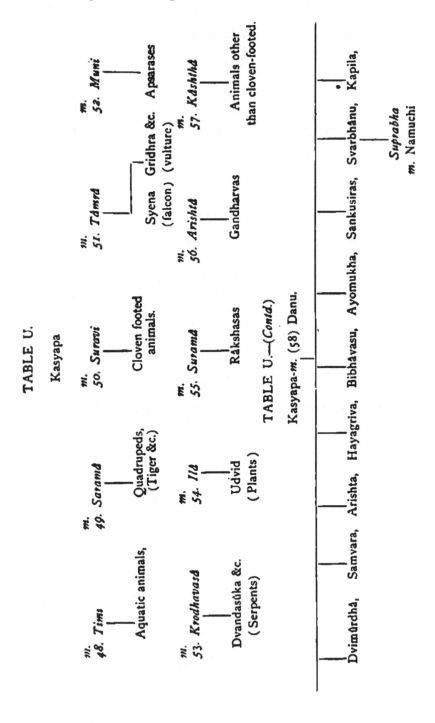

TABLE U.

Kasyapa

m. 48. *Timi*
Aquatic animals,

m. 49. *Saramd*
Quadrupeds,
(Tiger &c.)

m. 50. *Suravi*
Cloven footed
animals.

m. 51. *Tdmrd*
Syena   Gridhra &c.   Apearases
(falcon) (vulture)

m. 52. *Muni*

m. 53. *Krodhavasd*
Dvandasóka &c.
(Serpents)

m. 54. *Ild*
Udvid
(Plants)

m. 55. *Surand*
Rákshasas

m. 56. *Arishtd*
Gandharvas

m. 57. *Kdshthd*
Animals other
than cloven-footed.

TABLE U.—(*Contd.*)

Kasyapa-*m.* (58) Danu.

Dvimördhá, Samvara, Arishta, Hayagriva, Bibhávasu, Ayomukha, Sankusiras, Svarbhánu, Kapila,

Suprabha
m. Namuchi

72

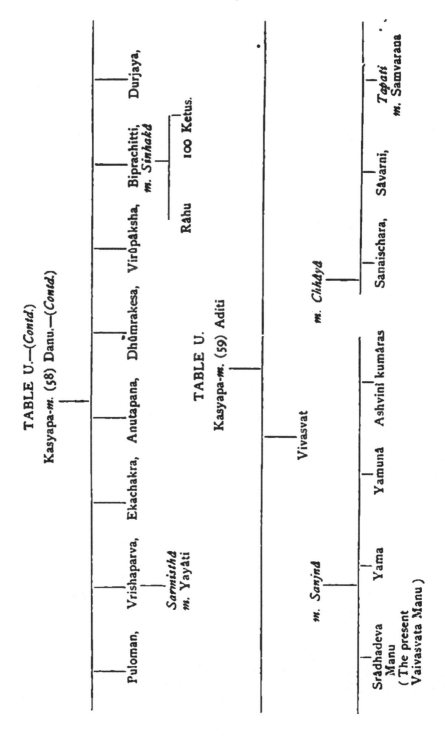

TABLE U.—(Contd.)

Kasyapa-m. (58) Danu.—(Contd.)

Puloman, Vrishaparva, Ekachakra, Anutapana, Dhûmrakesa, Virûpâksha, Biprachitti, Durjaya,
Sarmisthâ   *m. Sinhakâ*
m. Yayâti   Rahu   100 Ketus.

TABLE U.

Kasyapa-m. (59) Aditi

Vivasvat

m. Chhâyâ

m. Sanjnâ

Srâdhadeva   Yama   Yamunâ   Ashvini kumâras   Sanaischara,   Sâvarni,   *Tapati*
Manu   *m.* Samvarana
(The present
Vaivasvata Manu)

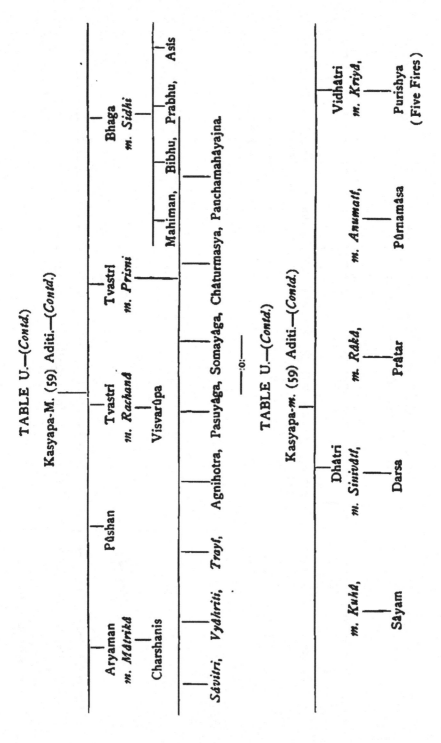

TABLE U.—(Contd.)

Kasyapa-M. (59) Aditi.—(Contd.)

TABLE U.—(Contd.)

Kasyapa-m. (59) Aditi.—(Contd.)

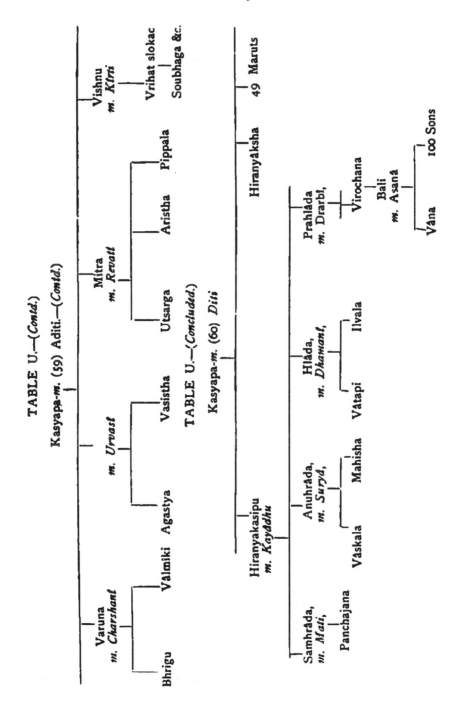

TABLE U.—(Contd.)

Kasyapa-m. (59) Aditi.—(Contd.)

Bhrigu

Varuna
m. Charshani

Valmiki   Agastya

Vasistha

m. Urvasi

Utsarga

Aristha

Pippala

Mitra
m. Revati

Vishnu
m. Kirti

Vrihat slokac
Soubhaga &c.

TABLE U.—(Concluded.)

Kasyapa-m. (60) Diti

Hiranyakasipu
m. Kayddhu

Samhrada,
m. Mati,

Panchajana

Vaskala

Anuhrada,
m. Suryd,

Mahisha

Hlada,
m. Dhamant,

Vatapi   Ilvala

Hiranyaksha

49 Maruts

Prahlada
m. Drarbi,

Virochana

Bali
m. Asana

Vana   100 Sons

75

GENERAL REMARKS ON THE TABLES.

These Tables must not be mistaken for human genealogies. The reader will have to carry himself in imagination to a time when there was a vast sheet of nebulous mass, when the globes and planets had not been formed, and the phenomena now known as day, night, year, month and season were still unknown.

The process known as Pralaya had absorbed the life energies of Trilokī, which remained latent in that intermediate plane between the higher and the lower Lokas known as Mahar Loka. When the creative process set in, and the ground was prepared for the manifestation of life, life energies streamed forth from the Mahar Loka, more as types than as individuals. These types are called Prajāpatis or the Lords of life kingdoms. They carry back to Trilokī all the life energies of the previous Kalpa. At Pralaya, they draw back unto themselves all the life energies of the dying Trilokī, and take a lasting sleep in the archetypal plane (Mahar Loka) to which they properly belong. The Prajāpatis of the First Manvantara become the Rishis of other Manvantaras. As the first Lords of creation bring back the life energies as well as the lost experiences of the previous Kalpa, so the Rishis bring back the lost knowledge of each Manvantara. This is fully explained in the fourteenth Chapter of the Eighth Skandha. The Kumārs are not Prajāpatis, as they come from a plane higher than Mahar Loka. In the first Manvantara, Marichī, Atrī Angirasa, Pulastya, Pulaha, Kratu, Bhrigu, Vasistha, Daksha, and Nārada are mentioned as the chief Prajāpatis. Of these, Nārada is not strictly speaking a Prajāpati, or Lord of creation, as he took no part in the work of creation, though he is called so having proceeded from Mahar Loka. Kardama, Ruchi and Visvakarmā are some of the other Prajāpatis.

Of the Prajāpatis, seven form distinct types by themselves. They preside over the seven stars, which form the constellation of Great Bear. They send forth their energies from the plane of the Seven Sages, and guide the course of life evolution that takes place in Trilokī. The sages are relieved every Manvantara by others who take up their place. The seven sages of our Manvantara, are different from the Prajāpatis of the first Manvantara. It is by great sacrifices and by great efforts that the highest Rishis of a

Manvantara attain the position of the Seven Sages. The Sages may become Prajāpatis, and Prajāpatis may become Kumāras. And men may become sages, if they follow the true path. The grades that divide men from sages or Rishis proper are many, and human evolution proceeds on the line of those grades.

Energies of another kind proceeded from Mahar Loka, energies known as Devas and Asuras. They work out, or rather they are intimately connected with, the tendency of life-evolution. There is a tendency in the Spiritual Jiva to acquire experience of the lower planes, through senses which they develop. The Asuras are connected with this tendency. There is the opposite tendency in the Jiva to get rid of the material taint and the material restriction earned in the efforts to acquire manifold experiences and to gain back the original state of purity after the acquisition of fresh spiritual treasures though the experiences of matter. The Devas are connected with this tendency.

These are the forms of life which then come into existence and work out their evolution in this Trilokī.

Life evolution proceeds on two different lines — that of globes and that of individuals. They are represented by the two sons of Manu — Priyavrata and Uttānapāda.

In the line of Priyavrata we find how the globes were formed in the solar system, through various cosmic fires originating from Visvakarmā, how this earth was formed, its continents and countries. The different divisions of the Bhūr Loka are presided over by different forms of intelligence, who are the sons of Priyavrata.

In the line of Uttānapāda we find the different life kingdoms passing through different stages of evolution.

First of all, we find a limit is put to life existence in Trilokī by Dhruva. Dhruva, son of Uttānapāda, presides over the Polar Star. That Star forms the farthest limit of Trilokī. Matter is so attenuated there that it can last for one Kalpa. We are speaking of a period when infant souls merged out to commence the race of life in the present Kalpa. They were spiritual and highly spiritual too. But they were carried away by the general current of creative tendencies. They were to limit themselves by sheath after sheath, so that they might acquire the experiences of Svar Loka, of Bhuvar Loka and of Bhūr Loka in succession. Dhruva, the infant soul, a child only five years old, however, resisted the common temptation. He would not go down, for he had an important service to render to the Universe. Who would advise him in this noble mission but Nārada. Nārada was out of element when the creative process was in full swing, and it was a necessity of life evolution. But there were instances of exception, instances of noble souls who would not go in with the general current, but would like to remain fixed in spiritual life, and Nārada was always to be found helping them with his advice.

Dhruva remained fixed in his early spirituality. That was a sacrifice, for he could not enrich himself with further spiritual experiences, through the senses, of the lower planes of life. But he had to keep up an abode which was to be resorted to by evolved souls in later days, souls that in due course would reach that high spiritual plane.

From that Kālpic plane and the dweller thereof, we come to lower planes and their dwellers, to the divisions of time that rule the lives of individuals and of lives adapted to these divisions of time. We come from the elementals of the Svarga plane, or the Devas, to the elementals of the Astral or Bhuvar plane, the Pitris, Bhūtas, Pretas and Pisāchas, till we reach the mineral kingdom, represented by Himalya, the Mountain king. At this point a turning point was reached in life evolution, and the goddess of life-evolution became the daughter of the Mountain king. Of this we shall know more hereafter.

We know of Daksha, first as the son of Brahmā, the creative Prajāpati when the life-process rapidly worked itself out in Elemental forms. Then there was no sexual procreation. Creation meant the materialisation of the Jiva. Satī, the daughter of Daksha, was the guiding energy of life-evolution. She became wedded to Śiva, the Lord of Bhūtas, Pretas and Pisāchas who by the infusion of their Tāmasic energies could bring down Jivas from their high spiritual plane.

When the process of materialisation was over, when the Jivas or Monads reached the lowest limits of materiality, the mission of Daksha came to an end.

Life evolution had now to pass through mineral, vegetable and animal stages, until at last the human stage was reached.

Satī now appeared as the daughter of the mineral king Himālaya. She gave the upward bent to life evolution and by the energy she imparted minerals were able to shake off the rigidity and stability of gross matter, to develop the sense of touch and to become vegetable at last. In like manner vegetable became animal, and animals at last became men.

Śiva, the husband of Bhagavati or Durgā, as Satī was now called, is the Purusha of Dissolution. Bhagavati is His Energy, Who guides the Monadic or Jiva Evolution of the Kalpa. It is the wear and tear, the process of destruction, that counteracts the cohesive strength of the particles forming mineral matter, which by its action becomes flexible and so receptive of outside influences.

Cells by division and death become capable of the life process in themselves. Vegetables grow by the rejection of cells, which necessitates a number of physiological processes. Death brings on life, waste, repair.

If animals exist in one and the same body, progress will be limited, further evolution will be impossible. It is by death that we evolve.

Bhagavatī works out the evolution of life in different kingdoms till the stage of humanity is reached.

At this point Aryaman, one of the Ādityas, comes to the help of humanity. Through his influence the sons of humanity become endowed with the power of reasoning, — the faculty of discrimination.

The sons of Aryaman are called Charshanis. The word Charshani literally means a cultivator. Its secondary sense given in the Vedic lexicon is one endowed with the discriminative faculty. The word Charshani is used in the Vedas for man. It is the equivalent of Arya or Aryan, the ploughman.

But it is not as ploughmen or cultivators, that the Aryans had their high place in humanity, but as men endowed with the power of discrimination. And this we owe to Aryaman. This is why, though an Āditya, he is called the chief of Pitris by Sri Krishna.

"I am Aryaman of the Pitris." — Bhagavat Gitā.

We have thus the first stage in life evolution, when the spiritual Jiva had to descend from the elemental to the mineral form. Next we have the second stage, when minerals passed through higher forms of life till the Human Kingdom was reached.

Then we have the third stage, when men became endowed with the power of discrimination.

In the exercise of the discriminative faculty men were helped by their elder brothers, the Rishis and Mahātmās of every period, and by Avatāras Who apeared from time to time.

Then the ground was prepared for further evolution. The Sacred Injunctions or the Vedas were revealed to men to give them a sense of right and wrong, of duties and prohibitions. The Vedas also held out to the developed sense of men the charming prospect of life in Svarga Loka with its lasting and alluring enjoyments. This may be called the stage of Karma Kānda. In following the stages of human evolution we have come down to Vaivasvatu Manvantara.

Side by side with the efforts made to raise humanity in the scale of evolution, sin was accumulating in the great Atlantean continent which spread over the whole of what we now know as the Bay of Bengal. The Atlanteans had acquired a mastery over the five forces of nature, which they used for selfish objects and against the cause and current of evolution.

Then there was a great revolution in Nature. The great Atlantean Continent went down with its load of sins. The sons of Sagar, the Atlantean king, became buried under the great ocean, which overtook the doomed continent, and to this day the sea is called in India, "Sāgar" or relating to Sagar.

There was a corresponding upheaval in the Himalayas, and the sacred river Gangā streamed forth from their sides, inaugurating the spiritual regeneration of the Universe. Much of what we now know as India must have been raised up at the time, and on its sacred soil appeared the great Avatāra Rāma, Who put an end to the disorganising, chaos-loving sons of Lankā. The people of Lankā were called Rākshasas as they were working towards the destruction of all order, all progress in the Universe, and rendered everything topsy-turvy in Nature.

Now it was time for Sri Krishna to appear, the greatest of all Avatāras in our Kalpa, Who gave the last bent to the progress of humanity. He wedded Himself with all the principles that enter into the constitution of man, so that man may come up to Him. He taught the basic unity of all beings, and laid down the path of Service and Devotion. He established the reign of spiritual life, and ever since His lotus feet sanctified the soil of India, the Scriptures only re-iterate His teachings, and they all sing His glory for ever and ever. We shall find in its true place the Service done by Lord Sri Krishna, and how by His Avatarship humanity has made one more advance in the scale of human evolution. When the Lord appeared, Bhagavatī made her appearance too as the daughter of Nanda. It is with Her energy that Sri Krishna performed the mission of His Avatarship.

This is a bare outline of what the Tables teach us, We shall consider them each in its own place. We shall find a detailed account as to how the Universe is preserved. We shall hear of great Rishis, of many Avatāras, of the part played by Devas and Asurus. We shall see how the Monads pass through different stages of evolution, till the idea of perfect humanity is presented by Lord Krishna.

The Tables sometimes speak of life Kingdoms, sometimes of human races, sometimes of types and principles, and sometimes of individuals. Sometimes, the names used convey a good deal of hidden meaning, sometimes they are used at random.

In the line of Priyavratra, we find how globes are formed, how continents and countries appear. The solidification of earth is indicated by the muteness of Bharata. Bhārata Varsa or India is called the first born of all countries, and other lands are enjoined to follow and to obey their eldest brother.

TABLE A.

SKANDHA IV. CHAP. 1.

The names of the first table have been considered before.

TABLE B.

SKANDHA IV. CHAP. 1.

Ruchi and Akuti both mean Wish, Desire. Yajna is sacrifice, Dakshinā means ordinarily the present made to a Brāhmana for officiating at a ceremony. It is also the present made for the performance of a Vedic sacrifice. No Vedic sacrifice is complete without the present of Dakshinā to the officiating priest. Dakshinā was married to Yajna, for they are inseparable. Possibly Yajna has reference to the elemental or Devic character of life forms in the first Manvantara. That also explains why there was no Indra separate from the Avatāra of the Manvantara.

The first Manvantara was one of Pravritti or Descent, Spirit could descend into matters only with the help of Desire. Desire is the father of Kāma — Kāma is the characteristic of Vedic Yajna. Yajna therefore guided the First Manvantara. He was the Avatāra of Vishnu as well as the Indra of the Devas.

The sons of Yajna were the Devas of the First Manvantarā. The Bhāgavata calls them Sushita or Bliss gods. The Vishnu Purāna calls them Yāma Devas. The Manvantara Devas have for their mission the carrying out of the cyclic work of the Manvantara.

TABLE C.

SKANDHA IV. CHAP. 1.

Marichi means literally a ray of light. The word is frequently applied to the sun's ray. As the sun's ray breaks up into the component colours, so the line of Marichi broke up into the life kingdoms. Kalā means a digit of the moon. Kasyapa was the son of Marichi and Kalā. He married the 13 daughters of Daksha, in the line Uttānapada. By his wives, Kasyapa was the father of Suras and Asuras, of elementals, vegetables, animals and men. He is directly connected with the Monads. Marichi and Kalā have a special significance in reference to Jivic evolution. Does the pair symbolise the sun's ray reflected on the Moon or the Atmic ray reflected on Buddhi? Any how Marichi and Kalā imply the divine ray in the Jivas or Ātma-Buddhi.

The monads of individuals are limited by the shells or bodies of Kasyapa's line. (The word Kasyapa means primarily bed, seat). They come through Pūrnima, daughter of Marichi. The sons of Pūrnima are Viraja and Visvaga.

Viraja is free from Rajas. Visvaga means one who goes all over the Universe. Viraja and Visvaga are Universal aspects of Jivic Intelligence.

(Viraja is the father of Vairājas). Devakulyā is the daughter of Purnimā. She flowed from the washings of the feet of Vishnu and became the divine river Gangā.

TABLE D.

SKANDHA IV. CHAP. 1.

Atri = *a* (not) + *tri* (three). Not three, but three in one. Anasuyā = (not)+ *asuyā* (envy, intolerance, jealousy).

Atri made severe Tapas for one hundred years for a son like unto the Lord of the Universe. The ascetic fire at last broke forth from his head and instantly Brahmā, Vishnu and Śiva appeared before him.

"Lords!" said Atri, "I had only one of you in my mind, but you have all Three come to me!"

The Trinity replied: — "We are three in one. You shall have three sons, one after each of us."

Anasuyā begot Sōma or the Moon after Brahmā, Datta or Dattātreya after Vishnu and Durvāsas after Śiva.

[The Moon is thus a sort of Brahmā or creator to the present Kalpa.]

Atri represents the Creative, the Preservative and the Destructive Intelligence in the individual, all united to carry out the complex process of evolution.

The Brihat Aranyaka certainly refers to one of his aspects in the following passage: —

"Speech is Attri; for by speech food is consumed; for Attri is verily derived from the root Attih (to eat, consume); he is the consumer of all." II-2-4.

TABLE E.

"Where was he, who thus established us? He Is within the mouth; hence is Ayāsya. He is Angirasa, because he is the essence of the members." Brihat Aranyaka I-3-8.

Commenting on this passage Sankarācharya says: "Life is also called Angirasa, the essence of causes and effects. Angirasa is a compound of Anga and Rāsa — Anga meaning members, causes, and effects, and Rāsa essence, substance; the whole meaning therefore is the substance, upon which causes and effects depend — It is the essence of every thing, because unless it were present, all would become without effect."

"He who abides in the mouth is Angirasa, for he is the essence (Rāsa) of the members (Anga). Life is the essence of the members. This is also Brihaspati. Speech is Brihati. Life is the preserver (pati) of Brihati, therefore it is Brihaspati."

B.A. I-3-19 and 20.

Brihaspati or the presiding deity of the planet Jupiter is called Angirasa *i.e.* the son of Angiras. The wife of Angiras is, according to the Bhāgavata, Sraddha or Faith, and, according to Vishnu Purina, Smriti or Memory. The latter is a more suggestive name. Brihaspati or Jupiter is the essence of all beings and of the Universe and is connected with the memory of the past.

Angirasa is the Rishi of the 5th Mandala of the Rig Veda. The Mantras of that Mandala are composed in the Brihati or big Metre. This accounts for the name Brihaspati (Brihati+pati).

Brihaspati or Jupiter, as the guide of the Devas, has to play a most important part in bringing about the life evolution of the present Kalpa according to the records of the past and the essence or Rāsa of all beings. The Āranyaka therefore calls him life itself.

Utathya, another son of Angiras, is *u+tathya. U* is an interjection, used as an expletive — *Tathya* means reality, truth — Utathya is said to be an incarnation of Vishnu. Both the brothers are said to have distinguished themselves in the Second Manvantarā. *Sinivāli* is the day preceding that of new moon or that day on which the moon rises with a scarcely visible crescent. Kuhā is new moon day when the moon is altogether invisible.

Rākā is the full moon day.

Anumati is the 15th day of the moon's age on which she rises one digit less than full.

The full moon and new moon days have thus a mysterious connection with the essence of all beings. On those days the herbs have their medicinal properties in full and even men have mysterious potencies, which have formed the subject of occult study.

TABLE F.

Pulastya = Pula + Stya.

Pula is large, wide. It also means a thrill of joy or fear.

Stya is he who collects, is connected with, remains in. Agastya = Aga + Stya.

Aga is mountain, unable to walk, fixed.

According to a Pauranik legend, the Vindhya mountain began to rise higher and higher so as to obstruct the path of the sun and moon. The gods being alarmed sought the aid of Agastya who was the teacher of Vindhya. The Rishi approached the mountain and asked it to bend down and give him an easy passage to the south and to retain the same position till his return. Vindhya obeyed the order of his teacher, but Agastya never returned from the south and Vindhya never attained the height of Meru.

According to the Bhāgavata, Agastya is the digestive fire of the stomach.

Visravas = Vi (signifying intensity) + Sravas (ear).

Kubera is literally deformed. IIe is the god of riches and Regent of the North. He is the king of the Yakshas and Kinnaras and a friend of Rudra. His abode is Kailāsa. He is represented as having three legs, only eight teeth and a yellow mark in place of one eye.

Rāvana, Kumbhakarna and Vibhishana are Rākshasas made famous by the Rāmayana.

Rāvana is one who makes a loud noise. The Rākshasas reached the height of their power in his time. The Yakshas, before his time, had occupied Lankā or Atlantis under Kubera, but Rāvana propitiated Śiva by his loud hymns, and acquired easy mastery over his kindred elementals. He ousted the Yakshas from Lankā and made it his own capital. Rāvana also controlled the higher Devas of Trilokī.

Kumbha karna = Kumbha (pitcher) + Karna (ear). This pitcher-eared brother of Rāvana is said to have devoured thousands of beings including sages and heavenly nymphs. He slept for six months at a time. He was ultimately slain by Rāma.

Vibhisana, meaning the Terrible, left his brother Rāvana and joined Rāma. After the death of Rāvana, Rāma installed him on the throne of Lankā. He is said to be still living.

The Rākshasas are said to have possessed Kāma Rupa *i.e.* they could assume any body at will.

In the line of Pulastya we have this strange combination — the digestive fire of stomach, ears, Yakshas and lastly the Rākshasas who could change their body at will. Altogether we may say, Pulastya is Intelligence which governs animal passions and Kāma.

TABLE G.

Pulaha = Pula + ha. *Ha* is one who gives up.

Gati is motion.

Karma-Srestha is one most skilled in karma or work.

Varīyas is excellent, preferable.

Sahishnu is patient, enduring.

Pulaha seems to be the higher aspect of Kāma — the impulses pure and simple, apart from their Kāmic generator, or perhaps Pulaha may represent Prānic activity.

TABLE H.

Kratu is a Vedic sacrifice, intelligence, power, ability. Kriyā is action.

Bālakhilyas — are a class of Rishis 60,000 in number, of the size of the thumb, and are said to precede the sun's chariot. The word literally implies stunted in growth like infants. These Rishis are said to burn brightly with the spiritual fire of asceticism. The number 60,000 is significant. It indicates a correspondence.

Perhaps the Rishis represent the sense perceptions which are guided by the Adhidevas who have their abode in the heart of the sun. The Balakhilya Rishis are therefore said to accompany the sun's chariot. Their connection with Vedic sacrifices is also intelligible, as they are generally directed to the Adhidevas.

TABLE I.

Vaśisthā is the Controller. He is the spiritual teacher of the Solar Race and represents spiritual Intelligence or Higher Manas. He is the controller of the senses and the lower mind.

Urjā is Energy. She is also called Arundhati.

TABLE J.

Atharvan — The Veda called by that name.

Dadhīchi — The name of a Rishi who accepted death In order to serve the Devas. Visvakarmān forged the thunderbolt with his bones and Indra defeated Vritra, the Asura King, with that weapon.

The line of Atharvan represents self sacrifice for universal good as well as magic or occult wisdom.

TABLE K.

Bhrigu — is the Dweller of Mahar Loka, or the Archetypal plane. Upon the Pralaya of Trilokī, the essence of that triple plane and its Karma become embedded in Mahar Loka. The creative process sets in again in strict conformity to the Karma of the past. Bhrigu is therefore father of:

Dhātā — or Universal Karma

Vidhātā — or Individual Karma, and

Sri or *Lakshmī* — the wife of Vishnu, the Energy of Preservation.

Ayati — or potency is the wife of Dhātā, Mrikandu and Markandeya, are in this line.

Niyati — or fate, is the wife of Vidhātā. Prāna and Vedasiras are in this line.

Kavi — is another son of Bhrigu and *Usanas* or *Sukra* is Kavi's son. But according to some authorities Kavi is the same as Usanas. It is a matter for reflection how Sukra or the presiding Rishi of the planet Venus is connected with Mahar Loka or the trans-personal plane. Mahar Loka is the first approach to universality and therefore may correspond to Higher Manas. However that be, Venus corresponds to the first plane of universality.

The consideration of Tables C to K has proved to be an interesting one. But readers are requested to remember that this is a mere study by an inquiring student and they are left to think for themselves. I might have dwelt at some length on this portion of the subject, but that would be going beyond the scope of the present work.

Briefly speaking then,

Marīchi — is Monādic ray or Ātmā-Buddhi,

Atri — is the adjustment of the creative, preservative and destructive tendencies in a Jiva,

Angiras — is the Essence of Creation, the auric repository of the Jiva,

Pulastya — is Kāmic Intelligence,

Pulaha — is higher Kāmic Intelligence, or it may be Prānic also,

Kratu — is lower Mānasic Intelligence,

Vasishtha — is Higher Mānasic Intelligence.

TABLE L.

Daksha — is the Able.

Prasūti — is the Mother, the Procreative Energy. During the First Manvantara Daksha had nothing to do with sexual procreation. He was the father of 16 primal energies. These energies were wedded to Dharma, Agni, the Pitris and Śiva — 13 to Dharma and one to each of the others.

Dharma — is that which binds the creation. Man and man, man and animal, animal and animal, all forms of creation are kept together by Dharma. The binding forces of creation are the wives of Dharma.

Sraddhā or Faith is the first wife of Dharma. Her son is *Satya* or Truth.

Maitri or Friendliness is the second wife. Her son is *Prasāda* or complacence.

Dayā or compassion is the third wife. Her son is *Abhaya* or Freedom from fear.

Sānti or Peace is the fourth wife. Her son is *Sama* or Tranquility.

The fifth wife is *Tushti* or contentment. Her son is *Harsha* or joy.

The sixth wife is *Pushti* or Fullness. Her son is *Garva* or Pride.

The seventh wife is *Kriyā*. Her son is *Yoga*.

The eighth wife is *Unnati* or Advancement. Her son is *Darpa* or Vanity.

The ninth wife is *Buddhi*. Her son is *Artha*.

The tenth wife is *Medhā* or Intellect. Her son is *Smriti* or Memory.

The eleventh wife is *Titikshā* or Forbearance. Her son is *Kshema* or Well-being.

The twelfth wife is *Lajjā* or Shame. Her son is *Vinaya* or Modesty.

The thirteenth and last wife of Dharma is *Mūrti* or Form. Her sons are Nara and Nārāyana, *i.e.* Humanity and Divinity. The Human Form constitute a Duality. It is in this dual form that Sri Krishna incarnated Himself.

From Dharma we pass to Agni.

[Agni is used in many senses. It means the channel of communication between different kingdoms in nature, specially between Man and Deva, as also a vehicle of consciousness, and sometimes consciousness itself. It also means the Rupa or form-giving principle in the Universe. It is frequently used in the Purānas in the last sense.]

Agni was wedded to *Svāhā*, the 14th. daughter of Daksha. His three sons are *Pāvaka* or the Purifier, *Pavamān* or that which is being purified and *Sāchi* or Pure. They have 45 sons who with their fathers and grandfather form the Forty-nine Fires. They are separately mentioned in the Vedic Sacrifices in honour of Agni.

Svadhā is the 15th. daughter of Daksha. She was married to the Pitris. Agnishvatvā, Barhishad, Sōmapa and Ājyapa are the names of the Pitris. They are with fire (Sagni) or without fire (Niragini). Svadhā bore two daughters to the Pitris, Vayunā and Dhārini. Both of them were well-versed in the Supreme wisdom.

[*Vayānā* is knowledge, wisdom, faculty of perception. *Dhārini* means that which bears, holds, carries, supports. Sometimes the word is used to mean the earth.

This two-fold classification means that some of the Pitris give the *body*, which is the receptacle or carrier, with its sub-divisions, and others give knowledge, wisdom and the faculties of perception].

Sāti is the last daughter of Daksha. She was wedded to Śiva. We shall specially notice her in the succeeding chapter.

THE QUARREL BETWEEN ŚIVA AND DAKSHA.

SKANDHA IV., CHAP. 2.

Of old the Prajāpaties performed a Yajna, and the Devas and Rishis all graced the occasion with their presence. Prajāpati Daksha entered the assembly, when all stood up to receive him, except Brahmā and Śiva. Daksha saluted his father Brahmā and with His permission took a seat. But he was so mortified by the conduct of Śiva that he could not contain himself, and indignantly broke forth thus: — "O you, Rishis, Devas and Agni! Witness this disgraceful conduct of Śiva my own son-in-law, rather my disciple. This senseless being would not do so much as rise up and receive me. He has no sense of respect and dis-respect, of purity and impurity. He is mindless of all injunctions and observances. Do you know, what he does? He roves like a mad man in the crematories, with his host of Bhūtas, Pretas and Pisāchas, sometimes laughing, sometimes weeping, his body covered over with the ashes of dead bodies, their bones serving for his ornaments. His name is Śiva (auspicious). But he is really A-Śiva (inauspicious). He is fond of intoxication, and his companions are the impure and senseless Bhūtas. Oh! that I have given my daughter Sāti in marriage to him. That was simply to obey the orders of Brahmā."

Śiva remained unmoved. Daksha went on abusing Him and at last he cursed Śiva saying "This vilest of Devas shall not participate in the sacrificial offerings to Indra, Upendra and others." He then left the place in a rage.

Nandisvara, the chief companion of Śiva, could not bear the gross and wanton insult done to his master. He retorted in angry tones the unkind words of Daksha and the approbation of some of the councillors. "Śiva bears malice to none. It is Daksha who makes differences, where there are none. Ignorant people follow him and blame Śiva. The Vedas deal with transitory objects. Worldly attachments receive an impetus from the Karma Kānda of the Vedas and they beget vices and evil deeds. This Daksha looks upon the body as the soul. He shall be as fond of women as a beast and his face shall be that of an Ajā (goat). Verily he deserves this, as he looks upon Avidyā as Tatvavidyā. He publicly insults Śiva. The Brāhmanas who follow him shall go through the repeated course of births and deaths and shall resort to the apparently pleasing Karma Kānda of the Vedas. These Brāhmanas shall have no scruples to eat anything and they shall make a profession of their learning, their Tapas and their austerities (Vrata). They shall consider their riches, their body and their Indriyas to be all in all. They shall beg about from door to door."

Bhrigu, the leader of the Brāhmanas, thus returned the curses of Nandi on the followers of Śiva: — "Those that will follow Śiva, shall be disregardful of the Sat (real) Śastras and shall be irreligious. With braids of hair on their head, and ashes and bones round their body, they shall frequent places where wine is indulged in. The Vedas have at all times laid down the approved path. The Rishis of old followed their injunctions and Nārāyana is at their very root. Those that forget all this shall only attain the Tāmasic Śiva, the Lord of Bhūtas and Pishachas."

Śiva with his followers then left the place. The Prajāpatis performed the Yajna for 1,000 years.

Sometime after, Brahmā made Daksha the head of the Prajāpatis, and his pride knew no bounds. He commenced a sacrifice called Vrihaspati Yajna and to it he invited all except Śiva and his own daughter Sāti. Sāti heard of the grand preparations made by her father and became impatient to witness the Yajna herself. Śiva at last yielded to her expostulations much against His own will. She left for Daksha's house accompanied by the attendants of Śiva. At last she reached her father's house and went to the place of sacrifice. But her father would not receive her. She did not find any offering to Śiva. She could easily make out that Daksha had disregarded her husband. No attention was also paid to her. She grew furious with rage and addressing her father said: — "With Śiva, all are equal. He has enmity with none. Who else but thee could be envious of his virtues? Thou hast attributed evil things to Śiva. But do not the Devas know all that and knowingly worship Him? If the devoted wife cannot kill her husband's calumniators, she must leave the place with ears closed with her hands. But if she is strong enough, she must in the first place sever the tongue of the calumniator from his body by force and then put an end to herself. Thou art the calumniator of Śiva. This my body is from thee, so I shall not keep it any longer. If prohibited food is taken, the best thing is to throw it out. True, there are the two Paths of Inclination (Pravritti) and of Renunciation (Nivritti). But one cannot adopt both the Paths at one and the same time. What action is there for Śiva? He is Brahmā Himself. Thou speakest of His ashes and bones. But hast thou any idea of His Yogic powers, in comparison with which thy powers as a performer of Vedic sacrifices are nothing? But there is no use wrangling with thee. I am ashamed of this body which has connection with thee. The sooner I get rid of it the better."

So saying Sāti gave up her body, and there was great uproar. Her attendants made ready for an attack, when Bhirgu, who acted as Adhvaryu, invoked the Ribhus. They appeared and beat the attendants of Śiva, who ran away on all sides.

Nārada informed Śiva of what had happened. Śiva bit His lips in anger and tore up a Jatā (matted hairtuft) from his head. The Jatā glowed with electric fire.

He threw it down on the earth and the terrible Virabhadra sprang from it. His tall body reached the high heavens. He was dark as the clouds. He had one thousand hands, three eyes burning like the sun, teeth terrible to look at, and tufts of hair bright as fire. He had a garland of human skulls round his neck and there were various weapons in his hands.

"What are thy behests, O Lord?" exclaimed Virabhadra. "Thou art clever in fight, child, thou hast nothing to fear from the Brāhmanas, for verily thou art part of myself. Go forth at the head of my army. Put an end to Daksha and his Yajna." Such was the command of Śiva. Virabhadra rushed forth with trident in hand, and the attendants of Śiva followed him with enthusiasm and noise. The priests, the Brāhmanas and their wives present at Daksha's sacrifice saw a huge dust storm, as it were, coming from the north. "Can it be the hurricane?" thought they, "but the wind is not strong. Can this be the march of robbers? But King Prāchinabarhi is still alive. In his reign there is no fear from robbers. No one is driving cattle. What can be the cause of this approaching volume of dust?" The attendants of Śiva arrived in no time. Some of them were brown coloured, some yellow. Some had their belly, some their face, like Makara. They broke the implements of sacrifice and scattered them around. They pulled down the buildings and put out the fires. They made all sorts of sacrilege, ran after the Rishis and Devas and frightened the women. Manimān caught hold of Bhrigu and tied him up. Virabhadra captured Daksha; Chandesa captured Sūryya and Nandisvara captured Bhaga. Seeing this, the other Brāhmanas and Devas took to flight, but they were grievously hurt by the stones cast at them by the followers of Śiva. Virabhadra began to uproot the beard of Bhrigu, for while scoffing Śiva he made his beard prominent. Nandishvara pulled out the two eye-balls of Bhaga, for he had encouraged Daksha by side glances. Virabhadra did not also spare Pūshan, and pulled out all his teeth. Pūshan had showed his teeth while smiling in approval of Daksha's abuse. But the crowning act of Virabhadra was still to come. He sprang upon Daksha and made several attempts to cut off his head. But the head resisted all his strokes. Wonder-struck, he took at last the weapons of sacrifice and easily severed the head of Daksha even as it were the head of a beast of sacrifice. Loud were the lamentations at the place of sacrifice when Virbhadra with his followers left it for Kailāsa.

The Devas after this signal defeat went to Brahmā. Brahmā and Vishnu knew what was to happen at Daksha's sacrifice, so they had kept themselves aloof. When the Devas had related their mishap, Brahmā explained to them that they had done wrong in not allowing Śiva to participate in the Yajna offering. There was no help now but to appease the Astral Lord, Who could destroy the Universe at His will. So saying Brahmā himself went with the Devas to Kailāsa the abode of Śiva. He found there higher beings than men perfected by birth, herbs, Tapas, Mantra or Yoga and Yakshas, Kinnaras, Gandharvas and Apsarasas. The river Nandā (Gangā) traced its course round Kailāsa. High up on the mount was the abode called Alakā and the garden called Saugandhika (sweet-scented). On two sides of Alaka were the two rivers Nandā and Alakanandā, sanctified by the dust of Vishnu's feet. Alakā is the abode of Kubera, the Yaksha king. The Kinnaras occupied the Saugandhika garden. Near it was a large fig tree (Vata) 800 miles (100 Yojanas) high, the branches spreading over 600 miles. Below that tree, the Devas found Śiva in deep meditation for the good of the Universe. Brahmā asked Him to pardon Daksha and his followers who had slighted Him by withholding Yajna offerings. "Through thy favour let the Yajna be completed now. Let Daksha get back his life. Let the eyes of Bhagadeva, the head of Bhrigu, the teeth of Pūshan, be restored. Let the Devas and the sacrificial Rishis be relieved of all pain in their broken limbs. Since now, the remnants of Yajna offerings are all Thine. Take Thy offerings, and let the sacrifice be completed this day."

Śiva replied with a smile thus: — "Daksha is a mere child. I do not even think of him as an offender. But I have to set right those that are led astray by Māyā. Daksha's head is burnt up. So let him have the head of a goat. Bhagadeva shall find his Yajna offerings through the eyes of Mitra. Pūshan shall have *pishta* (crushed or ground up things) for his offerings. In company with other Devas, however, he shall have the use of the sacrificer's teeth. Let the broken limbs of the Devas be rehabilitated. But those that have lost their limbs shall use the arms of Asvinikumāra and the hands of Pūshan. So let it be with the Rishis too. Bhrigu shall have the beard of a goat."

The Devas thanked Śiva for His great kindness and invited Him to the sacrifice. Brahmā accompanied Śiva. Daksha regained life and looked on Śiva with reverence. He acquired wisdom and became purified in mind. The sacrifice was duly performed. Daksha sat in meditation and, lo! Vishnu appeared on the back of Garuda.

All rose up and saluted Him. Spontaneous prayers broke forth from one and all. Vishnu participated in the Yajna offerings. Addressing Daksha He said: — "Only ignorant people see the difference between Me and Śiva. I, Śiva and Brahmā are Three in One. For the creation, preservation and dissolution of the Universe, We assume three different Names. We, as the triune Ātmā, pervade all beings. Wise men therefore look upon all others as their own selves."

Such is the story of Sāti's death. She took birth again as the daughter of Himālaya and became wedded once more — the union with Śiva this time was permanent.

THOUGHTS ON THE ABOVE.

Brahmā, Vishnu and Śiva are the three aspects of the Second Purusha.

Brahmā brings into manifestation the Prajāpatis, and the Prajāpatis bring into manifestation the individuals and life forms. The other Prajāpatis mostly represent the principles that enter into the constitution of life-forms, while Daksha represents the combination of principles forming a life unit.

Daksha had sixteen daughters — thirteen he gave in marriage to Dharma, one to Agni, one to the Pitris and one to Śiva.

Agni or the god of Fire is the Rupa or form-giving Deva. Fire is used in sacrifice, because it changes the form of things offered and makes them acceptable to the gods by change of form.

If Agni represents Rūpa Devas or Devas with forms, Dharma might represent Arūpa Devas or Devas without forms.

The Pitris, of whom four classes are only mentioned (Agnishvātvas, Barhishads, Saumyas and Ajyapas), are also divided into two classes, — one with fire and one without fire.

The attendants of Śiva were dwellers of the astral or Bhuvar plane.

For the sake of convenient reference we shall call the dwellers of Svarga Loka Devas and the dwellers of Bhuvar Loka, Astrals. The different classes of Devas and Astrals are described in the 20th. chapter of the 4th. Skandha. The Devas and Astrals were brought into manifestation by Daksha, whose position in creation was next to that of Brahmā. Therefore all stood up to receive him at the sacrifice except Brahmā.

Śiva first appeared as Kumāra Nīla Lohita or Rudra. And all beings thereafter got the potentiality of dissolution, phenomenal change, death and decay. But in the first stage of life process, phenomenal change, decay or dissolution was not in requisition, as Monads went on in their downward journey, not by dissolution, but by evolution. They remained what they were, and they acquired in addition a more material form. As the material form became prominent the Deva form and the astral form became suppressed.

Consciousness in Deva form manifests itself as mind, in the astral form as animal desire and sense perception. In the mineral form it can hardly show itself.

Śiva works out the decay and dissolution of mineral matter, so that the astral element may once more assert itself and there may be sense perception in the mineral metamorphosed into the vegetable. The process is carried further in the animal kingdom, and the animals get a constitution in which Kāma or animal desire can manifest itself. The animals evolve themselves by death. Death frees them from the trammels of one set of experience, and carries them onwards till the human body is reached.

The work of dissolution proceeds in various ways. Our sleep is partial dissolution. It is brought on by the astral attendants of Śiva.

Dissolution is caused by Tamas. Tamas begets inaction, and inaction causes death and decay. There is no phenomenal change without dissolution, death or decay.

There are so many material tendencies in us that they require rejection. Śiva gives us the power of rejection, as Vishnu, the power of preservation — preservation of all that is good in us. Death makes the man, where moral teachings fail, The Consort of Śiva is the Energy through Whom He guides the life process of Monads or Jivas. In the first stage of life process She is called Sāti or the Lasting. For the body of the Jiva was lasting during the period of evolution. But Her mission was to act on the Monad itself, to cause the material tendency in it by means of Tamas.

In the second stage, She is the Energy of dissolution, death and phenomenal change. In the third stage, she is over and above that the Energy of rejection (of all that is evil in us.) She is the kind mother, who has been nourishing all Jivas in their course of evolution.

When the Mineral form was reached by the primal elemental Jiva, the creative process had done its work and the process of dissolution was to assert itself. There was to be a revolution in the life process. Sāti gave up her own nature and became re-born in another character in the Mineral Kingdom. The creative process was materially changed. Daksha lost his original head, and he acquired the head of a goat. The goat symbolises sexual connection. All this happened during the reign of Prāchina-Barhis. The Prachetas brothers were his sons. Daksha reappeared as the son of the Prachetas brothers.

The Ādityas or gods of preservation who formed Daksha were Pūshava and Bhaga. They were the preserving deities of the first stage of life process. When the next stage came in, they lost their activity. This explains the breaking of teeth and the uprooting of eyes of two of the Ādityas. The subjoined Table of correspondences taken from the 11th. Chapter of the Twelfth Skandha shews that Pūshana and Bhaga correspond to the months of Pausha (December) and Māgha (January) when the rays of the sun are the least powerful. These Ādityas preserve Jivas in their downward course. Pūshana was a favorite god of the Aryan shepherd.

NO.	MONTH	ADITYA.	RISHI.	YAKSHA.	RAKSHAS.	NAGA.	GANDHARBA.	APSARAS.
	Chaitra ...	Dhatri.	Pulastya.	Rathavrit.	Heti.	Vasuki.	Tumburu.	Kritasthali.
2.	Baisakha ...	Aryman.	Pulaha.	Athaujas.	Praheti.	Kachnira.	Narada.	Punjikasthali.
3.	Jyaistha	Mitra.	Atri.	Rathasvana.	Pauresheya.	Takshaka.	Haha.	Menaka.
4.	Asarha	Varuna.	Vasistha.	Chitrasvana.	Sahajanya.	Sukra.	Huhu.	Rambha. (Sahajanya)
5.	Sravana	Indra.	Angiras.	Srotri.	Varya.	Elaptara.	Visvavasu.	Pramlocha.
6.	Bhadra	Vivasvat.	Bhrigu.	Asarana.	Vyaghra.	Sankhahala.	Ugrasena.	Anumlocha.
7.	Magha ...	Poshan.	Gautama.	Suruchi.	Vata.	Dhananjaya.	Sushena.	Ghritachi.
8.	Falguna	Parjanya. (Savitri)	Bharadvaja.	Ritu.	Vorcha.	Airavata.	Visva.	Senajit.
9.	Agrahayana.	Ansu. (Vidhatri)	Kasyapa.	Ritusena.	Vi tsatru.	Mahasankha.	Ritusena.	Urvasi.
10.	Pausha.	Bhaga.	Kratu.	Uma.	Sphurja.	Karkotaka.	Arishtanemi.	Purvachitti.
11.	Asvina	Tvastri.	Jamadagni.	Satajit.	Brahmapeta.	Kambala.	Dhritarashtra.	Tilottama.
	Kartika	Vishnu.	Visvamitra.	Saty.	Makhapeta.	Asvatara.	Suryavarcha.	Rambha.

TABLE M.

There is not much to detain us in this Table. It will be enough if readers will please note the meanings of the names used.

TABLE N.

We must divide this Table into the following heads: — I. The story of Dhruva, II. The story of Pirthu, III. The story of Prachina Barhis, IV. The allegory of Puranjana, and V. The story of the Prachetasas.

I. THE STORY OF DHRUVA.

SKANDHA IV. CHAP. 8-12.

Uttānapāda is one of the sons of the First Manu. Uttānapāda means "with uplifted foot". This perhaps refers to the period when the Jiva, having still the spiritual element strong in him, was not fixed in the course of material descent, but had one foot towards Mahar-Loka. Uttānapāda had two wives Suruchi (with good graces) and Suniti (of good morals). Uttama or the Highest was the son of Suruchi. Dhruva or the fixed was the son of Suniti. Once upon a time, Dhruva found Uttama on his father's lap and he wished to be there himself. For fear of Suruchi, Uttānapāda did not dare stretch forth his hands towards Dhruva, while Suruchi herself taunted the boy for his impudent aspiration. Stung to the quick by the bitter words of his stepmother Dhruva forthwith left the place and went straight to his mother and related to her his grievances. Suniti advised her son who was only five years old to make Tapas. Dhruva did not lose time but left home to make Tapas as directed by his mother. Nārada met him on the way. "Thou art a child Dhruva" said the great Rishi. "How is it possible for thee to find out Him by Tapas, Who is attainable by intense Yoga concentration and freedom from passion practised for several births. Desist my boy, for the present. Try, when thou hast enjoyed all the things of the world and hast grown old". But Dhruva was fixed in resolve and he importuned Nārada to teach him how to meditate. Nārada initiated Dhruva into the mysteries of the Mantra "Om Namo Bhagavate Vāsudevaya", told him how to meditate on Vāsudeva and asked him to make Tapas at Mathurā where Bhagavān permanently resides. Dhruva passed his days in austere asceticism, standing on one foot and living on air. The prince at last controlled his breath and with deep concentration saw the Divine Light in the heart. Bhagavān withdrew that Light from the heart, and on the break of Samādhi, Dhruva found the same Divinity outside, standing before him. Words he had none for a time. Bhagavān addressing him said: — "O Thou Kshatriya boy! I know thy resolve. Do thou ever prosper. I give thee a place which is ever bright and where Nirvana is constant. The planets and stars are all attached to that place. Those that live for a Kalpa will die, but that place shall never be destroyed. Dharma, Agni, Kasyapa, Indra and the seven Rishis with all the luminaries of the sky are constantly revolving round the place. Thou shalt succeed thy father on the throne and reign for 36,000 years. Thy brother Uttama shall disappear in a forest. Thy stepmother Suruchi shall die in pursuit of her son. The place where thou shalt finally go is my own abode, higher than that of the Rishis, and there is no return from it."

Dhruva returned to his parents and was placed by his father on the throne. He married Bhrami, the daughter of Siśumāra, and had two sons by her, Kalpa and Vatsara. He had another son Utkala by Ila. Uttama was killed by a powerful Yaksha while out on a hunt. Dhruva went out to the north to take revenge on the Yakshas for his brother's death. He killed several thousands of innocent Yakshas, Rākshasas and Kinnaras in battle. Manu took pity on them and asked his grandson to desist from fight. Dhruva bowed in obedience to Manu and so Kubera the king of Yakshas became much pleased with him and blest him too. After thirty six thousand years, Sananda and Nanda, two companions of Vishnu came with a chariot and took Dhruva to the promised abode.

Utkala was the eldest son of Dhruva and he was entitled to succeed his father. But he was a sage and had united himself with Brahmā. He declined the throne. Bhrami's son Vatsara became the king. Vatsara married Subithi and had six sons by her, — Pushpārna, Tigmaketu, Ishā, Urja, Vasu and Jaya. Pushpārna had two wives, — Pravha and Doshā. Prabhā had three sons, — Prātar, Madhyandina and Sayam, Doshā had three sons, — Pradosha, Nisitha and Vyushta. Vyushta married Pushkarini. His Son was Sarvatejas, afterwards called Chakshus. Chakshus had one son, — Nadvala Manu.

THOUGHTS ON THE ABOVE.

[The line of Uttānapāda, as I have said above, represents the appearance of individual life-forms. Limitation had to be put to the life-periods of individuals. We commence with Dhruva, who presides over the polar star, and lives for one Kalpa. His sons are Kalpa and Vatsara. "Vatsara" means year. The sons of Vatsara are the six seasons. "Pushpārna" is the flower season or spring. "Tigmaketu" means fierce-rayed. The word denotes summer season. "Isha" means full of sat and is the name of the month of Asvina. But it means here the rainy season. "Urja" is the name of the month of Kartika. It is indicative of autumn. "Vasu" meaning wealth is the season between autumn and winter, when paddy becomes ripe. "Prabhā" is light. "Doshā" is darkness. "Pratar," "Madhyandina" and Sayam are morning, midday and evening, respectively. "Pradosha" is first part of the night, "Nisitha" is midnight. "Vyushta" is day break. "Sarva-tejas" is all-fire. He was subsequently called Chakshus or eye. The names other than Chakshus indicate different capacities of individual life, ranging from portions of a day to the whole Kalpa. When the downward flow of Jivas was the rule, Dhruva had to make great sacrifice to remain fixed on the spiritual plane. Hence he worshipped Vishnu, as directed by Nārada. Sarva-tejas or Chakshus perhaps indicates the appearance of perceptive faculties. The son of Chakshus is glorified with the title of Manu. This is significant. He is called Nadvala, or one made of reeds. This marks a new era in the progress of Monads. As the reed is made up of sheaths over-lapping each other, so the sons of this Manu were constituted of overlapping principles. Why Nadvala is called Manu, has to be found out in the circumstances that attended the progress of the Monads from the mineral to the vegetable stage. The son of this Manu was Anga or the limbs. And Anga was wedded to the daughter of the death god. So there was no death up to the Nadvala form of life, and no limbs. It was something like the appearance of protoplastic matter, with all its potentialities of evolving life forms. Thus we can understand the importance of Nadvala as a Manu. Death or decay made the inorganic to develop organs or anga.]

II. THE STORY OF PRITHU.

SKANDHA. IV. CHAP. 13-23.

Nadvala had twelve sons; one of them being Ulmuka (fire-brand, torch). He had six sons, one of them being Anga or the members of the body. Anga married Sunitha, the daughter of Death. The iniquitous Vena was the son of Anga. When he became king, he issued a proclamation prohibiting all worship and sacrifices. The sages strongly remonstrated with him but when he turned a deaf ear to their words, they killed him with their incantations. The kingdom was now without a ruler and there was great disorder. The Rishis then churned the thigh of the dead body, until a dwarfish, deep black person came out. The Rishis told him to 'sit down and wait.' Hence he was called Nishada. They then churned the two arms, and a pair arose. "This male is an incarnation of Vishnu," said the Rishis, "and this female is an incarnation of Lakshmī. They shall marry each other. He shall be called Prithu and his wife, Archis. Prithu shall be the King and he shall preserve all beings." Prithu accepted the duty of preserving the people. He saw there was no vegetation on the earth. His subjects suffered from hunger. He thought that the earth had eaten up the seeds and was not bringing forth the plants. In anger Prithu took up his bow and aimed at the earth. She assumed the form of a cow and began to run away chased by the King. But she at last yielded and requested him to spare her life. "Thou art Lord of this Universe," exclaimed the earth, "Thou knowest very well that the forms of vegetable life created by Brahmā could not be used in Yajna so long. I have therefore preserved them within myself. If I had not done so, they would have been destroyed long ago and no Yajna could be performed in future. True, they are now rotting in me. But think about the best means to bring them out. Find out a calf, a milk-pot and a milker. I will secrete all desired objects as my milk. But first of all make my surface flat and level." Prithu rejoiced at these words. He made Svayambhuva Manu the calf and milked all vegetables into his own hands. Others followed him. The Rishis made Vrihaspati their calf and drew out the Vedas into their Indriyas.

The Devas made Indra their calf and milked out into their golden pot Amrita and energy of body, of mind and of the Indriyas.

The Daityas and Dānavas made Prahlāda their calf and milked out wine into their iron pot. The Gandharvas and Apsaras made Visvavasu their calf and milked out into their lotus vessel, fragrance, beauty and sweet words.

The Pitris made Aryaman their calf and extracted into their unburnt earth vessel the Kavya offerings. The Siddhas made Kapila their calf and milked out the Siddhis (animan &c). (And so other instances are given). Prithu was so glad that he called earth his daughter and hence she is called Prithivi or the daughter of Prithu. The King also crushed the mountains and made the earth's surface level.

Prithu then commenced a series of Asvamedha Yajnas. During the performance of the hundredth, Indra twice stole away the sacrificial horse, but Prithu's son restored it on both the occasions. The performer of one hundred Asvamedha sacrifices becomes an Indra. This was the cause of Indra's fear. Prithu could not bear the disgraceful conduct of Indra and he resolved to kill him. The Rishis dissuaded him and even Brahmā and Vishnu appeared to soothe the offended King and restore his friendship with Indra. Vishnu explained to Prithu that he had enough to do as a king of the earth and as a preserver of the people and that he should not aspire to become Indra, who had his duties as well.

Sometime after, the Sanat Kumar brothers appeared before the King and taught him the way to Mukti. He made over the kingdom to his son Vijitāsva and retired into the forest. At last he gave up the body and went to Vaikuntha.

THOUGHT ON THE ABOVE.

[We left the Monad in its protoplasmic state. The protoplasmic mass began to spread out limbs (Anga). But the development of limbs was not an unmixed blessing, for Anga became wedded to the daughter of Death.

There was no death in the protoplasm. The offspring of the first connexion with death was Vena.

The root *ven* means to move. The first moving protoplasmic mass had too much of unruliness in it, and it was not therefore fitted for *yajna* or evolution. It had to be brought under the law and the black element was churned out. That black element of Tamas had to wait till the time of the great dissolution. Vishnu had to incarnate at this stage as Prithu to suffuse the material mass with *satva* and thereby make it conscious. The course of evolution received a great impetus. The Monad had passed through elemental and mineral stages. Organic life had already appeared. Matter had passed through the grossness and immobility of Tamas and the irregular, impulsive and purposeless movements of Rajas, till it became permeated with Satva, when those movements assumed the regularity of conscious acts. The consciousness of Satva made the future evolution or *yajna* teem with big possibilities. Earth could no longer keep back the seeds of the vegetable creation in her bosom. Her surface became levelled and she looked green with vegetation. She brought forth all her latent life-energies and life-evolution commenced in right earnest under the guidance of the first King energised by Vishnu for the preservation of the universe. But that King was not to exceed the proper bounds. He was not to usurp the functions of Indra. The Devas are the executive officers of the Rishis in the cyclic administration of the universe and their work is more on cyclic than on individual lines. The kings however as representing Manu have to deal directly with Monads and Egos and have to guide them according to the light of the Rishis. Prithu was asked by Vishnu to keep himself within the bounds of kingly duties.]

III. THE STORY OF THE PRACHINA BARHIS OR BARHISHAD.

SKANDHA IV. CHAP, 24.

The eldest son of Prithu was Vijitāsva. He was so called for having restored the sacrificial horse stolen by Indra. Indra taught him the art of becoming invisible. Hence he was also called Antardhāna. He had four brothers — Havyaksha, Dhūmrakesha, Vrika and Dravinas. To them he gave the east, the south, the west and the north respectively. By his wife Sikhandini, Vijitāsva had three sons — Pāvaka, Pavamāna, and Suchi.

These fire-gods descended by the curse of Vasishtha but the descent was only temporary. Antardhāna had by his other wife Nabhāsvati one son, Havirdhāna. Havirdhāna had six sons — Barhishad, Gaya, Sukla, Krishna, Satya and Jitavrata. Of these, Barhishad was a great votary of Kriyā, (action) and he constantly performed Yajnas. Even while he was performing one Yajna, the place for another was preparing close by. Hence he was called Prāchina-Barhis. King Prāchina-Barhis married Satadruti, the daughter of the Ocean-god. And he had by her ten sons, all of whom were called Prachetas. The King ordered his sons to enlarge the creation. They went out to make Tapas for one thousand years. Nārada came to the King and told him that the way to Mukti was not through Kriyā Kānda. By performing sacrifices he was only acquiring new karma. The only way to attain liberation was to know oneself. The Rishi illustrated his teachings by the famous allegory of Puranjana. The King heard the story and its explanation from Nārada. He did not wait for the return of his sons. But he called his ministers together and delivered to them his mandate that his sons were to succeed him on the throne. He went to the Āsrama of Kapila for Tapas and attained liberation.

IV. THE ALLEGORY OF PURANJANA.

SKANDHA IV. CHAP. 25-29.

There was a king called Puranjana. He had a friend, but the king knew not his name nor his doings. Puranjana went in search of a place to live in. He went about on all sides, but found no suitable abode. At last while roaming south of the Himālayās, he found one Puri (town) in Bhārata Varsha (India), The marks were all favourable. There were nine gateways. In one of the gardens he found a most beautiful young lady. She had ten attendants. Each of them had hundreds of wives. One five-headed serpent was the warder of the town and he constantly guarded his mistress. The lady was on the look out for one to be her lord. Puranjana broke forth into words of love, and asked who she was. "O thou greatest of men!" exclaimed the lady, "I know not who I am or who thou art. Nor do I know who made us both. This only I know, that I now exist. I do not know even who made this town for me. These are my companions male and female. This serpent guards the town, even when we are all asleep. Luckily hast thou come here. I shall try with all my companions to bring to thee all objects of desire. Be thou the lord of this Puri for one hundred years. And accept all enjoyments brought by me." Puranjana entered the Puri and lived in enjoyment there for one hundred years.

Of the nine gateways, seven were upper and two lower — five on the east (Purva, which also means front), one on the south (Dakshinā), one on the north (Uttara) and two on the west (Paśchima). Two of them Khadyôta and Āvirmukhī were close to each other and Puranjana used them whenever he would go out to see Vibhrajita in the company of Dyumat.

Nalinī and Nālinī were also two passages built together. Puranjana used them with the help of Avadhūta in order to repair to Saurabha.

The Mukhyā passage was used for Apana and Bahūdana. Through the southern passage Pitrihū, Puranjana went with Srutadhara to Dakshinā Panchāla and through the northern passage Devahū, to Uttara Panchāla.

Through the western passage called Āsuri, Puranjana went with Durmada to Grāmaka. The other western passage was called Nir-riti, Through that passage Puranjana went with Lubdhaka to Vaiś-asa.

There were two blind gates *i.e.* without opening, viz: — Nirvak and Pesaskrita. Puranjana used them for motion and action. He went inside the town with Vishūchina. There he experienced Moha (delusion), Prasāda (contentment) and Harsha (joy), caused by his wife and daughters.

Puranjana became thus attached to Karma. He slavishly followed whatever the Queen did. If she heard, the King heard. If she smelt, the King smelt. If she rejoiced, the King rejoiced. If she wept, the King wept. Puranjana merged his self entirely in that of his wife.

Once upon a time, the King went out hunting into the forest Panchaprastha, His chariot had five swift going horses, two poles, two wheels, two axles, three flags, five chains, one bridle, one charioteer, one seat for the charioteer, two yoke ends, seven fenders, and five courses. He had a golden armour and an endless supply of arrows. Brihadbala was the commander of his forces. The King forgot his wife for the time being in the chase of deer. But he got tired and returned home. The Queen would not speak to him in feigned anger. The King appeased her with gentle and flattering words of love.

So passed the days in utter delusion. The King had 1100 sons and 110 daughters. He gave them in marriage to duly qualified persons. Puranjana's sons had 100 sons each. The kingdom of Panchāla became filled with the progeny of Puranjana. The King performed sacrifices for the welfare of his children and killed animals for the purpose.

Chandavega, a Gandharva king, had a strong force of 360 white Gandharvas. Each of them had one black wife. By turns these Gandharvas robbed the town of Puranjana. The serpent-warder could not fight long against such odds, it lost strength day by day. The King and all the citizens became extremely anxious.

There was a daughter of Kāla who went about the world for a husband. But no one received her for a wife. She went to Nārada and on the refusal of the sage cursed him to become a wanderer for ever. She was referred however by Nārada to Fear, the King of Yavanas. King Fear would not accept her for his wife. But he addressed her as his sister and assured her that she would enjoy all beings on earth, if only she attacked them unnoticed. His Yavana troops would always accompany her as well as his brother Prajvāra.

The Yavana troops of King Fear under Prajvāra and the daughter of Kala attacked the Puri of Puranjana. The old serpent gave way. The Puri was burnt up by Prajvāra. There was wailing all round. The Serpent left the Puri. Puranjana was dragged out of it. The sufferings he had caused to others in sacrifices or otherwise reacted upon him. Long he suffered forgetting even his old friends. His mind had been tainted by the constant company of women and he had thought of his wife till the last moment. So he became a female in the next birth. She was born as the daughter of the Vidarbha king. Malayadhvaja, King of Pāndya, defeated other princes in the fight for her hand and the princess became his wife. She bore to the King one black-eyed daughter and seven sons. The sons became kings of Dravida and each of them had millions of sons, Agastya married the daughter of the King, and had by her a son called Dridhachyta. His son was Idhmavāha. King Malayadhvaja divided the kingdom amongst his sons; and ascended the hills for devotional meditation. His wife accompanied him. One day the princess found the body of her husband cold in death.

With loud lamentations, she prepared the funeral pyre, placed the King's body upon it and put fire thereon. She then resolved to burn herself on the same pyre.

The former friend now appeared. Addressing the Queen he said: —

"Who art thou? Who is he lying on the funeral pyre that thou mournest aloud? Dost thou know me, thy friend, thy former companion? Dost thou remember even so much that thou hadst a friend, whom thou canst not recognise? Thou didst leave me in search of some earthly abode and enjoyment. We were two Hansas (swans) on the Mānasa Loka and we lived together for one thousand years. Desirous of worldly enjoyments thou didst leave me for the earth and there didst find a town with a woman as its mistress. The company of that woman spoiled thy vision and effaced thy memory. Hence thou hast attained this state. Thou art not the daughter of the Vidarbha King, nor is this King thy husband. Nor wast thou the husband of Puranjana. By my *māyā* thou misconceivest thyself as a man or a woman. But in reality both myself and thyself are Hansas. Wise men find no difference between us. If there is any difference between a man and his image, that is the difference between me and thyself."

The other Hansa now regained his lost consciousness and was reawakened to his former state.

This is the story of Puranjana. Now its explanation by Nārada: —

Puranjana is Purusha — he who illumines the Pura with consciousness.

The unknown friend is Īshvara.

The Pura or Puri or town is the human body.

"The marks were all favourable" — there were no deformities in the body.

"The nine gateways" are the nine openings of the body.

The young lady Puranjani is Buddhi.

She is the mistress of the body.

The ten male attendants are the five *jnanendriyas* or organs of perception and the five *karmendriyas* or organs of action.

The wives of the attendants are the functions of the Indriyas.

The five-headed serpent is Prāna. The five heads are its five sub-divisions.

"One hundred years" is the full term of man's life.

"Khadyota," literally glow-worm, is the left eye, for, it has not the illumining capacity of the right eye.

"Āvirmukhi" or the great illuminator is the right eye.

"Vibhrajita" is Rupa or object of sight.

"Dyumat" is the perceiving eye.

"Nalini" and "Nālini" are the left and right nostrils respectively.

"Avadhūta" is Vāyu. In the story, it means the perceiving nose.

"Saurabha" is Gandha or smell.

"Mukhya" is mouth.

"Apana" is speech.

"Bahūdana" is eating.

"Panchāla" is Pancha (five) + ala (capable) that which is capable of bringing to light such of the five objects of the senses, as cannot be otherwise cognised; Śastra or spiritual teachings.

The right ear is stronger than the left ear. Therefore it is more prominent and useful in *hearing* the Śastras, of which the first to be heard is Karma Kānda.

A man by the observance of Karma Kānda is called to the Pitris, *i.e.* he reaches, after death, the path called Pitriyāna.

"Pitrihū" is therefore the right ear. "Devahū" is the left ear corresponding to Devayāna.

"Uttara Panchāla" is Pravritti Śāstra or teachings of worldliness.

"Dakshinā Panchāl" is Nivritti Śāstra or teachings of renunciation.

"Nirriti" is death. The anus is called death, because ordinarily the Linga Sarira goes out through that passage after death.

"Lubdhak" is Pāyu.

"Vaisasa" is excrement.

"Nirvāk" is foot.

"Pesaskrita" is hand.

Of the Indriyas, hand and foot are blind, as there are no openings in them.

"Vishūchina" is mind.

Moha is the result of Tamas, Prasāda of Satva and Harsha of Rajas.

The aforesaid names indicate enjoyment in the Jāgrat or waking state.

The hunting represents enjoyment in the Svapna or dream state.

The "Chariot" is the body in dream consciousness.

The five horses are the five organs of perception.

The two poles are "I-ness" and "Mine-ness."

The two wheels are merit and demerit.

The axle is Pradhāna.

The three flags are the three Gunas.

The five chains are the five Prānas.

The bridle is Manas the seat of desires.

The charioteer is Buddhi.

The yoke-ends are sorrow and delusion.

The seven fenders are the seven Dhātus or essential ingredients of the body.

The five courses are the five organs of action.

The gold color of the armour is due to Rajas.

Brihadbala is the even perceiving mind.

The sons are the transformations of perception.

The daughters are the concepts following such transformations.

"Chandavega", the Gandharva king, is the year, every year of human life.

The Gandharvas are days.

Their wives are nights.

The 360 Gandharvas are the 360 days of the year. With their wives or nights they form the number 720.

The daughter of Kāla is Jarā or decrepitude.

The Yavanas are diseases or infirmities.

Fear is the King of all diseases and infirmities viz., Death.

Prajvāra is destructive fever.

As long as Purusha does not know his real self, but identifies himself with the Gunas of Prakriti, he becomes subject to births and deaths. The only remedy for this malady is pure devotion to Guru and to Bhagavān. By such devotion, dispassion and wisdom are both acquired.

"Darbha" is Kusa grass, symbolical of Yajna. "Vidarbha" is pure land. "Malaya" or the Deccan is famous for Vishnu worship.

"Malayadhvaja" is therefore a Vaishnava king.

[It appears that Vaishnavism had its rise and growth in the South of India before it overspread Northern India. This would be natural considering the hold of Vedic Brahmānism in Northern India.]

The daughter of Malayadhvaja is Devotion. The seven sons are the seven divisions of Bhakti, viz. —

1. *Sravana* or hearing the glory of Vishnu,

2. *Kirtana* or reciting the glory of Vishnu,

3. *Smarana* or constant remembrance of Vishnu,

4. *Pādasevana* or shewing respect to Vishnu,

5. *Archana* or worship of Vishnu,

6. *Bandana* or adoration of Vishnu,

7. *Dāsya* or consecration of one self to the service of Vishnu.

The other two divisions, *Saukhya* or companionship with Vishnu and *Ātmā nivedana* or complete resignation are not mentioned in this connection as they relate to a highly advanced spiritual state.

These modes of Bhakti worship are prevalent in Dravida.

The millions of sons are sub-divisions of Sravana, &c.

"Agastya" is mind.

"Dridhachyuta" is one confirmed in dispassion.

"Idhmavāha" is one who goes to Guru, fuel in hand, for instructions.

Īshvara, the unknown friend, called Himself and the Purusha two Kansas of the Mānasa Lake. Hansa is one absolutely pure. Mānasa Lake is the Heart.

"For one thousand years" — Both Jiva and Īshvara remained together as friends, the same in essence and in form, during the one thousand years of Mahā Pralaya, at the end of a Kalpa. During Manvantaric Manifestation, the Jiva parts from his Friend Īshvara and launches into a wild course of enjoyments, of joys and sorrows. The touch of that fascinating lady Buddhi destroys all previous remembrances and the Jiva plays several characters in the drama of life, in dream and delusion.

Nārada concluded his explanation of the allegory with this eloquent exhortation: —

"Know thou, O King, the deer, skipping in the flower-garden, in company with its sweet-heart, deeply attached to the sweets of that garden, devouring with eager ears the humming music of *bhramaras*, little caring for the wolves on its way or for the arrows of the huntsman that pierce its back.

"The flowers are but women who bloom only to droop. The fragrance and honey, the sweets of the garden, are the enjoyments brought on by the *karma* of another birth."

"The music of *bhramaras* is the pleasing conversation of women and others. The wolves are the days and nights. The huntsman who stealthily flings arrows at the deer is Death. The deer is thy own self."

"Consider Well the efforts of the deer. Concentrate *chitta* into the heart and all perceptions into *chitta*. Give up the company of woman. Turn a deaf ear to all idle talks. Be devoted to that one true Friend of Jivas — īśvara. Retire, retire from all others."

King Prāchina Barhis wondered why such beautiful teachings were with held by his teachers. Or forsooth, they knew not themselves. He requested

Nārada however to remove two doubts that were still lurking in his mind. — Purusha acquires *karma* in one body, but he reaps the fruits of that *karma* in another body. One body is the doer while another is the enjoyer and sufferer. To one body, the fruits of its own work are lost. To another body, there is an acquisition of fruits it did not sow. How can this be? This was the first doubt.

What is done is done. Nothing apparently remains of our *karma*. How can then the sequences be accounted for? This was the second doubt.

Narada replies: —

Purusha reaps the fruits in that very body without break in which it acquires *karma*, but that body is the Linga Sarira, inclusive of Manas. As in dream man works out the impressions of the wakeful state without changing the body, so he enjoys the fruits of *karma* created in one birth in the Karma-made body of another birth.

And the doer of Karma is verily the Manas and not the Sthūla body. "These are mine," "I am so and so," only such concepts of the mind produce re-birth, and not anything in the Sthūla body. So the mind sows and the mind reaps. The body is merely the vehicle of birth producing thoughts.

This is in answer to the first question. Now to the second.

How do you know there is chitta or mind? All the senses are at one and the same time in contact with the objects of all the senses. But still you perceive only one thing at a time. Hence you infer the existence of the mind. Similarly by marking the tendencies of the mind their connection with a former birth is inferred. Otherwise why should there be one mental affection at a time and not another?

Then, in this life you never realise a thing which you never heard or saw or felt before. How can the mind then reproduce matters you never experienced before?

The mind by its present characteristics gives an insight into the past as well as into the future.

It sometimes happens that things are perceived in the mind with strange combinations in time, space and action, as in dream.

But men are endowed with mind and the mind perceives one after another the objects of the senses in an enormous variety, and the perceptions are lost again. So (in the long run) not one experience is altogether strange.

(For instance, a man sees in dream that he is a king. He must have been a king in some birth or other. The present combination in the dream is untrue but not so the kingly experience. The experience is always true with reference to some time, some space, some action or other).

When the mind is intensely Sātvic (calm, pure and transparent) and becomes constantly devoted to Bhagavān, the whole universe is reflected on it.

In Jiva there is never a break in the egoistic experience as long as the Linga Sarira continues.

There is only a seeming break in sleep, swoon and-deep distress such as death and fatal illness, but such break is due to a collapse of the perceiving senses.

There is similarly a break in the fœtal stage and in extreme childhood. But such break is due to imperfection of the senses; The moon though not visible on the new moon night does still exist.

The connection with gross objects does not cease because there is a temporary absence of such objects. For, are not thoughts about objects potent in their effects in dream?

The Linga Sarira, consisting in their essence of the five pure elements (Tanmatra), subject to the three Gunas, extending over the sixteen transformations (of the Sānkhya category), permeated with consciousness, is called Jiva.

It is with this Ling Sarira that Purusha enters into a body or comes out of it, and it is with this Sarira that he experiences joy, sorrow, fear, misery and happiness.

As the leech has its hold on the first blade of grass till it connects itself with another, so the Jiva identifies itself with one body till it enters another.

Manas only acquires *karma* by its contemplation of the objects of the senses. The bondage is thus created by Avidyā.

Therefore do thou meditate on Hari to free thyself from all worldly attachments and to be fixed in Him for ever.

V. THE STORY OF THE PRACHETAS BROTHERS.

SKANDHA IV, CHAP. 30-31.

The Prachetas brothers left home in order to discover by Tapas the best mode of enlarging the creation. They went west-ward and had not gone far when Śiva rose from beneath a large lake and addressed them thus: — "Children, you are sons of Barhishad, I know your good resolve. Blessings be on you. By the performance of one's duty in life, one attains the state of Brahmā after many births. My abode is still further, inaccessible even to the virtuous. But the votary of Vishnu attains His holy state, only when this life is ended. I and the Devas shall also attain that state after the final break up of our Linga Sarira. Learn therefore this prayer to Vishnu. (Śiva then recited the prayer to Vishnu, known as Rudra Gitā). Concentrate your mind on this prayer, meditate on it and recite it constantly."

The Prachetas brothers entered the waters of the deep and there prayed to Vishnu for a thousand years. Vishnu appeared and asked them to chose a boon and without waiting for a reply addressed them thus: — "You are dutiful sons and shall ever be known as such. You shall have a son in no way inferior to Brahmā. All the three Lokas shall be filled with his progeny. Indra had sent Pramlochā to decoy Kandu Rishi in his penances and the Apsarā succeeded in winning the heart of the Rishi. She had by him one daughter whom she brought forth from her pores as she brushed against the tops of the trees. She left her child there and ascended to heaven. The moon nourished the child by putting his nectar-bearing forefinger into her mouth. Have that daughter of the trees for your wife. You are all alike in your virtues and she is like to you all. So she shall be the wife of all the brothers."

The brothers then rose up from the waters. They found the earth overgrown with innumerable plants, so high that they almost reached the high heavens. The Prachetas brothers were angry to find such growth in plants and they resolved to destroy them. They emitted fire and air from their mouths, which caused havoc in the vegetable kingdom. Brahmā came and pacified the sons of Barhishad. He advised the surviving plants to give their adopted daughter Mārisha in marriage to the Prachetas brothers. The offspring of this marriage was Daksha. He is the same as Prajāpati Daksha, son of Brahmā. His degradation was owing to his former disregard of Śiva. The Chākshusa Manvantara witnessed his work of creation.

The Prachetas brothers reigned for 1000 Deva years. They were succeeded by Daksha.

THOUGHTS ON THE ABOVE.

Consciousness in organic life had appeared with Prithu. The table of further evolution may be here reproduced for facility of reference.

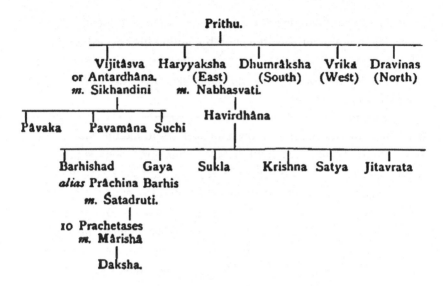

Vijitāsva could make himself invisible. This may have reference to the state of the body at that stage of evolution. The fires appeared as it is they that give forms. The object corresponding to elemental fire is Rūpa or form. Barhishad, the name of one class of Pitris, was the progenitor of the form-producing Linga Sarira with all its potentialities.

We find the senses developed in his sons the Prachetas brothers. "Pra" Means perfect and "Chetas" is the perceiving mind. But the mind perceives through the Indriyas, which are ten in number. Therefore they are ten brothers all alike; but they are wedded to one girl Mārishā.

There is some occult connection between water and sense perception. Barhishad was married to the daughter of the Ocean-god. The Prachetas brothers remained submerged for a thousand years in the waters. The protozoa and protophytes must of necessity be aquatic, as it were, for the development in them of sense perceptions.

It is in Touch that the sense perceptions find a common basis. Touch underlies all other perceptions. It is touch of the object by one sense or other that gives rise to one perception or the other. "Kandu" is primarily scratching or itching, secondarily touch. Mārishā was nourished by the moon and brought up by the plants.

The period refers to the stage of evolution when the vegetables formed the predominant creation. It corresponds somewhat to the geological period of tree-ferns and lycopods in our Manvantara.

The development of sense perceptions is the result of a communion with Vishnu, under the auspices of Rudra. This means a further infusion of Satva by Vishnu, which was made possible by the Dissolving influence of Śiva. And the son of the Prachetas brothers is verily Daksha, the Prajāpati of procreation, reincarnated under better auspices for the purpose of extending the creation. So we find the Trinity acting as three in one in the creative process.

With the appearance of Daksha Jiva evolution comes to an end in the first Manvantara.

TABLE V.

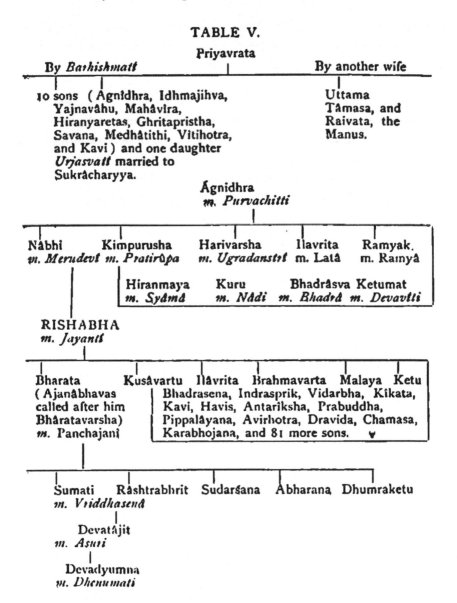

Priyavrata

By *Barhishmati* — By another wife

10 sons (Agnidhra, Idhmajihva, Yajnavâhu, Mahâvira, Hiranyaretas, Ghritapristha, Savana, Medhâtithi, Vitihotra, and Kavi) and one daughter *Urjasvati* married to Sukrâcharyya.

Uttama Tâmasa, and Raivata, the Manus.

Ágnidhra
m. Purvachitti

Nâbhi
m. Merudevi

Kimpurusha
m. Pratirûpa

Harivarsha
m. Ugradanstri

Ilavrita
m. Latâ

Ramyak.
m. Rainyâ

Hiranmaya
m. Syâmâ

Kuru
m. Nâdi

Bhadrâsva
m. Bhadrâ

Ketumat
m. Devavili

RISHABHA
m. Jayanti

Bharata
(Ajanâbhavas
called after him
Bhâratavarsha)
m. Panchajani

Kusâvartu Ilâvrita Brahmavarta Malaya Ketu
Bhadrasena, Indrasprik, Vidarbha, Kikata,
Kavi, Havis, Antariksha, Prabuddha,
Pippalâyana, Avirhotra, Dravida, Chamasa,
Karabhojana, and 81 more sons.

Sumati
m. Vriddhasenâ

Râshtrabhrit Sudarśana Abharana Dhumraketu

Devatâjit
m. Asuti

Devadyumna
m. Dhenumati

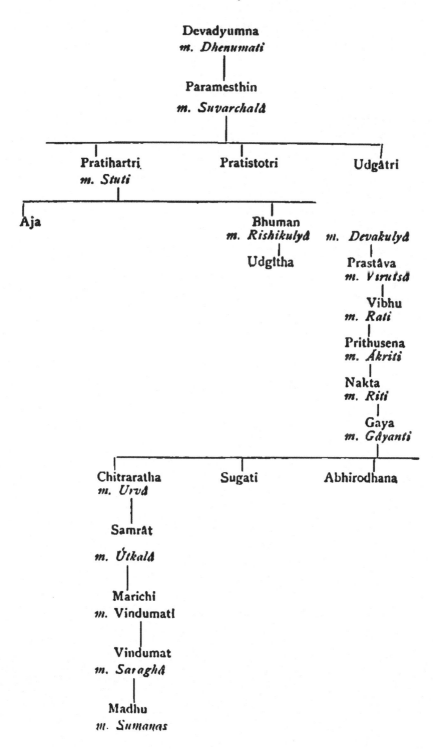

Devadyumna
m. Dhenumati

Paramesthin

m. Suvarchalá

Pratihartri
m. Stuti

Pratistotri

Udgátri

Aja

Bhuman
m. Rishikulyá

m. Devakulyá

Udgitha

Prastáva
m. Virutsá

Vibhu
m. Rati

Prithusena
m. Ákriti

Nakta
m. Riti

Gaya
m. Gáyanti

Chitraratha
m. Urvá

Sugati

Abhirodhana

Samrát

m. Útkalá

Marichi
m. Vindumati

Vindumat
m. Saraghá

Madhu
m. Sumanas

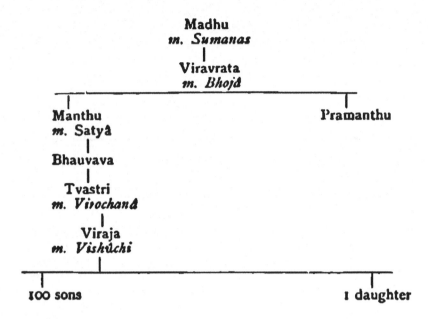

SKANDHA V.

TABLE V. PRIYAVRATA.

SKANDHA V. CHAP. 1.

Priyavrata was, from the beginning, under the influence of Nārada. So he declined to take part in the rule of the universe; till at last Brahmā persuaded him not to shirk his assigned work. King Priyavrata married Barhishmati, the daughter of Visvakarmā. By her he had ten sons Agnidhra &c., all names of Agni.

Of these ten, Kavi, Mahāvira and Savana were spiritually inclined and they became Parama Hansas (Parama Hansa is one who gives up the world entirely and becomes fixed in Brahmā). Priyavrata had by another wife three sons: Uttama, Tāmasa and Raivata. They all became Manus.

Priyavrata reigned for 400,000,000 years. The Sun-god Āditya moves round the Sumeru Mount and sends his rays up to the Loka-loka range, illumining half the regions while the other half remains dark. King Priyavrata in the exuberance of spiritual power determined to illuminate the dark regions and to make it all day and no night. He followed the Sun-god seven times with a chariot as swift and bright as that of the Sun-god himself even as though he were a second Āditya. Brahmā appeared saying "Desist, O Son, this is not thy assigned duty in the universe." The ruts caused by the wheel of Priyavtata's chariot are the seven oceans, which gave rise to the seven Dvipas — Jambu, Plaksha, Sālmali, Kusa Krauncha, Śāka and Pushkara.

Of these Dvipas, each succeeding one is twice as large as the one preceding it. The seven oceans respectively consist of:

1. Kshāra (Salt),

2. Ikshu (Sugarcane juice),

3. Surā (wine),

4. Ghrita (clarified butter),

5. Kshira (milk),

6. Dadhi (curd) and

7. Suddha (pure water).

They are like ditches round the Dvipas and their dimensions are the same as those of the corresponding Dvipas.

King Priyavrata divided the seven Dvipas among his seven sons thus: —

```
To Agnidhra,       he gave Jambu Dvipa.
 " Idhmajihva,     "   "   Plaksha Dvipa.
 " Yajnavāhu,      "   "   Sālmali Dvipa.
 " Hiranyaretas,   "   "   Kuśa Dvipa.
 " Ghritapristha,  "   "   Krauncha Dvipa.
 " Medhātithī,     "   "   Śāka Dvipa.
 " Vitihotra.      "   "   Pushkar Dvipa.
```

He gave his daughter Urjasvati in marriage to Śukra. The famous Devayāni was their daughter.

SKANDHA V. CHAP. 2.

King Āgnidhra presided over Jambu Dvipa. He saw the Apsarā Purvachitti and became love-stricken, so much so that he became a *jada* (Jada is
literally fixed, materialized hence idiotic, mad.)

The King had by her nine sons Nābhi, Kimpurusha, Harivarsha, Ilāvrita,
Ramyak, Hiranmaya, Kuru, Bhadrāsva and Ketumāla. Each of them
presided over the Varsha of his name. They were respectively wedded to
the following nine daughters of Meru, — Merudevi, Pratirūpā,
Ugradanstri, Latā, Ramyā, Śyāmā, Nari, Bhadrā and Devavīti.

SKANDHA V. CHAP. 4-6.

Nābhi had for his son RISHABHA an Incarnation of Vishnu. Rishabha
knew his Varsha to be the field of Karma. He married Jayanti and had by
her one hundred sons. The eldest and most qualified of his sons was
Bharata, Bhāratavarsha is named after him.

The chief amongst the remaining ninety-nine sons were Kusāvarta,
Ilāvarta, Brahmavarta, Malayaketu, Bhadrasena, Indrasprik, Vidarbha and
Kikata. These nine were the immediate successors of Bharata and were
attached to him.

Following them were Kavi, Hari, Antariksha, Prabuddha, Pippalāyana,
Ābirhotra, Dravida, Chamasa and Karabhājana. They were devoted to
Bhagavān. Their story will be related in the 11th. Branch of this Purāna.

The younger eighty one sons were devoted to karma and they were great
performers of Yajna.

Rishabha called his sons together and gave them proper advice. He taught
them Ātmā Vidya and revealed to them his own nature as the all pervading
Purusha, free from Avidyā.

"This my body is inconceivable. My heart is pure Satva. All impurities
were cast off by me. Therefore good people call me 'Rishabha' (primarily a
bull, secondarily the best). You are all born of my heart and so you all are

127

great; follow your brother Bharata willingly. By serving him you will do your duty by your subjects."

So saying, he made over the reins of government to Bharata and himself became a Parama Hansa. He took the vow of silence and never spoke again. He looked blind, dumb and deaf like one obsessed and mad. He went everywhere in this state, heedless of what others said. People flocked round him wherever he went. At last he thought the rush of people to be an impediment to yoga and took the vow of Ajagara life (Ajagara is a huge python that does not move, but eats whatever comes within reach of its mouth). He remained fixed at one place.

The yoga powers (Sidhis) sought him but he spurned them all. When he foresaw the end of his *prarabdha karma* Rishabha went about at will and travelled in Kanka, Venkata, Kūtaka and South Karnataka. While in the forest of Kūtaka he thrust some stones into his mouth. At that time the wind blew high and the bamboo tops caught fire and the body of the King was consumed. In Kali Vuga, King Arhat of Kanka, Venkata and Kūtaka will hear of the deeds of Rishabha and in the name of religion will introduce all sorts of sacrilegious practices as sanctioned by Rishabha's example.

SKANDHA V. CHAP. 7.

King Bharata married Panchajani, the daughter of Vīsva. He had by her five sons — Sumati, Rāshtrabhrit, Sudarśana, Ābharana and Dhūmraketu. This Varsha was formerly called Ajanābha. When Bharata became king, it was named after him Bhārata Varsha. King Bharata performed the Vedic Yajnas and made offerings to the Devas. But he knew the Devas as manifestations only of Vāsudeva. His mind became pure and filled with Satva. He lost himself in devotion to Vāsudeva. At last he divided his kingdom amongst his sons and himself went for Tapas to the hermitage of Pulaha in the *kshetra* of Hari on the Sacred Gandaki. He meditated in his heart on the lotus feet of Bhagavān and became suffused with ecstasy.

Bharata invoked the golden Purusha in the rising sun by a special Rik (Vedic Mantra) and addressed Him thus, "Let us attain the spiritual rays of luminous Savitri that are beyond Rajas and that are the generators of

Kārmic effects. By His Manas He created this universe. He preserves the Jiva again by permeating this universe."

SKANDHA V. CHAP. 8.

Once upon a time king Bharata had bathed in the Gandaka and after performing the daily practices was meditating on Pranava on the river-side. A deer came to drink water at the time. While the animal was quenching her thirst a lion roared not far off and she in terror jumped into the river. As she happened to be big with child, she was delivered of it at the time. Exhausted, the deer got back to the river side only to die. The new born fawn was being washed away, having no one to take care of it. Bharata took pity on the little fawn. He took it up and brought it to his hermitage. He brought it up as his own child and became deeply attached to it. He constantly thought of the deer-child, even so much so that when death approached he could not forget it and became re-born in another birth as a deer.

But though born as a deer, Bharata did not lose the memory of his former birth. He reflected that the mind that had been trained and controlled in the worship of Vāsudeva went astray only for the sake of one deer-child. He left the Kālanjara hills where he was born as a deer and sought for Sālagram, sacred with the Āsramas of Pulastya and Pulaha. He waited calmly for the exhaustion of Karma that had given rise to his deer life. He then gave up his body in the sacred waters of the Gandaka.

SKANDHA V. CHAP. 9.

A Brāhmana of the line of Angiras had nine sons by one wife. They were all well versed in the Vedas. He had one son by another wife and one daughter. This son was said to be an incarnation of Bharata. He was afraid of *sanga* (company), so much so that he would not even speak to any one for fear of acquiring new Karma. People took him for an idiot. His father strove hard to teach him the Vedas but did not succeed. His parents died and his half brothers had charge of him. Their wisdom was that of the Vedas. They had not learned Ātmā Vidyā. So they did not understand the nature of Bharata and neglected him. They gave him poor meals for the day's work in the fields.

At one time a thief wanted to propitiate the goddess Bhadra Kāli by human sacrifice in order that he might be blessed with a child. The victim that was procured somehow untied himself and fled. The attendants searched for him on all sides in vain. They at last fell upon Bharata who was watching in the fields in a peculiar way. They found him most suited for sacrifice and tied him up and carried him to the altar of Kāli. He was duly consecrated and the priest took up a sharp instrument to cut off his head. Kāli could no longer remain unconcerned. She rushed forth in rage from out of her image, wrested the knives from the hands of the thieves and cut off their heads.

Once upon a time Rāhugana King of Sindhu and Saubira was travelling in a palanquin. The chief palanquin bearer on reaching the river Ikshumati went in search of a bearer and on finding Bharata deemed him to be a god-send. He found his limbs strong and well-built and thought him capable of bearing the palanquin. He forced Bharata into the service. Bharata though quite unfit for this menial work did his utmost. But he was in the habit of looking forward for the distance of an arrow throw and then taking steps in advance, so that he might not unwarily kill some animal under his feet. He could not therefore keep pace with the other bearers and the palanquin lost its balance. King Rahūgana became angry and reproached the bearers. They complained against the new recruit. The king taunted Bharata with these words; "Oh my friend I dare say you are tired — for have you not carried me long and for a long distance too — and you appear to be thin indeed and weak. Are you suffering from decrepitude? Are not these your fellow-mates."

Bharata kept quiet. For these taunting remarks did not touch him. He was crystallised in wisdom and was no longer troubled with the false perceptions of "I and mine."

The palanquin again lost its balance. The king lost his temper and broke forth thus; "What is this? are you alive or dead? Do you thus disregard my orders and think of living? You must be a madman, like the Death-god I will punish your madness and bring you to your senses." King Rahūgana was proud of his learning and his kingship. He was inflated with Rajas and

Tames. He had therefore no hesitation in reproaching that lord of Yoga, Bharata.

Bharata smiled and thus replied: — "Thy taunts are true, O king! There is no doubt, I am neither tired nor did I travel long. For thy weight does not affect me nor have I any distance to travel. Nor could I be called fat. For the body is fat and not I. It is by falsely attributing the bodily attributes to self that one is said to have thickness, leanness, disease, hunger thirst, fear, enmity, desire, sleep, attachment, anger, egotism, pride and sorrow. But I have no such false perception.

"Thou sayest I am dead even when alive. But such is the case with all beings for they are all subject to constant transformations.

"Thou chargest me with disregarding the orders of my Master. But only if the relationship of Master and servant does really subsist, might there be command and obedience. But where is that relationship? If thou sayest, in the ways of the world, thou art my king momentary though these ways be, please tell me thy behests.

"Thou callest me a mad man and dost want to punish me and bring me to my senses. But I am not mad, though I may look so, for I am fixed in the meditation of Brahmā. But still if thou thinkest me to be a madman it will be useless to punish or to teach a senseless being."

So saying Bharata continued to carry the king. Rahūgana came down from the palanquin and fell at Bharata's feet. He expressed regret for having slighted such a sage in disguise and prayed for a fuller explanation of the philosophy involved in his weighty words. This led to an explanation by Bharata of the Advaita philosophy from the stand point of the Purānas, a denunciation of Vedic and Tāntric rites, and an allegorical description of the worldly life as trading in the forest (the world being the forest and the traders being men in search of wealth). The allegory was explained by Suka to Parikshit. [The enquiring student is referred to the original for details (V. 11-14.)]

SKANDHA V. CHAP. 15.

We must hurriedly refer to the line of Bharata. Sumati was the son of Bharata. Ill guided men in the Kali Yuga will call him a God. In his line Pratiha was master of Ātmā Vidyā. Coming lower down by far the most renowned king in the line of Bharata was Gaya Viraja was also well known. Of the hundred sons of Viraja, the eldest was Śatajit or the Conqueror of the hundred.

THOUGHTS ON THE LINE OF PRIYA VRATA.

Priya Vrata means literally one of welcome (*Priya*) deeds (*Vrata*).

Priya Vrata, was under the influence of Nārada from the beginning and he declined to go along the Descending path or Pravritti Mārga. He was wedded to the daughter of Vishva Karmā.

Vishva Karmā is the cosmic manufacturer. The work of this Prajāpati extends over the whole of Trilokī and he is the architect of all systems and chains included in the Trilokī — Priya Vrata, as we shall see later on, represents the earth chain only or the system known as Bhūr.

What we generally call the Solar system is a misnomer. For the sun stands between Bhūr Loka and Svar Loka and illumines both the Lokas with its rays. The Solar System is therefore properly speaking the whole of the Trilokī. In speaking of Priya Vrata, therefore, the Bhāgavata restricts itself to the regions illumined by the sun as well as by the moon (V-15-I.)

We shall enter into a detailed description of the whole system in the next chapter. Let us take here a passing glance of the line of Priya Vrata.

We take Priya Vrata to be the Earth chain complete in itself or rather the progenitor of the Earth chain.

Meru or Sumeru is the axis of Bhūr Loka, its highest point being the highest point of Bhūr Loka.

The sun god revolves round this central axis.

The Earth-god Priyavrata also revolved round Meru *i.e.* the Earth rotated round its own axis at a very rapid rate for some time during its infancy.

The rotation of the Earth was followed by the separation of layers. The part most removed from the centre was first affected.

In this way seven distinct layers were formed. The layer towards the circumference was the most spiritual. That towards the centre was the most material.

The reason of this is to be found in the action of the three Gunas and Tamas.

Satva is: on the material plane, light, transparent, with upward motion. On the mental plane, buoyant and cheerful, with true perception, spiritual.

Rajas is: on the material plane, constantly moving, translucent, with motion on the same plane, without levity or gravity.

On the mental plane, constantly active, partly joyful, partly sorrowful, with partially true and partially false perception, intellectual.

Tamas is: on the material plane, heavy, opaque, with downward motion.

On the mental plane indolent, melancholy, nonperceptive or dull.

The centripetal force is the action of Tamas and is connected with materiality. The centrifugal force is the action of Satva and is connected with spirituality.

Of the seven Dvipas, the central is the Jambudvipa, which is the most material.

The one farthest from the centre is the Pushkara Dvipa.

The spaces intervening between the layers or Dvipas are the seven oceans. They partake of the characteristics of the Dvipas, which they respectively surround. Thus the salt ocean surrounding the Jambu Dvipa is the most material. The materiality is indicated by the word "salt," which implies gross matter.

Priyavrata, it is said, went seven times round Meru, and at the time of each rotation, one ocean and its corresponding Dvipa were formed.

But when the Dvipas and the oceans were all formed that particular motion of the whole system was lost.

Since then days and nights are solely caused by the motion of the sun round Meru along the Manāsottara range.

The seven Dvipas may be the Globes A, B, C, D, E, F, and G of Theosophical literature.

The rulers of these seven Globes are seven sons of Priyavrata, named after Agni or Fire.

Agni is here the form-giving Energy of each Globe.

Of the ten sons of Priyavrata, seven only became Rulers of the Globes, but the other three Kavi, Mahavira and Savana, had nothing to do with the creative process. They are highly spiritual entities beyond the plane of the seven Globes.

The daughter of Priyavrata was Urjasvati. The word means full of Energy. She was wedded to Sukra, the presiding god of the planet Venus.

Her daughter is the renowned Devayāni, who was married to King Yayāti. She stands for Devayāna, the Radiant Path of the Upanishads, which transcends the Trilokī.

Of the sons of Priyavrata, we of Jambu Dvipa or Globe D are directly concerned with Āgnidhra, who presided over its earliest destinies.

The Bhāgavata does not relate the genealogy of the other sons as at present we have nothing to do with the life-evolution on these globes.

The process of materialisation is indicated by the Jada state of Āgnidhra on seeing the Apsaras Pūrvachitti.

The sons of Āgnidhra are the nine Varshas or Continents. We shall learn the details of these Varshas subsequently. Of these Varshas again, we are directly concerned with Nabhi. The word Nabhi means navel, which is at the centre of the body. The Nabhi Varsha is the pivot on which the other Varshas hang. The Nabhi Varsha is what we know as our Earth. The nine Varshas are also placed layer over layer, as the Dvipas are.

When Nabhi underwent further transformation, Rishabha became his son. In Rishabha, we come to a turning point. He is said to be an Incarnation of Vishnu. The word "Rishabha" means bull. But that meaning does not give us any help in understanding Rishabha and his work.

Priyavrata moved rapidly round Meru, till the globes were formed. This is in accordance with the Nebulous theory of Laplace. When the globes were formed, the Earth became denser. As the density increased, the movement of the Earth became irregular, till at last, the planet became fixed. This is not the western idea. The Pauranic idea is that the sun moves round the Earth, and the Earth remains fixed in its position. The story of Priyavrata's line is based upon this idea. Another idea of the ancients was that the planets had speech, till they became solidified.

Rishabha took upon himself the vow of silence. His son Bharata became speechless as a deer.

It was necessary to put a limit to the materiality of the Earth. The hard crust that formed the shell of the planet could not be allowed to affect its heart. The Earth was not to lose all spirituality. Therefore Vishnu incarnated in Rishabha so that spirituality might be stored in our planets, for the evolution of those Jivas that dwelt over it. Look at a Parama Hansa; the ascetic that neither speaks nor moves. Judging from outside, he is no better than a mute animal, but he is all spirituality within. Such is the nature of our mother Earth.

The thrusting of stones into the mouth of Rishabha is suggestive.

The sons of Rishabha are the countries of our Earth. Of these Bharata (India) was the first-born. The spiritual character of this holy land is shewn by the story of Bharata.

Bharata was obeyed and imitated by nine brothers, of whom Brahma-varta is well-known as described by Manu. Malaya is Malabar. Vidarbha is Berar and Kikata is Bihar.

The sons of Rishabha very likely include all the countries of the Earth.

Rishabha called his sons and asked them to follow Bharata. Will other lands now follow that advice?

THE EARTH CHAIN, BHUVANA KOSHA.

SKANDHA V. CHAP. 16.

Said Parikshit: — "Thou hast given the bare outline of these regions of the universe which are lighted by the sun and where the moon and the luminous starry host are also seen.

"Thou hast hereby mentioned the seven oceans and the seven Dvipas, but thou hast not given the details thereof." Suka replied: —

Imagine the Bhu-mandala or the Earth chain to be the pericarp of a lotus. Imagine there are seven sheaths immersed in it — the seven Dvipas. The central sheath is Jambu Dvipa. It is Niyut Yojanas in area (Niyut= 1,000,000 But Śridhara Svami here explains Niyuta as meaning one laksha or 100,000. So according to Śridhara the area of Jambu Dvipa is 800,000 miles). Jambu Dvipa is round like the lotus leaf.

There are nine Varshas in Jambu Dvipa, each nine thousand Yojanas in area completely divided by eight mountain ranges. (Bhadrasva and Ketumala form exceptions, for they extend over 34,000 Yojanas. Some take nine thousand Yojanas to be the expanse between the Nila and Nishadha ranges. The Vayu Purāna describes the position thus: — Two Varshas are situated like two bows north and south. Four are placed longways. Ilāvrita is as it were with four petals. *Śridhara*. This gives 7 x 9000 + 34000 = 97000).

ILAVRITA IS THE CENTRAL VARSHA.

Sumeru is situated in the navel of this Varsha. This king of mountains is gold all through. It is a laksha Yojanas high. If the Earth chain be taken to be a lotus, this Meru is its pericarp. It is 32,000 Yojanas as the top and 16,000 Yojanas at the foot and 16,000 Yojanas under the ground.

(By saying 16000 Yojanas at the foot, 84000 Yojanas are left out. Thus the Vishnu Purāna says — the Meru is 84000 Yojanas over the ground and 16000 under the ground, at the top 32000 and at the foot 16000. *Śridhara*. 16000 + 84000=100000).

On the north of Ilāvrita are the three mountain ranges Nila, Sveta and Śringavan in order. They are respectively the boundary ranges of Rāmayak, Hiranmaya and Kuru. They spread east and west up to the salt ocean. They are two thousand Yojanas wide. In length, each succeeding one is a little over one tenth part shorter than the preceding one. (There is no difference in height and in width. *Śridhara*).

So on the south of Ilāvrita are the three ranges Nishadha, Hemakūta and Himalaya spreading east and west like the preceding ones. They are 10,000 Yojanas in height. They are the boundary ranges respectively of Harivarsha, Kinpurusha and Bharata. (This — 10,000 Yojanas — is also the height of Nila, Sveta and Sringavnā. The width of these ranges again is that of Nila, and others. By Bhārata we are to understand Nabhi.

On the west of Ilāvrita is the Malyavat range and on the east lies the Gandha Madana range, These ranges extend north up to the Nila range and on the south up to the Nishadha range. They are two thousand Yojanas wide. They are the boundary ranges of Ketumala and Bhadrasva respectively. (East and west there is the Meru surrounded by Ilāvrita, then there are the two ranges Malyavat and Gandha Madana, and the two varshas Bhadrasva and Ketumala and nothing besides).

North and south, there is the Meru then Ilāvrita, 6 mountain ranges and 6 Varshas, 3 on each side and nothing else.

[Where do you then get a *laksha* of Yojanas? It is said: — Meru has a diameter of 16,000. Ilāvrita has 18,000. The 6 Varshas have 6 x 9,000 = 54,000. The 6 mountain ranges have together a width of 6 x 2,000 = 12,000. Thus north and south, we have 16,000 + 18,000 + 54,000 + 12,000 = 100,000.

East and west we have 34000 (9000 + 16000 + 9000) across Meru and Ilāvrita and the two mountain ranges 2 x 2000 = 4000.

The expanse of the two Varshas up to the ocean side is 62000. This gives us 34000 + 4000 + 62000 = 100,000. Thus there is no conflict. *Śridhara.*]

[This discussion of Śridhara throws immense light on the text. We find that the area is measured by the diameter. We find that 16000 is the diameter of Meru at the foot. We find that Ilāvrita has 9000 from Meru to Nila and 9000 from Meru to Nishadha. We understand also why Bhadrasva and Ketumala were said to be exceptions, their expanse being 34,000. A diagram will now best illustrate what we say.]

JAMBU DVIPA.

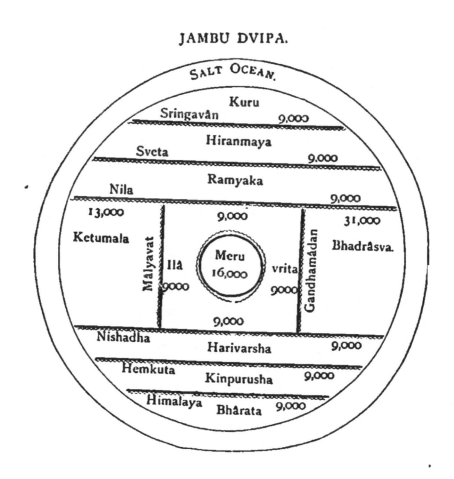

[Bhārata as a Varsha must not be mistaken for India. For Bhārata here stands for Nābhi or the whole of our known earth.

Bhārata Varsha extends from the base of the Earth opposite the Himalayas on the side of America to the highest point of the Himalayas.]

Kinpurusha Varsha, so called from its dwellers, extends from the highest point of the Himalayas as its base to the highest point of Hemakuta.

So with the other Varshas.

It will be seen, that we have no idea of any of the mountains, besides the Himalayas.

Ilāvrita stands on the same level with Ketumala and Bhadrasva. If these three be taken as one, we get the number 7. Five other Dvipas have 7 Varshas only.]

On the four sides of Meru are the four mountains — Mandāra, Meru Mandāra, Supārsna and Kumuā. They are ten thousand Yojanas in height and expanse.

(There are two mountains east and west, their expanse being north and south. There are other two north and south, their expanse being east and west. Otherwise if these mountains were to encircle Meru, Ilāvrita would not be in existence. *Śridhara*).

On these four mountains respectively are four big trees of Mango, Jamboland, Kadamba and the sacred Fig. They are the banners as it were of the Mountains. They are 11000 Yojanas high and they also spread over this area. Their width is one hundred Yojanas.

There is one lake below each of these trees: milk, sugarcane juice and pure water respectively. The use of these fluids gives natural Yogic powers to the Upadevas (lesser devas).

There are also four gardens of the Devas, *viz.* Nandana, Chaitraratha, Vaibhrājoka and Sarvato-bhadra.

The Devas, adored by the Upadevas amuse themselves in those gardens.

Big fruits with nectar-like juice fall from the mango tree on Mandāra.

(The Vayu Purāna gives the measure of the fruit. The Rishis who perceive truths give the measure of the fruits to be 108 cubits with the fist closed (*aratvi*) and also 61 cubits more. *Śridhara*)

When these fruits drop down, they give out a very sweet, very fragrant, profuse reddish juice which collects to form the river called Arunodā, having water of the color of Aruna or the morning Sun. This river waters the Eastern part of Ilāvrita. The use of its water gives such a sweet scent to the body of the female attendants of Durgā that the wind carries that scent to ten Yojanas around.

So the Jambu river is formed by the juice of the fruits that drop down from the Jambolova tree in Meru Mandāra. It waters the southern part of Ilāvrita.

The land on the banks of these rivers is soaked by their juice and worked on by air and light and is thus converted into gold called Jāmbūnada, which gives ornaments to the Devas.

Aruna is the morning Sun, as well as the color of the morning Sun. The river with Aruna water is also gold producing.

The Kadamba tree on Supārsva has cavities from which flow five streams of honey, each 5 Vyāmas wide (Vyāma = the space between the tips of the fingers of either hand when the arms are extended.) These streams water the western part of Ilāvrita. The fragrant breath of those that use them spreads over one hundred Yojanas all round.

The fig tree (Vata) called Satavolsa on the summit of Kumuda has branches which give rise to rivers that bring forth milk, curd, honey, clarified butter, molasses, edibles, carpets, cloths, ornaments, in fact all objects of desire. These rivers fall from Kumuda and water the northern part of Ilāvrita.

Those that use the waters of those rivers are free from all Infirmities, diseases, secretions, old age and death. They live in absolute bliss all their lives.

There are twenty more mountains on all sides of Meru, at its foot. They are Kuranga, Kurara, Kusumbha Naikovka, Trikuta, Sisira, Patanga. Ruchoka, Nishadha Sitivāsa, Kapila Sankha, Vaidūrya, Jārudhi, Housas, Rishabha, Nāga, Kālanjara, Nirada and others.

Two mountains, Jatharu and Devakūta, are situated on the east of Meru. They are two thousand Yojanas in height and in width. To the north they spread over 18,000 Yojanas.

So on the west there are the two mountains Pavana and Pāriyātra.

On the south there are Kailāśa and Karavira, which expand towards the east. So on the north, there are Trisringa and Makara. (If different measures are given in Vishnu and other Purānas, they are with reference to different Kalpas. *Śridhara*).

The sages say that in the central portion of the top of Sumeru is the abode of Brahmā, made of gold, 10,000,000 Yojanas in area, and of four equal sides.

Surrounding the abode of Brahmā are the eight abodes of the eight Lokapālas situated respectively in the directions presided over by these Lokapālas. Each of these abodes has the color of its own Lokapāla and each extends over 2 1/2 thousand yojanas. (The names of these abodes are given in other Purānas. Thus:

```
Manovatī is the abode of Brahmā.
Amarāvati    "    "      Indra.
Tejovati     "    "      Agni.
Sanyavati    "    "      Yāma.
Krishnāngana "    "      Nairita.
Sradhavati   "    "      Varuna.
Gandhavati   "    "      Vayu.
Mahodayā     "    "      Kubera.
Yasovati     "    "      Isa.
```

THE GANGES.

SKANDHA V. CHAP. 7.

The Avatāra Vāmana asked Bali, the Daitya King, for as much space as he could cover in three steps. The first step covered the earth. Vāmana then raised his foot over the heavens and the stroke of his left toe-nail caused a hole in the cosmic egg. Water entered the hole from outside, water that carried the washings of Vishnu's feet and that was consequently capable of purifying all the impurities of the world and that was in itself very pure, water that was then called Bhagavat pudi. In a thousand yugas the stream reached the highest point of Svar Loka, called Vishnupada.

Dhruva carried the stream on his own head with ever increasing devotion.

The seven Rishis (of the Great Bear) carry the sacred water in their braided tufts of hair, as something better than Mukti, for the stream of devotion flows from Vishnu direct.

Thence the stream passes through the path of the Devas, studded with thousands and thousands of starry chariots, till it overflows the lunar regions and fall down on the abode of Brahmā in Meru.

There the stream divides itself into four parts called Sitā, Alakanandā, Vankshu and Bhadrā.

The Sitā flows from the abode of Brahmā through the highest mountain ranges, she comes down to Gandha Mādana, thence through Bhadrāsva Varsha she falls into the salt ocean towards the east.

So the Vankshu flows through the Mālyavat range into Ketumala Varsha and falls on the west into the Salt ocean.

The Bhadrā flows north from the Sumeru peak through several mountain ranges down to Sringavat range and passes through Kuru in to the Salt ocean.

The Alakanandā flows south from the abode of Brahmā through several mountain ranges to Hema Kuta and thence to Himālaya till it reaches Bhārata Varsha (*i.e.* Nābhi Varsha) and at last flows through it into the Salt ocean.

There are a thousand other rivers and a thousand other mountains in each Varsha.

[The real source of the Ganges is not the melting of snow in the Himālāyas. That may be the source of the waters that swell the bed of the Ganges, as we see it. But the Ganges is something more than a volume of waters. There is a spiritual current underlying its waters. That current comes from regions higher than the highest peak of the Himālāyas. Hence the great sanctity attached to it].

THE MYSTERIES OF THE VARSHAS.

SKANDHA V. CHAP. 17-19.

Of the nine Varshas, Bhārata is the field of Karma (I must now once for all remind my readers that Bhārata when mentioned as a Varsha means Nābhi Varsha, the whole of this visible earth from the highest point of the Himalayas downwards). The other Varshas are places of fruition of the merits of those that go to Svarga. Hence they are called terrestrial (Bhouma) Svargas.

(Svarga is of three kinds: —

1. Divya viz. Svarga proper or Swar Loka.

2. Bhouma or terrestrial and

3. Bila or Pātālic.

Śridhara.)

Ilāvrita. — The dwellers of this Varsha live for ten thousand years of human measure. They are like Devas. They have the vitality of ten thousand elephants. Their body is strong like the thunderbolt. They enjoy

144

with women all their lives and only one year before death do the women bear children. They always live as it were in Treta Yuga.

Nārāyana — the Mahā Purusha pervades all the Varshas for their good, in different forms of His Chatur Vyūha (Vāsudeva, Sankarshana, Pradyumna and Anirudha).

In Ilāvrita, Bhava or Śiva is the only male. Other males do not enter that Varsha, for they know the curse of Bhāvanī (Durgā) that whoever should enter the Varsha was to become a female.

Bhava is adored by millions of women. He meditates on the fourth, the Tāmasa Mūrti of Mahāpurusha *viz.* Shankarshana. He recites the following mantra and runs about: —

"Om Namo Bhāgavate Mahā Purushāya Sarva-guna Sankhāynāya Anantāya Avyaktāya Namaha."

"Om, Salutations to Bhagavat Mahā Purusha, salutations to the manifester of all Gunas, the Endless, the Unmanifested."

Then follows a prayer to Sankarshana for which readers are referred to the original *Bhadtāsva.*

Bhadrasravas is the lord of Bhadrāsva. He and his followers dwell there, they meditate on the Hayaśirsha aspect of Vāsudeva, they recite the following mantra and run about.

"Om Namo Bhāgavate Dharmāya Ātmā-visodhanāya namah."

"Om salutations to Bhagavat Dharma; salutations to him who purifies the soul."

Then follows a prayer to Hayagrīva *Harivarsha.*

The renowned saintly Daitya Prahlāda with the dwellers of this Varsha adore Him and recite the following mantra.

"Om Namo Bhagavate Srī Nara Sinhāya Namastejastejase Āvirāvir bhava vajranakha vajra-danstra Karmā-Sayān randhaya randhaya tamo grasa om Svāhā Abhayam Abhoyam Ātmani bhūyisthūh om kshroum."

"Om salutations to Bhagavat Srī Hrisinha, Salutations to the fire of all fires! Manifest Thyself! Manifest thyself O thunder-nailed! O thunder-toothed! Burn up, burn up all desires! devour Tamas! Om Svāhā! Freedom from fear, freedom from fear be in us. Om! Kohrāum!"

Ketumāla.

Pradyumna or Kāmadeva presides over Ketumala in order to please Lakshmī Samvatsara (one year), the daughters of Samvatsara *viz:* the nights and Sons of Samvatsara*viz:* the days. The days and nights are 36,000 in number *i.e.* as many as are contained in the full term of a man's life (one hundred years). These days and nights are the lords of Ketumāla Lakshmī with whom the dwellers of Ketumāla adore Kāmadeva.

(The mantra and prayer are then given.)

Ramyaka.

Matsya (The Fish Incarnation) presides over Ramyaka. Manu is the King.

(Mantra and prayer follow)

Hiranmaya.

Kūrma (the Tortoise Incarnation) presides over Hiranmaya. Aryaman the chief of the Pitris dwells there with others.

(Mantra and prayer follow)

Kuru.

Varsha or the Boar Incarnation presides over Kuru. Bhūr with the dwellers of Kuru adore him.

(Mantra and prayer follow.)

Kinpurusha.

In Kinpurusha, Hanumān with the dwellers of the Varsha worship the Adipurusha Rāma, brother of Lakshamana and husband of Sitā.

(Mantra and prayer follow.)

Bhārat Varsha.

Nara Nārāyana presides over this Varsha. There are various (castes) and Āsramas in this Varsha. Nārada of great devotion leads the people of this Varsha. His object in so doing is to teach to Sāvarni, the coming Manu, the Sānkhya and Yoga (as related in the Bhagavat Gitā) together with the full realisation of Bhagavat (as related in the Pancharatras).

[This mission of Nārada is specially noteworthy.]

(Mantra and prayer follow.)

In this Bhārata Varsha there are many mountains and rivers.

Maloya, Mangalaprastha, Maināka, Trikuta, Rishava, Kutaka, Kōnva, Sahya, Rishyamūka, Srisaila, Venkata, Mahendra, Vāridhāra, Vindhya, Śaktimān, Riksha, Pāripātra, Drōna, Chitrakūta, Gobardhana, Raivatak, Kakubha, Nila, Gokāmukha, Indrakila, Kāmagiri and hundreds and thousands of other mountains are situated in this Varsha.

The following are the principal rivers Chandvavāsa, Tāmvaparni, Avatōda, Kritamālā, Vaihāyasi, Kāveri, Venūā, Payasvini, Sarkarāvartā, Krishnavenuā, Bhimrathi, Godābari, Nirvindhyā, Payoshni, Tāpi, Revā, Surasā, Narmadā, Charmanvati, Andha, Sōna, Mahānadi, Vedasmriti, Rishikúlyā, Trisāmā, Kousiki, Mandākini, Yamunā, Sarasvati, Drishadvati, Gomati, Saraju, Aghavati, Shasthavati, Saptavati, Satadru, Sushōma, Chandrabhāgā, Maruduridhā, Vitastā, Asikini and Visvā.

Those that acquire birth in this Varsha have recourse to Svarga, humanity and Naraka respectively, according as their Karma is White (Sātvic), Red (Rājasic) or Black (Tāmasic). The People acquire Moksha in this Varsha in accordance with their Varna (Caste). (This is because Karma according to caste prevails in this Varsha, not that Moksha is not otherwise attainable. *Śridhara*).

And what is moksha in this Varsha? It is the Companionship of Mahātmās (Mahāpurushas) brought about by the destruction of the bonds of Avidyā caused by various births. And that Moksha is in reality unceasing, unselfish devotion to the All-pervading, Indestructible, Causeless Paramātma Vāsudeva.

Even the Devas say: — "How fortunate are these people of Bhārat Varsha! For Hari is kind to them, even without many performances and they are so adapted for communion with Hari by devotion. We have attained Svarga by the performance of Yajna. But we shall have to be born again after the end of the Kalpa. What good is in this state, which does not bring us in direct communion with Vishnu? These people of Bhārat Varsha even with their short lives acquire the state of Hari. If there be any Karma left to us after the enjoyment of Svarga may we be born as men that we may worship Hari."

Some say there are eight upadvipas in Jambu Dvipa, formed by the sons of Sagara when they dug up this earth in search of the sacrificial horse. They are Svarna Prastha, Chandra Sukla, Āvartana, Rāmanaka, Manda-harina, Panchajanya, Sinhala and Loukā.

THE DVIPAS.

SKANDHA V. CHAP. 20.

Plaksha Dvipa

Jambu Dvipa is surrounded by the salt ocean on all sides. That ocean extends over Laksha Yojanas. That salt ocean is again surrounded on all sides by Plaksha Dvipa, which extends over 2 laksha of Yojanas.

There is one golden Plaksha tree in that Dvipa as high as the Jambu tree in Jambu Dvipa and the Dvipa itself takes its name from that tree. There Fire is seven tongued,

Idhmajihva son of Priyavrata ruled over this Dvipa. He divided the Dvipa into seven Varshas and named them after his seven sons each of whom ruled over the Varsha of his name.

Śiva, Vayasa, Subhadrā, Sānta, Kshema, Amrita and Abhoya are the Varshas.

Manikūta, Vajrakūta, Indrasena, Jyotishmat, Subarna, Hiranyasthiva and Meghmāla are the seven chief mountains.

Arunā, Nrimāna, Angirasi, Sāvitri, Supravātā, Ritambharā and Satyambharā are the seven great rivers.

Hansa, Patanga, Urdhāyana and Satyānga are the corresponding castes.

The dwellers of the Dvipa live for one thousand years. They look like Devas and procreate after Deva fashion. They worship the Sūrya (Sun-god) of the Vedas.

(The Mantra is given)

In Plaksha, Sālmali, Kusa, Krouncha and Śaka, the inmates have their age, Indriyas, strength, power and Budhi by their very birth and not by Karma.

The Dvipa is surrounded by the Sugar cane juice ocean which extends over 2 laksha of Yojanas.

Sālmali Divpa: — Twice as large as Plaksha Dvipa. The ocean of wine surrounding it is equally large.

Tree: — Sālmali (Bombax Malabaricum) as high as the Plaksha tree said to be the seat of Garuda.

King: Yajna-vāha son of Priyavrata.

Seven Varshas and seven sons of Yajnavaha: — Surochana, Soumanasya, Rāmanaka, Devvarha, Pāribhadra, Āpyāyana and Abhijhāta.

Seven principal mountains: — Surasa, Śata Sringa, Vamadeva, Kunda, Kumuda, Pushpa Varsha and Sahosra.

Seven great rivers: — Anumati, Sinivāti, Sarasvati, Kuhu, Rajani, Nandā and Rākā.

Divisions of people: — Srutidhara, Viryadhara, Vasundhara, and Ishundhara.

Presiding deity: — The Moon.

Kusa Dvipa: — Twice as large as Sālmali Dvipa surrounded by an ocean of clarified butter equally large.

Tree: — Clusters of Kusa grass glowing and glittering.

King: — Hiranyaretas son of Priyavrata.

Seven Varshas: — Vasu, Vasudāna, Dridharuchi, Nābhigupta, Satyavrata, Bikranama, and Devanāma.

Seven mountains: — Babhra, Chatur-Sringa, Kapila Chitra Kūta, Devānika, Urdharomau and Dravina.

Seven Rivers: — Raaskulyā, Madhukulyā, Mitravindā, Srutavindā, Deva Garbhā, Ghutachyntā, and Mantramālā.

Divisions of People: — Kusala, Kōvida, Abhiyukta and Kulaka.

Presiding Deity: — Agni (Fire-god).

Krouncha Dvipa: — Twice as large as Kusa, surrounded by an ocean of milk equally large. Named after the Krouncha Mountain. The Krouncha Mountain was attacked by Kārtikeya and injured too. But the Milk Ocean and the presiding deity Varuna saved it.

King: — Ghritaprestha son of Priyavrata.

Seven Varshas: — Ātmā, Madhuruha, Meghapristha, Sudhāwan, Bhrājistha, Lohitārna, Vānaspati.

Seven Mountains: — Sukla, Vardhamān, Bhajana, Upavarhaha, Nauda, Nandana and Sarvato-bhadra.

Seven Rivers: — Abhoya, Amritoughā, Āryukā, Tirthavati, Rupavati, Pavitravati and Suklā.

Divisions of people: — Purasha, Rishabha, Dravina and Devaka.

Presiding Deity: Āpas (Water-God.)

Sāka Dvipa: — 32 laksha Yojanas. Surrounded by an ocean of curds — equally extensive.

Tree: — Sāka (Teak wood tree) very fragrant.

King: — Medhātithi, son of Priyavrata.

Seven Varshas: — Purojava, Manojava, Vepamāna, Dhūmrānika, Chitrarepha, Bahurūpa and Visvā-dhāra.

Seven Mountains: — Isāna, Uru Sringa, Balabhadra, Sata Kesara, Sahasra-srotas, Devapāla and Mohānasa.

Seven Rivers: — Anaghā, Āyurdā, Ubhayaspriti, Aparājitā, Punchapadī, Sahasra Sruti and Nijadhriti.

Division of people: — Ritavrata, Satyavrata, Dānavrata and Anuvrata.

Presiding Deity: — Vayu (Wind-god).

Puskkara Dvipa: — Twice as large as Saka Dvipa surrounded by an ocean of pure water — equally extensive: There is a big Pushkara or Lotus plant with thousands of golden leaves. The Lotus is known as the seat of Brahmā.

Standing between two Varshas, eastern and western, is the Mānasattara Mountain ten thousand Yojanas high. On the four sides of this Mountain are four abodes of the Lokapālas = Indra and others.

Over these abodes the Sanvatsava or Uttarāyana Dakshināyana wheel (*chakra*) of the Sun's chariot moves in its course round Meru.

Vitihotra, Son of Priyavrata, is the king of this Varsha.

His two sons Rāmanaka and Dhātaka are the lords of two Varshas named after them.

The people of those Varshas worship Brahmā by Yajna performances.

Beyond the Ocean of pure water is the Lokāloka (Loka and Aloka) Mountain, dividing Loka, the regions lighted by the sun, from Aloka or the regions not lighted by the sun.

As much land as there is between Mānasottara and Meru, so much golden land is there on the other side of the pure water ocean. It is like the surface of the mirror. If any thing is thrown on that land, it is not regained. It is therefore forsaken by all beings. [The land between Mānasottara and Meru is one krore and a half *plus* seven and a half lakhs. There is as much land on the other side of the Pure Water Ocean. There are living beings in that land. Beyond that is the golden land. That land is eight krores and thirty nine laksha yojanas wide. It is thus that the distance between Meru and Lokāloka comes to be 12 1/2 krores as mentioned below. This is also said in the Śiva Tantra.

Two krores 53 lakshas and 50 thousand this is the measure of the seven Dvipas with the Oceans. Beyond that is the golden land which is 10 Krores of Yojanas. This is used by the Devas as their play-ground. Beyond that is Lokāloka. The ten krores include the previously mentioned land, "Forsaken by all beings" — this is to be understood with the exception of the Devas, for it is mentioned as the play-ground of the Devas. *Śridhara.*]

In order to understand the commentary of *Śridhara*, let us examine the figures.

Jambu Dvipa with Ocean on one side of Meru:

```
... ... 150,000 Yojanas
```

Plaksha Dvipa with Ocean on one side of Meru:
```
... ... 400,000
```

```
Sālmali   Do.  ... ... 800,000
```

```
Kusa      Do.  .. ... 1,600,000
```

```
Krouncha  Do.  .. ... 3,200,000
```

```
Sāka      Do.  .. ... 6,400,000
```

```
Pushkar   Do.  . ... 12,800,000
```

Deduct Pure water Ocean as it is not included between Meru and Mānasottara:

```
... ...   6,400,000
        18,950,000
```

Mānasottara stands half way in Pushkara, as it stands between two Varshas. Deduct distance between Mānasottara and Pure Water Ocean:

```
...  3,200,000
    15,750,000
```

The distance between Meru and Mānasottara is 1 1/2 Krores and 7 1/2 lakhs.

According to Śridhara, there is this much land on the other side of the Pure Water Ocean.

Beyond that land is the Golden land which according to *Śridhara* is:

```
                              ... ... 83900000 Yojanas

Thus we get Dvipas and Oceans     ... 25350000    "

Land beyond Pure Water Oceans     ... 15750000    "

The Golden land           ... ... 83900000    "
                                 125000000    "
```

Thus we get the 12 1/2 krores of Śrīdhara. Beyond the Golden land is the Lokāloka Mountain. This will also explain the quotation from Śiva Tantra. The following Diagram will partially illustrate the points.

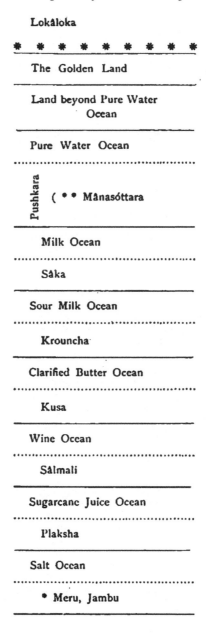

Lokāloka

The Golden Land

Land beyond Pure Water Ocean

Pure Water Ocean

Pushkara (• • Mānasóttara

Milk Ocean

Sāka

Sour Milk Ocean

Krouncha

Clarified Butter Ocean

Kusa

Wine Ocean

Sālmali

Sugarcane Juice Ocean

Plaksha

Salt Ocean

• Meru, Jambu

The Lokāloka is the boundary of three Lokas, Bhūr, Bhuvar, and Svar.

The rays of the numerous bodies from the Sun up to Dhruva illuminate the regions on the Triloka side of Lokāloka but they can never reach its other side. For such is the height and expanse of Lokāloka — (It is even higher than Dhruva. So it is the boundary of Trilokī. *Śridhara*).

The Bhu-Golaka or the Bhūr system measures 50 Krores. And Lokāloka is one-fourth of that *i.e.* 12 1/2 Krores (on one side of Meru. *Śridhara*).

Over this Lokāloka, Brahmā placed 4 Elephant Kings in four different directions *viz:* Rishabha, Pushkarachūra, Vāmana and Aparājitā. This is for the preservation of the Lokas.

Bhagavān Mahā Purusha (Vishnu) Himself remains there. He infuses various powers into the Elephant Kings and into the Lokapālas (preservers of the Lokas) Indra and others who are but His manifestations. He pervades all. He manifests His pure Satva. The characteristics of that satva are the eight Siddhis.

Dharma, Jnāna, Vairāgya, Aisvarya &c., Vishvaksena and His other Companions are with Him. His own weapons are in his hands. He remains there for the good of all Lokas.

To the end of the Kalpa, Vishnu remains in this way pervading all for the preservation of the Universe formed by His own Māyā.

The measure of Aloka is also 12 1/2 Krores (on one side of Meru. *Śridhara*).

Beyond Aloka is Visuddha (very pure region) where only masters of Yoga can go.

The Sun stands in the centre of the Egg. That is also the middle ground between Svar and Bhūr. Between the Sun and the Circumference of the Egg is 25 Krores.

The Sun is called Mārtanda (Mrita and anda) because in Mrita or dead matter he infused life as Vairāja. He is called Hiranya Garbha (Gold wombed) because he came out of the Golden Egg.

The sun divided space into Bhūr, Bhuvar and Svar. The Sun divides the regions of enjoyment and Moksha. He divides the Narakas and Pātālas. He is the Ātmā of Devas, men, animals, plants and other Jivas. He is the manifester of sight.

SVAR AND BHUVAR.

SKANDHA V. CHAP. 21.

The localisation, measure and other details of Bhūr have been given above. (By expanse 50 Krores and by height 25 Krores. *Śridhara*).

The measure of Svar is the same as that of Bhūr — Just as one cotyledon gives the measure of the other cotyledon in a flower.

Bhuvar is the connecting link of Bhūr and Svar.

THE SUN.

SKANDHA V. CHAP. 21-22.

The Sun from the Bhuvar Loka sends forth his rays to Trilokī.

(Here follow astronomical details which need not be given.)

When the Sun is between the Autumn and spring Equinoxes it is called Uttarāyana (or going towards the north.) Then the Sun's motion is said to be slow.

When the Sun is between the spring Equinox and Autumn Equinox, it is Dakshināyana (Going towards the south.) The Sun's motion is then said to be Quick.

When the sun is at the Equinoxes it is Vishuva. The Sun's motion is then said to be Even.

When it is Dakshināyana, the days increase. When it is Uttarāyana the nights increase.

The sages teach 9 Krores and 51 lakhs of Yojanas as the Circumference of Manāsottara.

[On both sides of Meru up to Manāsottara is 3 Krores and 15 lakhs. The Measure of the above circle is obtained from this (diameter). *Śridhara.*]

[A full diagram of the Bhūr system will now have to be given, to explain the above figures. For the sake of convenience, the Dvipa and its ocean are given as one.]

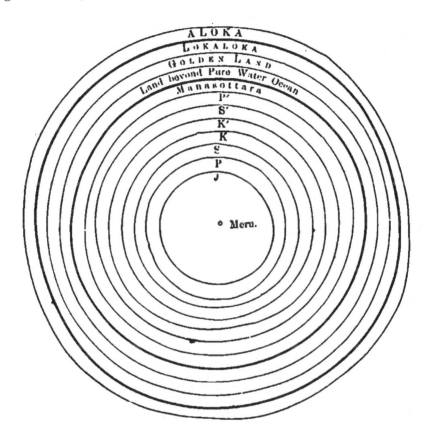

```
From Meru to Lokāloka on one side        ... 12 1/2 Krores
                  on both sides          ... 25        "
Loka loka on both sides                  ... 25        "
Measure of Bhūr system                   ... 50        "
Distance from Meru to Manasottora 15,750,000
On both sides                     ... 31,500,000
```

The Manāsottara range is a circle of which the last figure is the diameter.

The circle is obtained by multiplying the diameter by a little over 3.

The circle is thus given to be — 9 Krores and 51 Lakshas.

The Manāsottara is the path of revolution of the sun round Meru.

On the East side of Meru in the Manāsottara is the seat of Indra named Devadhānī.

On the South side is the seat of Yāma named Sanyamanī.

On the West is the seat of Varuna named Nimlochani.

On the North is the seat of the Moon named Vibhavarī.

Sunrise, midday, Sunset and night on those seats cause action and inaction in beings, according to the time with reference to the side of Meru.

(For those that live to the south of Meru, their east &c. commence from the abode of Indra, of those that live to the west from the abode of Yāma, of the northern people, from the abode of Varuna, of the eastern people from the abode of the Moon. *Śridhara.*)

Those that live on the Meru have the Sun always over their heads.

The Sun's chariot makes one round along Manāsottara in one year. The wheel or chakra of the chariot is therefore called Sanvatsara.

The 12 months are the 12 spokes of that wheel. The six seasons form 6 arcs.

The pole of that chariot extends to the top of Meru. The other end of the pole is on the Manāsottara. (It is either to be thought that the wheel is placed more than 50,000 Yojanas over the Manāsottara in the regions of air or the wheel is to be considered as high as that distance, otherwise the Manāsottara being 10,000 Yojanas high and Meru being 84 Yojanas high, 16 thousand being under ground, there will be a difference of planes in the Sun's revolution. *Śridhara.*)

There is another movement of the Sun round Dhruva. The radius of that revolution is one fourth the distance between Meru and Manāsottara. (*i.e.* 1/4 X 15,750,000 = 3,937,500).

The movement round Dhruva is caused by the action of air.

The seat within the chariot is 36 laksha of Yojanas wide. The yoke is also of the same measure. The seven horses are the seven Vedic metres (Gāyatri, Ushnik, Anustup, Vrihatī, Pankti, Tristup and Jagati). They are driven by Aruna.

The thumb sized Bālikhilya Rishis stand in front of the chariot and chant hymns in honor of Āditya.

THE PLANETS AND STARS.

SKANDHA V. CHAP. 22-23.

The moon is one laksha of Yojanas over the Sun. The growing Moon makes the day of the Devas and the waning Moon is the life of all Jivas, in fact he is Jiva.

He is Manomaya, Annamaya and Amritamaya. From him therefore proceed the life and advancement of Devas, Pitris, Men, Animals and Plants.

Two laksha of Yojanas over the Moon are the 27 Zodiacal constellations and also the star Abhijit (a mysterious star between Uttarāshādhā and Sravanā) attached to the wheel of time.

Two laksha of Yojanas over them is Sukra or Venus. His movements are like those of the Sun. He is ever favourable to men. His progression is generally accompanied by showers of rain. He also subdues those planets that counteract the rains.

Two laksha of Yojanas over Sukra is Budha or Mercury. He is much like Sukra in his movements and is generally favourable to men. But when he transgresses the Sun, there is fear of high winds, rainless clouds and drought.

Two laksha of Yojanas over Budha is Mangala or Mars. He moves round the Zodiac in three fortnights. He is generally unfavourable to men, causing miseries, unless he proceeds by retrogression.

Two laksha of Yojanas over Mars is Brihaspati or Jupiter. He moves in each sign of the Zodiac for one Parivatsara (year of Jupiter), if there is no retrogression. He is generally unfavorable to the Brāhmanas.

Two laksha of Yojanas over Jupiter is Sanaischara or Saturn. He loiters in each sign of the Zodiac for thirty months. He completes his round in thirty Anuvatsaras. He is generally unfavourable to all and causes unrest.

Eleven laksha of Yojanas over Saturn are the Rishis. Their influence is for the good of all people. They revolve round the Supreme abode of Vishnu.

Thirteen laksha of Yojanas beyond the Rishis is Dhruva, which is the Supreme abode of Vishnu.

All luminous bodies attached to the wheel of time move round Dhruva being propelled by Vāyu while Dhruva remains fixed.

The planets and stars remain fixed in their relative positions, under the union of Prakriti and Purusha by the future made for them by their Karma.

Some however say that the luminous bodies become fixed in their relative positions by the Yoga support of Vāsudeva, being held together in the shape of Sisumāra (the Gangetic porpoise). The Sisumāra has its face downwards and its body is coiled.

Dhruva is at the end of its tail. Prajāpati, Agni, Indra and Dharma are in the lower part of the tail. Dhāta and Vidhāta are at the root of the tail. The seven Rishis are in the middle. On the right side are the fourteen Stars from Abhijit to Punarvasu. On the left side are the 14 stars from Pushyā to Uttara Sārhā. So on, all the stars and planets. (For details refer to the original).

The Sisumāra is the Universal manifestation of Maha Purusha.

[The following Geo-centric diagram is given, as illustrative of the positions of the planets.]

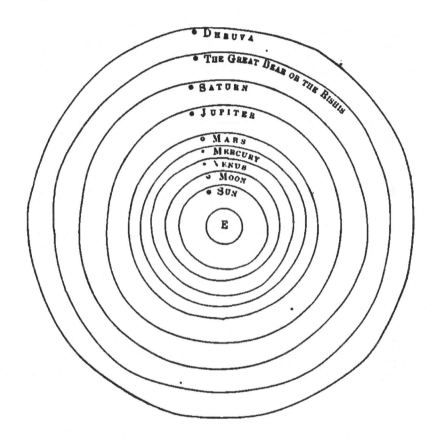

THE PĀTĀLAS

SKANDHA V. CHAP. 24.

Ten thousand Yojanas below the Sun is Rāhu, son of Sinhika. Though an Asura, by favour of Bhagavān he became a planet and immortal too like the Devas.

Ten thousand Yojanas below Rāhu is the abode of the Siddhas, Chāranas and Vaidyādharas.

Below that is the abode of the Yakshas, Rākshasas, Pisāchas, Pretas, and Bhūtas. This abode extends down to the regions of air and clouds.

One hundred Yojanas below that is the Earth. The details of the Earth's surface have been given above.

Underneath the Earth are the seven Patālas: — Atala, Vitala, Sutala, Talātala, Mahātala, Rasātala and Pātāla. They are ten thousand Yojanas apart from each other.

In these nether Svargas, Daityas, Dānavas and Nāgas dwell. Their enjoyments, power, joys and luxuries are even greater than those of the Devas of Svarga. Their houses, gardens and playgrounds are very rich. They are always joyous. They are attached to their wives, sons, friends and attendants. By the grace of īsvara, their desires are always gratified.

Māyā, the Dānava Magician, has built wonderful houses, gardens &c. in these regions with precious stones.

There are no divisions of time, as the Sun's rays do not enter those regions and no disturbances from such divisions. All darkness is removed by the light of the precious stones on the head of the serpent king.

The people of Pātāla use divine herbs and medicines, and consequently they have no infirmities, diseases, old age, languor and offensive secretions.

They have no death except by the Chakra of Bhagavān (*i.e.* final extinction).

Atala: — Bala, the son of Maya resides in Atala (Maya is a masculine form of Māyā the root Prakriti). He created here 96 forms of Māyā. The Māyāvins (those who practice Magic) still have recourse to those forms. When he yawns, three classes of women spring into existence viz:

1. Svairini (self willed loose women),

2. Kāmini (passionate women) and

3. Punschali (unchaste women).

If any one enters Atala these women completely allure him by their Hātaka (golden) charm, and when the man is completely overcome by their allurements, he says "I am īsvara", "I am Siddha."

[The women are only forms of Māyā because Māyā is personified as an alluring woman. A man in Atala is completely under the domination of Māyā and becomes estranged from spirit. So Māyā is all in all to him and he knows no other.]

Vitala: — Below Atala is Vitala. There Bhava (Śiva) the king of Gold reigns in company with his consort Bhavāni, attended by Bhūtas. He remains there for the benefit of the Prajāpati creation. The fluid of intercourse with Bhavāni gives rise to a river called Hātaki (Golden). Agni kindled by Vāyu drinks up that river and gives out the gold called Hātaka which is used in ornaments by the Asuras who dwell there.

(We have known Śiva as the Astral Lord. We find him here engaged in the work of creation. The text speaks of a mysterious connection between him and the gold called Hātaka. The occult varieties of gold such as Jāmvanada and Hātaka form a fit subject of study. Hātaka refers to the Prajāpati creation. There is duality in Vitala, as distinguished from the singleness of Māyā in Atala).

Sutala: — Below Vitala is Sutala. There the renowned Bali son of Virochana still dwells. Vāmana, the Dwarf Incarnation of Vishnu, took away the Trilokī from him and replaced him here. His enjoyments even here are greater than those of Indra. He performs Sva-dharma and worships Vishnu. His sins are all removed.

(A full account of Bali will be given below.)

Talātala: — Below Sutala is Talātala. Māyā, the Dānava king, rules there. His "Three Puras" (abodes) were destroyed by Śiva who is hence called Tripurari. But Śiva favoured him again and placed him in Talātala. He is the preceptor of all Māyāvins. He is preserved by Śiva and he has no fear from Sudarsana (the chakra weapon of Vishnu, which symbolises Time.)

(Bali and Māyā, Trilokī and Tripura, the seizure of one and the destruction of the other, the restoration of Bali to Sutala and of Māyā to Talātala, the favour shown to them in those regions, the correspondences of Sutala and Talātala are worth careful consideration. In the case of one, Vishnu or the Preservative aspect of the Second Purusha is the actor, and in the other, Śiva, the Destructive aspect.)

Mahātala: — Below Talātala is Mahātala. Many headed serpents, the progeny of Kadru, dwell there. The chief amongst them are Kuhaka, Takshaka, Kāliya, Sushena, and others. They are always afraid of Garuda, the Vehicle of Vishnu, and they are therefore seldom seen to indulge in pleasure-trips outside.

Rasātala: — Below Mahatala is Rasātala; Daityas, Dānavas and Panis, named Nivatakavachas, Kālakeyas and Hiranyapuravāsins dwell there. They are the enemies of the Devas. They are powerful from their very birth. They are subdued by the Sudarsana of Vishnu. They are like serpents. They fear even the threats of Saramā, the bitch of the gods who is Indra's messenger to them. They fear Indra also.

Pātala: — Below Rasātala is Pātala. The Nāgas dwell there. Vasūki is their chief. The other principal Nāgas are — Sankha, Kulika, Mahā Sankha, Sveta, Dhananjaya, Asvatara, and Devadatta. Their hood is very large and they are very furious. Some of them are five headed, some 7 headed, some 10 headed, some a thousand headed. The precious stones on their hoods dispel all darkness in Pātala.

ANANTA.

SKANDHA V. CHAP. 25.

At the root of Pātala, thirty thousand Yojanas beyond, is the Tamas aspect of Bhagavān called Ananta. Those that worship the Chaturvyūha aspect call him Sankarshana. He has a thousand heads. The earth held up on one of these heads looks but like a mustard seed. When the time for dissolution comes, Ananta assumes His Tamas form and becomes Rudra — other wise called Sankarshana, a host of eleven, with three eyes, three tufts of hair and with tridents on their heads. At other times, Ananta withdraws His Tamas and abides for the good of all Lokas. His eyes roll as it were by intoxication. His garments are blue. He has one ear-ring. He has a plough on his back.

THE NARAKAS.

SKANDHA V. CHAP. 26.

Where are the Narakas, O Rishi, asked Parikshit? Are they particular localities? Are they outside the Trilokī or inside?

Suka replied: —

They are inside the Trilokī on the south side below the earth, over the waters, where Agnishvāttā and other Pitris deeply meditate on the welfare of their respective descendants.

There, Yāma, the Death-god, metes out just punishment to the dead.

There are twenty-one Narakas: —

1. Tāmisra

2. Andha Tāmisara

3. Rourava

4. Mahārourava

5. Kumbhipāka

6. Kāla Sutra

7. Asipatravana

8. Sūkara Mukha

9. Andha Kūpa

10. Krimi bhajana

11. Sandansa

12. Tapta Surmi

13. Vajra-Kantaka Sālmali

14. Vaitarani

15. Pūyôda

16. Prānarodha

17. Vaisāsana

18. Lālābhaksha

19. Sārameyādāna

20. Avichi and

21. Ayahpāna.

There are seven other Narakas:

1. Kshāra Kardama

2. Rakshogana bhōjana

3. Sūlaprōta

4. Danda Sūka

5. Avata-nirodhana

6. Paryā vartana and

7. Sūchi mukha.

(For details of these Narakas, the reader is referred to the original. They are more for the exoteric than for the esoteric reader.)

There are hundreds and thousands of such Narakas in the realms of Yāma. The vicious enter them by turns. The meritorious go to Svarga. But the Karma of men is not exhausted in Svarga or Naraka. For that which remains unexhausted, they enter life again by re-birth.

(The mention of Pitris and Yāma connects the Narakas with the astral plane.)

SKANDHA VI.

THE STORY OF AJĀMILA

SKANDHA VI. CHAP. 1-3.

Rājā Parikshit asked how men could avoid Naraka.

SUKA replied: — It is by Prāyaschitta (expiation) that men can avoid Naraka. But it is not Vedic Prāyaschitta, not fasting by Chāndrāyana and other Vratas. These Vedic performances cannot root out vicious tendencies, for the performer is seen again to indulge in vices. They do not purify the mind. They simply counteract the Kārmic effect of the act for which Prāyaschitta is performed. The real Prāyaschitta is devotion to Vishnu.

Ajāmila was the son of a Brāhmana. He was dutiful, virtuous, modest, truthful, and regular in the performance of Vedic injunctions. One day in obedience to his father he went into the forests and there collected fruits, flowers, sacrificial wood and *Kusa* — on returning he saw a Sudra in company with a slave-girl. He tried much to subdue his passions but did not succeed. He spent the whole of his patrimony to win the love of that girl. He gave up his own wife and kept company with that slave girl. He had by her several sons of whom the youngest was Nārāyana. Ajāmila lost all his good qualities in low company and he forgot his daily practices. To support the woman and her children, he had recourse to all sorts of vicious and unlawful acts. Nārāyana was the favorite among his sons. He caressed him always. At last his end approached. He thought even then of his youngest son who was playing at a distance. Three fierce-looking messengers of Yāma appeared, with ropes in hand. Terrified at the sight Ajāmila cried out "Nārāyana, Nārāyana." Instantly the Messengers of Vishnu appeared. At the time when the servants of Yāma were drawing out the Jiva from the heart of Ajāmila, the attendants of Vishnu stopped them with a strong voice. "But who are you" said they "to interfere with the just sway of Yāma." The bright attendants of Vishnu only smiled and asked: "What is Dharma? Does your lord Yāma hold the sceptre of punishment against all who perform Karma? Is there no distinction made?"

The astral messengers replied: — "The performance of Vedic Injunctions is Dharma and their disregard is Adharma. This Ajāmila in his earlier days duly respected the Vedas. But in company with the slave-girl, he lost his Brahmānism, disregarded the Vedas and did things which a Brāhmana should not do. He justly comes for punishment to Yama."

The attendants of Vishnu expressed wonder at these words. "And you are servants of him, who is called the king of Dharma, and you do not know that there is something above the Vedas too. This Ajāmila consciously or unconsciously took the name of Nārāyana and that saved him from your clutches. It is in the nature of fire to consume fuel and so it is in the nature of Vishnu's name to destroy all sins. If one unconsciously takes some powerful medicine, does it not have effect? It matters not whether Ajāmila meant his youngest son or not but still he took the name of Nārāyana. So you must retire."

Wonder-struck the servants of Yāma left their hold over Ajāmila. They went away and complained to their Master. "There must be one law and one dispenser of that law. Otherwise some will be punished and others not. Why should there be this difference? We know Thee to be the sole dispenser of the Law for the vicious. But just now the attendants of Vishnu came and wrested from our hands a transgressor against the Vedas."

"True my sons", replied Yāma, "there is some one above me and it is Vishnu. His ways are mysterious.

"The whole Universe is in Him. His attendants always save His votaries. Only twelve of us know his Dharma, which is Bhāgavata and no one else. These twelve are Brahmā, Śiva, Sanat Kumāra, Nārada, Kapila, Manu, Prahlāda, Janaka, Bhishma, Bali, Suka and myself."

Ajāmila heard the conversation between the messengers of Yāma and Vishnu. He became sorely penitent (the repentance is strongly described). He overcame his attachments, left the house and went to Haridvāra. There he meditated on Vishnu with concentrated mind. The former attendants of Vishnu appeared once more and took him on a chariot to Vishnu Loka.

THE PROGENY OF DAKSHA.

SKANDHA VI. CHAP. 4-6.

[We left the line of Uttānapāda with Daksha, the son of the Prachetas brothers. We were told of his work of creation in the Chākshasha Manvantara. But we have to take up the line just now, to introduce the story of Visva Rūpa.]

Daksha first carried on the work of creation by Mānasic reproduction. But he found this sort of reproduction was not adequate for the enlargement of creation. He went to a place near the Vindhyas and prayed hard to Vishnu. Vishnu became pleased with his prayers and advised him to marry Asikni, the daughter of Prajāpati Panchajana. "Take her for your wife and have sexual intercourse with her. By sexual reproduction, you shall have a large progeny and that form of reproduction shall prevail among your sons too".

By Asikni, Daksha had at first 10 thousand sons called Haryasva. He asked them to take up the work of creation. They went westwards to where the river Sindhu falls into the ocean. They began to make Tapas there for their progeny. Nārada appeared before them and dissuaded them from Pravritti Mārga. He gave them instructions for obtaining Moksha and they followed the path of its attainment.

Daksha heard that his sons were killed by Nārada and he became very sorry.

He again had one thousand sons names Subalāsva. They also went out to the very same place and prayed to Vishnu for progeny. Nārada again dissuaded them and they never returned to their father.

Daksha became restless in sorrow and thus cursed Nārada on meeting him. "Thou shalt roam all over Trilokī and shalt find no resting place."

Daksha had then 60 daughters. Ten he gave to Dharma, 13 to Kasyapa, 27 to the Moon, two each to Bhūta, Angirasa, and Krisasva and four to Tārksha.

THE PROGENY OF DHARMA.

(1) *By Bhānu*: — Devar-shabha or the chief Devas.

(2) *By Lambā*: — Vidyota (flash of lightning)
                    |
            The clouds.

(3) *By Kakud*: — Sankata
            |
        Kikata (the elementals presiding over earth-cavities).

(4) *By Yāmi*: — Svarga.
            |
        Nandi.

(5) *By Visvā*: — The Visvadevas (Vedic-gods).

(6) *By Sādhyā*: — The Sādhyas — attainment of desires.

(7) *By Mavutvatī*: — Marutvat and Jayanta, otherwise called Upendra.

(8) *By Muhūrta*: — The Muhūrta Devas or Devas presiding over the moments.

(9) *By Sankalpā*: — Sankalpa (Desire).

(10) *By Vasu*: The eight Vasus (Vedic-gods), *viz*

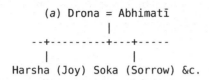

```
              (a) Drona = Abhimati
                     |
        --+---------+---+-----
          |             |
      Harsha (Joy)  Soka (Sorrow) &c.
```

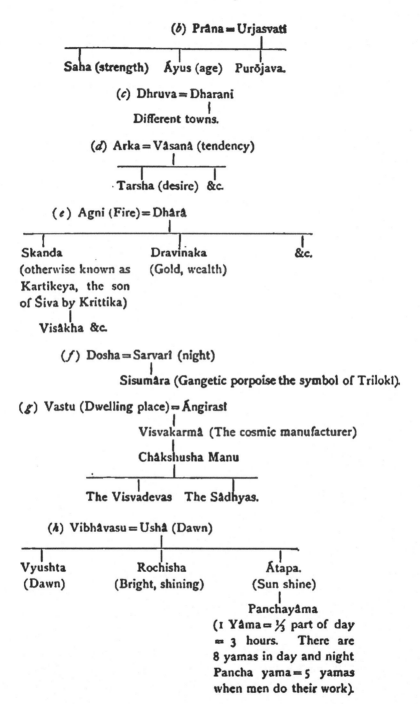

(*b*) Prâna = Urjasvatî

Saha (strength)   Âyus (age)   Purôjava.

(*c*) Dhruva = Dharani

Different towns.

(*d*) Arka = Vâsanâ (tendency)

· Tarsha (desire) &c.

(*e*) Agni (Fire) = Dhârâ

Skanda   Dravinaka   &c.
(otherwise known as   (Gold, wealth)
Kartikeya, the son
of Śiva by Krittika)

Visâkha &c.

(*f*) Dosha = Sarvarî (night)

Sisumâra (Gangetic porpoise the symbol of Trilokî).

(*g*) Vastu (Dwelling place) = Ângirasî

Visvakarmâ (The cosmic manufacturer)

Châkshusha Manu

The Visvadevas   The Sâdhyas.

(*h*) Vibhâvasu = Ushâ (Dawn)

Vyushta   Rochisha   Âtapa.
(Dawn)   (Bright, shining)   (Sun shine)

Panchayâma
(1 Yâma = ⅛ part of day
= 3 hours. There are
8 yamas in day and night
Pancha yama = 5 yamas
when men do their work).

[The 8 Vasus are sub-manifestations of Brahmā or the creative Purusha. They are energies that help creation in various ways. They find no place in the Hindu worship now. They are invoked only in marriage ceremonies when their appropriateness is evident. The Vedic gods can be analysed thus: —

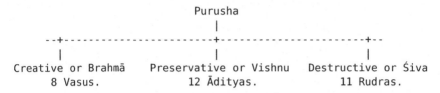

```
                          Purusha
                             |
  --+----------------------------+----------------------+--
    |                            |                       |
Creative or Brahmā    Preservative or Vishnu    Destructive or Śiva
   8 Vasus.                 12 Ādityas.               11 Rudras.
```

These are 31 gods. Then there are Prajāpati and Indra, making the number 33. The Brihat Āranyaka says that the 33 Krores of Devas are only sub rays of these primary 33].

THE PROGENY OF BHUTA.

By Sarūpā: — Millions of Rudras and the chief Pretas.

THE PROGENY OF ANGIRASA.

1. *By Svadhā*: — Pitris (comet).

2. *By Sāti*: — The Veda known as Atharva-Angirasa.

THE PROGENY OF KRISASVA.

1. *By Archis*: — Dhūma ketu (comet).

2. *By Dhishanā*: — Vedasiras, Devala, Vayuna and Manu.

THE PROGENY OF TARKSHA.

1. *By Vinatā*: — Garuda (the vehicle of Vishnu) and Aruna (the charioteer of the Sun.)

2. *By Patangi*: — Birds.

3. *By Yāminī.* — Moths and locusts.

4. *By Kadru*: — the serpents.

The Moon: The Moon married the 27 stars. But he is consumptive (*i.e.* he is consumed?). Therefore he has no progeny. (What is meant by the consumption of a planetary body like the Moon?)

THE PROGENY OF KASYAPA

1. *By Timi*: — Aquatic animals.

2. *By Saramā*: — Wild beasts, such as Tigers.

3. *By Surabhi.* — Cloven-footed animals.

4. *By Tāmrā*: — The Vultures.

5. *By Muni*: — The Apsarasas.

6. *By Krōdhavasa*: — Serpents such as Danda Suka and others.

7. *By Ilā*: — Plants.

8. *By Suramā*: — The Rākshasas.

9. *By Aristhā*: — The Gandharvas.

10. *By Kāsthā*: — Beasts other than cloven-hoofed.

11. *By Danu*: — 61 Dānavas the chief of them being Dvī Mūrdhā, Sāmbara, Aristhā, Hayagrīva, Vibhāvasu, Ayōmukha, Sanku Siras, Svarbhānu, Kapila, Putōma, Vrisha Pravā, Eka-Chakra, Anutapana, Dhūmra-Kesa, Virupaksha, Vipra-chitti and Durjaya.

Namuchi married Suprabhā, the daughter of Svar-bhanu.

King Yayāti married Sarmisthā, the daughter of Vrisha-parvan.

Vaisvanara was another son of Danu. He had four daughters. Upadanavi, Haya-siras, Puloma and Kalaka. Puloma and Kalaka had 60,000 valiant sons named Poulama and Kalakeya. Arjuna alone killed all of them in Svarga. Bipra Chitti had by his wife Sinhika 101 sons. The eldest of them is Rāhu. The other hundred are Ketus. They all became planets.

12. *By Aditi*: — The 12 Ādityas — Vivasvat, Aryaman, Pūshan, Tvastri, Savitri, Bhaga, Dhātri, Vidhātri, Varuna, Mitra, Indra, and Vishnu. *Vivasvat* had by his wife Sanjnā two sons Srāddhadeva Manu and Yāma (the death god), and one daughter the river Yamunā. This Sanjnā became also a mare and produced the twin Asvini Kumāras. He had also by Chaya two sons Sanaischara (Saturn) and Sāvarni Manu and one daughter Tapatī. Tapatī had for her husband Sanvarana. Mātrikā is the wife of *Aryaman*. He had by her sons called Charshani. (For Charshani *vide Suprā*.) The human race has been moulded after them by Brahmā. Pūshan is childless, and broken toothed. He partakes only of powdered food. This has been related in the story of Daksha. Rachanā is the wife of *Tvastri*. She is the daughter of a Daitya. Prajāpati Tvastri had by her one son Visvarūpa. Though connected on the mother's side with the Asuras, Visvarūpa was made a Purohita by the Devas, when Brihaspati (Jupiter) their former preceptor left them.

SKANDHA VI. CHAP. 18.

Savitri had, by his wife Prisni, three daughters, Sāvitri (Gāyatri), Vyāhriti (Bhūr, Bhuvar, Svar, Mahar &c.) and the Trayi; (Rik, Yajur, and Sāman). His sons were Agnihotra, Pasu Yāga, Sōma Yāga, Chaturmāsya Yāga and the 5 Mahā Yajnas.

Bhaga had, by his wife Siddhi, three sons Mahimart, Vibhu and Prabhu and one daughter Āsis.

Dhātri had, by his wife Kuhu, one son Sāyam (evening), by his wife Sinivaū, Darsa (the new moon day), by his wife Rākā, Prātar (morn) and by his wife Anumati, Pūrnamāsa (full Moonday).

Vidhātri had, by his wife Kriyā, five Agnis called Purishya. Charshani is the wife of *Varuna*. Bhrigu incarnated as his son. It is said that the great

Rishi Vālmika is also Varuna's son. Mitra and Varuna once felt love for Urvasī. Agastya and Vasishtha were then born of that Apsaras.

Mitra had, by Revati, Utsarga, Arishta and Pippala.

Indra had, by Paulomī, Jayanta, Rishabha and Midhusha.

Vishnu, as son of Aditi, is known as the Vāmana incarnation. He had by his wife Kirti one son Brihat Śloka (great fame). His sons were Sambhoga and others.

13. *By Diti*: Hiranyakasipu, Hiranyāksha and the Maruts.

THE STORY OF VIVSVARŪPA.

SKANDHA VI. CHAP. 7-8.

Indra surrounded by the Devas, was seated on the throne of *Trilokī*. He felt the pride of his position. Brihaspati, the preceptor and guide of all Devas came, but Indra did not rise up to receive him. Thus insulted, Brihaspati left the place at once and abandoned the Devas. The Asuras took this opportunity to put down the Devas and carried on a severe struggle under the lead of Sukra. The Devas were worsted in the fight and they went to Brahmā for redress. Brahmā advised them to accept the guidance of Visvarūpa, son of Tvastri. They gladly went to Visvarūpa and he consented to be their preceptor. Visvarūpa initiated Indra into the mysteries of Nārāyana Kabacha (an invocation to Vishnu which preserves one against all danger. The invocation must be read in the original, so no attempt has been made to render it into English). With the help of that Kabacha, Indra easily conquered the Asuras and firmly established once more the Kingdom of Trilokī.

Visvarūpa had three mouths. With one he used to drink Sōma, with another he used to drink wine and with the third he used to take his food. While performing Yajna, he openly gave oblations to the Devas, but secretly reserved some for his mother's relations the Asuras. Indra once found out this treachery. He became angry and cut off the three heads of Visvarūpa. The Sōma drinking head became Chātaka (the Swallow, supposed to live only on rain drops). The liquor imbibing head became Chataka (the Sparrow). The food eating head became Tittiri (the francoline partridge). The sin of killing a Brāhmana attached to Indra. He divided it into equal parts and distributed them between earth, water, trees and woman. Earth accepted her part on receiving the boon that her cavities would be filled up by nature. But the sin manifests itself in the barren lands. The trees took their part in return for the boon that the wounds on their cuticle should naturally heal up of themselves. But the sin shows itself in the exudation. Water was persuaded by the boon that it could mix with any other substance. But the sin shows itself in bubbles and foam.

THE STORY OF VRITRU.

SKANDHA VI. CHAP. 9-13.

Tvastri became enraged at the death of his son. He gave offerings to Agni for the destruction of Indra. A huge and fearful Asura rose out of the sacrificial fire. The Devas threw their weapons at him, but he swallowed them all. Wonderstruck they prayed to Vishnu for help. Vishnu asked them to go to Dadhīchi and pray for his body and assured them that the weapon made of his bones by Visvakarmā would cut off the head of Vritra. The Devas went to Dadhīchi and got his body. Visvakarmā made the thunderbolt instrument (Vajra) out of his bones. Indra went with this instrument at the head of the Devas to fight with Vritra. *The fight took place at the commencement of Treta Yuga in the first Yuga cycle of Vaivasvata Manvantara,* on the banks of the Narmadā. After a severe fight, the chances shewed themselves favourable to the Devas. The Daitya and Dānava chiefs began to shew their backs to the enemies. "What is this my companions?" exclaimed Vritra, "Is not death inevitable? And what death is more enviable than that with honor and glory? There are two modes of death, rare though they be, that are given the palm in all religious books — one is by control of the Prānas by means of Yoga and the other is by facing enemies foremost of all, in the battle field."

But the Asuras heeded him not. The Devas ran after them. "O ye cowards?" exclaimed Vritra, "What glory do you gain by running after those that fly away. Come and approach those that are in the field." So saying he attacked Indra. Indra in anger threw a large club at him. Vritra easily took it up with his left hand. He struck it with force on the head of Airāvata, the elephant of Indra. The elephant receded 28 cubits and vomitted blood, The magnanimous Vritra seeing the distress of the animal did not strike it again. Indra softly touched the injured animal, trying to give it relief and he took respite for some time. Vritra remembered the wicked deeds of Indra and addressed him thus "O thou assassinator of a Brāhmana! Thou didst kill thy own Guru, my brother Visvarūpa. Thou didst raise faith and trust in my brother's mind and still thou didst kill that innocent, wise Brāhmana, your own Guru, having been initiated by him in Yajna. Your karma makes you worse than even Rākshasas. It is meet that I shall kill thee with this Trident and make over thy body as food for vultures. And if thou, O Indra, cuttest off my head, I shall be free from the bond of Karma, by offering my body as Bali (sacrificial food) to the animals. Here I stand before thee. Why dost thou not strike with the Vajra. Thou hast been favoured by Vishnu and by Dadhīchi. Victory and all the virtues always follow Vishnu. I will do as advised by my deity Sankarshana and attain after death the state of Yogins by sacrificing this body. O Bhagavat, may I ever and ever remain in the Service of thy votaries. This I deem a thousand times more desirable than the attainment of the Supreme Abode, or of Siddhis or of Mukti."

Vritra then took the trident in hand and attacked Indra — Indra then had recourse to Vajra and he easily cut off both the trident and one hand of Vritra. Vritra took a club in the other hand and struck both Indra and the elephant. The Vajra slipped out of the hands of Indra and he felt ashamed to pick it up in the presence of his enemy. "Pick it up, O King of Devas, and kill your enemy. This is no time for shame or sorrow. It is not you or I that are the real actors. Bhagavān is guiding us all. He guides the whole Universe. Look at me. I have been worsted, hand and weapon gone, still I am trying my best to kill you. This our fight is but like the game of dice in which the life of one of us is the stake."

Indra could not help wondering at the wisdom and magnanimity of Vritra. He exclaimed "O king of Dānavas! thou hast got over the Māyā of Vishnu. The Asura nature has altogether- left thee and thou art fixed in devotion to Vishnu. Verily thou art a Mahatma now."

They again engaged in fight. This time Indra cut off both the club and the other hand with the help of Vajra — Vritra then opened his mouth and swallowed Indra. There was loud wailing and lamentation all round. But Indra broke through the interior of Vritra with the help of Vajra, and he then forcibly applied the bolt to cut off the head of Vritra. The bolt though actively employed could only sever the head of the Asura King in 360 days. The flame of self from Vritra's body merged in Shankarshana in the presence of the Devas.

The sin of killing a Brāhmana a second time followed Indra in the form of a hideous old outcaste woman. He fled away into the Mānasa lake and entered the filament of a lotus stalk. He remained there concealed for one thousand years. King Nahusha reigned in Svarga during that time. But as he became maddened in pride, Sachi the wife of Indra made him a serpent. The Brāhmanas then called back Indra to Svarga, and he reigned there again.

THE STORY OF CHITRAKETU.

SKANDHA VI. CHAP. 14-17.

Chitraketu, the King of Sūrasena had ten millions of wives, but he had no son. Rishi Angiras once came to him. The King expressed regret for his childlessness. Angiras performed a Yajna in honor of Tvastri, and gave the sacrificial remnants to the eldest wife. "You shall have a son, O King!" said Angiras. "But he will give you joy and sorrow both." In time the eldest Queen bore a son. Her co-wives grew jealous and poisoned the child. Chitraketu was deeply moved, and he wept profusely. At the time Nārada and Angiras came to him. They taught him the worship of Shankarshana. Chitraketu became fixed in the meditation of this second manifestation of Chaturvyuha, and this made him very powerful. He became the King of the Vidyādharas.

Once Chitraketu was roaming over the firmament on the chariot given him by Vishnu, when he saw Śiva surrounded by his attendants openly embracing His consort Bhāvanī. Chitraketu made some taunting remarks in the hearing of all. Śiva simply smiled, and so did His attendants. But

Bhāvanī cursed Chitraketu with an Asura birth. Chitaketu accepted the curse with an unruffled mind, saying it was the way of all beings to meet with things pleasant and unpleasant in this perishable world, and he only asked Bhāvanī to pardon him, if he had offended her. "Look how bold the followers of Vishnu are!" exclaimed Śiva, "They fear no body in this world. I am also a follower of Vishnu. So I took no offence at the words of the King Vidyadhara."

Chitraketu became Vritra by this curse, but his magnanimity and devotion to Vishnu were not lost.

THE DAITYAS.

SKANDHA VI. CHAP. 18.

THE DAITYAS.

Skandha VI. Chap. 18.

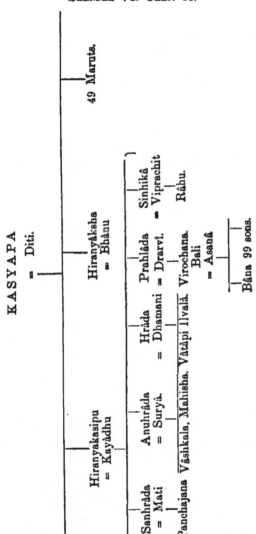

THE MARUTS.

SKANDHA VI. CHAP. 18-19.

Diti was very much grieved by the loss of her sons, caused by Indra. She ardently wished to have a son who could kill Indra. With this object, she served Kasyapa with all her heart and pleased him much. Kasyapa offered to give her any boon, and she prayed for an immortal son that would kill Indra. Sorely perplexed in mind, the Rishi thought within himself of a device. He said "I grant you the boon, but you shall have to observe Punsavana Vrata for one full year." This is a Vaisnava Vrata, the performance of which requires absolute purity of body and mind. Kasyapa related the details to his wife, (for which refer to the original). His object was to give an immortal son to Diti and to purify her mind by this Vrata, so that she might cast, off all enmity against Indra. He also thought it possible that his wife might not observe the strict rules for such a long time. Diti however accepted the conditions, and she bore a son. Indra became very much frightened, and he closely watched his step mother to discover a breach of the rules. He followed and served Diti always and tried to please her. One day Diti became very much tired, and she fell asleep after eating before she could wash her hands, mouth and feet. Finding this opportunity, Indra, by his Yogic powers entered the womb and split the child into 7 parts. The Maruts wept and requested their half-brother not to kill them. Indra consoled them saying that they need have no fear from him, and he would make them his companions. He then split each of the seven into as many parts again. By the favour of Vishnu, the Maruts were not destroyed, but came out all alive from the womb of Diti. It was a little short of one year still. Indra made them drinkers of Sōma and his chief companions. Diti woke up, and she was astonished to find 49 sons by her. "Tell me Indra if thou knowest" said she, "how is it I have these 49 sons instead of one. Pray do not conceal any thing." Indra gave the whole story to Diti and expressed great repentance. He assured Diti that the Maruts would be his best companions. Diti's mind had been purified, and she allowed her sons to become Devas. Thus the Maruts, though born as Daityas, became immortal Devas. (Marut Vayu air. Vayu corresponds to the sense of touch and to vital energy).

SKANDHA VII.

THE MYSTERIES ABOUT THE SURAS AND THE ASURAS.

SKANDIIA VII. CHAP. 7-1.

Rājā Parikshit said: — "To Bhagavān, all beings are equal, and He is the dear friend of all. Why did he kill the Daityas for the sake of Indra, as if He was not above partiality. Supreme Bliss Himself, He had nothing to gain from the Devas. Being above the control of the Gunas, He had no fear from the Asuras, and he did not bear any unfriendly feeling for them. We are in doubt as to the virtues of Nārāyana. Please clear up the doubt."

Suka replied: — Void of Gunas, without beginning, without manifestation, beyond Prakriti, Bhagavān pervades and permeates the Gunas of His Māyā. Hence His seeming relations. Satva, Rajas and Tamas are not His Gunas, but they are the Gunas of Prakriti. These attributes or tendencies of Prakriti do not all prevail at one and the same period; but they have got their periods of increase and decrease. (That is, since the beginning of the universe, the general tendency which guides all beings is different at different times. Thus at the very outset there was inertia, Tamas. This inertia was got over by Rajas, which predominated in the Prajāpatis, and the life-forms appeared on the globes. There was Tamas again in the mineral kingdom, which had to be conquered by Rājasic activity. And Rajas was in full swing till humanity reached a certain stage. Then Satva manifested itself for the evolution of men. The spiritual regeneration will be brought about by the ever increasing prevalence of Satva).

When Satva prevails, Bhagavān favours the Devas and Rishis. When Rajas prevails, He favours the Asuras. When Tamas prevails, He favors the Yakshas and Rākshasas. He follows in fact the periodic tendency.

It is Kāla (Periodicity) that now brings up Satva. So the Lord seems to favour the hosts of Devas, in whom Satva prevails. He also seems to put down the hosts of Asuras, who are opposed to the Devas being full of Rajas and Tamas.

It is also to favour the Asuras that He kills them. For we have seen above, how the gate-keepers of Vishnu became Hiranyāksha and Hiranyakasipu by the curse of the Kumāra brothers. They had to become Asuras for three successive births. In the second birth, they became Rāvana and Kumbhakarna, when they were killed by Rāma. In their last birth, they became Shishupāla and Danta-vakra, when they were killed by Sri Krishna. Then they became finally liberated and restored to their place in Vaikuntha.

(The Spiritual ascent commenced finally on the appearance of Sri Krishna. It was to prevail for the remaining life period of the universe. The Asuras had done their work by this time, and therefore they finally returned to Vaikuntha).

THOUGHTS ON THE ABOVE.

The Daityas and the Dānavas are both called Asuras. But there is a radical difference between the two classes.

The Daityas are opposed to the Ā-dityas. The root verb *dā* means to cut to pieces, to separate. *Diti* is that which separates. *Aditi* is that which does not separate. Jivātmā is the same in all beings. One life principle animates all the forms of creation. The idea of separateness did not exist from before. The elementals that began life in this Kalpa from the spiritual plane, have hardly any idea of separate existence. The Devas and Pitris are described as classes (*ganas*), and not as individuals. In the Mineral Kingdom, again, there is no individual existence. Individuality has to be worked out, and the sons of Diti bring about this great work in the evolution of life forms.

When we have the sense of separate existence strong in us, we become capable of further evolution. By our individual experiences, we know what is right and what is wrong, what is pleasurable and what is painful. Things that give joy give pain as well. It is the measure of pleasure or pain that teaches us what to covet and what to shun. Then we have the fact that by our very existence we have duties to perform. The teachings of other ages that are revealed to the Rishis and proclaimed by them, give us a better idea of things, and they tell us more than we can know of by our own experience. The Asuras lead us on and on, till we reach the highest point that, with a sense of individuality, we may attain.

When the individual soul gathers all experience that may be acquired by the idea of separateness, it traces back its way to that spiritual home whence it came. In the return journey, it is helped by the Ādityas, who gradually efface the idea of separateness, by an ever increasing infusion of Satva: Vishnu himself became Āditya and taught men the unity of all souls.

The Ādityas who guided the early elementals had to be crushed, so that separateness might grow. Pushan and Bhaga were therefore overpowered by the attendants of Śiva at the sacrifice of Daksha.

The Ādityas who guide humanity in their return to spirituality are themselves high spiritual energies, the highest Devas of our Trilokī.

Our evolution is thus two-fold — individual and non-individual. When we work as individuals, we are under the influence of Daityas. When we want to cast off separateness, we are under the influence of the Ādityas.

In both cases, however, it is the bliss element in us that is worked on by the Daityas and A-dityas. This bliss element is our eternal heritage from Īshvara, and it is this element that saves us in our contact with manifold matter. The measure of bliss, (*ananda*), enables us to judge what matter to accept and what not.

Individuality developed under Hiranyakasipu, and all sorts of blissful experiences were acquired. The sons of Hiranyakasipu were all called Bliss (Hrāda), but the perfection of Bliss (Pra-Hrāda) was in Prahlāda. He found out that the worldly joys were unreal, and that the real joy could be had only from Him above, who was joy itself.

But Prahlāda did not realise that there was one life underlying all beings, and that all beings were essentially one and the same. He was separate in his devotion, though unselfish to the extreme. He knew that men had separate existences, and while he attained perfection, others did not. It was therefore his duty to raise others to his level. With all unselfishness and devotion, Prahlāda was an Asura, because he worked from the stand point of individual life. The foster-father of Sri Krishna was Nanda, the word meaning also bliss. But the bliss of Gopas and Gopis consisted in forgetting self altogether. The bliss that was then evolved will draw humanity to the highest level of spirituality in our Kalpa.

The reign of the Daityas may be divided into three periods: —

1. — The period of Hiranyāksha and Hiranyakasipu.

2. — The period of Rāvana and Kumbhakarna.

3. — The period of Shishupāla and Dantavakra.

I. *Hiranyāksha and Hiranyakasipu.*

Jaya and Vijaya are the outer aspects of Vishnu. Vishnu preserves the universe, and He preserves all beings. Existence, consciousness and bliss all proceed from Vishnu, and it is these essential attributes that bring about the involution and evolution of all beings. In minerals, there is existence, but it is Tāmasic. Consciousness and bliss are completely eclipsed by the Tāmasic opacity of gross matter.

In the vegetables, there is existence and something more — the bare dawning of perceptive consciousness. There is predominating Tamas in the vegetables also. But Rajas also tries to manifest itself.

In the animals, Rajas asserts itself by increasing activity, and by the action of the senses. The animals exist, they are conscious and they have blissful experiences.

In men, Rajas plays the most important part. Through the ever increasing activities of mind and the development of consciousness, man runs after all sorts of experience, pleasurable and painful, till at last the idea of lasting and real bliss settles down in him, and he knows more of bliss than any other being in the universe. The future evolution of man lies in the permanence of spiritual bliss, which is purely Sātvic in its character.

Vishnu preserves all beings in their Tāmasic, Rājasic and Sātvic stages. For preservation means the maintenance as well as the improvement of beings. Therefore preservation is Sātvic, and Vishnu is the Preserver. We live and move onwards in all stages of our being. But in Rājasic and Tāmasic stages, it is the attendants of Vishnu, the door-keepers, that preserve us, and the Daityas are the lower manifestations of Jaya and Vijaya. One is Tāmasic and the other Rājasic.

Hiranyāksha is Tāmasic. He represents the original inertia of matter, its primary resistance to the onward process of evolution. There was existence after Pralāyic sleep But it was homogeneous existence, with little or no phenomenal change. Varāha got over this homogeneal tenacity by the killing of Hiranyāksha, and he set going the process of planetary and individual life.

Hiranyakasipu came next. He was the favoured son of Brahmā. He helped the evolution of individual life. Minerals became vegetables. Vegetables became animals, and animals became men. The intellectual power of men rapidly increased, and there was material and moral progress. The limit of moral progress was reached by Prahlāda. But the ideal of Prahlāda was based upon the conception of differences and of individualities. It is for this reason that Varna and Ashrama Dharma, or the separate duties of life for separate classes of men, is dealt with in the discourses with Prahlāda.

But though Prahlāda was a son of Hiranyakasipu, he was an exception to the general run of material evolution which was fostered by Hiranyakasipu. Hiranyakasipu hated the development of Sātvic virtues, he hated Hari, the embodiment of Satva. Nrisinha killed the great Daitya, and Satva made its appearance in men.

Hiranya means gold.

Hiranyāksha is gold-eyed.

Hiranyakasipu is gold bedded.

II. *Rāvana and Kumbhakarna.*

Hiranyakasipu represented the gradual development of material and intellectual evolution, till the highest point was reached.

Then there was a period of intellectual abuse. The Intellect of man tried to get a supremacy over the established order of things: Rāvana sought to make Nature subservient to his own purposes. The universe existed for man, and not man for nature. This was the perverse idea that guided the people of the Atlantean Continent. The intellectual giants, maddened by this material grandeur, did not look for any world beyond the one they lived in. They cared not for Svarga, nor for the sacrifices that led to Svarga. The flow of evolution, the breath of Īshvara seemed to stand still for a time as it were. The human will tried to override the divine will. There was chaos and disorder, which tended to cause dissolution in the universe. Hence Rāvana was a Rākshasa. The Tāmasic Kumbhakarna with his six-monthly sleep was the back ground of Rāvana.

The spiritual forces that were called forth to put an end to this state of things were equal to the occasion. The great Atlantean Continent was washed away by the sea. The sacred Gangā came rushing forward from the heights of the Himalayas, and eventually Rāma appeared to give a finishing stroke to the evolutionary work of the time.

Vishvāmitra and others had paved the way for the great work undertaken by Rāma. They propounded the Karma Kānda of the Vedas.

Men who knew nothing but the joys and sorrows of this short span of earthly life, and whose ideas and aspirations were all confined to that life, made a great advance when they were taught of an existence after death. When they further knew that life in Svarga was infinitely happier and far more lasting than what they called life on this earth, they made the beginning of a really spiritual life. The Vedic Devas are permanent dwellers in Svarga, and the Vedic Sacrifices establish communion with them by means of Apurva, a spiritual force generated by the performance of sacrifices, and life in Svarga becomes prolonged for a very very long period. People took time to understand this truth, but in time they accepted the performance of Vedic Sacrifices as the only religion for man.

There was however a re-action. The intellectual giants, called Rākshasas, looked down upon Vedic Sacrifices, and they did not care for any life after death. They were the worst enemies of the Vedic Rishis.

Vishvāmitra took the help of Rāma in protecting the Rishis in the peaceful performance of Yajnas.

But people had grown old in their ideas about Vedic sacrifices. The first seceders were some Kshatriyas. They did not understand why Vedic Sacrifices should be the monopoly of Brāhmanas, and they aspired to the position acquired by them. The foremost of these Kshatriyas were the Haihayas and Tālajanghas. But they were defeated by Parashurama, who re-established the supremacy of the Brāhmanas.

But a silent revolution was going on, in which the Kshatriyas and Brāhmanas equally took part. King Janaka and Rishi Yajnavalkya gave the finishing stroke to the Upanishad movement, and side by side with Karma Kānda grew up the Jnāna Kānda of the Vedas. Rāma brought the two divisions of the Vedas into closer union, as he was himself the resting place of both. And as Vishnu himself, He became the object of Upāsanā. The three Paths appeared, that of Karma, Bhakti and Jnāna. Vedic Sacrifices held their own, and a school grew up which accepted these as the highest Karma which man could perform. Another school, following the very old teachings of Kapila, dissected the transformable parts in man and discriminated the same from the non-transformable. A sister school followed up the teaching with practices in conformity to these, and taught how to concentrate the mind on the discriminated Atmā. Another school confined itself to the properties of matter and mind, soul and oversoul, and remained wonder-struck at the superior properties that divided Jiva from Īshvara. Schools of independent thought grew up. Each school had its followers. There were differences and dissensions. There was disunion, self-sufficiency, pride, envy, jealousy and other evil traits of human character that thinks too much of itself. Every one followed his own faith and hated the follower of other faiths. This was the cycle of Shishupāla and Dantavakta.

Jarāsandha performed Vedic sacrifices, and he put in chains the Vaishnava kings. There were those who believed in the existence of two primary causes, (*Dvivid*). Men, like the king of Kashi, prided themselves on mock wisdom. Religious faiths existed in all possible shades, and their difference was accentuated by dogmatism and mutual jealousy. "The Vedas are different, the Smritis are different. He is not a Muni, who has not some distinctive opinion of his own." This well known verse related strictly to the period of which we are now speaking. Shishupāla had respect for the Munis. He was essentially a man of the period.

Sri Krishna taught harmony. He gave the essence of all religions, the eternal truths that formed the ground work of all faiths. He proclaimed in the clearest language possible the One underlying the Many, the eternal Brahmān as forming the essence of Jiva and Īshvara. He particularly emphasised the relations of man, Īshvara and the universe, and the duties that followed from these relations. Religion became a science, the law universal, and all teachings found there respective places in the universal religion which He proclaimed. The Rishis bowed down their heads before Him. The Upanishads were never explained so lucidly before. The key-note of all truths and all religions was unravelled beyond all doubt. Such knowledge could proceed only from Īshvara Himself. The Rishis recognised Sri Krishna as the Lord. But Shishupāla was slow to believe in this novel revolution. He did not understand why the Rishis gave the first place to Sri Krishna at the Rajasūya sacrifice performed by Rājā Yudhisthira. The difference formed a religion with Shishupāla. But the age of differences was doomed. The age of unity, of harmony, of spiritual glory was now to reign in the Universe. Hundreds and hundreds of years have passed away, but the scriptures one and all proclaim the glory of the Lord Sri Krishna. What He has done for our universe, we shall see later on.

Danta-vakra was the Tāmasic counterpart of Shishupāla.

The Asuras advanced as the Kālpic age advanced. There was no end of advancement from the standpoint of self. There is no big jump from individual self to universal self. Though the essential idea of spirituality is unity and the essential idea of materiality is diversity, the one idea develops into the other idea, by an ever widening view of things. Our duties enlarge. Our relations increase. The range of life widens, till it includes the life in Svarga. Vedic Yajna is then performed, though from a pure motive of self-advancement. The advanced self comes very near to the universal self. The performance of Vedic sacrifices is Asuric in so far as it is selfish, but it minimises the self of earthly existence, and gives a transitory character to our worldly joys and sufferings, and it gives the idea of an enlarged self, of widened existence and of higher duties. The Karma Kānda of the Vedas therefore opens the door widely to real spiritual life.

This explains why Vishvarupa, an Asura, guided the Devas for some time. The three heads of Vishvarupa represent the three Vedas. The swallow head is the Rik, the sparrow head is the Sāman, and the Tittiri head is proverbially the Yajur. This refers to the prevalence of Karma Kānda. But when better times came, Indra killed Vishva-rūpa. The place of Vishva-rūpa was however speedily taken, up by Vritra. And Indra had recourse to Atharva, the fourth Veda and to Dadhīchi, a votary (represented as the son) of Atharva Veda, the very ideal of self-sacrifice.

And who is this Vritra? The Vedas say: — *"Sa imān lokān Avrinot etat Vritrasya Vritratvam."*

He spread over (*vri*) all these Lokas, this is the Vritraship of Vritra.

The Bhāgavata says: — "These Lokas are spread over by him in the form of Tvashtri's Tapas. Hence he is called Vritra." VI. — 9-xviii.

The invocation of Tvashtri is thus described in the Bhāgavata: — "Rise up, O Indra — Shatru, never give up enmity." VI — 9-xii.

The word *shatru* means enemy. Tvastri meant to say "he who is to become the enemy of Indra." But by proper grammatical construction, the expression means, he of whom Indra is to become the enemy. The invocation was therefore defective and it produced a contrary result. Pānini points this out as an apt illustration of what bad grammar leads to.

The Vedas thus speak of the invocation: — "As he said-*Svāha*! O Indra-Shatru! rise up — so Indra became the enemy of Vritra." Notwithstanding his wisdom, Chitra-ketu was anxious to have a son. He wept bitterly, when the son was lost. He was a votary of Sankarshana, who presides over Ahankāra or Egoism. So by devotion he became the king of the Vidyādharas. This selfish devotion, the worship of Gods for the gratification of selfish aspiration, which is so universal, is Vritra.

Vritra was killed by a weapon made of the bones of Dadhīchi the Rishi of self-sacrifice. We want to kill thee for thy bones, for they will be of service to the universe, so said the Devas. And Dadhīchi felt the height of pleasure in giving himself completely up, that the universe might prosper.

We are told that the fight with Vritra took place in the Vaivasvata Manvantara. The readers will easily understand why this is so.

The fight between the Devas and the Asuras is only a counterpart of struggles on our earth between the forces of materiality and spirituality. With the appearance of Lord Krishna, the ascendancy of the Asuras is virtually over, and however self-seeking we may be by our nature, we bow down before the ideal of unselfishness, of One Life pervading all beings, so prominently held before us by that greatest of all Avatāras, and the circle of those that follow this ideal is daily increasing.

But why is Atharva Veda spoken of as the Veda of unselfishness? The popular idea about that Veda is quite the contrary.

People resort to it for Tāntric malpractices. The Vajra or thunderbolt is an electric current, which in the hands of Indra has the power of spiritualisation. The Asuras dread the subtle forces of nature which reach them even in the regions of Pātāla. Who knows what purpose the electric discharges serve in the economy of nature? Who knows of the subtler currents of spiritual forces that silently bring about the grandest revolutions in nature? Atharva Veda inculcates an intimate acquaintance with the subtle forces of nature. It opens the door alike to White as well as Black Magic. But at the present day, the Black Magic only survives, making the Atharva a name of opprobrium and reproach.

Marut is Vāyu. The Maruts are forms of Pranic energy. They are 49 in number, corresponding to the 49 forms of Agni. These 49 forms include all sorts of Pranic energy in the spiritual, intellectual and material planes. As the whole process of evolution is dependent on life activities, and as life itself is essentially divine, the Maruts are the companions of Indra. As by life, we understand individual life as imprisoned in Jivic centres, the Maruts are by birth Daityas.

We have lingered so long over the Daityas. The Dānavas are also called Asuras, but they are essentially different from the Daityas. Every individual has got two aspects — Prākritic and Purushic. The Purusha aspect in him is limited by the individual Prakriti. The individual limitation appertains to the Daityas. The Prākritic element in man is Dānavic. The chief Dānava, Māyā, is an aspect of Māyā. Māyā is a great magician, as the essence of Prakriti is illusion. Duryodhana and his brothers could not discriminate between the illusory aspect of the assembly-ground prepared by Māyā. To the Pāndavas, the followers of Sri Krishna, there was no illusion. The Dānavas lead men away from spirituality, so much so that they may be estranged completely from their spiritual nature. These dark forces in nature have no redeeming feature in them. Fortunately for the history of the universe, we do not hear much of them.

THE STORY OF HIRANYAKASIPU.

SKANDHA VII. CHAP. 2-4.

Upon the death of Hiranyāksha, Hiranyakasipu collected his companions and told them that Vishnu was no longer keeping that neutrality and impartiality which he had observed of yore. On the contrary, he had taken the side of the Devas, under the pretence of Upāsana.

He then consoled his nephew and his brother's wife by words of wisdom explaining to them the transitory character of the world and the permanence of Ātmā. He also told them several stories to illustrate the point.

Hiranyakasipu vowed enmity to Vishnu. He prayed hard for immortality and supremacy over the Trilokī. Brahmā became pleased with his asceticism and enquired what boon he wanted. Said Hiranyakasipu: — "Let me have no death from any one created by Thee. Let not those that are not created by Thee kill me inside or outside, by day or by night, with any weapon, either on the earth or in the air. Let no man or animal, with or without life (asu) Deva, Daitya or serpent kill me. As thou art without a rival in battle, the one glorious lord of all beings and all Lokapālas, so let me be too. Let me possess all the Siddhis, (Anima &c.)" Brahmā said, Amen.

Hiranyakasipu then ruled the Universe. He took the place of Indra. All the Devas worshipped him.

Brāhmanas and other Grihasthās performed Yajna in his honor and gave offerings to him. The earth yielded plenty even without much effort. There was prosperity all around. The Shastras were however not duly respected. (All this is a description of the material period, the reign of Materiality). A long, long time passed on in this way. At last the Lokapālas could bear it no longer. They prayed to Vishnu for relief. The Devas heard a voice from heaven "Wait ye all. The time has not yet come for the fall of Hiranyakasipu. He shall be the enemy of his own son. I kill him then." — Assured by these words, the Devas went to their own place.

HIRANYAKASIPU AND PRAHLĀDA.

SKANDHA VII. CHAP. 4-9.

Hiranyakasipu had 4 sons. Of these Prahlāda was great in his virtues. He was respectful, well-behaved, truthful, self-controlled, friendly to all beings, and great in his devotion. Even in his infancy, he gave up play and constantly meditated on Vāsudeva. The things of the world had no relish for him. In the exuberance of devotional feelings, he sometimes laughed, sometimes wept, sometimes sang and sometimes danced. At times when the feelings were profound, he remained quiet with hair standing on end while tears flowed down his cheeks.

Shanda and Amarka, sons of Shukra, had charge of the education of Prahlāda. He heard and learned whatever they had to say, but he inwardly did not like the teachings about mine and thine and about the transitory things of the world.

Once Hiranyakasipu placed Prahlāda on his lap and asked him — "What do you consider to be righteous (*Sādhu*)?"

Prahlāda replied: — "Human souls enshrined in bodies are always distracted on account of false perceptions. O great Asura, I therefore consider it righteous to leave the house, which like a dark well causes the downfall of Ātmā, in order to go to the forest and take the shelter of Vishnu."

Hiranyakasipu smiled and said: — "It is thus that boys are spoiled by others. Take him back to the house of his teachers and let them see that Vaishnavas in disguise may not confound his Buddhi."

The teachers brought him to their house and asked him in gentle and sweet words: — "Child, do not conceal any thing from us. We are your teachers. Tell us whether this perversity is spontaneous in you or whether it is acquired from others." Said Prahlāda: — "I and others, this is mere false perception caused by the Māyā of Bhagavān. So salutations to Him. When Bhagavān becomes kind, it is then only that the difference-making perception of men disappears. As the iron moves of itself in the presence of a magnet, so the distraction in my Budhi, if you like to call it so, rises of itself in the presence of Vishnu."

"Get the cane," said one of the teachers, "This wicked boy will put us all to shame. He is a disgrace to his family. It is but meet to punish him. The Daityas are sandal trees and this boy is a thorn plant amongst them. Vishnu is the one for the extirpation of the sandal forest, and this boy is his handle."

They threatened Prahlāda in various ways and taught him Dharma, Artha and Kāma, and the different devices to subdue one's enemies. At last they thought Prahlāda had been well trained. So they took him to the king.

The king embraced the child and said "Prahlāda, my boy, you have been so long with your teachers. Tell me what you have learned, as the best of all."

Prahlāda replied: — "Hearing of Vishnu, recital of His glory, constant remembrance of Him, attendance on Hari, His worship, adoration, service, and friendship, and offering oneself entirely to Him this is ninefold Bhakti. This Bhakti is to be offered to Vishnu and acted upon. This I deem to be the best teaching."

Hiranyakasipu reproved the teachers in anger. They told him, it was neither from themselves nor from any one else that Prahlāda had these teachings, but that they were spontaneous with him. The Asura king then addressing his son said: — "If you have not learned these things from your teachings, whence could you have such a vicious inclination."

Prahlāda replied: — "Inclination for Vishnu does not come to the Grihasthā either from himself or from any other. One blind man cannot lead another. It is the company of Mahātmās alone that can give such an inclination."

Hiranyakasipu could bear it no longer. He threw down the child from his embrace, and asked the Asuras to kill him at once or expel him. They cried out "kill him, kill him," and struck the five year old child with their spears. But Prahlāda was deeply concentrated in Bhagavān, so he felt not the spears at all. This put Hiranyakasipu in fear, and he devised means to kill the boy.

He tried big elephants, venomous serpents, Tāntric practices, throwing down the child from the hills, enclosing him in cavities, poisoning, starvation, cold, air, fire, water, but failed to kill his innocent son. He then thought his end was near at hand and became melancholy. Shanda and Amarka told him not to entertain fears, but to wait till Shukra came. The king asked them to take charge of the boy once more. They again commenced to teach him their sciences. One day the teachers left the house on business. The boys were all engaged in play, and they invited Prahlāda into their midst. Prahlāda took the opportunity to instruct the boys. He explained to them in eloquent terms the transitoriness of all joys and sorrows and the vanity of all worldly attachments. He taught them the imperishable character of Ātmā, and dilated on its relation to the body and the universe. He then preached in glowing words friendliness to all beings and devotion to Bhagavān. He then told the boys that he had learned these things himself from Nārada.

The boys expressed wonder, for they knew Prahlāda to have been always under the tuition of Shanda and Amarka.

Prahlāda informed them that when Hiranyakasipu had gone to the Mandāra mountain for prayer, the Devas attacked his kingdom, and Indra carried away his wife. Prahlāda was then in her womb. Nārada kept Hiranyakasipu's wife in his own Ashrama till he had taught to her, more for the child in the womb than for the mother, the whole of Ātmā Vidyā.

Prahlāda again continued the discourse and impressed on his companions in the most eloquent words, full of wisdom, the utility and nature of devotion. (The original discourse will repay perusal).

The teachers returned and found the contagion of Vaishnavism had also spread amongst other boys. They instantly reported the matter to Hiranyakasipu. The king became all wrath and angry. He sent for Prahlāda. Prahlāda approached him with all respect and humility. The king thundered forth thus: — "What makes thee so often disobey me, thou vile enemy of thy own race? Dost thou not know that I will instantly put thee to death? All Trilokī dreads me and trembles when I am enraged. But thou dost break my words without the least fear in thy mind."

"Father," said Prahlāda, "Bhagavān is my only strength. He is not only my strength, but also yours and that of the whole world. Look upon all as your own self, father."

"Unfortunate that thou art", said Hiranyakasipu, "Tell me, who else is there besides myself whom thou callest Bhagavān or Īshvara. Where is he?" Said Prahlāda, "He is everywhere."

"Why not then in this pillar?"

"Yes, I see him there."

"Well, let me sever your head from your body and see how your Hari can preserve you."

So saying, Hiranyakasipu took sword in hand and violently struck the pillar with his fist. A great noise was heard at the time, and the fearful Nrisinha came out of the pillar, half man, half lion. Hiranyakasipu with wonder saw He was neither man nor animal. Nrisinha placed the Asura king on his thighs and tore him with His nails to death. (For a description of Nrisinha and of the fight refer to the original).

The Devas all collected and prayed to Him one after the other. But Nrisinha was still in a rage and they dared not approach Him. Brahmā at last sent Prahlāda to pacify Him.

Prahlāda approached Him slowly and prostrated himself at His feet; Nrisinha became full of tenderness and placed his hand on the head of Prahlāda. That divine touch removed all evil from Prahlāda and illumined his mind with Brahmā Vidya. He then broke forth into a prayer, (perhaps the most sublime in the Bhāgavata Purāna).

THE PRAYER OF PRAHLĀDA

SKANDHA VII. CHAP. 9.

"Brahmā and other Devas, Rishis and wise men, full of Satva, have failed to adore Thee in suitable words. How can this Asura boy please Thee, O Hari: But I think, it is not wealth, good birth, beauty, asceticism, learning, power, intellect, or even Yoga that is so much suited for the worship of Parama Purusha as Bhakti. It is by Bhakti that the elephant king pleased Bhagavān. *Even a Chandāla, (an outcaste) is much superior to a Brāhmana, who has all the 12 virtues, but has no devotion to Vishuu.* For the Chandāla who offers his Manas, his words, his Karma, his wealth and even his Prāna to Vishnu, purifies not only himself, but his whole line, while, the proud Brāhmana does not even purify himself." (Without devotion, the virtues only serve to increase pride. They do not purify the mind. *Śridhara*.)

(The Almighty Vishnu does not want any offering from the ignorant for himself. He is possessed of all things. But the man who gives offerings to Him can alone keep them to himself, for verily the paintings on the real face are to be seen in the image. The self in man is only a reflection of Ātmā or Manas. Therefore if a man does any thing that affects his Manas only, it does not concern his real self. If an offering is made to Īshvara, that reaches his real self).

"Therefore though of low birth, I have no hesitation in reciting thy glory as much as I can, for such a recital is sure to purify a man.

"Withdraw, O Lord! this terrible form, and be cooled. Look! the world trembles at Thee.

"I am not afraid, however, even of this form, as I am afraid of the wheel of births. Give shelter at thy feet, that I may gain Moksha.

"I have been scorched by the fire of misery in all births. The only remedy is devotion to Thy service. For Thy servant by Thy favor gets the company of Mahātmās. By their company, he gets rid of all worldly attachments and sings the glory of Bhagavān. Then the miseries of life cannot overpower him.

"The parents are not the protectors of the child; medicine is not the remedy for the diseased; the boat is not a shelter for the drowning; for they cannot save from a recurrence of evils. And even the little that others do is promoted by the Prompter of all.

"When Purusha wishes, Māyā disturbed by Kāla creates the Sūkshma Sharira, headed by Manas. That Manas is drawn into a world of recurring births, characterised by the transformations of Māyā": (5 Jnanendriyas, 5 Karmendriyas, 5 Bhūtas and Manas). "I am being squeezed in this wheel, like the sugar-cane in the mill.

"Draw me unto Thee, O Lord! or I am lost in the whirl."

(Some platitudes and a short account of the part taken by Vishnu in the creation follow).

"Thou dost incarnate as man, animal, Rishi and Deva in order to guard all beings, to destroy the enemies of the world and preserve Dharma, according to the requirements of every Yuga. But in Kali Yuga, Thou concealest Thyself. Hence (from manifestating only in three Yugas), Thou art called Triyuga.

"Lord of Vaikuntha, this mind does not take pleasure in discourses about Thee, as it is vitiated, prone towards the outside, unmanageable, passionate and affected by the three promptings — joy, sorrow and fear. How can I with such a mind think of Thee?

"I am drawn on all sides by the Indriyas, and I am as miserable as a man with many wives.

"I am not the only sufferer. Look! all men remain fallen by their own karma in the Vaitarani (River at the gate of Yāma) of recurring births. They are afraid of births and deaths and of danger from each other. They are mutually both friends and enemies. Take pity on these bewildered creatures, O Thou that art on the other side of the river, and preserve them this very day by taking them across the Vaitarani (*i.e.* the relativity's of Trilokī existence).

"O guide of the Universe! what is thy difficulty in saving all men? For Thou art the cause of the creation, preservation and destruction of the Universe. Thou hast much kindness for the ignorant. Thou art the friend of the afflicted. What then by saving us only who serve thy favorite men the Mahātmās (for, those who serve the Mahātmās are already saved).

"O Thou Supreme, I am not the least anxious for myself about the Vaitarani (Trilokī existence), however difficult to cross it may be, for my mind is plunged in the nectar ocean of singing thy glory. But I mourn for the ignorant, those that care only for the gratification of the senses and for the means of such gratification while they remain estranged from Thee.

"Generally, O Deva! the Munis are desirous of their own Moksha, they hold their tongue, and roam in solitude without caring for the good of others. But I do not like to be liberated alone, leaving behind me the afflicted round me; I find no other shelter for these misguided people, besides Thee.

"They are not happy, O Lord, in the enjoyment of the objects of the senses. For like itching, it is not a pleasure by itself but seems to be so, as long as Thou art not known.

"It is said that holding the tongue (*mouna*) vowed observance (Vrata), sacred knowledge (Sruta), austerity (Tapas), reading (Adhyayana), the observance of rules pertaining to one's caste (Sva Dharma), exposition of Shastras (Vyākhyā), living in solitude (Rahas), recital of Mantra (Japa), and Samādhi also lead to Moksha. But generally it is seen that these are only means of livelihood for those that have no control over their senses. And for proud people they are sometimes the means of livelihood and sometimes not. But pride in itself is not a good thing.

"Thou art not separate from the Universe. Both cause and effect are thy forms. It is not by avoiding the ways of Universe but by seeing Thee everywhere by means of Bhakti, that the right course is followed. It is by striking one stone against another that fire comes out, and not otherwise."

[Let the words of the Asura boy resound from one end of India to the other. Let the sublime words of compassion and universal love be written in characters of gold, and let them be engraven in the hearts of all Indians]. Prahlāda was made the king of the Asuras.

VARNA AND ASHRAMA.

SKANDHA VII, CHAP. 11 TO 15.

Nārada related the story of Prahlāda to King Yudhisthira at the Rajasūya sacrifice. That story revealed the highest devotion that was possible for a Jiva to attain with the idea of separate existence. But separation also gives rise to the idea of difference. And as differences become established in society, duties and relations become manifold. Yudhisthira therefore appropriately asked Nārada about the Varnāsrama duties.

The general rules to be observed by all castes are first given, ethical, spiritual and devotional. The specific duties and indications of each caste are then given, much the same as given in Manu Sanhitā, as also the duties of women. The following significant passage occurs at the end: —

"The indications of each caste are given above (e.g. restraint of the senses, contentment, &c., for Brāhmanas; courage, strength, &c., for Kshatriyas; reverence, energy, &c., for Vaishyas; and humanity, service &c., for Shudras). If however the indications of one caste are found in a man belonging to another caste, he is to be specified by the caste of his indications and not the caste of his birth." VII — 35.

The commentary of Śridhara is explicit on this passage. This shews the liberality of the Bhāgavata Purāna. According to this Purāna, the divisions of caste at the present day, (for one must not forget that the Vaishnava movement belongs comparatively to a later period), are not to be determined by birth, but they are indicated by the virtues of each particular individual.

The duties of each Āsrama are next enumerated in detail. The enumeration follows the Smritis, with a word for Bhakti Yoga where necessary. Some very useful hints are given for a Grihasthā, for which please refer to the original.

The paths called Pitriyāna and Devayāna are next described. Hints on Yoga and the recital of Pranava are also given.

SKANDHA VIII.

YAJNA.

SKANDHA VIII. CHAP. 1.

An account has been given above of the progeny of Devahūti and Prasuti. Yajna is the son of Akuti. In the First Manvantara, when Asuras and Rākshasas were going to devour Manu, Yajna killed the former, with the help of his sons, the Yāma Devas. He ruled over Svarga as the Indra of that Manvantara.

[This brings us to the end of the 1st Manvantara. The narration at several places took us to later Manvantaras, and the account of the Asuras especially took us to Vaivasvata Manvantara. The account of the first Manvantara is illustrative of the succeeding Manvantaras. Details have therefore been given at times which might not properly pertain to the 1st Manvantara, but which fit in with other Manvantaras at those stages of the narration. Necessarily the account of the succeeding Manvantaras is very meagre.]

END OF THE FIRST MANVANTARA.

THE SECOND MANVANTARA.

SKANDHA VIII. CHAP. 1.

Svārōchisha is the 2nd Manu. (Svārōchisha = Self refulgent). He is the son of Agni; Dyumat, Sushena, Rochishmat and others are the sons of this Manu. (Dyumat and Rochishmat also mean bright, refulgent). Rochana was the Indra (Rochana = bright illuminating). Tushita and others were the Devas. Urjastambha and others were the seven Rishis well versed in Brahmā Vidyā.

There was one Rishi named Veda Siras. His wife was Tushitā. He had by her *Vibhu*, the Avatāra of this Manvantara. Vibhu took the vow of Brahmācharya and never married. 80,000 Rishis learned his Vrata.

(The Second Manvantarā is in Theosophical language the second ascending half of the 1st round. The spiritual character of this Manvantara is manifest from the use of words meaning "bright," "refulgent." The Avatāra is Vibhu or All-pervading. The vow of Vibhu also denotes spirituality. Agni also, the father of the Manu, is almost a name for spirituality).

THE THIRD MANVANTARA.

SKANDHA VIII. CHAP. 1.

The third Manu is Uttama, son of Priya Vrata. Pavana, Srinjaya, Yajnahotra and others were his sons. The sons of Vasistha, Pramada and others, were the seven Rishis.

Satya, Veda Sruta, and Bhadra were the Devas. Satyajit was Indra.

Dharma had by Sunritā one son named Satya-Sena. He was the Avatāra of this Manvantara. He was born with others called Satya-Vrata. He killed wicked Yakshas and Rākshasas given to falsehood, and Bhūtas who injured others.

[The characteristic mark of this Manvantara which is the first half of the second Round is Truth. Satya or Truth enters into the names of one class of Devas, of the Indra and of the Avatāra. The name of the Avatāra's mother was also truth. The Yakshas and Rākshasas were given to falsehood].

THE FOURTH MANVANTARA.

SKANDHA VIII. CHAP. 1-4.

The fourth Mann was Tāmasa, brother of Uttama. He had ten sons, Prithu, Khyāti, Nara, Ketu and others.

Satyaka, Hari and Vira were the Devas. Triśikha was Indra.

Jyōtirdhāman and others were the seven Rishis. The Vedas had been lost in time. The sons of Vidhriti, called Vaidhritis, however preserved them by their own energy. They are also the Devas of this manvantara.

The Avatāra Hari incarnated as the son of Harimedhas by Harini. He saved the Elephant king from the crocodile.

THE STORY OF THE ELEPHANT KING.

SKANDHA VIII. CHAP. 2-4.

An elephant king resided on the summits of Trikūta. He roamed about with his female herd, intoxicated with the juice that exuded from his temples. Finding a lake, he plunged himself into its waters and quenched his thirst. He then took water in his trunk and passed it on to the young herd and the females. A powerful crocodile attacked him in rage. They fought for one thousand years, each trying to draw the other unto him. The elephants on the bank raised a piteous cry, but they could not be of any use to their companion. The Elephant King got tired at last, but the crocodile being in his own element did not feel any fatigue. The elephant devoutly and ardently prayed to the supreme Purusha. In response to that prayer, Hari appeared with the Devas, seated on the back of Garuda. He drew out the crocodile, cut off its head with the chakra and thus saved the Elephant King.

The Elephant was a Gandharva, named Hūhū. He was playing with his wives in a tank. Rishi Devala went there to bathe. The Gandharva drew the Rishi himself by his feet. The Rishi cursed him to become a crocodile. The elephant was king Indradyumna of Pandya. He was under a vow of silence while engaged in meditation. Rishi Agastya came with his disciples, but the king could not receive him with any word of welcome. "O thou of untrained intellect like an elephant, be an elephant thyself." Such was the curse of the Rishi to him.

[The Elephant represents the characteristic Jiva of this Manvantara. The elephant becomes excited and mad when the juice exudes from his temples. In the story, madness represents the prevalence of Kāma. The elephant was passionately attached to his wives. The Jiva had given himself too much to Kāma, and he was carried away helplessly by the demon, he knew not where. His better sense could not prevail without some extraordinary help and that help was given by Hari, an incarnation of Vishnu. Possibly the story represents the development of animal instincts].

THE FIFTH MANVANTARA.

SKANDHA VIII. CHAP. 5.

Raivata was the fifth Manu. He was the brother of Tāmasa. His sons were Arjuna, Bali, Vindhya and others. Vibhu was Indra. Bhūttaraya and others were the Devas.

The seven Rishis were Hiranya-romay, Vedasiras, Urddhabāhu and others.

The presiding deity of Vaikuntha incarnated in partial manifestation as the son of Subhra and Vikuntha. He was the Avatāra of this Manvantarā. [This is the first half of the Third Round. The incarnation of the Lord of Vaikuntha may have some significance, but what is not clear from the text.]

THE SIXTH MANVANTARA.

SKANDHA VIII. CHAPTER 5.

The Sixth Manu was Chākshusha, son of Chakshus. Pūru, Pūrusha, Sudyumna and others were his sons. Mantra Druma was Indra. Apya and others were the Devas; Haryasma, Dviraka and others were the Rishis.

The Avatāra was Ajita, son of Vairaja by Deva-Sambhūti. He assumed the form of Kūrma or the Tortoise, and helped in the churning of the Milk Ocean.

THE CHURNING OF THE OCEAN.

SKANDHA VIII. CHAP. 5-12.

In the fight with the Asuras, the Devas lost their lives. They fell down and did not rise up again. By the curse of Durvāsas, Indra and the three Lokas became shorn of Srī or Lakshmī (wife of Vishnu in Vaikuntha: Preservative energy). Consequently there were no performances such as Yajna. (Durvasas once saw Indra on the elephant Airavata. He gave him the garland of his own neck. Indra proud of his own Srī or wealth, placed the garland on the head of the elephant. The elephant threw it down and tore it to pieces with his feet. Durvāsas got angry and cursed Indra that he and his Trilokī were to lose Srī). Indra did not know what to do and the Devas all went over to the seat of Brahmā on the top of Meru. Brahmā, saw the Lokapālas lifeless and lustreless, as it were, the Lokas beset with evils and the Asuras full of life and energy. He meditated on Parama Purasha with concentrated mind and then addressed the Devas thus.

"Purusha has resort to Rajas, Satva and Tamas respectively for Creation, Preservation and Dissolution. This is just the time for Preservation. For the good of all beings, He shall now be possessed of Satva. So let us take the shelter of the guide of the universe. He shall now befriend the Devas and do what is best for us."

The Devas with Brahmā then went to Ajita. Brahmā prayed to Him as the Preservative aspect of Virāt Purusha. Vishnu appeared before the Devas and addressed them thus: —

"The Asuras favored by Sukra are now victorious. Make peace with them so long as you are not strong yourselves. Lose no time in churning the

Milk Ocean for Amrita in concert with the Asuras. By drinking Amrita
even dead persons become immortal. Throw all creepers and herbs into
that ocean. Make Mandāra mountain the churning rod and make Vasūki the
rope. Then with my help, churn the ocean with all diligence. The Asuras
shall have all the trouble to themselves, while you shall reap the fruits. If
the Asuras ask for any concession, you had better approve of that. Do not
be afraid of any poison that may arise. Have neither greed nor anger nor
desire in respect of the things that will arise."

So saying Vishnu disappeared. The Devas went to the Asura King Bali and
Indra explained to him what Vishnu had said about the churning. The
Asuras approved of the plan and made friends with the Devas. They then
went together and uprooted the golden mountain Mandāra and carried it
towards the ocean. After going a long way, they felt fatigued and dropped
the mountain. Several Devas and Asuras were crushed by its fall. Vishnu
appeared on Garuda and revived them all. He then easily placed the
mountain on the back of Garuda and went towards the ocean, followed by
the Devas and Asuras.

The Serpent King Vasūki was assured of a share in Amrita and he
consented to become the rope. The Mountain was then surrounded by
Vasūki. Vishnu followed by the Devas held the mouth of the serpent. But
the Asuras said: — "We have learned the Vedas, we know the Sāstras, it is
improper for us to hold the tail of a serpent. We will not do that. It is
inauspicious." Vishnu smiled. He and the Devas gave up the mouth end
and held the tail.

The churning then commenced. The Mountain was however heavy and it
sank down to the bottom of the ocean. The Devas and Asuras became
mournful. Vishnu then assumed the form of a Tortoise, went into the water
and raised the Mountain. He then remained like a Dvipa one lakhsa
Yojanas in expanse with the mountain on his back. He infused his
influence all round. Energised by Him, the Devas and Asuras vigorously
carried on the churning. At last fire and smoke came out from the thousand
mouths of Vasūki. This overpowered the Asuras and the Devas — but the
Devas were refreshed by clouds, rains, and winds sent by Vishnu.

After a good deal of churning, poison came out first. It spread out on all sides and the Prajāpatis and their progeny in terror took the shelter of Śiva. Śiva felt compassion for them and with the approval of Durgā, he drank up the whole of the poison. It made his throat blue.

The Churning recommenced. Out came Surabhi (the fabulous cow of plenty). The Vedic Rishis took that Cow for the necessaries of Yajna. Then came the horse Uchchaih-Sravas. Bali desired to have it. But Indra as directed by Vishnu made no desire. Then came the elephant Airavata, then the 8 space elephants and their 8 female partners.

Next arose Kaustubha, the celebrated lotus-colored gem. Vishnu wished to have it as an ornament for His breast. Next came Pārijāta, then the Apsaras.

Illumining all sides with her lustre arose Lakshmī. All paid homage to her. She looked on all sides, but found none, whom she could accept. If there was an ascetic he could not control his anger. If there was a Jnāni (sophist) he could not get over attachments. There might be a Mahātmā, but he had not conquered his passion of love. How could he be called īsvara, who depended on others, (and no one but īsvara could claim Lakshmī). If there was Dharma any where, there was not friendliness for all beings. If there was sacrifice, it was not for liberation. There was power but it could not resist the flow of time. If there was one void of likes and dislikes, he did not take a companion. If there was any one long lived, he had neither good nature (*Sila*) nor auspiciousness (*Mangala.*) If one had good nature and auspiciousness, he was not long lived. If one had all the Virtues he was out of his element with her. If he was all that she wanted he did not want her.

Considering everything, Lakshmī at last accepted Vishnu for her husband. He placed her on His breast. She favored the Devas, so they became possessed of all the virtues. She showed indifference to the Asuras, so they lost their might, energy and modesty and became greedy.

Then arose a lotus eyed girl called Vāruni (Spirituous liquor.) The Asuras accepted her.

Then arose Dhanvantari, part of a part of Vishnu, with a pot of Amrita in hand. Seeing the pot of Amrita, the greedy Asuras took that by force. They quarrelled with each other, some saying "First myself," "First myself," others saying "Not you" "Not you," whilst the weaker amongst them finding that they were going to be deprived, cried out in jealousy "The Devas are also entitled to an equal share. They have also toiled with us."

At this time Vishnu became a most beautiful young woman. She filled the hearts of the Asura Chiefs with passion. They asked the tempting girl to settle their differences and to make a proper distribution of Amrita amongst them. "But how can you trust a woman," said the girl. But the Asuras had fallen in love with her, so they made over the Amrita pot to her without further thought. She consented to distribute Amrita on the condition that the Asuras should put up with whatever she did, right or wrong. The Asuras consented. She then made the Devas and Asuras sit in two separate rows. She distributed the whole of the Amrita amongst the Devas. Only one Asura, named Rāhu, sat with the Devas. The Sun and the Moon pointed him out to the girl Vishnu. Vishnu then and there severed the head from the body of the Asura, but as the head had touched Amrita, it became immortal. Brahmā made it a planet. Rāhu still pursues the Sun and Moon at eclipses out of enmity.

When the Amrita was wholly spent, Vishnu assumed His own form and in the presence of all left the place on the back of Garuda.

The Asuras found they had been deceived and they became very angry. They could not bear the success of their enemies but they instantly engaged in fight with them. The fight was personal between the chiefs of both sides. (It is interesting to note the antagonistic names, as they give the correspondences between the Deva and Asura chiefs.) Indra fought with Bali, Kārtikeya with Tāraka, Varuna with Heti, Mitra with Praheti, Yāma with Kalanābha, Visvakarmā with Māyā, Tvastri with Sāmbara, Savitri with Virochana, Aparajita with Namuchi. The Asvini Kumāras with Vrishaparvan, Sūrya (Sun) with the hundred sons of Bali, Vāna and others, Chandra (Moon) with Rāhu, Vāyu with Puloman, Bhadra Kali with Sumbha and Nishumbha, Vrishākapi with Jambha, Vibhavasu with Mahisha, the sons of Brahmā with Ilvala and Vatapi, Brihaspati with Sukra, Sani with Naraka, the Maruts with the Nivātakavachas, the Vasus with the Kaleyas, the Visvadevas with the Poulamas and the Rudras with the Krōdhavaśas. (Those who want to make a deep study will do well to note these correspondences as they will serve to explain points which I have not touched upon as beyond the scope of the present work).

The Asuras used all the weapons of tempting Māyā and conquered the Devas, Vishnu then came to their rescue and they became victorious (The details of the fight might be interesting from an occult point of view, for which the reader must refer to the original.)

Śiva heard that Vishnu had assumed an enchanting female form. To satisfy his curiosity he went to Him with Bhāvanī. Vishnu assumed that form again to satisfy Śiva. The Astral Lord became passionate and ran after that female form and embraced her. The female Vishnu got out of the embrace and re-assumed His own form. Śiva was then restored to himself.

THOUGHTS ON THE ABOVE.

We have already seen that the ascent of spirit commenced in the Vaivasvata Manvantara. If the fourteenth Manvantara or the second half of the Seventh Round he left out of consideration, as the Manvantara of Dissolution or Pralaya, the middle of the remaining 13 Manvantaras will be in the Vaivasvata Manvantara. But the ascent could not commence without preparation. That preparation was made in the Chākshusha Manvantara or during the latter half of the Third Round.

Srī or Lakshmī is the Sātvic energy of preservation. This energy was so much overpowered by Materiality, that she was not to be found in Trilokī. The spiritual forces, the Devas, lost life and energy. The Asuras were at the height of their power. But as the ascending arc was near at hand, the Devas were promised Amrita *i.e.* immortality for the remaining part of the Kalpa. But that Amrita was to be obtained, the arc of spiritual evolution was to be raised by the churning of the ocean of Milk.

The ocean of Milk does not appertain to Jambu Dwipa, but it is the ocean of Saka Dwipa. The seven oceans are transformations of Prakriti, differing in the admixture of Satva, Rajas and Tamas and determining the character of the globe they surround. Vishnu, as the Third Purusha, is the divine source of evolution in every Jiva. The seat of that Vishnu is the ocean of Milk, the ocean where Satva prevails.

It is Vishnu who from His seat in the Ocean of Milk sends down Prānic Energy and the mineral becomes a vegetable. He sends down the power of perception and then the power of conception and the vegetable becomes an animal and at last a man. Throughout this course of evolution, there is a development of the self element in us. There is no idea of self in the mineral or in the vegetable. It faintly asserts itself or rather makes an effort to assert itself in the animal kingdom. The early history of humanity is the development of the selfish element in him. The Jiva has two sides in himself and non-self. The self side is caused by limitation due to his own senses They put him in contact with the outside world, and make him a centre of sense perceptions. He becomes lost entirely in the sense products, which form a world by themselves. The non-self side of a Jiva, is his spiritual nature. He begins with this spiritual nature. But the development of selfishness eclipses this nature, the true, the real nature of Jiva, and he identifies himself entirely with the acquired and false nature.

Then comes a crisis in the evolution of Jivas. Were men to be lost for ever to their spiritual, their real nature? Were they to be tempted away by the senses, which had done their work of training, past all chance of return?

Vishnu, the God of human evolution, willed otherwise. He caused a re-adjustment of the Daivic and Āsuric forces, and the Devas by His help got the better of the Asuras. This is the churning of the Ocean of Milk. It averted a crisis and is therefore a great event in the history of the Universe.

The Asura element could not be altogether wiped away. For the Deva or spiritual nature evolves out of Asura or selfish and material nature. Unselfishness grows out of selfishness, spirituality rises out of materiality.

In the act of churning, the Devas could not do without the Asuras. Churning itself, implies the action and reaction of two contending forces. "Make peace with them, as long as you are not strong yourselves." The compromise of the Devas with the Asuras is the development of spiritual faculties out of the personal element in man. It is the grafting of higher Manas on lower Manas. The element of mind is in the Asuras as well as in the Devas. But the Asuric or lower mind thinks of self as separate from other selves. The Daivic or higher mind breaks through the trammels of personality and finds oneness all round.

To use a better expression, we shall say higher self and lower self, rather than self and non-self.

Jivas are carried on in their course of life evolution by the force of past tendencies, and nature unaided produces the personal man. But when the past tendencies are exhausted, there is nothing to keep on the Jivas in their course of evolution.

Kūrma comes to the help of humanity at this stage. He gives a new power to men, the power of discrimination. With this power men become free agents, and they become responsible for their actions. They then generate new Karma for themselves, which takes them through infinite births and becomes a most potent factor in their future evolution.

The three Purushas have three Oceans as their correspondences. The first ocean (Kārana) gives the materials of the Jiva body. The Second ocean (Garbhoda), gives the germs of all Jivas. The third (Kshira) is the ocean of Jiva evolution. This ocean is churned for the spiritual evolution of Jivas, and it yields all that is necessary for that evolution. Vishnu himself appears as Kūrma and becomes the sustaining force of that evolution.

It is a Kālpic revolution. Vasūki sustains the earth and its inhabitants for one Kālpic period. The thousand hoods represent the thousand Maha yugas of every Kalpa. The Asuras held the mouth end of the serpent king and the Devas held the tail end. And the Devas acted wisely. For as the Kalpa waned, they got the supremacy.

The tortoise thrusts out its limbs and draws them in. Man is drawn outside by his senses during material descent and he is drawn in by his spiritual ascent. It is by the power of discrimination when fully developed that a man returns to his higher nature.

Srī or Lakshmī is the divine energy of Vishnu. She is the Energy of preservation, of evolution and progress She works out all that is good, all that is beautiful, and all that is powerful in this Universe. The possibilities of purely material development or of Nature's own evolution, are limited, and they are worked out in time. Then there is a void. There was this void in our universe and Trilokī become deprived of Sri. This was the curse of Durvasas, an Avatāra of Śiva.

The Churning took place as a remedy for this evil. Fresh forces had to be brought into requisition, fresh elements that could secure the spiritual evolution of the universe. Lakshmī herself reappeared in a most enchanting form, as the energy of a new evolution, the very best that man was capable of. The necessaries of this evolution also appeared and became powers in the hands of those that had to take part in the spiritual evolution of the universe.

All evolution is preceded by dissolution. Unless we give up the evil element in us, we can not acquire the good. The evil has to be destroyed and the Lord of destruction, in his infinite compassion, accepted this poison for himself, to do away with the evils of the Universe.

The Poison only opens the door for Amrita, the spiritual nectar. The famous Purusha Sukta says: — "He placed Amrita or eternal bliss in the higher three Lokas." The Bhāgavata renders this famous saying into the eighteenth sloka of the 6th. chapter of the Second Skandha. Commenting on this sloka, Śridhara says, bliss in our Trilokī is only transitory and the dwellers of Mahar Loka have also to leave their abode for the higher Jana Loka, when they are oppressed by the fire of Kālpic dissolution. Amrita was secured to the higher Lokas, as there is no selfishness in them. (III. 10-9.) Could the Asuras, the gods of selfishness, aspire to have life immortal and unlimited bliss. Vishnu decided otherwise.

The way was thus prepared for the Vaivasvata Manvantara, when men learned to discern between right and wrong.

THE SEVENTH MANVANTARA.

SKANDHA VIII. CHAP. 13.

Srāddha Deva son of Vivasvat or Sūrya is the seventh Manu. He is reigning at present. Ikshvāku, Nabhaga, Dhrishta, Saryāti, Narishyanta, Nābhāga, Dishta, Tarusha, Prishadhra, and Vasumat are his ten sons.

The Ādityas, the Vasus, the Rudras, the Visvadevas, the Maruts, the Asvini-kumaras and the Ribhus are the Devas. Purandara is their Indra. Kāsyapa, Atri, Vasistha, Visvāmitra, Goutama, Jamadagni and Bharadvāja are the seven Rishis.

The Avatāra of this Manvantara is Vāmana, the youngest son of Aditi by Kāsyapa.

(The Purāna will revert to this Manvantara after giving a general account of the succeeding Manvantaras).

THE EIGHTH MANVANTARA.

SKANDHA VIII. CHAP. 13.

Sāvarni is the son of Vivasvat by his wife Chāyā. He shall be the eighth Manu — Nirmoka, Virajaska (without Rajas) and others shall be his sons. Sutapas, Viraja (without Rajas) and Amrita Prabha shall be the Devas. Bali, son of Virochana, shall be the Indra.

Gālava, Diptimān, Parasurāma, Asvatthāma, Kripa, Rishya Sringa and Vyāsa shall be the seven Rishis.

Sārvabhouma, son of Devaguhya by Sarasvati, shall be the Avatāra. He shall wrest the kingdom of Svarga Loka from Purandara and make it over to Bali.

(The eighth Manvantara is the Second half of the Fourth Round and should be the spiritual half according to Theosophical ideas. But we find the

Asura King Bali, who was removed from the kingdom of Trilokī in the Vaivasvat Manvantara, restored to the kingdom of Svarga).

Amongst the Rishis we find Parasurāma who fought with Rāma and Asvatthāma and Kripa who ranged themselves against the Pāndava brothers in the battle of Kurukshetra.

All this shews that spirituality was developed out of materiality. The sons of Manu are Nirmoka and Virajaska. *Moka* is the cast off skin of an animal and may well represent the sthūla body. Nirmoka is one without Moka.

Virajaska is without Rajas. So the course of evolution shews a tendency in the first place to cast off the sthūla body and to overcome the Rajas.

THE NINTH MANVANTARA.

SKANDHA VIII. CHAP. 13.

The ninth Manu is Daksha Sāvarni. He is the son of Varuna Bhūtaketu, Diptaketu and others shall be his sons. Pāra, Marichi garbha and others shall be the Devas and Adbhūta their Indra. Dyu timat and others shall be the Rishis.

Rishabha, son of Āyushmat by Ambudhārā, shall be the Avatāra.

THE TENTH MANVANTARA.

SKANDHA VIII. CHAP. 13.

Brahmā Sāvarni is the tenth Manu. He is the son of Upaśloka. Bhūrishena and others shall be his sons. Havishmat, Sukrita, Satya, Jaya, Mūrti and others shall be the Rishis; Suvāsana, Aviruddha and others shall be the Devas and Sambhu their Indra.

Vishvaksena, son of Visvasrij by Visūchi, shall be the Avatāra.

THE ELEVENTH MANVANTARA.

SKANDHA VIII. CHAP. 13

Dharma Sāvarni is the eleventh Manu. Satya-Dharma and others shall be his ten sons. Vihangama, Kālagama, Nirvāna-ruchi and others shall be the Devas, Vaidhrita their king, and Aruna and others the Rishis. Dharma-Setu, son of Āryaka by Vaidhritā shall be the Avatāra.

THE TWELFTH MANVANTARA.

SKANDHA VIII. CHAP. 13.

Rudra-Sāvarni is the twelfth Manu. Devavat, Upadeva, Devasrestha and others shall be his sons (men shall be evolved into Devas In this Manvantara). Harita and others shall be the Devas, Ritadhāman their Indra. Tapomūrti, Tapasvin, Agnidhraka and others the Rishis; Svadhāman, son of Satya-sahas by Sūnritā, shall be the Avatāra.

THE THIRTEENTH MANVANTARA.

SKANDHA VIII. CHAP. 13.

Deva Sāvarni is the thirteenth Manu. Chitra Sena, Vichitra and others shall be his sons, Sukarma and Sutrāma the Devas, Divaspati their Indra and Nirmoka, Tatvadarsa, and others the Rishis.

Yogesvara, son of Devahotra by Vrihati, shall be the Avatāra.

THE FOURTEENTH MANVANTARA.

SKANDHA VIII. CHAP. 13.

Indra Sāvarni is the fourteenth Manu. Uru, Gambhira, Vradhna and others shall be his sons.

Pavitra and Chākshusha the Devas, Suchi their Indra, Agni, Vāhu, Suchi, Suddha Māgadha and others the Rishis.

Brihat-bhānu, son of Satrāyana by Vitānā, shall be the Avatāra (*i.e.* the great sun shall absorb everything.)

THE ADMINISTRATION OF A MANVANTARA

SKANDHA VIII. CHAP. 14.

Said Rājā Parikshit: — Tell me, O Rishi, what are the respective duties of Manu and others in the Manvantaras.

Suka replied: — The *Avatāra* of each Manvantara guides the Manu, the sons of Manu, the Rishis, the Indra and the Devas of that Manvantara. (Each Manvantara has its own place in the history of the Kalpa, and the general evolution has to be worked out in the way best adapted to that Manvantara. The administration of each Manvantara is in the hands of a separate set of kings and ministers. Vishnu incarnates in each Manvantara, as the king of all who serve as administrative officers of that Manvantara and he is as such called the special Avatāra for that Manvantara. The divine kings, the Rishis, the Devas, all work under His direction. He gives the law that is to be administered. He shews the path, which evolution is to take in any particular Manvantara.)

Yajna and others are Avatāras of Purusha. Guided by them, Manu and others lead the course of the universe.

Rishis: — At the end of every four Yugas, the Srutis become devoured by time. (The human races have a life period timed to the four Yugas. They have their infancy, as it were, in Satya Yuga, and they have to be guided by wise sayings, which form the Srutis of those races. The Srutis become better understood with the growth of racial intelligence and other texts take the place of old ones. When the races do not require the help of the earlier texts, those texts become lost in time. When the races begin another life cycle, they require again the help of teachings, which become revealed to the Rishis. The Rishis then give those teachings to the races.) The Rishis find out the Srutis, by means of Tapas. The eternal Dharma proceeds from the Srutis. (People know their duties from the scriptures.)

Manus. — The Manus then take up the Dharma, and each in his own time devotedly promulgates it on the earth.

Manu's sons. — The sons of Manu preserve the Dharma, generation after generation, till the end of the Manvantara.

Devas and Indra. — Indra, with the Devas that participate in sacrificial offerings, protects the three Lokas and gives rains.

(Besides this general administration, there are other ways also of managing the affairs of the universe and these are mentioned incidentally in the following slokas. *Śridhara.*)

Hari appears as the Siddhas (Sanaka and others) and expounds divine wisdom (Jnāna) in every Yuga. He appears as Rishis (Yājnavalkya and others) and expounds Karma. As Lords of Yoga (Dattātreya and others), He expounds Yoga.

THE STORY OF BALI.

SKANDHA VIII. CHAPS. 15-23.

Bali, son of Virochana and grandson of Prahlāda, was once defeated by Indra. His Guru, Sukra, advised him to perform the Visvajit sacrifice. When *ghee* was offered at the sacrifice, one chariot, some green coloured horses, one lion-marked flag, one golden bow, two quivers with an inexhaustible store of arrows, and one divine *kavacha* (protective charm) arose from the fire. Bali gladly accepted these things. Prahlāda also gave him a fresh garland and Sukra gave him a conch.

Equipped with these things Bali attacked Svarga. Brihaspati told Indra the time was inauspicious and the Devas could not succeed without the help of Vishnu. He advised them to give in and to remain concealed somewhere, till the time came for their ascendancy. The Devas followed the advice of Brihaspati and Bali became the king of Trilokī.

Sukra advised Bali to perform one hundred Asvamedha sacrifices.

Aditi became disconsolate at the down-fall of her sons. She asked her husband Kasyapa what to do for her sons. The Prajāpati advised her to observe Payōravata in honor of Vishnu (for details, see the original). She observed the Vrata for 12 days when Vishnu appeared before her and assured her He would incarnate as her son.

Vāmana was born of Aditi at midday, on the 12th day of the moon, during the white quarter in the month of Bhādra, while the moon was in the first part of Sravanā, in the Abhijit.

(Vāmana = Dwarf). Vāmana heard that Bali was performing Asvamedha on the banks of the Narmadā. He went there and Bali received him duly and enquired what he wanted, expressing his willingness to gratify him fully. Vāmana asked for only three paces of ground. Bali laughed at this modest prayer and asked him to take more land. But Vāmana excused himself, saying a Brāhmana should be content with small things only. Bali laughed again and at once said "Then accept." He then took the water pot to make the formal gift. Sukra perceived the object of Vishnu. He tried to dissuade Bali from carrying out his promise. "This is not a dwarf Brāhmana but Vishnu Himself. By one pace he will cover the whole of Bhūr Loka and Bhuvar Loka. By the second pace, He will cover Svar Loka and what then will become of the third pace? You will have to go to Naraka for not being able to fulfil your promise. And where shall you yourself remain after giving over all you have? Therefore desist from what you are doing. No doubt truth is preferable. But the Vedas also allow untruth in extreme cases."

Bali replied: — "The grandson of Prahlāda shall never speak an untruth. I will give to this Brāhmana boy what I have promised, even if he be Vishnu and my enemy too."

Sukra said in anger — "You disregard the words of your Guru. So you shall forthwith lose everything."

Bali remained unmoved. He worshipped the Brāhmana boy and read out the formal Mantra of giving over three paces of land. Vindhyāvali, the virtuous consort of Bali, at this time placed a golden pitcher filled with water before her husband. He washed the feet of Vāmana with that water, and sprinkled it over his head. Then Vāmana wonderfully grew in size. The whole Universe became visible in him. He seized the whole of Bhūr Loka with one pace the whole of Bhuvar Loka with his body, and the directions in space with his hands, so that even the whole of Svar Loka became insufficient for the second pace. But nothing remained for the third pace. For the second pace of Vāmana passed through Mahar Loka, Jana Loka, Tapas Loka and reached even Satya Loka.

The Asuras exclaimed: — "By what an unjust device has our king been deprived of all! It is no sin to fight with this disgrace of a Brāhmana, this deceitful Vishnu." So they engaged in fight with the followers of Vishnu, but were defeated by them.

Bali told his followers there was no use fighting, for Kala was against them. The same Bhagavān who had favored them was now in opposition.

Garuda, knowing the intention of Vishnu, tied Bali with the noose of Varuna.

Vāmana then addressing Bali said: — "Where is your promised ground for my third pace? You have told a lie. You do not carry out your promise to a Brāhmana. For this you will have to go to Naraka."

Bali said: — "Do not think I told an untruth or that I mean to deceive thee. Here is my head for the third pace. I am not so much afraid of the Naraka thou art speaking of, nor of this noose, nor of any troubles I may undergo, nor of any punishment thou mayest inflict on me as I am afraid of doing anything for which good people will blame me. I deem this punishment an act of favor a favor shewn perhaps out of consideration for my grand-father Prahlāda. For this kingdom only maddened me with power and made me forget my end. And what shall I do with this body too? True thou art my enemy, but this loss of kingdom has brought me nearer to thee."

Prahlāda appeared at this time. He bowed down to Vāmana and said: — "It is thou that didst give the kingdom of Trilokī to Bali and it is thou that hast taken it away and really thou hast shewn him a favor by doing so. For power maddens a man and blinds him as to his real self."

Vindhyāvali said: — "O Lord, Thou art the Creator, the Preserver, and the Destroyer of Trilokī. Who else could own it besides Thyself? It was the height of presumption to pretend to give the Trilokī to you." Brahmā said: — "O Deva of Devas, all-pervading Lord, thou hast taken away everything from this Bali. He has also given himself up entirely to Thee, without being moved in the least. He does not now deserve to remain tied up."

Bhagavān said: — "O Brahmā, I take away all his riches from him whom I favor. For one proud of riches disregards both myself and others. When after many births the Jiva happens to become a man, and when in that birth he is found not to entertain any pride of birth, karma, age, beauty, wisdom, power, wealth and other things, you should know that to be my favor. One constantly devoted to me is not led away by anything apt to beget pride.

"This king of Dānavas and Daityas has now conquered Māyā. So he is not beside himself even in grief. His wealth gone, his position lost, himself overpowered and chained by enemies, forsaken by friends, reviled and cursed by his own preceptor, and what not, this Bali did not give up Truth.

"I will give him a place, difficult for others to attain. He shall be the Indra of Sāvarni Manvantara. Till then let him reside in Sutala. By my wish, the dwellers of Sutala shall have no mental or bodily pain, no fatigue, no sleepiness, no defeat and no misfortune. Bless thee, O Maharaj, go to Sutala with thy clan. Sutala is even wished for by those that dwell in Svarga. Even the Lokapālas shall not be able to overpower thee. What of others? If any Daitya does not follow thee, I will kill him by my Chakra. By all means I will preserve thee and thy followers. There you shall always find me at your door. Thy Asura nature shall be there entirely destroyed under my influence."

Prahlāda was also ordered by Bhagavān to accompany Bali to Sutala. So they all went to Sutala.

THOUGHTS ON THE ABOVE.

We now find Bali shorn of all materialism and restored to spiritual purity. We can well understand the removal of Bali from the kingdom of Trilokī, for the cyclic movement was tending that way since the last Manvantara, and the Devas were to have supremacy over Trilokī. We have to study the future of Bali, as holding further light for us.

We must repeat here the distinction made between the two classes of Asuras: Daityas and Dānavas. The Daityas trace their origin to the gate-keepers of Vishnu. They had inherent Satva in them, which was eclipsed in their downfall. Therefore, though they acted as materialistic forces following the cyclic tendency, they were themselves not incapable of spiritual development Thus we find words of wisdom and spirituality in Vritra, in Hiranyakasipu, unselfish devotion in Prahlāda, and complete resignation in Bali. Hiranyāksha and Hiranyakasipu went back to their old place in Vaikuntha. Vritra became united with Sankarshana. Prahlāda is immortal in his unselfish mission, and we have just heard the future of Bali. The Maruts become Devas after their very birth.

Therefore there is no extinction for the Asuras, except for those that do not follow Bali and do not place themselves under the influence of Vishnu. The cyclic weapon or Chakra is ever ready to destroy those that hopelessly go against the law.

Now a word about Sutala. The arrangement of Pātālas as given in the text is the reverse of what they should be in point of spirituality, for Atala is the most and Pātāla the least removed from spirituality.

The influence of Vishnu does not extend beyond Sutala, and nothing can save those that transgress the limits of this nether plane. For in Vitala the destructive Purusha reigns and a passage to that plane is only a door to utter extinction. And in Atala there is not a trace of spirituality, the work of destruction is already done, and mother Nature dissolves the material elements for some better use in future.

The special provision for Sutala is therefore a cyclic necessity. For Jivas have to be preserved from an undesirable end. Therefore Bali was given a post, the proud privilege of seeing that Jivas do not undergo utter extinction. Sutala was also fortified with an accession of spirituality.

The example of self-abnegation, the ideal of self-sacrifice, Bali is to become the king of Devas in the succeeding Manvantara.

THE MATSYA AVATARA.

SKANDHA. VIII. CHAP. 24.

Towards the end of the previous Kalpa, Brahmā was falling asleep and the Vedas fell from his mouth. The Asura Hayagrīva took them up. Seeing this Vishnu became a small fish. King Satyavrata was making Tarpana (*i.e.* offering libations of water), when the fish found its way into his hands. He threw it into the river. The fish implored the King to preserve him. So he took it home and placed it in a small waterpot. The fish increased in size so much that all tanks and rivers were tried, but they could not contain it. At last the king took the fish to the sea, but it implored him not to throw it away into the sea. The king then said: — "This fish must be the Deity Himself, otherwise how could it grow so large?" The fish then addressed the king thus: "On the seventh day from this, the Trilokī shall be plunged into the Pralaya waters. Then a big Ark shall come to thee. Take all plants, all seeds, all animals, and the seven Rishis with you and get into that ark. When the wind shakes that ark, tie it with a serpent to myself. I will remain with that ark in the Pralaya Ocean till the awakening of Brahmā. I will manifest supreme wisdom in thee."

So saying the fish disappeared and on the seventh day the Pralaya waters deluged the Trilokī. Satya Vrata did as he was told. He got the highest wisdom from the Fish Incarnation.

That Satya Vrata is Srāddhadeva, our present Manu.

SKANDHA IX.

THE VAIVASVATA MANVANTARA.

SUDYUMNA.

SKANDHA IX. CHAP. 1.

Srāddhadeva Manu had no child for some time. Vasistha performed a sacrifice in honor of Mitra-varuna that he might obtain progeny. Sraddha, wife of the Manu, went to the chief priest and asked for a daughter. So Manu had a daughter named Ilā. He took Vasistha to task for having had a daughter. Vasistha thought the priest had done something wrong. He prayed to Bhagavān for the change of Ilā's sex. So Ilā became a male named Sudyumna and in company with others went on horse back to the chase. He entered a forest called Sukumāra, below the Meru, which is the play ground of Śiva and his consort. He and his companions were all transformed into females, for such is the mandate of Śiva for those that enter the forest. In this changed condition, Sudyumna with his female companions went to Budha. Budha took a fancy for Sudyumna and had by her one son Purūravas.

Vasistha took pity on Sudyumna again and prayed to Śiva to change his sex. By the favor of Śiva, Sudyumna became a male for one month and a female for another month. He had three sons. Utkala, Gaya and Vimala.

IKSHVĀKU BROTHERS.

SKANDHA IX. CHAP. 2.

Manu prayed to Vishnu for one hundred years for other sons. He got ten sons like unto himself. Ikshvāku was the eldest:

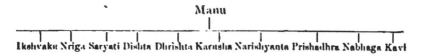

(8). PRISHADHRA.

While residing in the house of his Guru, Prishadhra was placed in charge of cattle. It was raining one night, when a tiger entered the fold. The cattle strayed about in fear and bellowed aloud. Prishadhra ran after the tiger. The night was dark. He missed his aim and cut off the head of the cow, which the tiger had seized. He found out the mistake in the morning and informed his Guru about it. The Guru said: — "You shall become a Sudra, as the fruit of your Karma." Prishadhra accepted the curse. He became an ascetic, and roamed about the earth as the friend of all beings. Eventually He ended his life in fire.

(10). KAVI.

Kavi attained wisdom in his youth. He did not marry.

(6). KARUSHA.

The sons of Karūsha were the Kārūshas, a race of pious Kshatriyas, who guarded the north.

(5). DHRISHTA.

Dhārshtas were the sons of Dhrishta. Though born as Kshatriyas, they became Brāhmanas on this earth.

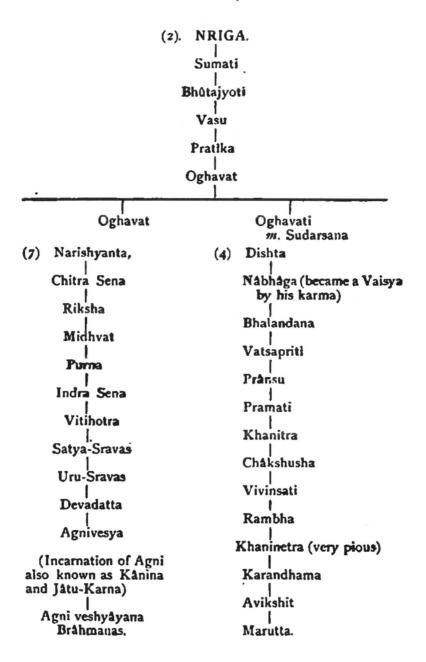

(2). **NRIGA.**

Sumati

Bhûtajyoti

Vasu

Pratîka

Oghavat

Oghavat	Oghavati
	m. Sudarsana

(7) Narishyanta,

Chitra Sena

Riksha

Midhvat

Purna

Indra Sena

Vitihotra

Satya-Sravas

Uru-Sravas

Devadatta

Agnivesya

(Incarnation of Agni
also known as Kânina
and Jâtu-Karna)

Agni veshyâyana
Brâhmanas.

(4) Dishta

Nâbhâga (became a Vaisya
by his karma)

Bhalandana

Vatsapriti

Prânsu

Pramati

Khanitra

Châkshusha

Vivinsati

Rambha

Khaninetra (very pious)

Karandhama

Avikshit

Marutta.

Sambarta, Son of Angiras, officiated at the Yajna performed by Marutta,
The Devas took direct part in the Yajna,

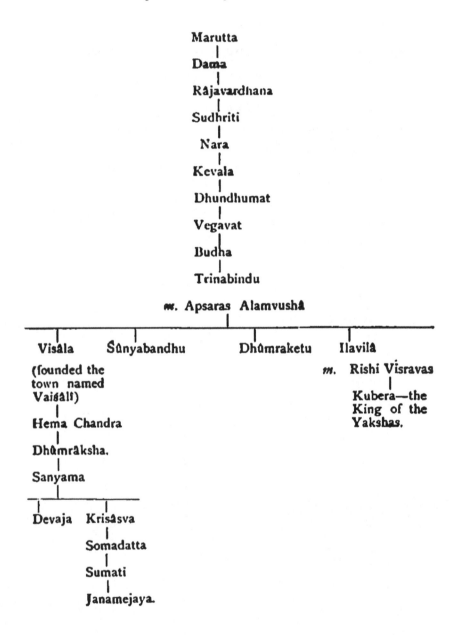

(3). SARYĀTI.

SKANDHA IX. CHAP. 3.

Saryāti was well versed in the Vedas. He had one daughter, Sukanyā. He went with her one day to the Āsrama of Chyavana Rishi. Sukanyā found there two streaks of light as from glow-worms, issuing from within a mound of earth, thrown up by white ants. She pricked those portions with a thorn and blood oozed out. The party of Saryāti found that their usual secretions were stopped. The king thought some one had offended Chyavana. The girl then told her story. The king found the Rishi underneath the mound of earth and asked his pardon. The Rishi wanted the hand of the girl in marriage and Saryāti consented. So Sukanyā became the wife of Chyavana.

One day the Asvini Kumāras came to Chyavana. The Rishi asked them to give him youth and beauty and promised in return to give them offerings of Sōma, though they had no part in Sōma Yāgas, The Asvini Kumāras took the Rishi inside a tank and all the three came out young and beautiful and looking all alike. Sukanyā could not recognise her husband and she prayed to the Asvini Kumāras to remove her confusion. They were pleased with her chastity and pointed out her husband.

One day king Saryāti came and found his daughter sitting with a young man. He reproved Sukanyā for her supposed unchastity. The girl then related the story of her husband's attaining youth and the king became very much pleased.

Chyavana made offerings of Sōma to the Asvini Kumāras. This offended Indra. He held up the Vajra to kill Chyavana, but the son of Bhrigu paralysed the hands of Indra. From that time the Devas consented to give a share in Sōma to the Asvini Kumāras.

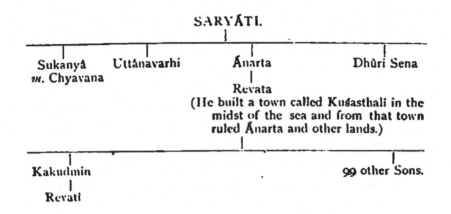

SARYÂTI.

Sukanyâ m. Chyavana	Uttânavarhi	Ânarta	Dhûri Sena

Ânarta
|
Revata
(He built a town called Kuśasthali in the midst of the sea and from that town ruled Ânarta and other lands.)

Kakudmin	.	99 other Sons.

Kakudmin
|
Revati

Kakudmin took his daughter Revati with him and went to Brahmā loka to enquire of Brahmā, who should be her husband. The Gandharvas were singing at the time and Kakudmin had to wait for a moment. He then saluted Brahmā and made the enquiry. Brahmā laughed and said: — "O king, the men of your choice are dead and gone. I do not hear even of their sons and grandsons. Twenty seven yuga cycles have now passed away. Therefore go back to thy place and give thy daughter to Baladeva, who has now incarnated as an Ansa (part) of Vishnu for the good of Bhūr-loka." And so the king did. (The Present is the 28th. Yuga cycle. Baladeva is the brother of Sri Krishna.)

NABHAGA.

SKANDHA IX. CHAPS. 4-6.

Nabhaga remained long with his Guru. So his brothers thought he had become a Brahma-chārin. They reserved no share for him at partition. Nabhaga at last returned to his house and asked for his share in the patrimony. The brothers pointed out their father Manu as his share. Nabhaga asked his father — "How is it my brothers have reserved thee for my share?" Manu replied: — "Child, do not believe them. The clan of Angiras are performing Yajna. They get confounded on every sixth day. This is the sixth day. Give them two Vaisvadeva Sūktas. When they go to Svarga after completion of their Yajna they will leave all their sacrificial wealth to you." Nabhaga did as he was told. The Angirasas left all the property remaining on the sacrificial ground to Nabhaga. As he was going to take those things, a dark Purusha appeared from the north and said. "These are mine."

"But the Rishis have given them to me" said Nabhaga.

"Go to your father then and ask for the solution" said the dark Purusha.

"Yes, the remnants of a Sacrifice belong to Rudra" said Manu.

Nabhaga returned and said "Yes these remnants of sacrifice all belong to thee. So my father told me."

"I am pleased with thee and thy father. Both of you have spoken the truth" said Rudra, "I give thee supreme wisdom. I also give thee these remnants. Take them now."

```
   NABHAGA
      |
   NĀBHĀGA.
      |
   AMBARISHA
```

King Ambarisha had discrimination and dispassion. His devotion was great. His mind was fixed on the lotus feet of Vishnu, his words were all about the glory of Vaikuntha, his hands were engaged in cleansing the temples of Vishnu, his ears only heard about the glory and the works of Vishnu, his eyes intently looked on the symbols of Vishnu wherever found. His body felt pleasure in the touch of Vaishnavas, his nose smelt the sweet fragrance of Tulasi proceeding from the feet of Vishnu, his tongue tasted only food offered to Vishnu, his feet traversed the places sacred to Vishnu and his head was devoted to the salutation of Vishnu. If he enjoyed things of this world, it was for service to Vishnu and not for the sake of enjoyment. If he had attachment, it was only for those that were devoted to Vishnu. The fruits of his action he offered to Him. By devotion and by the unselfish performance of duties pertaining to his sphere of life (Svadharma), he pleased Bhagavān and by degrees he gave up all desires. Vishnu was so much pleased with the King, that he gave him His own Chakra for protection.

Ambarisha with his wife once undertook to perform Dvādasi Vrata for one year. (Dvādasi is the twelfth day of the Moon. The Vrata consists in fasting on the eleventh day of the Moon and in breaking the fast on the 12th day). On one occasion he fasted for 3 consecutive days. He bathed himself in the Yamunā and worshipped Vishnu at Mathurā. He gave plenty of riches and cattle to the Brāhmanas. He then fed the Brāhmanas and asked their permission to eat himself. At the time Durvāsas appeared as his guest. The king received him duly and requested him to take his meals. The Rishi consented and went to bathe himself in the river and perform his daily rites. The king waited long for him but he did not return. There was only half a muhurta now remaining of Dvādasi. If the king did not eat any thing, his Vrata would not be observed. If he ate, he would shew disregard to a Brāhmana. At this juncture, the king decided to serve both ends by taking a little water, for the Brāhmanas call that both eating and non-eating. Durvāsas came back. By spiritual vision, he knew what had happened and became highly enraged. He tore up a hair tuft and charged it to kill Ambarisha. The king remained unmoved. The chakra of Vishnu consumed the destructive force sent by Durvāsas and went even to destroy him. The Rishi ran in every direction. The Chakra followed him wherever he went. He went to Brahmā and prayed to be saved. "It is not in my power to save thee" said Brahmā. "Thou hast offended a votary of Vishnu." He went to Śiva. "Child" said Śiva "this weapon of Vishnu is too much for me even. Go thou to Vishnu." Durvāsas went to Vishnu and prayed to be pardoned and saved. Said Vishnu: "O Brāhmana, I am dependent on my Bhaktas. I am not free. My heart is in the possession of my Bhaktas. I am dear to them. Without these my Bhaktas I do not even want myself, nor my absolute powers, for I am their sole and supreme resort. They forsake their wives, homes, children and wealth for my sake. How can I forsake them. Their heart is chained to me. They look on all with equal eyes. By devotion they win me even as chaste wives win their husbands. My service is all in all to them. They do not even desire the four Muktis, Sālokya and others, though these come within their easy reach. What perishable objects can they have desire for? The Sādhus are my heart. I am the heart of the Sādhus. They do not know any one besides me nor do I know any one besides them. O Brāhmana, hear what is thy only remedy. Without delay go to him who has caused this fear in thee. When force is used against Sādhus, it reacts on him who uses the force. True asceticism and wisdom are both for the salvation of the Brāhmanas. But in one untrained, they produce the contrary effect. Therefore go thou to the son of Nābhāga. Beg his pardon and thou shalt be saved." Durvāsas went back to Ambarisha and touched the feet of the king. Ambarisha became non-plussed at this act of a Brāhmana and knowing the object of the Rishi, he prayed to the Chakra to desist from its course and to save the Brāhmana. The Chakra had just commenced its work of destruction, but it withdrew its energies upon the prayer of Ambarisha. Durvāsas was extremely thankful and he thus praised the king. "I see this day the greatness of Vaishnavas, O king. Thou didst pray for my welfare, though I had offended thee. There is nothing strange for those that have conquered Vishnu Himself. Thou hast been very kind to me. Thou hast favored me much. Thou didst not even think of my offence, but thou hast saved my life." The king had waited for Durvāsas all this time. He now fell at the feet of the Rishi and requested him to take his meals. The Rishi gladly did so, and also made the king take his food.

Durvāsas then went to Brahmā Loka. He did not return for one year and the King lived upon water only all this time, being so anxious to see the Rishi back. Such is the holy story of Ambarisha.

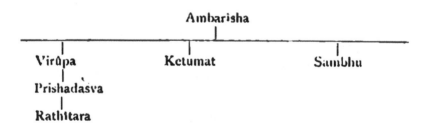

Rathitara had no children. At his request Rishi Angiras produced certain sons by his wife. They were known both as Rathitaras and Āngirasas.

[Durvāsas had cursed Indra, and Indra lost all power. But after the great churning, times were changed. The divine law favoured the Devas and the worshippers of Vishnu. Those who assumed a power, independently of Vishnu, were sure to find disappointment, however eminent their position might be.]

IKSHVĀKU.

SKANDHA IX. CHAPS. 6-13.

Ikshvāku was born out of the nostrils of Manu when sneezing. He had one hundred sons. Vikukshi, Nimi, and Dandaka were the eldest born. Twenty five of them ruled on the east of Āryāvarta, twenty five on the west and twenty five in the middle. The others ruled else where. For the performance of Ashtakā Srāddha, Ikshvāku once ordered Vikukshi to get some good flesh. Vikukshi had a bagful of good game. But he was hungry and ate one rabbit out of his store. Vasishtha found fault with this and Ikshvāku had to reject the whole of the game. The King became angry at this and he expelled his son from the kingdom. When Ikshvāku died, Vikukshi returned. He succeeded his father as king and was known as Saśāda or Rabbiteater. Puranjaya was the son of Saśāda. He was also called Indravāha and Kakutstha. The Devas had a fight with the Asuras and Indra asked for the help of Puranjaya. Puranjaya wanted Indra to be his carrier, and the King of the Devas became a bull. Puranjaya ascended the bull on its hump. He is therefore called Indravaha or Indra-vehicled and Kakutstha or the mounter on the hump. He defeated the Asuras.

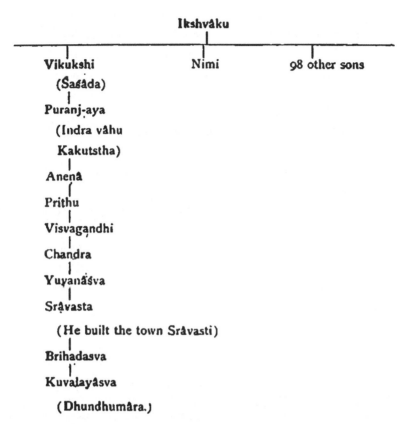

Ikshvâku

- Vikukshi (Saśâda) — Nimi — 98 other sons

Vikukshi
(Saśâda)
|
Puranj-aya
(Indra vâhu
Kakutstha)
|
Anenâ
|
Prithu
|
Visvagandhi
|
Chandra
|
Yuyanâśva
|
Srâvasta
(He built the town Srâvasti)
|
Brihadasva
|
Kuvalayâsva
(Dhundhumâra.)

With his 21 thousand sons, Kuvalayâsva killed an Asura called Dhundhu, for the good of Rishi Utanka. But the Asura killed all his sons, except three, with fire from his mouth. Those three were Dridhâsva, Kapilâsva and Bhadrâsva.

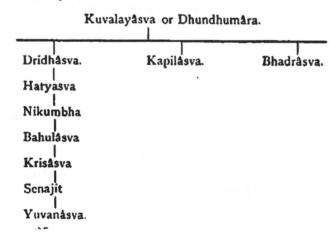

Kuvalayâsva or Dhundhumâra.

- Dridhâsva. — Kapilâsva. — Bhadrâsva.

Dridhâsva.
|
Hatyasva
|
Nikumbha
|
Bahulâsva
|
Krisâsva
|
Senajit
|
Yuvanâsva.

Yuvanāsva had no son. So the Rishis performed a sacrifice directed to Indra. One night Yuvanāsva became very thirsty and entered the Yajna house. He found all the Rishis sleeping at the time. He thought it improper to rouse the Rishis and drank whatever water he found near at hand. By chance that happened to be the consecrated water with the power of producing a son. When the Rishis rose up they did not find the water. On enquiry, when they knew what had happened, every one wondered what the outcome would be. In time the king brought forth a son from his right side. The little thing cried out for milk. Indra said "Do not weep, child, you shall *drink wine* ('*Mān Dhātā*')" So saying he offered the child his fore finger. From this, the child was called Māndhātā. Yuvanāsva, by the blessing of the Rishis, did not meet with death at delivery. Māndhātā was a very powerful king. The thieves dreaded him much. He performed many sacrifices and made many gifts. He married Indumatī, daughter of Sasabindu. He had three sons Purukutsa, Ambarisha, and the Yōgin Muchukunda. He had also fifty daughters.

Rishi Soubhari made Tapas in the waters of the Yamunā. One day he saw the pairing of a couple of fish and became excited. He requested king Māndhātā to give him one daughter in marriage. The king said: "By Svayamvara, you may get my daughter" (*i.e.* the girl must choose her own husband from amongst a number of men offering themselves as husbands.) The Rishi thought because he was old and decrepit therefore the king wanted to put him off. So Soubhari by yogic powers became young and beautiful. All the fifty daughters then accepted him for their husband. The Rishi prepared for himself all the enjoyments of life and passed his days in company with his 50 wives. He then became disgusted with this sensual life and afterwards attained Moksha with his wives.

Yuvanāsva adopted his grand son Ambarisha. Ambarisha had one son Youvanāsva. His son was Hārita. These three, Ambarisha, Youvanāsva and Hārita were the founders of the chief clans of the Māndhātā Dynasty.

The elemental serpents gave their sister Narmodā in marriage to Purukutsa. Purukutsa accompanied Narmodā to Rasātala at the request of Vasūki. There he killed such Gandharvas as deserved to be killed. Those who remember this story have no fear from serpents. Such was the blessing of the elemental serpents.

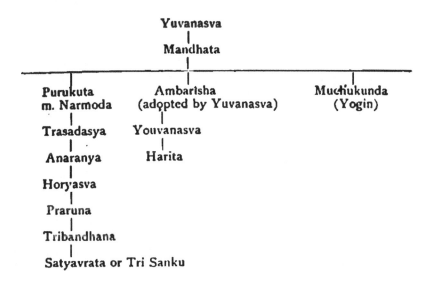

Tri Sanku became a Chandāla by the curse of his father. Rishi Visvāmitra lifted him up to Svarga in his own mortal body. Tri Sanku is still visible in the heavens. The devas turned him with his head downwards and attempted to throw him down. Visvāmitra by his power has retained him there.

[Tri Sanku is a constellation in the southern hemisphere.]:

```
Tri Sanku
    |
Haris Chandra
```

Haris Chandra had at first no issue. He prayed to Varuna for a son, promising to offer him as a sacrifice to the Water-god. The king had a son named Rohita (Red). Varuna asked for his victim. Ten days passed away. "Without teething the child will not be pure." There was teething. "When these milk teeth fall away, then will be the time." The milk teeth fell off. "Let other teeth grow." Other teeth did grow. "But he is a Kshatriya boy. He can be pure only when he is fit to put his armour on."

The king put off Varuna from time to time in this way, out of affection for his son. Rohita came to know of his father's promise. To save himself, he took a bow and went to the forest. There he learned that his father had an attack of dropsy, the disease caused by Varuna. So he prepared himself to go back, but Indra prevented him by persuasive words. He was put back from year to year by Indra, till his 6th. year. He then made his way to the king. He purchased from Ajīgarta his second son Sūnahśepha. He saluted his father and offered the child. King Haris Chandra appeased Varuna by human sacrifice and got rid of his dropsy. In that sacrifice, Visvāmitra was the Hōtā, Jamadagni was the Adhvaryu, Vasistha Brahmā and Ayāsya was the Udgāta. Indra being pleased gave a golden chariot to the king. Visvāmitra taught Ātmā Vidya to Haris Chandra and he attained liberation.

[The story of Haris Chandra in this Purāna follows the vedic version. The gist of the story is that in the course of further evolution the Devas were to be propitiated by human sacrifice. But this sacrifice did not mean killing. It was the complete offering of oneself up to the service of the gods. The mission of the human victim is to constantly work for the good of the Universe and to extinguish his own personality. Sūnahśepha was not killed in the sacrifice. He was offered up to the service of the gods. After the sacrifice, he was called Devarāta i.e. one offered to the Devas. Visvāmitra adopted Devarāta as his own son and he asked his hundred sons to accept him as their eldest brother. He disowned those sons that did not obey him (Bhāgavata IX-16). Therefore Visvāmitra took the principal part in this sacrifice and not Vasistha, though he was the family preceptor.]

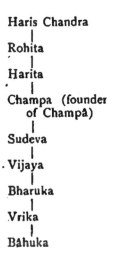

Haris Chandra
|
Rohita
|
Harita
|
Champa (founder
   of Champâ)
|
Sudeva
|
. Vijaya
|
Bharuka
|
Vrika
|
Bâhuka

His enemies dispossesed Bahuka of his kingdom. He went to the forest accompanied by his wives. When he died, the eldest queen prepared herself for death also. Rishi Aurva knew her to be big with child, and dissuaded her from accompanying her husband on to the funeral pyre. The co-wives of the queen, out of jealousy, gave her poison. The child was born with this poison, therefore he was called Sagara (Sa = with, gara = poison.) Sagara became a great king. The Seas were dug by his sons. He was prevented by Rishi Aurva from taking the lives of the Tālajanghas, Yavanas, Sakas, Haihayas, and Barbars. But he made them change their outward look. He performed an Asvamedha sacrifice as advised by Aurva and Indra stole the sacrificial horse.

Sagara had two wives Sumati and Kesini. The 60 thousand sons of Sumati searched for the horse on all sides. They dug the earth's surface and made the Seas. They found the horse near Kapila. They took him to be the stealer of the horse and abused him. For this they were all burnt up.

Kesini had one son Asamanjas by Sagara. Anśumat was son of Asamanjas. He was attached to his grandfather Sagara. Asamanjas was a Yogin in his former birth. He therefore wanted to avoid company by means of provoking acts. He threw down some children into the Saraju. His father

Sagara was thus compelled to forsake him. By Yogic powers, he brought back the children thrown into the Saraju, and left his father for ever.

Anśumat was also sent by Sagara to search for the horse. He found the horse and a heap of ashes near Kapila. He saluted Kapila and glorified him. The Avatāra was pleased. He permitted Anśumat to take away the horse. He also informed him that his burnt-up Pitris could only be saved by the water of the Gangā.

Sagara completed the sacrifice with the horse. He made over the kingdom to Anśumat and attained Mukti.

Anśumat made Tapas for the downward flow of Gangā but without success. He was followed by his son Dilipa. He also did not succeed. Bhagiratha was the son of Dilipa. He prayed hard and Gangā appeared in person before him. "Child, I am pleased with thee. What boon do you ask for"? Bhagiratha told her what he prayed for. "But who shall arrest my course, when I fall down. If not arrested I will pierce the earth and reach Rasātala. Again if I pass over earth, men will wash away their sins in my waters. Where shall I wash away those sins, O King? Therefore do thou ponder well what to do." Said Bhagiratha: — "The touch of Sādhus shall take away thy sins. For Vishnu, the destroyer of sins, remains in them. Thy downward course shall be arrested by Rudra." Śiva was pleased by the prayer of Bhagiratha, and he consented to hold Gangā.

Gangā came rushing down and she was taken by Bhagiratha to where the ashes of his Pitris lay. The very touch of her waters purified the sons of Sagara and they went to Svarga.

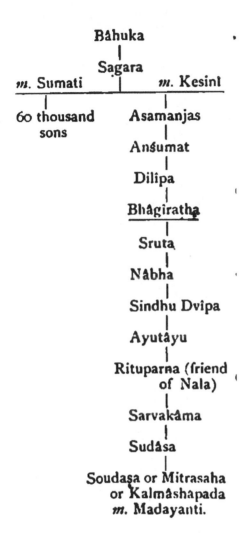

Bāhuka
|
Sagara
m. Sumati — | — *m.* Kesinī
| |
60 thousand   Asamanjas
sons |
Anśumat
|
Dilīpa
|
Bhāgiratha
|
Sruta
|
Nābha
|
Sindhu Dvipa
|
Ayutāyu
|
Rituparna (friend
of Nala)
|
Sarvakāma
|
Sudāsa
|
Soudaṣa or Mitrasaha
or Kalmāshapada
m. Madayanti.

Once there lived two Rākshasas. Soudāsa killed one and did not kill the other. The surviving Rākshasa, bent on taking revenge, entered the service of Soudāsa as a cook. When the king entertained Vasistha, he gave him human flesh to eat. The Rishi became angry and caused Soudāsa to become a Rākshasa. When he learned however it was the doing of a Rākshasa, he reduced the king's Rākshasa life to 12 years. The king also held out water for the execration of Vasistha. His queen prevented him. So he threw the water at his own feet. His feet became black with sin. While living as a Rākshasa, the king saw a Brāhmana and his wife in their privacy, and he attacked the Brāhmana. The wife reminded the king of his former birth and requested him not to deprive her of her husband at the time of enjoyment. The king heeded not her words but devoured the Brāhmana. The Brāhmana woman cursed Soudāsa so that he should meet with death whenever he had female connection. On the expiry of 12 years, Soudāsa reverted to his former birth, but for fear of the curse he had no connection with women. Vasistha at the request of Soudāsa produced a son by his wife, Madayanti. The conception lingered for 7 years. Vasistha struck the womb with a stone (Aśman) and the son was hence called Aśmaka. The son of Aśmaka was Bālika. He was the surviving kshatriya, after the extirpation of that caste by Parasurāma. Hence he was called Mūlaka also (the root of a race).

Soudāsa
|
Aśmaka
|
Bālika or Mūlaka
|
Daśaratha
|
Aidaviḍi
|
Visvasaha
|
Khatvānga

Khatvānga was a very powerful king. He killed Daityas as a friend of the Devas. The Devas offered him a boon. The king wanted to know how much longer he was to live. Learning it was a Muhurta only, he returned forthwith to his place and concentrated his mind on Bhagavān. He attained Mukti.

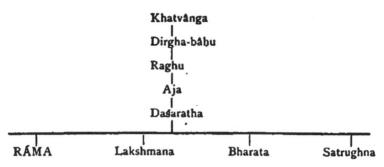

Khatvânga
|
Dirgha-bâbu
|
Raghu
|
Aja
|
Daśaratha

| RÁMA | Lakshmana | Bharata | Satrughna |

(The story of Rama as told in the Râmâyana is widely and universally known. It is therefore unnecessary to repeat that story from the Bhâgavata Purâna.)

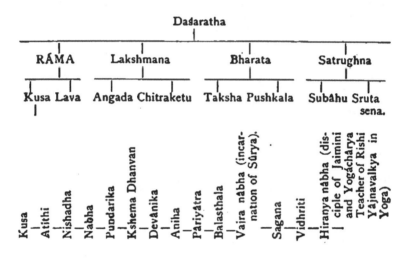

Daśaratha

| RÁMA | Lakshmana | Bharata | Satrughna |

| Kusa Lava | Angada Chitraketu | Taksha Pushkala | Subâhu Sruta sena. |

Kusa – Atithi – Nishadha – Nabha – Pundarika – Kshema Dhanvan – Devânika – Aniha – Pariyâtra – Balasthala – Vaira nâbha (incarnation of Sûrya). – Sagana – Vidhriti – Hiranya nâbha (disciple of Jaimini and Yogâchârya Teacher of Rishi Yâjnavalkya in Yoga)

Pushpa – Dhruva Sandhi – Sudarsana – Agni varna – Sighra – Maru

Manu has matured in Yoga. He now resides at Kalapa. Towards the end of

Maru	Vatsa-Vriddha	Sutapas
Prasusruta	Prativyōma	Amitrajit
Sandhi	Bhânu	Brihadrai
Amarshana	Divâka	Barhi
Mahasvat	Sahadeva	Kritanjaya
Visvabâhu	Brihadasva	Rananjaya
Prasenajit	Bhânumat	Sanjaya
Takshaka	Pratikaśva	Śakya
Brihadbala, killed at the battle of Kurukshetra by Abhimanyu	Supratika	Suddhôda
	Marudeva	Langala
(Time of Parikshit)	Sunakshatra	Prasenajit
	Pushkara	Kshudraka
Brihat-rana	Antariksha	Sumitra
Vatsa-vriddha	Sutapas	

Kaliy uga he shall restore the Solar dynasty.

Sumitra shall be the last of the Ikshvāku dynasty in this Kali Yuga.

Nimi was the second son of Ikshvāku. He asked Vasistha to officiate at his Yajna. But the Rishi had been pre-engaged with Indra. So he asked the king to wait till he came back. Considering the uncertainty, Nimi did not wait for his family Purohita. But engaged another priest. Vasistha on returning became offended and cursed Nimi with the loss of his body. Nimi gave the same curse to Vasistha. So both gave up their bodies. Vasistha was reborn shortly after as the son of Mitravaruna by Urvasi. The Rishis picked up the body of Nimi and placed it with the scented things of

Yajna. On the completion of the Yajna, the Rishis prayed to the Devas for the vivification of the body. But Nimi said from within the scented things that he did not want to be encumbered with the body any more. The Devas said: "Then remain in the eyes of all beings as winking." So Nimi remains in the twinkling of eyes.

The Rishis churned the body of Nimi and a son was born. He was called Janaka. As he was born, when his father was bodiless (*videha*) he was also called *Vaideha*. The churning also gave him the name of Mithila (Manth = to churn). He built the town Milhilā. (Mithilā is the modern Tirhut).

```
NIMI                        Maru
  |                           |
Janaka                     Pratipa
  |                           |
Udâvasu                    Kritaratha
  |                           |
Nandivardhana              Devamirha
  |                           |
Suketu                     Visruta
  |                           |
Devarâta                   Mahadhriti
  |                           |
Brihadratha                Kritirâta
  |                           |
Mahâvirya                  Mahârôman (large-haired)
  |                           |
Sudhriti                   Svarnaroman (gold-haired)
  |                           |
Dhrishtaketu               Hrasvaroman (short-haired)
  |                           |
Haryasva                   Sira-Dhvaja
  |
Maru
```

While ploughing the ground for sacrifice, Sira-Dhvaja got Sita at the end of the plough. Therefore Sira (plough) being his Dhvaja (flag, proclaimer of fame), he was called Sira Dhvaja.

(This Sira-Dhvaja is the renowned Janaka of Ramayana.)

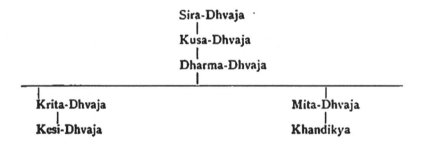

```
                    Sira-Dhvaja
                        |
                    Kusa-Dhvaja
                        |
                    Dharma-Dhvaja
                        |
        _____
        |                              |
  Krita-Dhvaja                    Mita-Dhvaja
        |                              |
  Kesi-Dhvaja                     Khandikya
```

Kesi Dhvaja was versed in Ātmā-vidya, Khandikya was versed in Vedic Karma, Kesi Dhvaja overpowered Khandikya and he fled away.

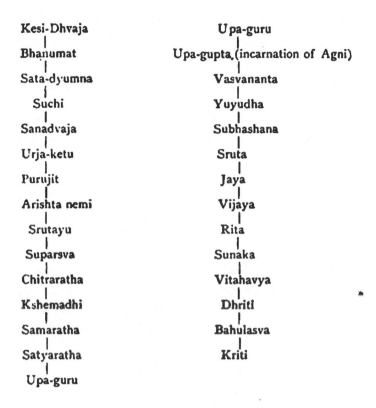

Kesi-Dhvaja	Upa-guru
Bhanumat	Upa-gupta (incarnation of Agni)
Sata-dyumna	Vasvananta
Suchi	Yuyudha
Sanadvaja	Subhashana
Urja-ketu	Sruta
Purujit	Jaya
Arishta nemi	Vijaya
Srutayu	Rita
Suparsva	Sunaka
Chitraratha	Vitahavya
Kshemadhi	Dhriti
Samaratha	Bahulasva
Satyaratha	Kriti
Upa-guru	

These kings of Mithila were well versed in Ātmā-vidya.

THE LUNAR DYNASTY.

SKANDHA IX. CHAP. 14.

Sōma (the Moon) was born out of the eyes of Atri. He carried off Tāra, the wife of Brihaspati (Jupiter). Brihaspati asked for his wife several times, but Sōma would not give her up. Sukra (Venus) was not on good terms with Brihaspati. So he took the side of Sōma, with his disciples, the Asuras. Śiva with his Bhūtas took the side of Brihaspati. Indra with the Devas also sided with their preceptor. The two parties engaged in fight. After some days of fight, Angiras informed Brahmā about every thing that transpired. Brahmā reproached Sōma. So he returned Tāra to Brihaspati. Brihaspati found that Tāra had conceived. "Immediately throw out the seed of another man in my field," cried he. Tāra feeling bashful brought forth at the time a lustrous son, Both Brihaspati and Sōma desired to have the son, each saying "It is mine not yours." When they quarrelled with each other, the Devas and Rishis asked Tāra who was the father of the child. The child reproved his mother for the delay in answering. Brahmā took Tāra aside and learned from her that Sōma was the father of the son, Sōma then took the child. Brahmā seeing the deep wisdom of the child named him Budha (Mercury).

Budha had by Ilā one son Pururavas. Nārada related his beauty and his virtues to the Devas in Svarga. Urvasi heard all that and took a fancy for the king. By the curse of Mitra Varuna, she had then a human form. Both the king and the Apsaras became attached to each other and they lived as husband and wife. But Urvasi laid down two conditions of her company with the king — (1) that the king was to preserve two rams, which the Apsaras had brought with her and (2) that the king was never to expose himself before her except in privacy. Indra sent the Gandharvas in search of Urvasi. They found her out and took away her two rams. She had a maternal affection for these animals and she cried out in despair. The king hurriedly took his arms and ran after the Gandharvas. They left the rams and fled away. The king brought them back. But in the hurry, he had forgot to cover himself and Urvasi left him. The king became disconsolate, and roamed about in search of her. After some days he found her on the banks of the Sarasvati with her 5 companions. He entreated her to come back. She promised to give her company to the king one night every year and informed him of her delicate state of health.

Urvasi came after a year, with one son. She advised the king to entreat the Gandharvas for her hands. The king did so and the Gandharvas became pleased with him. They gave him one Agnisthāli (pot of fire). The king took the Agnisthāli to be Urvasi and roamed with it in the forest. (The Gandharvas gave him the fire for the performance of sacrifice necessary for the attainment of Urvasi). The king found out his mistake at last. He then placed the fire in the forest, went home and meditated every night on Urvasi. On the approach of Tretā, he was inspired with the three Vedas (Karma-Kānda). He then went to the place of fire and found there one Asvatha tree (the sacred fig) grown from inside a Śami tree (Śami is the name of a tree said to contain fire). He decided that the fire must be within the Asvatha tree. He took two pieces of wood (technically called Arani) from that tree and produced fire by their friction. He deemed one piece to be Urvasi and another piece to be himself and the space between the two pieces to be his son. By friction, the fire called Jatavedas came out. (*Vedas* is wealth, enjoyments in general. *Jāta* is grown. Jata-vedas is that fire from which enjoyments proceed that which gratifies all sense-desires. It is the chief fire of the Karma-kānda of the Vedas). By the invocation of the three vedas, that fire became three fold. (Āhavaniya, Gārhapatya, and Dakshinā are the three fires perpetually kept in the household. *Āhavaniya* is the eastern fire which represents the relations of the house holder with the Devas. *Gārhapatya* is the sacred fire which the householder receives from his father and transmits to his descendants and from which fires for sacrificial purposes are lighted. It represents household and family duties. *Dakhina* is the southern fire. It represents all classes of duty to the Pitris). The king imagined this threefold fire to be his son (The son by his offerings sends his father's soul to Svarga. The sacrificial fire also sends the performer to Svarga). With that fire, he performed Yajna desiring to reach the Loka (plane) of Urvasi. Prior to this in Satya Yuga, Pranava was the only Veda, Nārāyana was the only Deva, there was only one fire and only one caste. The three Vedas came only from Pururavas, at the beginning of Treta Yuga. The king attained Gandharva Loka by means of the fire. (In Satya Yuga, Satva generally prevailed in men. Therefore they were all fixed in meditation. But in Treta Yuga, Rajas prevailed and by the division of the Vedas, Karma Mārga made its appearance. *Śridhara.*)

[The true history of the origin of the three Vedas is thus given in veiled words. They originated in the strong desire of men in Treta Yuga for the possession of heavenly things. This gives us about two millions of years at the present day. The origin of the Vedas must not be confounded however with their existence in the present form. For that we must refer to the sacrifice of Haris Chandra, the adoption of Sunah sepha by Visvāmitra and the division amongst the Madhu Chandas brothers.]

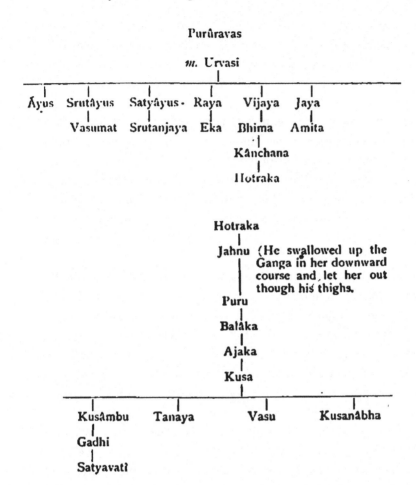

Rishi Richika asked for the hand of Satyavati. Gadhi did not consider him to be a fit husband for his daughter. He therefore wanted to put him off and said: — "Give a dower of one thousand horses, with the lustre of moon all over their body and with one of their ears dark-coloured (Śyama). For we are sons of Kusika."

The Rishi went to Varuna and got the horses. He gave them to the king and married Satyavati.

Satyavati and her mother both asked Richika to prepare *Charu* for the birth of a son to each. (*Charu* is an oblation of rice, barley, and pulse, boiled together. It is offered to Devas and Pitris). Richika prepared two charus and consecrated one with Brāhmana Mantra and the other with Kshatriya Mantra. The Rishi then went to bathe himself. In the meantime, the mother thought, the daughter's Charu must be superior to hers. So she procured that from her daughter and the daughter partook of her mother's Charu. When the Rishi returned and learned what had taken place, he said to his wife: — "What an improper thing you have done by this exchange of Charus! You shall have a fierce and terrible son, while your brother shall be the greatest in divine wisdom."

Satyavati prayed to her husband, saying "Let it not be so." The Rishi then said, "Then your grandson shall be all that."

Jamadagni was born of Satyavati. She became the river Kausiki.

Jamadagni married Renukā the daughter of Renu.

Jamadagni had several sons, Vasumat and others. The youngest was Rāma (Parsurama). He is said to be an Incarnation of Vishnu. He destroyed the Haihaya Kshatriyas. He cleared the earth of Kshatriyas twenty one times.

Kārtaviryarjuna was the chief of the Haihaya clan. He got yogic powers from Datta-Atreya and also one thousand heads. He was very powerful. He was hospitably received one day by Jamadagni, with the objects yielded by his Kāma-Dhenu (a cow that yields all objects of desire). The king longed to have the cow and forcibly carried her away. Parasurāma killed the king in battle and carried back the cow. The sons of the king out of revenge killed Rishi Jamadagni while Parasurāma and his brothers were out. Incensed by this conduct of the Haihayas, Parasurāma killed all the Kshatriyas on account of their iniquities.

Jamadagni on his death became the Seventh Rishi in the constellation of the Seven Rishis.

Parasurāma will become one of the Seven Rishis in the next Manvantara. He bides his time, with axe in hand, on the Mahendra mountain.

Gadhi had his son Visvāmitra. Though a Kshatriya, he became a Brāhmana by his Tapas. He had one hundred sons. The mid son was Madhuchhandas.

But they were all called Madhuchhandas. Visvāmitra adopted as his son Sunahsepha, son of Ajigarta of the clan of Bhrigu after he had been offered up to the Devas and the Rishi asked his sons to accept him as their eldest brother. Śunahśepha had been purchased as the victim of Haris Chandra's sacrifice. He prayed to the Devas and to Prajāpati and got liberation. In the clan of Gadhi, he was known as Devarāta. In the clan of Bhrigu, he was called Sunahsepha. The elder sons of Visvāmitra did not accept him. So the Rishi cursed them to become Mlechhas. Madhuchhandas with the youngest 50 did as asked by the Rishi.

The other sons of Visvāmitra were Ashtaka, Harita, Jaya, Kratumat and others.

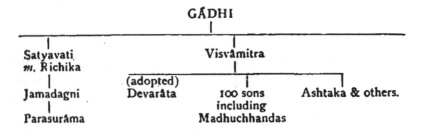

THE LUNAR DYNASTY (Continued).

SKANDHA IX. CHAP. 17.

Āyus was the eldest son of Pururavas. His line is now given.

THE LUNAR DYNASTY.

SKANDHA IX. CHAP. 17.

Áyus was the eldest son of Pururavas. His line is now given.

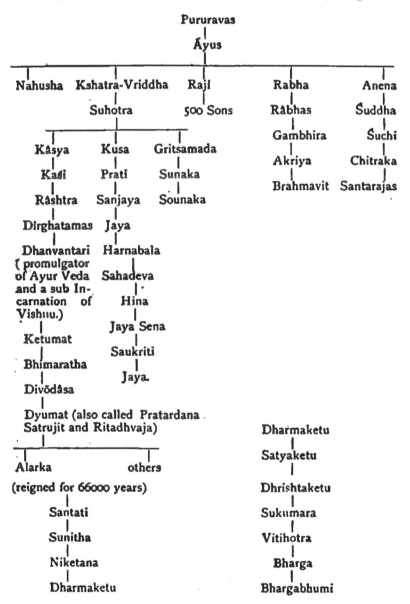

Pururavas
|
Áyus

Nahusha	Kshatra-Vriddha	Raji	Rabha	Anena
	Suhotra	500 Sons	Rábhas	Suddha
			Gambhira	Suchi
Kâsya / Kusa / Gritsamada			Akriya	Chitraka
			Brahmavit	Santarajas

Kâsya — Kusa — Gritsamada
|
Kaśi — Prati — Sunaka
|
Râshtra — Sanjaya — Sounaka
|
Dirghatamas — Jaya
|
Dhanvantari — Harnabala
(promulgator
of Ayur Veda — Sahadeva
and a sub In-
carnation of — Hina
Vishnu.)
| — Jaya Sena
Ketumat — Saukriti
|
Bhimaratha — Jaya.
|
Divödâsa
|
Dyumat (also called Pratardana
Satrujit and Ritadhvaja)

| |
Alarka   others
(reigned for 66000 years)
|
Santati
|
Sunitha
|
Niketana
|
Dharmaketu

Dharmaketu
|
Satyaketu
|
Dhrishtaketu
|
Sukumara
|
Vitihotra
|
Bharga
|
Bhargabhumi

257

Raji defeated the Asuras and made over Svarga to Indra. Indra placed Raji in charge of Svarga. Raji died and his sons did not return the kingdom of Svarga to Indra. Brihaspati made invocation against them and they were all easily killed.

SKANDHA IX. CHAPS. 18-19.

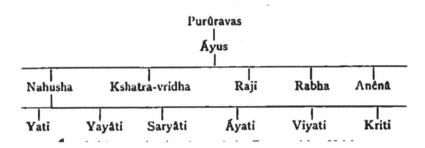

Śarmistha was the daughter of the Dānava king Vrishaparvan. Devayāni was the daughter of Sukra, the preceptor of the Dānavas. They quarrelled whilst playing with each other and Śarmistha threw Devayāni into a well. King Yayāti happened to pass by the way and he rescued her. She became attached to the king and married him. Sukra became displeased with the Dānavas for the ill treatment of his daughter by Śarmistha. And to please the preceptor and his daughter, Vrishaparvan had to make over his daughter and her companions to Devayāni as her constant attendants. So they accompanied Devayāni to the place of Yayāti. Sukra warned Yayāti however not to have any intercourse with Śarmistha. But the king did not heed the warning. He had two sons Yadu and Turvasu by Devayāni and three sons, Druhya, Anu and Puru by Śarmistha. Devayāni complained to Sukra and by the curse of the Rishi the king was attacked with the infirmities of old age. The Rishi was subsequently pleased to say that the king might exchange his infirmities with another. Yayāti called his sons one by one and they all declined to comply with his request except the youngest son Puru. So he exchanged his infirmities with Puru and lived as a young man. At last he found that no amount of gratification of the senses produced satiety and being disgusted with the pleasures of life, made over to Puru his youth and took upon himself his own infirmities. He made over the south east to Druhya, the east to Yadu, the west to Turvasu and the north to Anu. He then made Puru his successor and went into the forest.

SKANDHA IX. CHAP. 20.

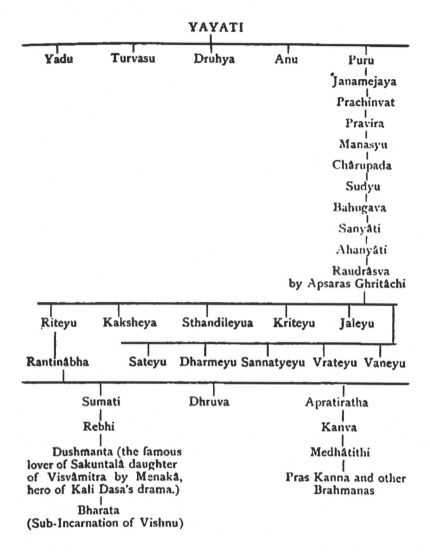

YAYATI

| Yadu | Turvasu | Druhya | Anu | Puru |

Puru
|
Janamejaya
|
Prachinvat
|
Pravira
|
Manasyu
|
Chârupada
|
Sudyu
|
Bahugava
|
Sanyâti
|
Ahanyâti
|
Raudrâsva
by Apsaras Ghritâchi

| Riteyu | Kaksheya | Sthandileyua | Kriteyu | Jaleyu |

| Rantinâbha | Sateyu | Dharmeyu | Sannatyeyu | Vrateyu | Vaneyu |

Sumati   Dhruva   Apratiratha
| |
Rebhi   Kanva
| |
Dushmanta (the famous   Medhâtithi
lover of Sakuntalâ daughter |
of Visvâmitra by Menakâ,   Pras Kanna and other
hero of Kali Dasa's drama.)   Brahmanas
|
Bharata
(Sub-Incarnation of Vishnu)

Bharata had three wives, all of Vidarbha. One of them bore a son to the king, but he pronounced the child to be unlike himself. The wives of the king killed their children for fear of their being called illegitimate. Bharata gave Yajna offerings to the Maruts and to Sōma (Moon) that he might be blessed with a Son. The Maruts gave him Bharadvāja as his son. Brihaspati (Jupiter) produced Bharadvāja on Mamatā (Egoism), the wife of his brother Utathya. The parents deserted the child and he was brought up by the Maruts. Bharadvāja being adopted by Bharata was called Vitatha.

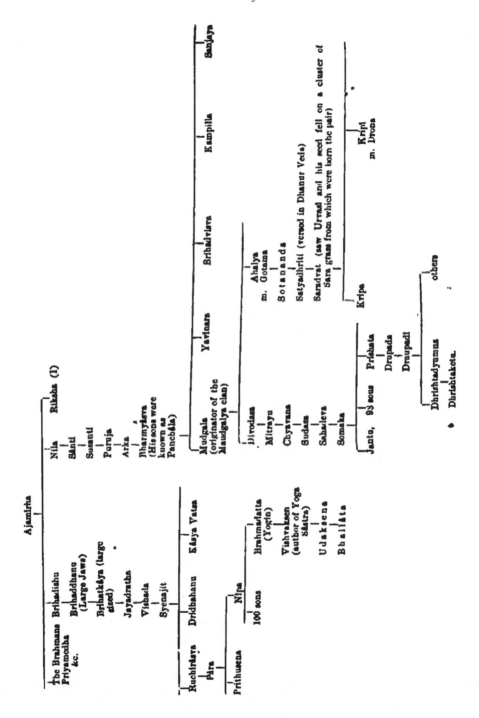

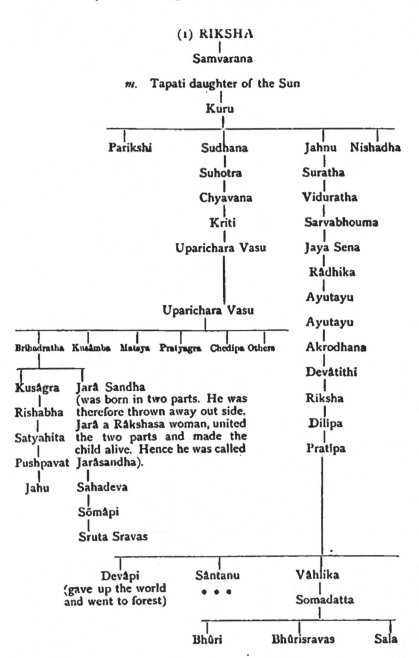

(1) RIKSHA
|
Samvarana

m. Tapati daughter of the Sun
|
Kuru

Parikshi — Sudhana — Jahnu   Nishadha

Sudhana
|
Suhotra
|
Chyavana
|
Kriti
|
Uparichara Vasu

Jahnu
|
Suratha
|
Viduratha
|
Sarvabhouma
|
Jaya Sena
|
Rādhika
|
Ayutayu

Uparichara Vasu

Brihadratha   Kusāmba   Matsya   Pratyagra   Chedipa   Others

Ayutayu
|
Akrodhana
|
Devātithi
|
Riksha
|
Dilipa
|
Pratīpa

Kusāgra
|
Rishabha
|
Satyahita
|
Pushpavat
|
Jahu

Jarā Sandha
(was born in two parts. He was
therefore thrown away out side.
Jarā a Rākshasa woman, united
the two parts and made the
child alive. Hence he was called
Jarāsandha).
|
Sahadeva
|
Sōmāpi
|
Sruta Sravas

Devāpi   Sāntanu   Vāhlika
(gave up the world   • • • |
and went to forest)   Somadatta

Bhūri   Bhūrisravas   Sala

Santana had in his former life the power by pass of his hands to make an old man young. He was therefore called Sāntanu in this life. When he became king, there was drought for 12 years. The Brāhmanas ascribed this to Sāntanu's overlooking the claims of his eldest brother Devāpi. Sāntanu went to his brother. But in the meantime his minister had sent certain Brāhmanas to Devāpi and they dissuaded him from Vedic Dharma. He thus became unfit to be a king and the Devas then rained. *But Devāpi is waiting at Kalāpa for his future mission. The lunar dynasty will come to an end in the present Kaliyuga and Devāpi will be the progenitor of the lunar Dynasty in the next Satyayuga.*

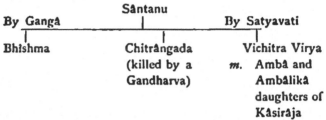

Satyavati was the daughter of Uparichara Vasu by Matsyagandhā. Before her marriage with Sāntanu, Rishi Parāśara had by her one son Krishna Dvaipāyana, the renowned Vyāsa, father of Suka, the propounder of the Bhāgavata Purāna.

As Vichitra Virya had no son, Satyavati asked Vyāsa to produce sons on his wives. They were Dhritarāshtra, Pāndu, and Vidura.

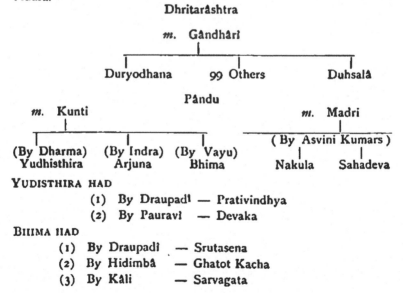

YUDISTHIRA HAD

    (1) By Draupadī — Prativindhya

    (2) By Pauravi — Devaka

BIIIMA IIAD

    (1) By Draupadī — Srutasena

    (2) By Hidimbā — Ghatot Kacha

    (3) By Kāli — Sarvagata

ARJUNA HAD

    (1) By Draupadi — Srutakirti
    (2) By Ulûpî — Irâvat
    (3) By the princess
        of Manipur — Vabhruvâhana
    (4) By Subhadrâ — Abhimanyu
                m. Uttarâ
                  |
            Parikshit

NAKULA HAD

    (1) By Draupadî — Satânika

    (2) By Karenumatî — Naramitra

SAHADEVA HAD

    (1) By Draupadî — Sruta Karman

    (2) By Vijayâ — Suhotra

Arjuna—Abhimanyu—Parikshit—Janmaejaya—Satânika—Sahasrânika—Asvamedhaja—Asima Krishna—Nemi Chakra (Hastinâ pura shall be washed away and he shall reside at Kousâmbi)—Upta—Chitraratha—Suchiratha—Vrishtimat—

Vrishtimat—Susena—Mahipati—Sunitha—Nri Chakshus—Sukhinala—Pariplava—Sunaya—Medhâvin—Nripanjaya—Durva—Timi—Brihadratha—Sudâsa—Satânika—Durdamana

Durdamana—Mahinara—Dandapâni—Nimi—Kshemaka

Kshemaka shall be the last of this approved line in the Kali Yuga.

Now as to the **Magadha kings.**

Jará Sandha – Sahadeva – Marjari – Srutasravas – Yutáyu – Naramitra – Sunakshatra – Brihat Sena – Karmajit – Satanjaya – Vipra – Suchi – Kshema – Suvrata – Dharma Sutra – Sama

Sama – Dridhasena – Sumati – Subala – Sunitha – Satyajit – Visvajit – Ripunjaya

This line shall he extinguished one thousand years after the death of Parikshit. (The future tense is used in the text with reference to the time of Parikshit.)

SKANDHA IX. CHAPS. 23.

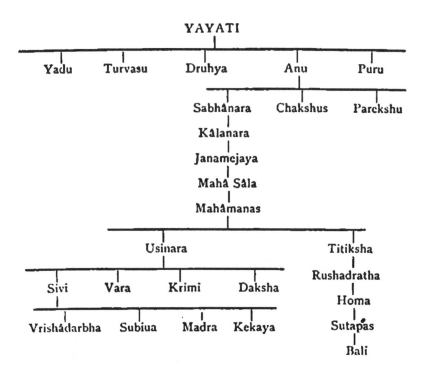

YAYATI

Yadu   Turvasu   Druhya   Anu   Puru

Sabhánara   Chakshus   Parekshu

Kálanara

Janamejaya

Mahá Sála

Mahámanas

Usinara   Titiksha

Sivi   Vara   Krimi   Daksha   Rushadratha

Homa

Vrishádarbha   Subiua   Madra   Kekaya   Sutapas

Bali

265

Dirghatamas Rishi produced on Bali's wife Six sons — Anga, Banga, Kalinga, Sambhu, Pundra and Odhra. These six sons founded kingdoms in their own names in the East.

(Anga is the country about Bhāgalpur. Banga is modern Bengal. Kalinga is the country between Jagannatha and the Krishna. Odhra is part of modern Orissa.)

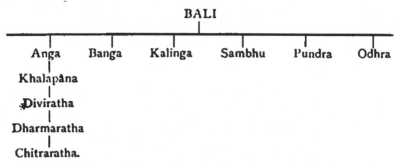

BALI

Anga   Banga   Kalinga   Sambhu   Pundra   Odhra

Khalapâna

Diviratha

Dharmaratha

Chitraratha.

Chitratha was also called Rōmapâda. He had no son. Dasaratha (father of Rama) was his friend. He gave his daughter Sântâ to Romapâda. Sântâ was married to Rishi Rishya Sringa. That Rishi made a Yajna for Romapâda and he had a Son Chaturanga born to him.

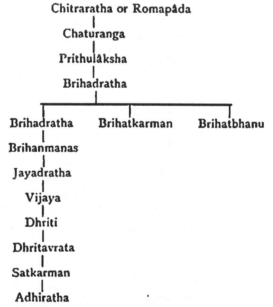

Chitraratha or Romapâda

Chaturanga

Prithulâksha

Brihadratha

Brihadratha   Brihatkarman   Brihatbhanu

Brihanmanas

Jayadratha

Vijaya

Dhriti

Dhritavrata

Satkarman

Adhiratha

(He adopted Karna of the Mahâbhârata as his son, when he had been left by Kunti.)

Chitratha was also called Rōmapāda. He had no son. Dasaratha (father of Rāma) was his friend. He gave his daughter Sāntā to Rōmapāda. Sāntā was married to Rishi Rishya Sringa. That Rishi made a Yajna for Rōmapāda and he had a Son Chaturanga born to him.

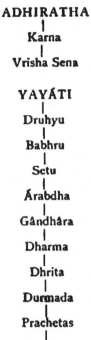

ADHIRATHA
|
Karna
|
Vrisha Sena

YAYÁTI
|
Druhyu
|
Babhru
|
Setu
|
Árabdha
|
Gándhára
|
Dharma
|
Dhrita
|
Durmada
|
Prachetas
|
One hundred sons inhabiting the north as a Mlechcha race

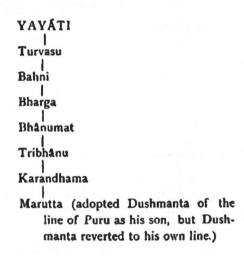

YAYÁTI
|
Turvasu
|
Bahni
|
Bharga
|
Bhánumat
|
Tribhánu
|
Karandhama
|
Marutta (adopted Dushmanta of the
line of Puru as his son, but Dush-
manta reverted to his own line.)

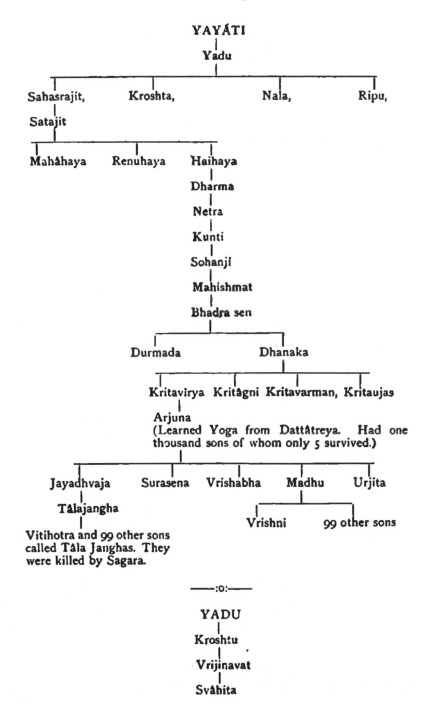

YAYÁTI
|
Yadu
|

| Sahasrajit, | Kroshta, | Nala, | Ripu, |

Satajit
|

| Mahâhaya | Renuhaya | Haihaya |

Dharma

Netra

Kunti

Sohanji

Mahishmat

Bhadra sen
|

| Durmada | Dhanaka |

Kritavîrya Kritâgni Kritavarman, Kritaujas
|

Arjuna
(Learned Yoga from Dattâtreya. Had one
thousand sons of whom only 5 survived.)

| Jayadhvaja | Surasena | Vrishabha | Madhu | Urjita |

Tâlajangha
|

| | Vrishni | 99 other sons |

Vitihotra and 99 other sons
called Tâla Janghas. They
were killed by Sagara.

——:o:——

YADU
|
Kroshtu
|
Vrijinavat
|
Svâhita

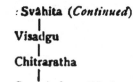

: **Svåhita** (*Continued*)

|

Visadgu

|

Chitraratha

|

Sasavindu. (Had ten thousand wives
and one laksha sons by éach wife. Of these sons, six were famous
Prithu Sravas, Prithu Kirti, Punyayasas etc.,)

——:o:——

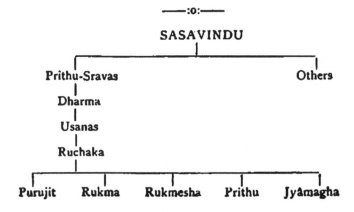

SASAVINDU

Prithu-Sravas — Others

Dharma

Usanas

Ruchaka

Purujit — Rukma — Rukmesha — Prithu — Jyamagha

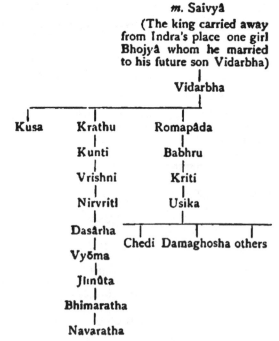

m. Saivyâ
(The king carried away
from Indra's place one girl
Bhojyâ whom he married
to his future son Vidarbha)

Vidarbha

Kusa — Krathu — Romapâda

Kunti — Babhru

Vrishni — Kriti

Nirvriti — Usika

Dasârha — Chedi Damaghosha others

Vyôma

Jimûta

Bhimaratha

Navaratha

270

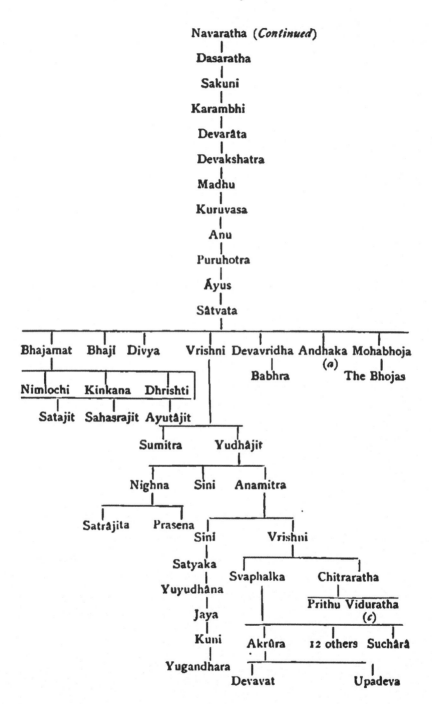

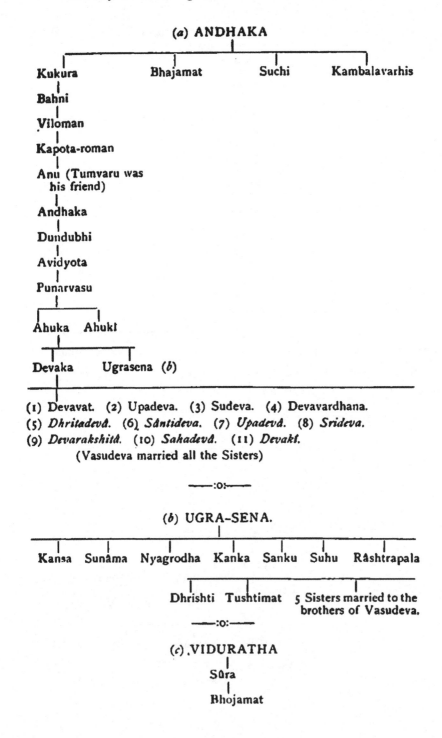

(a) ANDHAKA

Kukura   Bhajamat   Suchi   Kambalavarhis

Kukura
|
Bahni
|
Viloman
|
Kapota-roman
|
Anu (Tumvaru was his friend)
|
Andhaka
|
Dundubhi
|
Avidyota
|
Punarvasu
|
Ahuka   Ahukl
|
Devaka   Ugrasena (b)

(1) Devavat. (2) Upadeva. (3) Sudeva. (4) Devavardhana.
(5) *Dhritadevâ.* (6) *Sântideva.* (7) *Upadevâ.* (8) *Srideva.*
(9) *Devarakshitâ.* (10) *Sahadevâ.* (11) *Devakî.*
(Vasudeva married all the Sisters)

——:o:——

(b) UGRA-SENA.

Kansa   Sunâma   Nyagrodha   Kanka   Sanku   Suhu   Râshtrapala

Dhrishti   Tushtimat   5 Sisters married to the brothers of Vasudeva.

——:o:——

(c) VIDURATHA
|
Sûra
|
Bhojamat

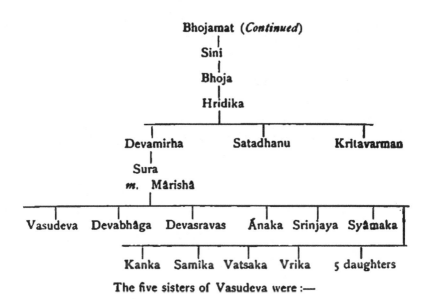

Bhojamat (*Continued*)

Sini

Bhoja

Hridika

Devamirha   Satadhanu   Kritavarman

Sura
m. Mârishâ

Vasudeva   Devabhâga   Devasravas   Ánaka   Srinjaya   Syâmaka

Kanka   Samika   Vatsaka   Vrika   5 daughters

The five sisters of Vasudeva were :—

(1) *Prithâ*, married to Pându

(2) *Srutadeva*, married to Vriddha Sarman
Dantavâkra

(3) *Sruta Kîrti*, married to Dhrishtaketu

Santardan   4 sons

(4) *Sruta Sravas*, married to Damaghosha of Chedi

Sisupâla

(5) *Râjâdhidevi*, married to Jayasena

Vinda   Anuvinda

The five sisters of Kansa were married to the 5 brothers of Vasudeva. They were :—

(1) *Kansâ*, married to Devabhâga.

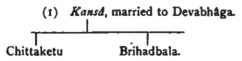

Chittaketu   Brihadbala.

(2) *Kansavatî*, married to Deva Sravas.

Suvira   Ishumat

(3) *Kankâ*, married to Kanka.

Vaka   Satyajit   Purujit.

(4) *Râshtrapâlî*, married to Srinjaya.

Vrisha Durmarshana Others.

(5) *Sûrabhûmi*, married to Syâmaka.

Harikesa   Hiranyâksha.

As to the other brothers of Vasudeva, Vatsaka had by Apsaras—Misrakesi, Vrika and other sons.

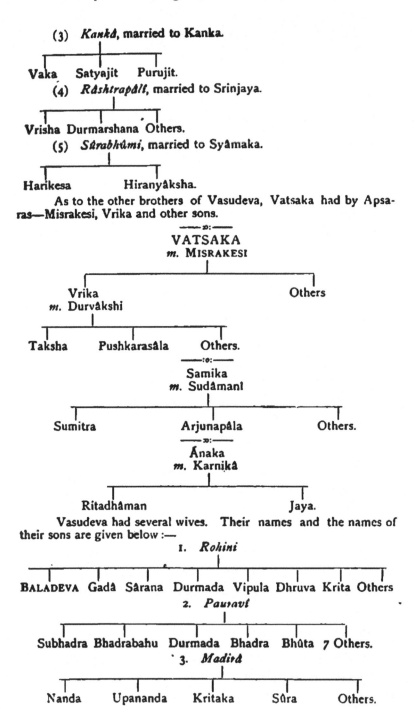

VATSAKA
m. MISRAKESI

Vrika   Others
m. Durvâkshi

Taksha   Pushkarasâla   Others.

Samika
m. Sudâmanî

Sumitra   Arjunapâla   Others.

Ânaka
m. Karnikâ

Ritadhâman   Jaya.

Vasudeva had several wives. Their names and the names of their sons are given below :—

1. *Rohini*

BALADEVA Gadâ Sârana Durmada Vipula Dhruva Krita Others

2. *Pauravî*

Subhadra Bhadrabahu Durmada Bhadra Bhûta 7 Others.

3. *Madirâ*

Nanda   Upananda   Kritaka   Sûra   Others.

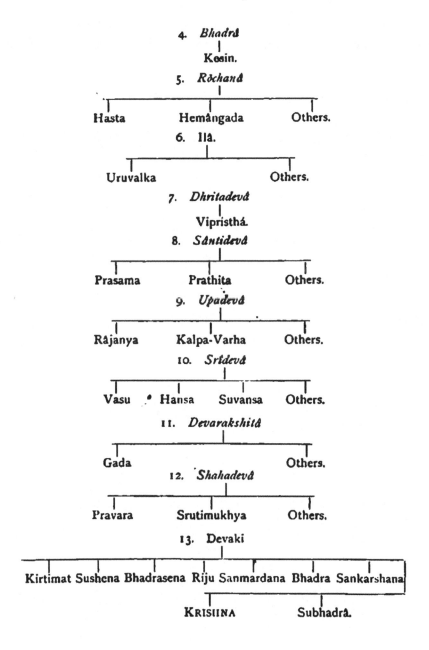

4. *Bhadrá*
|
Kesin.

5. *Róchaná*
|

Hasta — Hemángada — Others.

6. Ilá.
|

Uruvalka — Others.

7. *Dhritadevá*
|
Vipristhá.

8. *Sántidevá*
|

Prasama — Prathita — Others.

9. *Upadevá*
|

Rájanya — Kalpa-Varha — Others.

10. *Srídevá*
|

Vasu — Hansa — Suvansa — Others.

11. *Devarakshitá*
|

Gada — Others.

12. *Shahadevá*
|

Pravara — Srutimukhya — Others.

13. Devaki
|

Kirtimat Sushena Bhadrasena Riju Sanmardana Bhadra Sankarshana

KRISHNA — Subhadrá.

With the birth of Sri Krishna, we come to the end of the Ninth Skandha of the Bhāgavata Purāna. But for the completion of the racial account, we give here only the 1st. Chapter of the 12th. Skandha.

SKANDHA XII. CHAP. 1.

We have seen Ripunjaya to be the last of the Magadha kings. He will be also called Puranjaya (The future tense, it must be remembered, is used solely with reference to the time of Parikshit). His minister Sunaka shall kill him and place his own son Pradyōta on the throne.

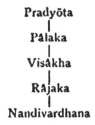

Pradyōta

Pâlaka

Visâkha

Râjaka

Nandivardhana

These 5 kings of the line of Pradyota shall reign for 138 years.

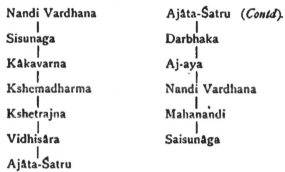

Nandi Vardhana	Ajâta-Satru (*Contd*)
Sisunaga	Darbhaka
Kâkavarna	Aj-aya
Kshemadharma	Nandi Vardhana
Kshetrajna	Mahanandi
Vidhisâra	Saisunâga
Ajâta-Satru	

These ten shall reign for 360 years—Mahânandi shall have a son, Nanda, by a Sudra woman. He shall be the next king. One Brâhmana Chânakya shall kill Nanda and his eight sons and shall place Chandra Gupta on the throne.

Chandra Gupta — Vârisâra — Asokavardhana — Suyasas — Dasaratha — Sangata — Salisuka — Soma-Sarman — Satadhanvan — Brihadratha

These ten kings called Mauryas shall reign for 137 years. Pushpamitra, Commander of Brihadratha's forces, shall kill his master and be king himself. He shall be the founder of the Sunga dynasty.

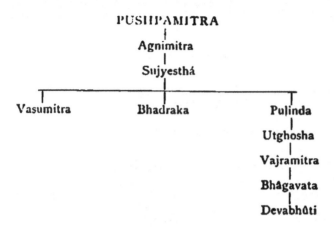

PUSHPAMITRA
|
Agnimitra
|
Sujyesthá

Vasumitra — Bhadraka — Pulinda
|
Utghosha
|
Vajramitra
|
Bhágavata
|
Devabhûti

These (10) ten kings of the Sunga dynasty shall reign for 112 years. Vasudeva, the minister of Devabhûti, shall kill his master and become himself the king.

VASUDEVA
|
Bhûmitra
|
Nárâyana
|
Susarman

These four kings shall be called Kânvas. They shall reign for 345 years. Susarman shall be killed by his servant Balin, a Sudra of the Andhra clan, who shall himself usurp the throne. Balin shall be succeeded by his brother.

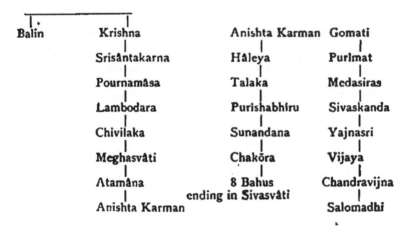

Balin	Krishna	Anishta Karman	Gomati
	Srisântakarna	Hâleya	Purlmat
	Pournamâsa	Talaka	Medasiras
	Lambodara	Purishabhîru	Sivaskanda
	Chivilaka	Sunandana	Yajnasri
	Meghasvâti	Chakôra	Vijaya
	Atamâna	8 Bahus	Chandravijna
	Anishta Karman	ending in Sivasvâti	Salomadhi

These thirty kings of the Andhra dynasty shall rule the earth for 456 years. Seven Ābhiras, kings of Avabhriti, ten Gardabhins (men of Gardabha) and sixteen Kankas shall then be the rulers. They shall be followed by 8 Yavanas, 14 Turushkas and ten Surundas. These 65 kings shall reign for one thousand and ninety nine years. Eleven Moulas shall then be the kings for 300 years.

Bhuta-Nanda, Bangiri, Sisunandi and Yaso-Nandi shall then become kings. Their sons, all known as Bāhlikas, shall succeed them. Then Pushpamitra shall be the king, then his son Durmitra. Seven Andhras, seven Kosalas, Vidurapatis and Nishadhas shall then become kings, at one and the same time, over the lands of these names. They shall be the descendants of the Bāhlikas.

Visvasphūrji, otherwise called Puranjaya, shall be the king of the Magadhas. He shall make havoc of the caste system. His chief town shall be Padmavati (Modern Patna) but his kingdom shall extend from Hardwar to Pryag.

Then there shall be Sūdra and Mlechcha kings.

THOUGHTS ON THE VAIVASVATA MANVANTARA.

The study of the Vaivasvata Manvantara can be pursued, as to minor details, from more than one stand-point. But I am at present concerned with only the broad outlines of its esoteric aspect.

We are to understand, in the first place, that there are certain types of human races in this as in other Manvantaras. Each of these types has a history of its own. Each has its stages of growth, rise and decline, and some have their periods of revival in this Manvantara as well. Each racial type has to be studied separately.

The connection of the races with the Sun and the Moon requires a little consideration.

Those who are acquainted with Hindu astrology know that the life time of a man is divided into certain divisions, each division being under the influence of one planet. Each planetary period again has its sub-divisions, in each of which there is a secondary run of the planets.

According to the Bengal School, the main planetary run takes 108 years for its completion, and according to another school, it takes 120 years.

The following is the order of planetary succession according to the second school, which prevails all over India, except in Bengal: —

Sun 6 years, Moon 10, Mars 7, Rāhu 18, Brihaspati 16, Saturn 19, Mercury 17, Ketu 7 and Venus 20. Thus if a man lives for 120 years, all the planets will in turn have influenced his life in the above order, commencing from the planet of his birth. Again there will be corresponding sub-runs of all the planets during each planetary run. The races are also governed by such planetary influences.

The Solar Dynasty means that the particular type of humanity so denoted was born under the influence of the solar planet. When all the planets have in turn exercised their influence over this Dynasty, it disappears for a time and is re-born under the influence of the Sun.

Similarly there will be a revival of the Lunar dynasty — that which commenced under the influence of the Moon.

The law of planetary influence over the human races is not as clearly known as that over individual men. Otherwise the future history of each race would not be the sealed book to us which it is.

The humanity of the present Manvantara was first born under the influence of the Solar Planet. Our Moon is the son of the Sun-God.

The races that first appeared were called Solar races.

Other races appeared under the influence of the Moon. In these races we find first the influence of Brihaspati or Jupiter, through his wife Tāra, then of Budha or Mercury, and lastly of Sukra or Venus, through his daughter Devayāni.

This planetary succession may be only a Sub-run of the planets. We read, in the account of the previous Manvantaras, of the appearance of Sukra as the guide of the Daityas, and of Brihaspati as the guide of the Devas. We have also read of the appearance of Rāhu in the sixth Manvantara. This shews that the main planetary round has to be found in the Kalpa itself.

Our knowledge on the whole subject is however so poor that it is unsafe to make any distinct suggestion.

Now we shall take the Solar Races, or the sons of Vaivasvat Manu, in order of their treatment in the text. *Prishadhta* and *Kavi* were the first spiritual races. They did not marry *i.e.* there was no sexual reproduction among them.

Next in order was the *Kārusha* race inhabiting the north.

The *Dhārshtas* were also a spiritual race (Brāhmanas).

The descent towards Materiality commenced with Nriga. He is said to have been transformed into a lizard. His grandson was *Bhūtajyotī*, Bhūtas being different forms of matter. *Vasu* is a God of Material wealth. *Pratīka* means the reverse or opposite (*i.e.* the reverse of spirit.) *Ogha* means a current. The current of materialism set in with the line of Nriga.

The next line, that of Narishyanta, shews further materiality. Midhvat is that which wets (the root *mih* means to pass water). *Viti* is production, enjoyments. Vitihotra is the name of a sacrificial fire. *Agnivesya* is an incarnation of Agni or the Fire-God, but he is nick-named Kānina or son of an unmarried woman and also *Jātukarna* (the name of a Vedic Rishi). There seems to have been sexual procreation in this line. The incarnation of Agni further indicates that the present human form was complete, for Agni is the form-giving energy in Nature.

In the next line of *Dishta* we have *Vatsapriti* or affection for children, *Pransu* or tall, *Pramati* or full-grown intellect, *Khanitra* or digger,

Chākshusha or the eyed, and*Khaninetra* or the hollow-eyed. This line represents the race of the earliest diggers, very tall, with the hollow eye predominant in them as a characteristic feature; this race was very powerful and capable of direct communion with the Devas, and the gods acted as waiters in the Yajna of Marutta.

The line of Saryāti refers to Ānarta and a town named Kusasthalī, built in the midst of the Sea. Evidently the continent on which the race flourished is now under water. Ānarta is supposed to be Sourāshtra (modern Surat.) But the site of Kusasthalī cannot be ascertained. There were remnants of this race till the time of Krishna, for Balarām married Revati, the daughter of Kakudmin (hump-backed). The line of Nabhaga is a short one and it merged itself into that of Angiras who was the father of Brihaspati or Jupiter. Ambarisha is the prominent figure of this period.

Then we come to the line of *Ikshvāku*. This is the best known line of the Solar races. It flourished during the last Tretayuga. *Ikshvāku* is called the eldest son of Manu. Perhaps this has reference to the appearance of the Race in the previous Manvantaras.

The eldest son of Ikshvāku is Vikukshi (*Kukshi* is womb.) He is also called Sasada or the Rabbit-eater. The Moon is called Rabbit-marked.

Puranjaya is the son of Vikukshi. He is called Indra-Vāha or Indra-Vehicled. Several of the kings of this dynasty befriended the Devas of Svar Loka.

Further down we find King *Purukutsa* forming an alliance with the elemental serpents, and holding communion with the dwellers of Rasātala. The river Narvadā is mentioned in connection with Rasātala.

Māndhātā is a traditional name that has been preserved upto this time in common parlance in the saying "As old as king Māndhātā." The line of Māndhātā was divided into three different branches. *Muchukunda* represented a branch of Yogins. The long, unbroken sleep of Muchukunda is traditional and he is credited also with Yogic powers. Another branch that of Ambarisha, Youvanāsva and Hārita represented a spiritual sub-race. But we have to follow the history of the Atlanteans through Purukutsa. The connection with Rasātala, or the plane of Material ascendancy, affected the destiny of this line. In Trisanku, the aspiration ran very high. He became a Deva, but had his head turned downwards, *i.e.* turned towards materiality. With the powers of a Deva, but with the aspirations of an Asura, the ground was prepared for the downfall of this line. For a time, however, the Race flourished in all its materiality. The alliance between Devas and men became cemented by the performance of Vedic sacrifices. This was the first spiritual advance of the human race, through the temptations of Svarga life.

The time of Haris Chandra is the Vedic era, when the earliest Riks of what we know as Rigveda were composed. Visvāmitra and his disciples were the Vedic Rishis of this age. The Vedas tried to curb the riotous course of materiality by prescribing a number of restrictions on the enjoyment of material desires. Elaborate rules were laid down as to how the desires might be best gratified for a prolonged period in Svargaloka, by the performance of sacrifices or Yajna. The whole of the life of the regenerate classes was regulated by rigid laws and a glowing picture was given of life in Svarga after death. The sacred injunctions were not, however, potent enough to check the Kāmic tendencies of the race and the cyclic law which now required the spiritual evolution of humanity was continually disregarded by the race. This was poison (*gara*) to the system of humanity and king Sagar imbibed this poison. Hence he was called the Poisoned. He had two wives. The sons of one wife were 60 thousand in number. They offended Kapila, an Incarnation of Vishnu, and thus were all consumed. They reached the limit of material degradation, where final extinction awaited the race. The number 60,000 is suggestive.

The extinction of Sagara's sons was attended with great changes on the earth's surface. It is said they dug the earth and made the seas in their search for the sacrificial horse. Hence the sea is called Sāgara. This may refer to the sinking down of Atlantis when a large portion of that great continent became a sea-bed. There was a corresponding upheaval of land and the Himalayan chain reared up its head, as we can easily infer from the first appearance of the Ganges. The first flow of Gangā indicated a many sided revolution in the appearance of the earth's surface. A new continent was formed to which India was attached as the prominent link. Spiritual sub-races grew up on the banks of the sacred river who more than atoned for the sins of their fathers. The fore-runner of the race of spirituality was Asamanjas (rising above the ordinary run). He was a Yogin not led away by the material tendencies of the age. His son was Ansumat (having the ray or light in him). Ansumat pacified Kapila.

Gangā is said to be a spiritual stream flowing from the feet of Vishnu. With the advent of this stream, the spiritual rebirth of humanity commenced in right earnest, for the remaining period of the Kalpa. Already the path had been paved by the Karmakānda of the Vedas, which put restrictions on the wanton and reckless performance of Karma or action. The pure magnetism of the holy river helped on the process of regeneration. But this was not in itself sufficient to cope with the forces of materiality. Accordingly we see*Kalmasha* or sin appearing in the line of Bhagiratha. King Kalmashapāda became a Rākshasa. A Rākshasa is an elemental of destruction. When mind becomes too much identified with the gross body and its desires, its connection with the Higher Self is liable to be cut off by the action of the Rākshasas. These forces of Tamas act in different ways to serve different purposes in the economy of the Universe. When the material downfall of man reaches its furthest limit in the Kalpa, the Rākshasas become Tāmasic forces in man and he is unconscious of his higher nature. That sleep in time becomes a permanent sleep, and the lower man becomes dead to his real Self. This is the real death of man, when the ray sent forth by Īshvara comes back to Him, without any spiritual harvest, and what constituted the personality of man dissolves into the Material Universe.

The time had come when a fresh departure was necessary in the methods pursued by the Lilā Avatāras for the spiritual regeneration of the Universe. They had now to appear amongst men, as ordinary beings, to give direct teachings to their votaries, to infuse as much Satva as possible into humanity and to retard by all means the further extinction of the human race.

For a time the Rākshasas reigned supreme, but not over the new continent, permeated as it was by the sacred waters of the Ganges. Their stronghold was Lankā, the remnant of the Atlantean continent. Following the descent of Gangā therefore, Vishnu incarnated himself as Rāma, one of the greatest of his manifestations. The Rākshasas of Lankā were killed. Vibhishana only survived, but he was allied to Rāma and so became immortal in spirituality. The Rākshasa survives in us but its energy of dissolution does not militate against the evolution of man. It was Rāma who first gave the idea of Īshvara to the degraded human races of the present Manvantara. They knew, for the first time, that there was one greater than all the Devas — the Gods of the Vedas — and that there were planes higher than even Svarga. The path of devotion was proclaimed. And it became possible for men to cross the limits of death and of Trilokī by this quality. The downfall was stopped no doubt; but the ascent was only permanently secured by Lord Sri Krishna as we shall see later on.

After Rāma, there is little of interest in the line of Ikshvāku. The decline commenced and the line became extinct with Sumitra, but it is said one king Maru of this line became an adept in Yoga and retired to Kalapa, where he bides his time to revive the solar dynasty towards the end of the Kaliyuga. We may take him to be the originator of another race which will be the re-incarnation of the Ikshvāku race.

We have considered the line of Ikshvāku's descendants through Purukutsa. There is another line of his descendants through Nimisha. Then we come to the Lunar Dynasty.

The Lunar races first appeared while the descendants of Ikshvāku were still flourishing, though on the eve of their decline. They had immense possibilities of spiritual evolution, and the great Aryan race seems to be connected with them. The appearance of these races is almost simultaneous with the first flow of the Ganges. For we find Jahnu, who swallowed up the Ganges in her first terrestrial course, is only sixth in the line of descent from Pururavas.

The Lunar dynasty originated in the union of Tārā, the female principle of Brihaspati (Jupiter), and the Moon. The issue was Budha (Mercury), the direct progenitor of the Lunar dynasty.

The son of Budha was Pururavas. He married Urvasi, the renowned Deva nymph.

Pururavas had six sons. But we are concerned with only two of them, Āyus and Vijaya.

Vijaya gave the Adept line of the race and Āyus, the ordinary humanity.

In the line of Vijaya, we find Jahnu, purified by the assimilation of Gaṅgā, Visvāmitra, pre-eminently the Rishi of the Rig Veda and one of the seven sages who watch over the destiny of the present Manvantara, Jamadagni, another of the seven sages of our Manvantara and Parasurāma one of the coming sages of the next Manvantara. We have already mentioned the part taken by Visvāmitra and his sons in the composition of the Vedic Mantras.

Coming to the line of Āyus, we recognise the forefathers of the Aryan races.

In the short-lived branch through Kshatra-vriddha, we find the Vedic Rishi Gritsamada, his son Sūnaka, the renowned Sounaka, Dirghatamas and Dhanvantari, the promulgator of Āyur-veda.

But the longest history of the Race is through the descendants of Yayāti.

King Yayāti married Devayāni, the daughter of Sukra, the presiding Rishi of the planet Venus, and had by her two sons, Yadu and Turvasu. Sukra is the son of Bhrigu, the Rishi of Mahar Loka. Devayāna, is the path leading beyond Trilokī, after death.

But the King had also connection with a Dānava girl, who brought forth three sons, Druhyu, Anu and Puru. For his Dānava connection, King Yayāti had in youth to undergo the infirmities of age. This evil was transmitted to Puru, the youngest son of the Dānava girl.

The line of Puru was short-lived. But it is this line that gave some of the renowned Vedic Rishis, viz. Apratiratha, Kanva, Medhātithi and Praskanva. Dushmanta, the hero of Kalidasa's renowned drama also came of this line. Vishnu incarnated in part as Bharata, son of Dushmanta.

Then there was a revolution. Bharata found that his sons were not like unto himself. So the direct line of Puru came to an end. What followed is a little mysterious. Bharata adopted Bharadvāja as his son. Bharadvāja was begotten by Brihaspati (Jupiter) on the wife of his brother Utathya named Mamatā (Egoism).

Bharadvāja is one of the seven presiding Rishis of the present Manvantara. His name is connected with several Mantras of the Rig Veda.

The great actors in the Kurukshetra battle were the descendants of Bharadvāja. We find much diversity of spiritual characteristics among them. The material and spiritual forces were gathered together, in all possible grades from the Pāndavas downward to the sons of Dhrita-rāshtra and their allies. The poetical genius of the author of the Mahābhārata has called forth characters in the Drama of the Kurukshetra battle, that stand out in all the details of real life and find a permanent place in the genealogy of the Lunar dynasty. The study of the racial account of the line of Bharadvāja becomes therefore extremely difficult.

The Lunar dynasty will be revived by Devāpi, a descendant of Bharadvāja, who is biding his time at Kalāpa.

The early inhabitants of Bengal, Behar and Urishyā were the sons of Anu, the second son of Sarmisthā. The famous Kāma, one of the heroes of Kurukshetra, also belonged to this line.

The eldest son of Sarmisthā by Yayāti was Druhyu. Prachetas of this line had one hundred sons, who inhabited the north as Mlechha races.

But the greatest interest attaches to the line of Yadu, the eldest son of Yayāti by Devayāni. The early descendants of this line were the Haihayas, killed by Parasurāma, and the Tālajanghas, killed by Sagar — both of the Solar Dynasty. The Mahābhārata has given an importance to the overthrow of these early Yadu classes as a victory of the Brāhmanas over the Kshatriyas. Next to the Brāhmanas in intelligence were the Kshatriyas. They eagerly accepted the teachings of Rāma, who incarnated as one of them. They knew Īshvara as higher than the Devas and the Brāhmanas. They thought they could profitably employ their time in seeking after the knowledge of Brahmān. This necessarily offended the orthodox Brāhmanas, who performed the Vedic sacrifices and had no higher ambition than to resort to Devaloka. The Kshatriyas thus represented a religious evolution, of which the Upanishads were an outcome. In time, some Brāhmanas even became disciples of Kshatriyas. Both Rāma and Krishna incarnated themselves as Kshatriyas. We are to understand that by Kshatriyas, during this period of Puranic history, is meant seceders from Vedic Karma Kānda more or less.

The early seceders, the Haihayas and Tālajanghas were put down by the Brāhmana Parasurāma and by the Kshatriya King Sagar, who espoused the cause of Vedic Karma Kānda and of the Brāhmanas, represented by Rishi Aurva of this time.

Parasurāma did not like any meddling with Vedic Karma Kānda by persons not perfected in wisdom. Even Rāma had to respect the Vedic Rishis and had to protect them in the performance of Vedic sacrifices from the attacks of Asuras and Rākshasas. When Lord Krishna appeared on the scene, the Asuras still survived; the Vedic Rishis denied offerings to Him, Vedic Karma had a strong supporter in Jarāsandha, there was hypocrisy in the name of religion, and there were pretensions in various forms. On the other hand great improvements had been made in the proper understanding of the realities of life and of the laws of nature. Intellect overflowed in many channels of thought, and the religious nature of man found vent in all directions from atheism to religious devotion.

Leaving this general resumè, we may now enter upon a closer study of the history of religious movements in our present Manvantara, so that we may understand the great work done by Lord Sri Krishna. The races live as individuals live. However developed an individual may be, when he is re-born after death, he first becomes a child as any other child. There is much of spiritual life in the child, and sometimes pictures of heavenly life are presented to his spiritual vision, which are denied to to the grown-up man. The child begins his life when he is grown up, and then his individual characteristics soon manifest themselves. We do not read much of the man in the child. Hence the history of the early spiritual races, who were infants in the racial life, does not teach us anything. We find some of them had communion with the Devas of Svarga Loka, but that is more on account of their infant spirituality than any thing else.

When the races developed in time, they became most intellectual as well as most material at the same time. Manvantara after Manvantara was taken up in developing the physiological (Pranic) activities, the sense (Indriya) activities, and then the lower mental activities of the Jivas. The personal man was fully developed in the sixth Manvantara and the great churning only opened the door for another line of development. The possibility of spiritual activity was secured to men by Kūrma.

When the races of the Sixth Manvantara therefore became reborn in the Seventh Manvantara, they were the most intellectual of all races, but they had also the power given to them of developing spiritual faculties. They could not however shake off the Asuric element all at once. They were extremely fond of material joys, and they devised all means, which human intellect could contrive, of gratifying material desires. That was right which gave material gratification; that was wrong which militated against material enjoyment.

Bhuvar Loka is the plane of animal desires. The human beasts go after death to Bhuvar Loka. They do not possess anything which could take them to Svarga Loka.

The Svarga Loka is for those who develop in themselves the faculty of discriminating between right and wrong, and who do or attempt to do what is right. Far more it is for those who love others and who do good to them. For service and love pertain to planes higher even than Svarga. But in the higher planes, service is unselfish and love is divine. The lower forms of service and love pertain to the plane of Svarga. In Svarga there is selfishness, but it is mixed with spirituality. It is only the good, the virtuous, the devoted that go to the plane of the Devas and there gratify their higher desires to their heart's content. There are divine music, divine beauty, divine objects of gratification in Svarga Loka — allurements enough for a man of desire. And if his merits be great, he enjoys the things of Svarga Loka for an enormously long period.

But a man by bare intellectuality can not cross the threshold of Svarga. The Devas reject the intruder. However much Trisanku might aspire to have the enjoyments of Svarga, and however great his intellect might be, he was not allowed to enter the coveted plane, without the passport of spirituality. Humanity had still to learn the proper means of securing life in Svarga.

Poor and chance spiritual acquisitions give only a passing life in Svarga and that not of a superior character. So all the knowledge as to attaining Svarga life had to be revealed in time.

The Rishis made great efforts to improve humanity by securing for them a prolonged existence in Svarga, most of all Rishi Visvāmitra, one of the seven sages of our Manvantara. Visvāmitra failed in his attempt to send Trisanku to Svarga. He then tried with his son Haris Chandra. It is said he advised the Rājā to make a human sacrifice to Varuna. But we find the victim Sunah-sepha living after the sacrifice, under the name of Deva-rata, or one given up to the gods, and some of the Riks even were revealed to him. Haris Chandra succeeded in entering Svarga. That was a great victory for Rishi Visvāmitra. The Vedas were revealed to the Rishis and sacrifices came to be known.

Nārada also helped the cause in another away. He related the beauty and the virtues of king Purūravas to the Devas in Svarga. Urvasi, the famous Deva nymph, hearing all that, became enamoured of the king. She had then, by the curse of some god, a human form. So she could keep company with the King. The king was enchanted by her beauty. When she left, he followed her advice and pleased the Gandharvas. The Gandharvas gave him the fire, with which the king could perform sacrifice. The fire became threefold. With one he could perform his duties to the Devas and go to Svarga Loka. With another, he could perform his duties to the Pitris. With the third fire, he could perform the duties of a house-holder. Thus sacrifices meant duties. And it is by the performance of duties that men can perform Vedic sacrifices and go to Svarga Loka.

The Vedas laid down injunctions and prohibitions. They regulated the actions of men, propelled by Kāma or desire. Men must eat meat. The Vedas said this meat was prohibited, but that could be used. Men mixed with women. The Vedas laid down restrictions. Even they regulated the relations between man and wife. Then the Vedas laid down the duties which men owed to all classes of beings. In order to induce men to accept the Vedic injunctions, the Vedas held out Svarga as the reward of Vedic

Karma. They even favoured the belief, that there was to be immortal life in Svarga gained by the performance of Vedic Karma. Detailed rules as to the performance of Vedic sacrifices were given. So long as men did not aspire to become Indra, or the ruler of Svarga, the Devas were pleased with the sacrifices; they helped the performer as much as they could, giving them all objects of desire, and they welcomed them to Svarga, when they passed to that plane after death. The Devas were as friendly to the performer of Vedic Karma as they were unfriendly to the immature Trisanku.

The Vedic Karma Kānda became thus fully revealed. The revelation was made in the last Treta-yuga of the present Manvantara. "At the beginning of the Treta Yuga, the three Vedas were revealed through Pururavas." IX. 14-49. "The path of Karma was promulgated in Treta Yuga, by the division of the Vedas." *Śridhara*.

The great churning was justified. The Devas asserted themselves for the good of humanity. The Rishis got the revelation and helped men to place themselves in active relationship with the Devas. Men learned to regulate themselves and to give up the wantonness of material life. And they had a strong inducement to do so in the prospect of eternal life in Svarga. The great actor in this Vedic movement was Rishi Visvāmitra, (Hallowed be his name!) Others followed him in quick succession, and there was a brilliant combination of Vedic Rishis who propounded the whole of the Karma Kānda of the Vedas, as it was revealed to them by the force of Kālpic necessity.

At all times there have been two parties, one following the current of evolution, and another going against it. At all times there have been cavillers and sceptics.

The Haihayas and Tālajanghas were confirmed materialists and great sinners. They ridiculed the Brāhmanas, who performed Vedic Karma, and often set themselves in opposition to them. They were very troublesome to the Brāhmanas. King Sagar wanted to extinguish the race, but he was prevented from doing so. Possibly Atlantis was the country inhabited by these races and Nature helped the cause of evolution by dragging down the continent itself under water. The sacred Gangā also flowed at this time, spreading purity over all lands lying on her banks.

The Haihayas however still flourished; and they had a great leader in Kārta-Viryārjuna. Then came one of the great Avatāras, Parasurāma. He extirpated the Haihaya Kshatriyas, and went on killing the Kshatriyas till Rāma appeared, and it was then that he thought his mission was over.

If there were some Kshatriyas who disregarded the Vedas, there were others who found transitoriness, even in Svarga Loka, and honestly thought that the complete wisdom was not to be found in the Karma Kānda. They were for further revelations At first, the Brāhmanas did not look with favour upon these Kshatriyas. But when it was found that the Kshatriyas got real light, they were soon joined by the Brāhmanas. The foremost of these Kshatriyas was Janaka, and the foremost of the Brāhmanas was Yājnavalkya. The further revelations were called the Upanishads.

King Janaka found Sitā, the consort of Rāma, at the end of his plough. Yājnavalkya defeated all the Brāhmanas of his time in discussions held at the court of king Janaka.

When Rāma incarnated, there existed the people of Lankā, a remnant of the Atlantean continent, who had inherited a mighty material civilisation, but who were called Rākshasas, on account of their gross iniquities. They reached the last point of material downfall, and lost all spirituality. They were called Rākshasas as final extinction was their lot, and as the force of dissolution was strong in them.

Then there were the regenerate classes, who performed Vedic sacrifices. There were a few again, who accepted the Upanishads as a teaching, but they could not boldly declare themselves against the performance of sacrifices.

Rāma finally did away with the Rākshasas. The bard who sang his glory, the great Vālmiki, thus began his lay: — "O Killer of birds, thou shalt not live for ever, as of the pair of storks thou hast killed the male, so passionately attached to his consort." Verily the Purusha in us, the ray of the supreme Purusha, becomes passionately attached to the element of Prakriti in us, so that we may acquire spiritual experiences through the body. And it is a cruel act to separate our Prākritic individualities completely from him by turning ourselves persistently away from the

Purusha. But when Rāma became an Avatāra, the fate of the separator was sealed.

When the Rākshasas were killed, the Rishis were left free to perform the Vedic sacrifices.

Rāma did something more. He married the daughter of Janaka, and by this act openly espoused the cause of the Upanishads.

Lastly Rāma offered Himself as an object of worship. This was the beginning of Vishnu worship, which makes no distinction between classes and castes. Rāma openly made friendship with Guhaka, belonging to the lowest class, whom it was an abomination to touch, for Guhaka was devotedly attached to Him, as an Incarnation of Vishnu.

The world admired Rāma. No man could reach such eminence. He must be something more than a man. In time men accepted him as an Avatāra. At any rate, he was an example to others in every respect. The ethical standard he laid down in his own life was unimpeachable. The world had never seen such sacrifices in the performance of the duties of life. A model king, a model son, a model husband, a model brother, a model warrior, a model friend, the model of models, Rāma left an indelible mark as a religious and moral teacher, on the age in which he lived, and on all succeeding ages.

The example was not lost on the world. The many-sided picture, that Rāma presented, produced a spirit of enquiry, which has never been rivalled in this Kalpa. Men thought on different lines. They studied the Upanishads, which had been favoured by Rāma. They could not forget also that Rāma taught salvation for the performers of Vedic sacrifices. Then there was the teaching of his own life. The light was manifold. Independent schools of thought grew up, notably the six schools of philosophy. Each school tried to find its authority in the Upanishads and the divine scriptures supplied texts enough for all the schools. Every school found a part of the truth but not the whole truth. Yet each school regarded its own part as the whole. So they quarrelled. The Mimānsākas said that the performance of Vedic sacrifices was all in all. It had the sanction of time-honored texts and of the most ancient Rishis. And Jaimini supplied the reasoning by which the practice could be supported. The Sānkhyas said that the chief duty of a man was to discriminate between the transformable and the non-transformable element in him, and when that was done, nothing more was needed. The followers of Patanjali said that mere discrimination was not sufficient, but a continued practice was required. The Vaiseshikas studied the attributes and properties of all objects and sought by differentiation to know the truths. There were others who worshipped the Bhūtas, Pretas and Pisachas, so that they might easily acquire powers. Others worshipped the dwellers of Svarga Loka. Some worshipped Īshvara. But mostly the worship of Śiva was prevalent. Gifts and charities also were not unknown, in fact they were very extensive in some instances. But generally the object of all religious observances was self-seeking more or less.

Amidst this diversity of religious ideas and religious observances, seemingly so contradictory, Sri Krishna, the greatest of all Avatāras, appeared and He brought the message of peace and reconciliation. He laid great stress on the fact that the performance of Vedic sacrifices could lead us only to Svarga Loka, but when our merits were exhausted, we were bound to be born again on Bhūr Loka, our Earth. While on Earth, we form fresh Karma, which gives rise to other births. The performance of Vedic Karma does not therefore free us from the bondage of births, for, as the Lord said, there is object-seeking in these performances. Object-seeking for one's own self does not find a place in the higher Lokas. Its highest limit is Svarga Loka. So long as man remains self-seeking, he can not transcend the limits of Trilokī. In the higher Lokas, there is no recurrence of births and re-births. Once you are translated to Mahar Loka, you live for the whole of the remaining period of the Kalpa, passing through a gradual evolution to the higher Lokas. And if you form a devotional tie with the Lord of many Brahmāndas, the First Purusha, even the Kālpic period does not restrict your existence. Liberation is a relative term. It may be from the bondage of births and re-births in Trilokī. It may be liberation from the bondage of Bvahmandas or solar systems. Those who worship only material objects remain chained to this earth. Those who worship the dwellers of Bhuvar Loka (Bhūtas, Pretas, Pisachas and Pitris) or cultivate aspiration for them become allied to them and they pass only to Bhuvar Loka after death. Those who worship the Devas and cultivate this aspiration go to Svarga Loka after death. Those who worship Hiranya-garbha go up to Satya or Brahmā Loka. Those who worship the Lord of all Brahmāndas pass beyond even the Brahmānda.

The first thing that a man should do is to transcend the limits of Trilokī. This he cannot do as long as he is self-seeking. He should therefore perform his actions *unselfishly*. And the Lord said as follows: —

1. There is the perishable and the imperishable element in us. Karma or actions appertain to the perishable element. The perishable element constantly changes, so it cannot be our real self or Ātmā. From the standpoint of our real self, we can dissociate ourselves from our actions, which relate to our transitory nature. Here the system of Sānkhya came into requisition.

2. But by this discrimination, we can not forcibly stop the performance of actions. For the actions are propelled by (*a*) active tendencies which form an inseparable part of our present nature, and (*b*) by the necessity of our very existence. So by stopping actions, we force the tendencies to mental channels, and cause more mischief by producing mental germs for the future. And we cannot stop all actions, as some are necessary for our bare existence.

3. Therefore we are to perform actions, and we can perform them unselfishly, if they are done from a pure sense of duty. We are to take duty as a law of our very existence. *Yajna* is only another name for this law. The Lord of beings, having created all beings with the Yajna, said of yore, — "You shall prosper by the performance of this Yajna and this Yajna shall be the producer of all desired objects for you." Yajna consists of mutual sacrifices, as all beings are dependent on one another. "Think of the Devas by means of Yajna, and the Devas shall think of you." All our actions may be classed under duties — duties which we owe to the Devas, the Pitris, the sages, the animals and to other men. If we perform our Karma for the sake of Yajna only, we perform it unselfishly.

4. As discrimination is useful in realising the real self, so restraint is necessary to put down the acquired self. The tendencies of the acquired self, if left to themselves, prompt men to ever recurring actions, which again produce their own effects, some of which develop into fresh

tendencies or strengthen the pre-existing tendencies. So restraint is to be constantly practised. The object of restraint is to free the mind from thoughts of the object world and to fix it on the real self, Ātmā. Here the system of Patanjali comes into requisition. But the system is to be accepted with this reservation that Yoga does not necessarily mean renunciation of Karma. It includes the unselfish performance of Karma and, for the average humanity, renunciation of Karma is harmful as an expedient of Yoga. Though there may be some who do not require Karma for themselves, yet they should not renounce it, if they want to set an example to others and not to confound their intellect.

5. But the Pūrva Mimānsākas say: Vedic Karma is all in all, and the authority of the Vedas is supreme. Here Sri Krishna had to assert Himself as an Avatāra, and He asked people to accept His own authority. He said there was self-seeking in Vedic Karma, and one could not therefore avoid the recurrence of births by the performance of Vedic Karma. So Sri Krishna said to Uddhava: — "If the Vedas say that men attain Svarga by the performance of Vedic Karma, it is simply by way of inducement, and not as pointing out the supreme end. The father says; 'Boy, eat this bitter medicine and I will give thee this cake in my hand.' The boy takes the medicine for the sweet thing. But that really leads to his recovery from the disease. So the Vedas mean final liberation as the end. But to enforce restraint, they hold out the prospect of Svarga, which is most agreeable to men." (Elaboration of XI. 21. 23.)

Many were unwilling to accept the authority of Sri Krishna, and the chief amongst them was Sisupāla.

This was the teaching of Karma Yoga by Sri Krishna. But the unselfish performance of Karma is not all. It is only a negative virtue. It purifies the mind and frees it from the taint of selfishness. The mind then becomes prepared for the higher planes and becomes fit for the direct influence of Īshvara.

So Sri Krishna gave to His disciples the true conception of Īshvara. He told them Īshvara was One, the source of all existence, all knowledge and all bliss. He told them how one Īshvara pervaded the whole universe and became thus manifested through the Universe. He also pervaded all beings, and became manifested through these beings. The Universe and the Jiva were His Prakritis or bodies as it were. The Universe body was eight-fold in its character, beginning with that most susceptible to His influence and ending with the division most obtuse to that influence. This eight-fold Prakriti also entered into the constitution of Jiva. But there was something more in Jiva, — the consciousness, the knower. This element was Īshvara Himself, as limited by Jiva Prakriti, or Jiva body. The whole universe being the body of Īshvara, His knowledge and powers were unrestricted, whereas the body of the Jiva, being limited and restricted, his powers and knowledge were also restricted.

This highest conception of Īshvara is not adapted for all. So Sri Krishna gave the conception of Īshvara, as manifested by His powers, and as manifested in Time and Space, and lastly as He is manifested in the human body with four hands and the Crown, symbolising His lordship over the whole Universe.

But this conception of Īshvara is not enough. As man owes a duty to all beings, the performance of which is Karma, so he owes a duty to Īshvara, and that duty is Upāsanā. All beings make sacrifices for one another, and so they owe duty to one another. But Īshvara makes the greatest sacrifice for all beings and He holds all beings close to His bosom in each Kalpa, that they may work out their evolution under the most favorable circumstances. He waits for those that give up everything for His sake, and give themselves entirely up to Him, so that He may bear their Karma upon Himself and hasten their evolution to such an extent, that they may approach His own state. As Īshvara gives Himself to the service of the Universe, so do His Bhaktas too. Men owe the highest duty to Īshvara, and this they discharge by means of Upāsanā. Upāsanā is the law of being for all Jivas, when they reach the state of manhood. Surrender is the essence of Upāsanā, and this Sri Krishna taught to Arjuna.

When a man by performing his duties to other beings and to Īshvara becomes purified and single minded, he is entitled to receive the final teaching, and not before. And Sri Krishna gave that teaching at the very last to Arjuna. He said that Jiva and Īshvara were one in essence. It is the difference in Prakriti that makes all the difference between Jiva and

Īshvara. When all the bonds of Prakriti are broken through, only Brahmān remains, the one reality, underlying both Īshvara and Jiva. When we become fixed, in this wisdom all is Brahmān, and final liberation is attained. This is the real teaching of the Upanishads, as embodied in Uttara Mimānsā. In this connection, Sri Krishna pointed out the fallacy of the Vaiseshika system in attempting to know the Attributeless, through the attributes.

The highest wisdom of the Kalpa was revealed and the world resounds with all glory to Sri Krishna. The Rishis and Mahātmās took up His work. All the religious movements and religious writings that have followed only reproduce His teachings.

There was something however wanting in these teachings as given in the Mahābhārata — the relation of Sri Krishna to His own Bhaktas. What He did for the Universe and how He did it are fully related in the great Epic. But what He did for those that had already given themselves up entirely to Him, who did not require the teaching of Karma, Upāsanā and Jnāna, who were His own people, who knew no other Dharma than Himself, who had followed Him through ages, and who simply took births as He appeared on this earth, what Sri Krishna did for these Bhaktas, what His relations were with them, are not described in the Mahābhārata at all. The lordly side is given but not the sweet side. The picture of the Lord edifies and overawes, that of the Lover enchants and enthrals. The Bhāgavata sings what the Mahābhārata left unsung. That is the peculiar significance of the Tenth Skandha which follows, the Skandha that maddens the hearts of all real devotees.

THE TENTH SKANDHA.

VRINDĀVANA LILĀ

THE BIRTH OF SRI KRISHNA.

SKANDHA X. CHAP. 1-3.

Said Suka: — The goddess Earth, being oppressed by the heavy load of tens of thousands of Daitya hosts, who were born as arrogant kings, sought the shelter of Brahmā. She took the form of a cow, and with tears running down her cheeks, piteously related her grievances to the Lord of Creation. Brahmā took Śiva and the Devas with him, and went over to the Ocean of milk (Kshīra Samudra), the abode of Vishnu. There he adored the Lord of Preservation and heard the Divine voice, which he thus explained to the Devas: —

"Even before this, the Lord knew about the grievances of the goddess of Earth. Go, take your births, as parts of yourselves, in the clan of the Yadus. The Lord of Lords, by governing His Kāla Śakti, shall appear on the Earth and relieve her pressure. The Supreme Purusha Himself shall be born in the family of Vāsudeva. Let the Deva girls take their births for His gratification. The thousand-mouthed, self-illumining Ananta, who is only a part of Vāsudeva, shall be the elder-born, that he may do what pleases

299

Hari. Bhagavati, the Māyā of Vishnu, who keeps the whole world under delusion, shall also incarnate in part, as desired by the Lord, for doing His work."

Saying all this to the Devas, and giving words of consolation to the goddess of Earth, Brahmā went back to his own abode.

Śura Sena, the chief of the Yadus, ruled over the town of Mathurā. Hence it became the chief seat of the Yadu kings. It is a sacred town, the constant seat of Hari.

Once upon a time, at Mathurā. Vāsudeva drove in his chariot with his newly married wife Devaki. The marriage presents were innumerable. Kansa, the son of Ugrasena, held the reins of the horses himself, so eager was he to please his sister Devaki.

On the way, an incorporeal voice, addressing Kansa, said: —

"O ignorant one! the eighth child of her whom thou art now driving shall be thy slayer."

The cruel Kansa instantly took sword in hand and caught Devaki by her hair.

Vāsudeva pacified him with these words: —

"Thy virtues are well known. Why shouldst thou kill a female, thine own sister, at marriage. Death is certain, this day or a hundred years hence. Man takes body after body under the action of Karma, as he takes step after step in walking, or even as the leech takes blade after blade of grass in moving.

"As in dream there is a reflex perception of what is seen and heard in waking, and as in that perception the man forgets his former self and becomes a reflex of that self, so a man gives up his former body and becomes forgetful of it.

"To whatever body the mind is drawn by fruit — bearing Karma, the Jiva assumes that body as its own.

"The wind shakes the water and the Son or moon, reflected on its bosom, appears as if shaken. So by ascription, the Purusha has the attributes of the body. He who does evil to another has to fear evil from others.

"This girl, thy younger sister, is motionless with fear. Thou art not entitled to kill her."

But persuasion was of no avail, as Kansa was under the influence of the Daityas.

Vāsudeva then thought how he could ward off the present danger, leaving the future to take care of itself.

Addressing Kansa he said: —

"But, O King, thon hast no fear from her: Surely I would make over to thee her sons, from whom thou hast fear." Kansa desisted from his cruel act and Vāsudeva went home with his bride, pleased for the time being.

In time Devaki brought forth eight sons and one daughter.

The truthful Vāsudeva presented his first son Kirtimat to Kansa. The king admired the firmness of his brother-in-law and smilingly said: — "Take back this child. I have no fear from him. From your eighth born my death is ordained." "So let it be" exclaimed Vāsudeva, and he took back his son. But he had very little faith in the words of Kansa.

Kansa learned from Nārada that Nanda, Vāsudeva and others of their dan, their wives and even the clansmen of Kansa, his friends and relatives, were partial incarnations of the Devas. He further learned from the Rishi that preparations were being made for the lolling of the Daityas, whose power menaced the Earth.

When the Rishi left Kansa, he took all the members of the Yadu clan for Devas and every child of Devaki for Vishnu that was to kill him. He now confined Vāsudeva and Devaki in his own house and put them in fetters. He put to death every son that was born to them.

He knew himself to be Kālanemi who had been, in another birth, killed by Vishnu. He fell out with the Yadus, deposed his own father Ugra Sena and became himself the King.

With the alliance of the Māgadhas (people of Magadha or ancient Bihar) and with the help of Pralamba, Baka, Chānūra, Trināvarta, Agha, Mushtika, Arishta, Dvivid, Pūtanā, Kesi, Dhenuka, Vāna, Bhouma and other Asuras, Kansa tormented the Yadus. They fled away to the kingdoms of Kuru, Pānchāla, Kekaya, Sālva, Vidarbha, Nishadha, Videha, and Kausala. Some only remained behind and they followed the behests of Kansa.

Six sons of Devaki were killed, one by one, by Kansa.

The seventh, the abode of Vishnu, whom they call Ananta, appeared in the womb of Devaki, causing both joy and grief to his parents.

Vishnu, the Ātmā of all beings, knew the sufferings of His own followers, the Yadus, at the hands of Kansa. He summoned Yoga Māyā and commanded her as follows. "Go forth, blessed Devi! to Vraja, which is adorned by Gopas and Gos (*Go* is ordinarily a cow. *Gopa*, go and pa is a preserver of cow, a cowherd. Vraja or Go-kula was the chief town of Nan da, the king of the Gopas). Rohini, wife of Vāsudeva, dwells in Gokula the kingdom of Nanda. Other wives of Vāsudeva lie hidden at other places, for fear of Kansa. The child in the womb of Devaki is my Sesha named abode. Draw it out and place it in the womb of Rohini. I shall myself become the son of Devaki as a part of myself. Thou shalt be born of Yasodā, the wife of Nanda. Men shall worship thee as the giver of all desires and boons, with incense, presents and sacrifices. They shall give thee names and make places for thee on the Earth. Durgā, Bhadrakali, Vijayā, Vaishnavi, Kamadā, Chandikā, Krishnā, Madhavi, Kanyakā, Māyā, Nārāyani, Īsāni, Sāradā and Ambikā — these shall be thy names. For thy *drawing out (Sankarshana)* the child shall be called Sankarshana, He shall be called Rāma, from his attractiveness (*ramana*) and Bala from his uncommon strength (*bala*)."

"So let it be, Om!" said Bhagavati, and she carried out the behests of the Lord. By inducing the sleep of Yoga, she removed the child from the womb of Devaki to that of Rohini. People thought Devaki had miscarried.

Then Bhagavān, the Ātmā of the Universe, the dispeller of all the fears of his votaries, entered the Manas of Vāsudeva in part. Devaki bore in her Manas this part of Achyuta, even as the East bears the moon. Her lustre being confined to the prison-room could not please others, even like fire confined as heat or like Sarasvati confined in the cheat who keeps his wisdom to himself. Kansa saw an unusual glow round his sister such as he had never witnessed before. He exclaimed "Surely Hari is born in this womb, He who is to take away my life. What shall I do this day? He comes on a mission and His energy will be all directed towards that end. Am I then to kill my sister? But the killing of a pregnant female, my own sister, will ruin my fame, my wealth and my life. By the performance of such a heinous act, one becomes dead even when alive. Men curse him for his evil deeds and after death he enters the regions of absolute darkness."

Kansa by his own persuasion restrained himself from doing any violent act and he waited with feelings of bitterness for the time when Hari was to be born. But whether sitting or lying down, eating or walking, he thought of Vishnu and saw Him everywhere in the Universe.

Brahmā, Śiva, the Rishis, the Devas adored Vishnu in the womb of Devaki. "True in thy will, attainable by Truth, the one Truth before, after and in creation, the root of the Universe, and underlying the Universe as its only Reality, Thou from whom all true sayings and true perceptions do proceed, Truth Thyself, we take Thy shelter."

"The primal Jiva tree stands on the field of Prakriti. Joy and sorrow are its fruits. The three gunas (Satva, Rajas and Tamas) are its three roots. Dharma (the means of attaining objects), Artha (the objects), Kāma (desires) and Moksha (freedom from desires), these are its fourfold juice, the five senses are its sources of perception, the six sheaths form its chief feature, the seven constituents of the physical body (*dhātus*) form its skin, the five Bhūtas, Manas, Buddhi and Ahankāra are its eight branches, the nine openings are its holes, the ten Prānas, or physiological functions, are its leaves and Jivātma and Paramātmā are the two birds sitting on this tree.

Thou art the one root of this tree, it ends in Thee and it is preserved by Thee. Those that are deluded by Thy Māyā see manifold forms in place of Thy real self, but not so the wise. Thou art consciousness itself. For the good of the world, Thou dost assume Satva-made forms, which bring joy to all good people and woe to the evil-minded."

"O Lotus-eyed, thou art the abode of Satva. Thy votaries, by concentrating their minds on Thee and by resorting to Thy feet which serve as boats to them, make an easy ford of this Ocean of recurring births (*Sansāra*)."

"O Self manifest, the Ocean of recurring births, which is formidable and unfordable to others, gives way before Thy votaries, even at the mere touch of the boat of Thy feet. So while they cross themselves, even without the boat, they leave that boat for others, for they have boundless compassion for other beings." (*i.e.* Thy votaries lay down the path of Bhakti. *Śrīdhara*.)

"There are others (followers of the Path of wisdom) who consider themselves liberated (*Mukta*). But their intellect is impure as they have no Bhakti in Thee. By ascetic efforts they rise to (near about) the Supreme abode, but (being overpowered by obstacles) they fall down, by their disregard of Thy feet."

"But Thy votaries, O Madhava, never slip away from Thy path for they are bound by their attachment to Thee and Thou dost preserve them. So fearlessly they tread over the heads of Vināyaka hosts. (The Vināyaka are elementals who are supposed to cause obstacles to all good works)."

"Thy body is pure Satva, for the preservation of the Universe. That body becomes the means of attaining the fruits of (devotional?) karma. It is by reason of that body that men are able to worship Thee by means of Veda, Kriyā Yoga, Tapas and Samādhi." (There could be no worship, if no body had been assumed. Hence there could be no *attainment of the fruits of Karma, Śrīdhara*. This is not intelligible, if ordinary Karma is meant.)

"If this Satva body of Thine had not existed, direct perception would not be possible. For through Thy manifestations in (the world of) the Gunas, thoughts can (at last) reach Thee. The Gunas only relate to Thee and are themselves manifested by Thee." (By devotion to the pure Satva body, the mind partakes of its character *i.e.* becomes purely Sātvic. Then by the favor of Vishnu, there is direct perception, *i.e.* the form is not the object of direct perception but the means of direct perception. But these forms only serve the purpose of devotion. The Purusha can not be known by these forms. Hence the following Śloka, *Srīdhara*).

"Thy Name (nāma) and Thy Form (rūpa) are not however to be known by Thy attributes, births and deeds. For Thou art their Seer and Thy Path is beyond the reach of Manas and speech. Still in the act of devotion, Thy votaries realise Thee. By hearing, uttering, causing others to remember and by meditating on Thy blessed names and forms in devotional practices, one becomes fixed in mind on Thy Lotus Feet and does not then stand the chance of another birth."

"By Thy birth, the pressure on the Earth is removed. The marks of Thy feet already adorn her. Heaven and Earth look favored by Thee."

"What else can be the cause of Thy birth but a mere fancy on Thy part, for even the birth, life and death of Jivātmas are but seeming things caused by Thy Avidyā."

"The Fish, the Horse, the Tortoise, the Man Lion, the Boar, the Swan, in these and in Kings, Brāhmanas and wise men, Thou hast incarnated. As thou dost preserve us and preserve this Trilokī, so dost Thou take away the load from off the Earth. Our salutations to Thee."

"And mother Devaki, the Great Purusha Himself is in Thy womb in part, for our good. Fear not then from Kansa, whose death is near at hand. Thy Son shall be the Saviour of the Yadus."

Having thus adored the Lord, the Devas left the place.

In time, when all nature looked still and there was joy in heaven and earth, Sri Krishna was born under the influence of the Rohini constellation. It was all dark at dead of night. He had four hands bearing Sankha, Chakra, Gadā, and Padma. The mark of Srivatsa the Kaustubha gem, the yellow cloth, the crown on the head glittering with stones, the brilliant ear-rings all marked Him out as the Purusha, and Vāsudeva and Devaki adored Him as such. Devaki asked him to withdraw his lordly form with four hands.

Said Bhagavān, addressing Devaki.

"In the Svayambhuva Manvantara, thou wert called Prisni, and this Vāsudeva, Prajāpati Sutapas. Commanded by Brahmā to beget progeny, thou didst make austere Tapas and prayed for a son even like unto my own self. So I was born of thee as Prisni-Garbha. This was my first Incarnation. When you two were Aditi and Kasyapa, I was born of you as Upendra, otherwised called Vāmana (the Dwarf). This was my second Incarnation. In this my third Incarnation, I am again born unto you. This form is shown to thee to remind thee of those previous births. Thou shalt attain my supreme state by meditating on me both as a son and as Brahmā."

Then He assumed the form of an ordinary child.

Directed by Him, Vāsudeva took Him to Vraja, the Kingdom of Nanda. The fetters loosened. The gate opened wide. The gate keepers fell into deep sleep. Though there was a heavy downpour of rain, the serpent Sesha gave shelter under his thousand hoods. The river Yamunā, deep in flood, fretting and foaming under the storm, made way for Vāsudeva. The Gopas were all fast asleep in Vraja. Vāsudeva placed his own son by the side of Yasodā and took her new born daughter away and placed her near Devaki. He then put on his fetters and remained confined as before. Yasodā knew that she had a child, but the labour pains and sleep made her quite forget the sex of the child.

COUNSEL WITH THE DAITYAS.

SKANDHA X. CHAP. 4.

The gates closed again, the gate-keepers woke up and, on hearing a child's voice, they forthwith informed their King. Kansa had been anxiously waiting for the birth of this child. So he lost no time in getting up and appearing before Devaki. He snatched away the child from her. Devaki remonstrated with her brother praying for the life of her daughter. Kansa heeded not her words. He raised the child aloft and cast it down to strike it against a stone. The child slipped away from his hands, and rose high up. This younger born of Vishnu appeared with eight hands, bearing eight weapons, — Dhanus (bow) Sūla (spear) Isha (arrow), Charma (hide protector), Asi (sword), Sankha (conch), Chakra (Disc), and Gadā (club). She had divine garlands and garments and was adorned with ornaments. Siddhas, Chāranas, Gandharvas, Apsarasas, Kinnaras and Nāgas worshiped her with profuse offerings.

"Fool that thou art" she thundered forth, "What if I am killed. He who shall make an end of thee, thy former enemy, is born somewhere else. Do not kill other children in vain."

The Goddess Māyā then became known by different names in different parts of the earth.

Kansa was wonder-struck. He removed the fetters of Vāsudeva and Devaki and begged their pardon, saying, "Like a Rākshasa, I have killed your sons. I do not know what fate awaits me after death. Not only men tell lies, but the Devas too."

Kansa then called the Daityas together. These sworn enemies of the Devas heard their master and then broke forth thus: —

"If it be so, O King of Bhoja, we will kill all children, whether ten days old or not, whether found in towns, villages, or pasture grounds. What can the Devas do, cowards in battle? They are always afraid of the sound of thy bow. Dost thou not remember how, pierced by thy arrows, they fled for their lives. The Devas are only bold when they are safe, and they indulge in tall talk outside the battle ground. Vishnu seeks solitude. Śiva dwells in forests. Indra has but little might. Brahmā is an ascetic. But still the Devas are enemies. They are not to be slighted. Therefore engage us, your followers, in digging out the very root of the Devas, for like disease and sensuality when neglected at first, they become difficult of suppression. Vishnu is the root of the Devas, and he represents the eternal religion (Sanatana Dharma i.e. Dharma that follows the eternal course of time, or is based on the eternal truths of nature, hence eternal religion, a term applied to Hinduism proper). And the roots of Dharma are the Vedas, the Cows, the Brāhmanas, Tapas and Yajna. Therefore by all means, O King, we shall kill the Deva-knowing, Yajna-performing and ascetic Brāhmanas and cows that supply the sacrificial ghee. Brāhmanas, Cows, Vedas, asceticism, truth, restraint of the senses, restraint of the mind, faith, kindness, forbearance and sacrifices these are the parts of Vishnu's body. Therefore the best way to kill him is to kill these. Vishnu, who pervades all hearts, is the guide of all Devas, the enemy of Asuras. He is the root of all Devas, including Śiva and Brahmā."

Kansa approved of this counsel. He directed the Kāmarupa bearing (*i.e.* bearing forms at will) Asuras to oppress all good people and they readily took to their work.

NANDA AND VASUDEVA.

SKANDHA X. CHAP. 5.

Nanda performed the birth ceremony of his son with great pomp. His gifts knew no bounds. Vishnu was worshipped and there was plenty in Vraja. The time came for payment of the year's dues to Kansa. So Nanda left Gokula (*i.e.* Vraja) in charge of the Gopas and himself went with the dues to Mathurā. Vāsudeva learned of Nanda's arrival and went to meet him. Nanda stood up to receive him and embraced him heartily. Said Vāsudeva: —

"Brother, you grew old and gave up all hopes of having a child. Luckily a son is now born unto you. It is indeed a new birth to you, that you are blessed with the sight of a lovely son. Friends cannot live pleasantly together as their manifold Karma, like a strong wind, forces them asunder. Is it all right with the big forest, with the pasture lands where you now dwell with friends? Is it all right with my son (Balarāma) who lives at your place with her mother, and who looks upon you as his parent?"

Nanda replied: —

"Alas! your sons by Devaki were all killed by Kansa; even the daughter that was born last has ascended to the heavens. Surely man is governed by the unseen. Those that know are not deluded." Said Vāsudeva: —

"You have paid your yearly dues and have also met me. Now do not remain here any longer. For evils befall Gokula."

Nanda left Mathurā for Gokula.

PUTANĀ

SKANDHA X. CHAP. 6.

With evil forebodings, Nanda made his way to Vraja, for he thought Vāsudeva would not tell a lie. And he was right. By Kansa's orders, the fierce Putanā went about killing children in towns, villages and pasture lands, for verily she was a killer of children. That wanderer of the skies entered Gokula at will, assuming the form of a woman most beautiful to look at. So no one stopped her passage. She moved freely here and there and at last entered the house of Nanda. She looked like a kind mother and Yasodā and Rohini were so much struck by her fine exterior that they did not stop her access to Krishna. Putanā placed the child on her lap and gave him milk from her breast full of deadly poison. The divine child knew who Putanā was and what she was about. He held fast her breast with both hands and in anger drank in the very life juice of the Asura woman. She screamed forth "Let go", "Let go", "No more". Her eyes expanded. She cast up and down her hands and feet again and again in profuse perspiration. Her groans made heaven and earth tremble and space itself resounded on all sides. At last she fell dead like a great mountain, crushing down trees within an ambit of twelve miles. Fearlessly the boy played on her body.

The Gopa ladies hurried to the place with Rohini and Yasodā. They bathed the boy in cows' urine and dust from cow's feet. They pronounced the twelve names of Vishnu (Kesava and others) over twelve parts of his body. Then after touching water, they duly uttered the root mantras over their own body and that of the child. Lastly they invoked Vishnu by different names to protect the child from danger of all sorts. (The protective mantra uttered by the mother with passes of the hand over different parts of the body was supposed to shield the child from danger. Latterly the custom has been to get the mantra written, with due ceremonies, by a qualified Brahmān, on the sacred bark (Bhūrja) and then to tie it round the hand.)

Yasodā then placed the child on her lap and gave him milk.

By this time Nanda had returned to Vrindabana. He saw the huge body of the Asura woman and realised the force of Vāsudeva's warning.

The people of Vraja cut the body into parts and burnt them with fuel. The smoke was sweet-scented, as the touch of Krishna's body purifies even the enemy.

THE UPTURNING OF THE CART.

SKANDHA X. CHAP. 7.

The ceremony observable on the child being able to stand on his legs and the birth-day ceremony were observed together and there was a great feast at the house of Nanda. Yasodā placed the child near a cart, containing brass vessels with articles of food, and became busily engaged in receiving her guests. The child wept but she did not hear. He then raised his feet aloft, weeping for his mother's milk, and struck the cart with his feet. The cart was upset, the brass vessels broken and the wheel and axle upturned. The Gopa ladies could not account for this wonderful phenomenon. The boys, who sat near the child, told all that they saw, but people could not easily believe what they said.

TRINAVARTA OR THE WHIRLWIND.

SKANDHA X. CHAP. 7.

The child was once on the lap of Yasodā when he suddenly became so heavy that Yasodā had to throw him on the ground. The Asura Trināvarta or Whirlwind made an attack on the child and a violent dust storm overtook Gokula. The Asura had scarcely raised Krishna to a certain height, when his weight almost crushed him to death. Krishna did not let go his hold and the Asura breathed his last and fell dead. Yasodā kissed her son again and again, but when he opened His mouth, the mother saw the whole Universe within it.

THE NAMES "KRISHNA" AND "RAMA."

SKANDHA X. CHAP. 8.

Garga, the family priest of the Yadus, came to Vraja at the request of Vāsudeva. Nanda duly received him and said: — "You are versed in the Vedas and you are the author of an astrological treatise. Please perform the Naming ceremony of the two boys." Garga replied: "I am known as the priest of the Yadus and, if I officiate at the ceremony, Kansa might suspect your son to be the eighth son of Devaki." Nanda promised strict privacy, and the Rishi performed the ceremony. Addressing Nanda, he then said: —

"This son of Rohini shall be called Rāma or the charming one, as he shall charm his friends by his virtues. He shall be called Bala, from possessing excessive strength. From his bringing together the Yadus, he shall be called Sankarshana.

"This other boy, taking body, yuga after yuga, had three colors, White (*Sukla*), Red (*Rakta*) and Yellow, (*Pīta*). Now he has got the black color (*Krishna*). In the past, he was born as the son of Vāsudeva. So those that know call him Srimat Vāsudeva. He has many names and many forms, according to his deeds and attributes. Neither I nor other people know them all. He shall give you the greatest blessings and protect you against all dangers. In days of yore, good people conquered the ill-doers by his help. Those that are attached to him are not conquered by enemies, even as followers of Vishnu are not conquered by the Asuras. Therefore this son of Nanda is equal to Nārāyana by his virtues, powers and fame."

PRANKS OF THE BOY.

SKANDHA X. CHAP. 8.

With growing childhood, Krishna became very naughty. Once the Gopa women made the following complaints. Krishna would untie their calves before the milking time. He would steal their milk and curds and divide the remnants, after eating, among the monkeys. If they did not eat, he would break the pot. If he did not get the things he wanted, he would curse the inmates and other boys. If the pots were out of reach, he would raise himself on seats or husking stools and bear those hanging pots away to get at their contents. He would illumine the dark room by the glitter of his own body and that of his jewels, to serve his purpose. He would talk insolently, and spoil the ground. The Gopa women exclaimed: — "But now how innocent he looks before you." Krishna betrayed fear in his eyes. Yasodā would not beat him. So she only smiled.

One day Rāma and other boys complained to Yasodā that Krishna had eaten earth. The mother remonstrated. "They have lied" exclaimed Krishna "Or if they have spoken the truth, then examine my mouth." "Open it," said Yasodā. But what did she find within that mouth? The Seven Dvipas, the planets, the stars, the three Gunas and all their transformations, even Vrindāvana and herself. "Is this dream or delusion or is this all the power of my own son? If Thou art then the Unknowable, my salutations to Thee. I take the shelter of Him, by whose Māyā I seem to be Yasodā, this Nanda my husband, this boy my son, the Gos (cows) Gopas and Gopis to be mine." She had the true knowledge, but it was soon eclipsed by the Māyā of Vishnu and Yasodā again knew Krishna to be her own son.

Rājā Parikshit asked: —

"What did Nanda do that Krishna would be his foster son? And what did Yasodā do, that Krishna should suck her breast? Even his own parents did not witness the deeds of the child of which poets have sung so much."

Suka replied: —

"Drōna, the chief of the Vasus, with his wife Dhārā shewed great obedience to Brahmā. 'When born on Earth may we have the highest devotion for Him.'" Such was their prayer to Brahmā and it was granted. Drōna was born as Nanda and Dhārā as Yasodā.

THE TYING.

SKANDHA X. CHAP. 9.

One day Yasodā was churning curdled milk and singing the deeds of her son. Krishna came up and, desirous of sucking milk, held the churning rod. Yasodā placed him on her lap and gave him milk to suck. But the milk that was boiling on the oven overflowed the pot and she hurriedly left her son. In anger Krishna bit his lips, broke the milk pot with a stone, took the fresh butter to a retired corner and there partook of it. Yasodā came back after a while and found the pot broken. Her son had left the place and she could easily see that it was all his doing. She found Krishna seated on the husk stand, freely dividing the contents of the hanging pots among the monkeys, and she quietly approached him with a stick. Krishna hurriedly got down and ran away as if in fear. Yasodā ran after him and caught him at last. Finding him fear-stricken, she threw down the stick and tried to fasten him to the husking stand. The rope fell short by the breadth of two fingers (say two inches). She added another rope. The gap remained the same. She added rope after rope, as many as she had of her own and of her neighbours, but could not bridge over the distance. She stood baffled at last, amazed and ashamed. Finding that his mother was perspiring in the effort and that her hair had become dishevelled, Krishna allowed himself to be fastened to the stand.

THE ARJUNA TREES.

SKANDHA X. CHAP. 10.

The Yaksha King Kuvera had two sons — Nalakūvara and Manigriva. They became maddened with power and intoxicated with drink. Nārada passed by them while they were playing with Gandharva girls stark naked in a river bath and they heeded him not. Nārada thought how best he could reclaim them. "Poverty is the only remedy for those that lose their heads in wealth. These sons of the Lōkapāla Kuvera are deep in ignorance, insolence and intoxication. Let them become trees. But they shall not lose memory by my favor. After one hundred Deva years, the touch of Sri Krishna shall save them." These sons of Kuvera in consequence became a pair of Arjuna trees in Vrindāvana.

While Krishna was fastened to the husking stand, the pair of Arjuna trees drew his attention. He was bent on making good the words of Nārada. So he approached the trees, drawing the husking stand behind him by force and, placing himself between them, uprooted the trees. They fell down with a crash and lo! two fiery spirits came out, illumining space by the splendour of their bodies. They prayed to Krishna and then rose upwards.

The Gopa women had been engaged all this time in their household duties and the crash attracted the attention of all the Gopas and Gopis. The boys told what they had seen. But some were loath to believe that all this could be done by the boy Krishna.

THE FRUIT SELLER.

SKANDHA X. CHAP. 11.

One day Krishna heard a woman crying out "Come ye buy fruits." He took some paddy and hastened to her side. The woman filled both his hands with fruits and lo! her basket became full of gems and precious stones.

VRINDAVANA.

SKANDHA X. CHAP. 11.

Seeing that calamities befell Brihat Vāna (Vraja or Gokul) so often, the elders put their heads together to devise the best course to adopt. Upa Nanda, one of the oldest and wisest of them, said: —

"We that wish well for Gokula must hence get away. Evils befall that bode no good for the children. This boy was with difficulty saved from that child-killing Rākshasa woman. It is only by the favor of Vishnu that the cart did not fall on him. When he was taken high up by the whirlwind Asura, and when he fell down on the rock, it was the Deva Kings that saved him. If this boy and others did not perish when they were between the two trees, it was because Vishnu preserved them. Ere this Vraja is visited by fresh calamity, let us go elsewhere with the boys and all attendants.

"There is a forest called Vrindāvana with fresh verdure for cattle, where Gopas, Gopis and Gos will all enjoy themselves. The hills, grass and creepers are all holy there. This very day let us go to that place. Make ready the carriages. Let the cows precede us, if it pleases you all."

With one heart, the Gopas exclaimed: — "Well said! Well said!" They prepared their carriages and placed on them the aged, the young, the females and all household articles. They drove the cows in advance. They blew their horns and beat their drums. Accompanied by the priests, the Gopas went on their way. The Gopa girls, seated on chariots sang the deeds of Krishna and Yasodā, and Rohinl attentively listened to them.

At last they entered Vrindāvana, which gives pleasure at all times, with the carriages; they made a semi-circular abode for the cattle.

Rāma and Krishna saw Vrindāvana, the hill Govardhana and the banks of the Yamunā and then became very much pleased. In time they became keepers of calves (Vatsa). They tended the calves in the company of Gopa boys on pasture lands near at hand. They played with other boys as ordinary children.

VATSA OR THE CALF.

SKANDHA X. CHAP. 11.

One day Rāma, Krishna and other boys were looking after their calves when an Asura, with the intention of killing them, assumed the form of a calf (Vatsa) and got mixed among the herd. Krishna pointed this out to Balarāma and silently moved behind the Asura. He held it aloft by the hind feet and tail and gave it such a whirl that its life became extinct. The boys, cried out "Well done! Well done!" and the Devas rained flowers on Krishna.

BAKA OR THE CRANE.

SKANDHA X. CHAP. 11.

One day the Gopa boys went over to a tank to quench their thirst. They saw a huge monster in the form of a Baka (crane). It rushed forth and swallowed Krishna. Krishna caused a burning in its throat and the Asura threw him out. It made a second attack and Krishna held the two beaks and parted them asunder as if they were blades of grass, And the Asura died.

AGHA OR THE SERPENT.

SKANDHA X. CHAP. 12.

One day Krishna was playing with the boys in the forest. Agha, the youngest born of Putanā and Baka, the Asura whom even the Devas, rendered immortal by *Amrita,* dreaded, burning with a spirit of revenge at the death of his brother and sister, thought of killing Krishna and all his attendants. He stretched himself forth as a huge serpent, spreading over one yojana, the extremities of his open mouth touching the clouds and the earth. The Gopa boys took the Asura to be the goddess of Vrindāvana. "Or if it really be a serpent opening its mouth to kill us, it will instantly be killed like the Asura Vaka." So with their eyes fixed on Krishna they clapped their hands and with a smile entered the mouth of the serpent, even before Krishna had time to warn them. The Asura still waited with its mouth open for Krishna. Krishna thought how he could kill the serpent and at the same time save his companions.

On reflection, he himself entered the mouth of the serpent and stretched himself and his comrades. The Asura lost breath and breathed his last. A shining spirit emerged from the Asura body and entered the body of Krishna. Krishna gave fresh life to his comrades by his Amrita bearing looks.

Krishna killed Agha in his fifth year, but the Gopa boys who witnessed the act said, when Krishna entered his sixth year, that the act was done that very day.

"How could that be?" enquired Parikshit.

Suka explained this with reference to the following story.

BRAHMA AND KRISHNA.

SKANDHA X. CHAP. 13-14.

When the Asura Agha was killed, Krishna went with his companions to the river bank and said: —

"We are hungry, the hour is late. Let us have our meals here. Let the calves drink water and graze on near lands." The Gopa boys spread out their stores and improvised plates for eating. While they were engaged in eating, the calves strayed away. The boys became anxious and were about to get up, when Krishna stopped them, saying he would find the calves. He left his companions and went on the search. Brahmā, who had been witnessing from the high heavens all the deeds of Krishna, even the killing of Agha, with wonder, wanted to have still one more manifestation of his divine powers. Finding opportunity, he removed the calves as well as the Gopa boys to some secure place and disappeared. Krishna could not find the calves and on returning he could not find his companions. He then knew it was all the act of Brahmā. To please Brahmā, as well as to please the mothers of the Gopa boys, He Himself became so many calves and so many Gopa boys of their very size and form to the minutest detail. The mothers thought they had got their boys and they became even more attached to them. The cows thought they had got their calves and their fondness knew no bounds.

Krishna went on playing his manifold parts for one year. Five or six days remaining till the completion of the year, Balarāma saw one day that the cows were grazing on the summits of Govardhana, while the calves were grazing at some distance near Vraja. The cows impelled by a fit of attachment breathlessly ran towards the calves even those that had quite lately brought forth younger calves and caressed them profusely. The elder Gopas who were in charge could not restrain them with all their efforts. They felt shame and vexation. But when they themselves approached the calves and their own sons, their anger melted away in deep affection.

Balarāma thought for a moment. "Never was such love witnessed by me before — this attachment for calves that had been weaned long ago. The people of Vraja have even increasing affection for their own sons even as they had of yore for Krishna. These calves no longer appear to be the incarnations of Rishis, their keepers the Gopa boys do not appear any longer to be the incarnations of the Devas. They look all like thee O

Krishna! Wherein lies the mystery?" Krishna explained to Rāma what had happened. Brahmā appeared after a Truti (fraction of a moment) of his own measure. He saw the boys, he saw the calves. He could not make any distinction between those he placed under his own Māyā and those brought into existence by the Māyā of Krishna. The foggy darkness is overpowered by the darkness of the night. The light of the glowworm vanishes before the light of the day. To delude Krishna, Brahmā became deluded himself. In another moment Brahmā saw the calves and the boys each and all bearing four hands, the divine weapons and all the divine powers. They shone in resplendent glory. Brahmā became overpowered, stupefied. Recovering himself, he found once more Sri Krishna alone, searching for the calves and boys in Vrindāvana. He fell at the feet of Krishna, again and again, his four heads with their crowns rolling on the ground and with tears in his eyes, he glorified Krishna.

(The glorification is a long one. Only one sloka is given here.)

"It is only he who lives on, anxiously looking out for Thy favor, bearing through the workings of his own Karma as a matter of course and making obeisance to Thee in heart, words and body, that can get the heritage of Mukti (As one must be living, so that a particular heritage may vest in him, so the Bhakta must keep up his individuality to get the heritage of Mukti)."

Parikshit asked. "How could the people of Vraja have greater love for Krishna than for their own sons?"

Suka replied: —

"Self, O King, is the most beloved of all things not so beloved are one's sons or wealth. Therefore, O king, people love themselves better than they do their sons, their riches or their homes. Those that deem their body to be their own Ātmā or self, love that body more than anything else.

"But the body only becomes dear as it pertains to self. It can not be as dear as self. For when the body wears away, the desire to live on is still strong.

"Therefore Ātmā or self is most dear to all beings and the whole of this Universe is for that self.

"But know thou this Krishna to be the Self of all selves, the Ātmā of all Ātmās. For the good of the Universe, he also looks by Māyā as one possessed of a body. Those that know Krishna know that all movable and immovable beings are but His forms and that nothing else exists.

"Of all things, the ultimate reality is 'Existence'. Krishna is the reality of Existence itself. So there is nothing besides Krishna."

Here ends the Kumāra Lilā of Krishna. The Pouganda Lilā is now to commence. (Kumāra is a boy below five, Pouganda is boyhood from the 5th to the 16th year).

END OF KUMARA LILĀ

DHENUKA.

SKANDHA X. CHAP. 15.

On attaining the Pouganda age, Rāma and Krishna were placed in charge of cows. Vrindāvana looked gay and Krishna amused himself with his companions in the forests. One day Sridāman, Subala, Stoka and other companions spoke to Rāma and Krishna "Not far off is a forest of palm trees (Tāla). Tāla fruits fall in abundance there, but one Asura Dhenuka, with many of his kin obstruct all access to them. The Asura has the form of an Ass. We smell the fragrance of the fruits even from here. They are very tempting indeed." Rāma boldly entered that forest and gave a shake to the Tāla trees, and Tālas fell in abundance. Roused by the noise, the Ass rushed forth and kicked Rāma with its hind feet. The Asura brayed and made a second rush, when Rāma held it by the hind feet and whirling it round in the skies threw It dead on the trees. The kith and kin of the Asura then came rushing forth, but they were one and all killed by Rāma and Krishna. When they returned to Vrindāvana the Gopis who had been feeling the separation went out to receive them and, being pleased to see them, cast bashful glances at them.

THE KĀLIYA SERPENT AND THE FIRE.

SKANDHA X. CHAP. 16-17.

The Nāgas or serpents made offerings to Garuda on appointed days. Kāliya, proud of his own valour, did not make any offering himself and snatched away the offerings made by others. Garuda attacked him and, being overpowered in the fight, Kāliya sought shelter in a deep pool of water in the Yamunā.

Of yore, Garuda had caught a fish in that pool of water and was about to eat it, when Rishi Soubhari asked him not to eat, but Garuda heeded not his words. The wailings of the fish moved the tender heart of the Rishi and for their future good he cursed Garuda with death, if he entered the pool any more.

Kāliya knew about this and he therefore sought protection in that pool of water with his family. The water became deadly poison and even the adjoining air breathed poisonous death.

One day Krishna went with all his companions, other than Rāma, to the Yamunā side. The Gopa boys and the cows being very thirsty drank the water of that pool and met with instant death. Krishna cast his amrita pouring looks at them and they got up, being restored to life. They looked at each other, very much surprised.

To purge the river, Krishna got upon a Kadamba tree and jumped into the pool of water. Kāliya fiercely attacked him and stung him to the quick. The serpent then twined round Krishna. The cows wept, the Gopa boys became senseless. There were evil portents in Vrindāvana. Nanda and other Gopas came out in search of Krishna. They saw him in the grasp of the powerful serpent and made loud wailings. A moment after, seeing how they all grieved for him, Krishna eluded the grasp of the serpent and moved dancing round him. The serpent, somewhat fatigued, also kept moving with its overspread hoods, fixing its looks on Krishna. Krishna then got upon the hoods one thousand in number, one hundred being the chief, and danced on them putting down the hood that tried to raise itself. It was a lovely sight and the Devas sang in joy and rained flowers. The serpent king was overpowered. He vomited blood. His body was broken. In his heart of hearts, he sought the protection of Nārāyana. The serpent girls also glorified Krishna and prayed for their husband's life.

Krishna said: — "Go hence O serpent, dwell in the sea. Men and cows shall use the water of the river. You left Rāmanaka Dvipa for fear of Garuda. But now as your heads bear the marks of my feet, Garuda shall not touch you." Kāliya left the Yamunā with his wives and the water of that river has been pure ever since.

The people of Vrindāvana embraced Krishna and shed tears of joy. They were all so much put out that they stopped that night on the river bank. At midnight, a fire broke out from a castor plantation and it surrounded the people on all sides. The Gopas and Gopis cried out: "O Krishna, O Rāma, we are yours. Krishna! Save us from this fire. We are not afraid of our lives, but it will pain us to part from Thy feet."

Krishna ate up the whole fire.

PRALAMBA.

SKANDHA X. CHAP. 18.

It was summer. But Vrindāvana was cool with its shade, its water-spouts and its river.

Rāma and Krishna were tending the cattle with their companions. An Asura named Pralamba disguised himself as a Gopa boy and mixed with the other boys. The All-knowing Krishna found him but he feigned friendship, with the object of killing the Asura. Krishna proposed two parties for play. The defeated party had to carry the members of the victorious party on their backs. Krishna became the leader of one party and Rāma that of the other. The party of Krishna were routed near the Bhāndiraka forest. Krishna carried Srīdāmana on his back, Bhadrasena carried Vrishabha and Pralamba carried Balarāma. Pralamba ran with Balarāma beyond the mark. Balarāma suspected something evil. Then composing himself, he hit a blow on the head of the Asura and Pralamba lay down dead.

THE FOREST CONFLAGRATION.

SKANDHA X. CHAP. 19.

The cattle strayed away from the Bhāndarika forest, when suddenly there was a fire. They ran bellowing into a forest of rushes. The Gopa boys went in search of them and found them from a distance. Krishna called them out and they responded to the call. At the time a general conflagration in the forest overtook the cows and the Gopa boys and they helplessly turned to Krishna. Krishna asked the boys to close their eyes. They did so, but when they looked again they found themselves once more in the Bhāndarika forest. Seeing this Yoga power in Sri Krishna, they knew him to be a God. The older Gopas and Gopis, hearing all the wonderful deeds of Rāma and Krishna, knew them to be Devas.

THE RAINY SEASON.

SKANDHA X. CHAP. 20.

The *rainy season* followed summer. There was joy and plenty. (For a graphic and highly poetical description of the rainy season please refer to the original. The details of the description are somewhat important from the esoteric standpoint and the Season itself is suggestive as to a new era in spiritual development.)

THE AUTUMN.

SKANDHA X. CHAP. 20.

The AUTUMN came and it was all *calm, clear* and *transparent.*

The clouds disappeared. The water became pure. The wind became gentle. With the advent of lotus-bearing Autumn, the waters regained their tranquillity, even as distracted Yogins the calm of their minds by fresh resort to Yoga. The Autumn removed the clouds from the skies, promiscuous living from the animals, mud from the soil and dirt from the water — even as Bhakti in Krishna does away with the impurities attaching to the four Āsramas. The clouds gave up rainy moisture and looked beautifully white, even like Munis who give up all desires. The hills sometimes gave pure water from their sides and sometimes not, as wise men pour forth the nectar of their wisdom sometimes and not often. The animals that frequent shallow water did not know that the water was subsiding, as deluded men living in family circles do not realise the daily expiry of their lives. And they suffered like sensuous men from the rays of the Autumn sun. Day by day the soil gave up its muddiness as the wise give up their Mine-ness and the creepers got over their immaturity as the wise get over their I-ness. The Sea became calm as a Muni no longer distracted by Vedic performances. The farmers stored up waters in the paddy fields by making strong embankments, even as Yogins store up Prana by withdrawing it from the Indriyas. The moon gave relief from the inflictions of sun-burning, even as wisdom relieves the misery caused by connection with the body, and as the sight of Sri Krishna removes all the sorrows of the Gopis. The clear skies gave a brilliant view of the stars, as the mind purified by Satva makes manifest the conclusions of the Mimānsa Darsanas. The full moon shone above with all the stars as Sri Krishna shone on earth with the circle of Yadus.

SRI KRISHNA AND THE GOPIS.

SKANDHA X. CHAP. 21.

Krishna roamed in the fresh forest with the cattle and his companions. He played upon the flute and the Gopis forgot themselves in hearing his music. They saw before their mind's eye the dancing Krishna filling the holes of the flute with nectar flowing from his lips, the peacock feather on his head, Karnikāra flower on his ears, his cloth yellow like gold and the Vaijayanti garland round his neck.

Some exclaimed: — "What better could the eyes feed upon than the lovely faces of Rāma and Krishna, with the flutes touching their lips and their smiling glances."

Some said: — "How beautiful they look with garlands of mango twigs, peacock feather and blue lotus. In the assembly of Gopas, they look like heroes on the theatrical stage."

Others said: — "What did that bamboo piece of a flute do that it should drink so hard the nectar flowing from Krishna's lips, the special possession of the Gopis, that nothing should remain but the taste thereof. The water that nourished it is thrilling with joy and the plant of which it is a shoot is shedding joysome tears."

Some said: — "Look, O companions! how lovely does Vrindāvana look from the touch of Sri Krishna's lotus feet! Look there, the peacock madly dances to the tune of the flute and other animals stand dumb on the summit of the hills and witness the scene. There is no spot on the earth like Vrindāvana."

Others said: — "How blessed are these female deer that In the company of their husbands hear the music of the flute and make an offering of their loving looks!"

Other Gopis said: — "So tempting is this form of Krishna and so alluring is the music of his flute that even Deva girls become lost to themselves. Look, how the cows drink that music with ears erect. And even the calves stand with their mothers' milk in their mouths, eagerly listening to that sound. Those birds are no worse than Rishis, for they sit high on trees whence they can have a full view of Krishna and with eyes closed they silently hear the sweet music of the flute. Even the rivers shew the love transformation of their hearts by their whirls and they stop their course to embrace the feet of Krishna with their raised billows serving as hands and offering lotus flowers at those feet. The clouds give shadow and they shed dewy flowers on Krishna. Most fortunate is Govardhana, for Krishna drives cattle on its sides and it makes its offerings of edibles and drink."

The Gopis became full of Krishna (Tanmaya).

THE STEALING OF CLOTHES.

SKANDHA X. CHAP. 22.

In the first month of the DEWY SEASON (Agrahāyana), the girls of Vrindāvana worshipped Kātyāyani (a name of the Goddess Durga, wife of Śiva). The observances lasted for a month. The girls prayed to Kātyāyani that they might get Krishna for their husband. They bathed early in the morning every day in the river Yamunā. One day they left their clothes on the bank and went down into the river to bathe. Krishna took away their clothes. He asked the girls to come up and take them. They did so and the clothes were returned. Krishna then addressing the Gopis said:

"O virtuous girls, I know your resolve. It is to worship me. I also approve of it and you must succeed. The desires of those that are absorbed in me do not bear Kārmic fruits. For fried or burnt paddy does not germinate. Go back to Vraja. Your object in worshipping Kātyāyani is gained. These nights (*i.e.* on nights to come. *Sridhāra*) you shall enjoy with me."

KRISHNA AND VEDIC YAJNA (SUMMER AGAIN.)

SKANDHA X. CHAP. 23.

Krishna went over to a distant forest driving cattle with his companions. The summer sun was fierce and the trees gave shade. "Look, O companions" said Krishna, "how noble minded these trees are. They live for others. Themselves they suffer from the winds, the rains, from the sun and frost but they protect us from these. They do not send away one disappointed. They offer their leaves, their flowers, their fruits, their shade, their roots, their bark, their fragrance, their juice, their ashes, their fuel, their buds, and what not. Of all living beings, such only justify their birth as do good to others by their lives, their wealth, their wisdom and their words." (This is introductory as an attack upon the selfish performances of Vedic Brāhmanas. *Sridhāra*.)

The boys became hungry and they complained to Rāma and Krishna.

Krishna said: — "The Brāhmanas are performing Āngirasa Yajna. Take our names and ask them for food."

The boys did as they were told but the Brāhmanas heeded them not. Narrow were their desires which did not extend beyond Svarga. But for these, they went through elaborate Karma. Ignorant as they were, they thought themselves to be wise. Yajna was all in all to them but they disregarded the Lord of Yajnas, the direct manifestation of Parama Purusha. They looked upon Krishna as an ordinary man and as Brāhmanas they deemed themselves to be superior to Him. They said neither yea nor nay. So the boys returned unsuccessful to Krishna and Rāma. Krishna smiled and asked them to go to the wives of the Brāhmanas. This they did. The Brāhmana women had heard of Krishna and they were eager to see him. Notwithstanding the protests of their husbands, brothers, sons and friends, they hastened to Krishna with dishes full of eatables of all sorts. The ears had heard and the eyes now saw. And it did not take the Brāhmana women long to embrace Krishna and forget their grievances.

Knowing that the women had given up all desires for the sake of seeing Ātmā, Krishna said smilingly: — "Welcome O you noble-minded ones, take your seats. What can we do for you? It is meet that you have come to see us. I am Ātmā and therefore the most beloved. Those that care for their Ātmā or self bear unconditional and unremitting Bhakti towards me. The Prānas, Buddhi, Manas, the relatives, the body, wife, children and riches all become dear for the sake of self or Ātmā. What can be therefore dearer, than Ātmā? Now that you have seen me, go back to your husbands. They have to perform the sacrifices with your help."

The Brāhmana women replied: — "Lord, thou dost not deserve to speak so cruelly to us. Make good thy words ('My Bhakta does not meet with destruction' or 'He does not again return' *Śridhāra*.) We have taken the shelter of thy feet, throwing over-board all friends, that we may bear on our heads the Tulasi thrown from Thy feet. Our husbands, parents, sons, brothers, and friends will not take us back. Who else can? Grant us, O conqueror of all enemies, that we may have no other resort but Thee. (We may not have such resorts as Svarga &c. for which our husbands are striving. We want to serve Thee. *Śridhara*)."

Sri Krishna replied: — "Your husbands will not bear any grudge against you. By my command all people, even the Devas (in whose honor the sacrifices are made) shall approve of your conduct. Direct contact is not necessary for love. Think of me with all your heart and you shall speedily obtain me."

The Brāhmana women returned to their husbands and they were received well. The Brāhmanas repented. But for fear of Kansa, they could not go to Vrindāvana. They worshipped Krishna at home.

INDRA AND THE RAISING OF GO-VARDHANA. THE INSTALLATION.

(THE RAINY SEASON AGAIN.)

SKANDHA X. CHAP. 24-27.

There were great preparations for Yajna in honor of Indra. "What is this all about, father?" asked Krishna of Nanda. "What is the outcome of this sacrifice? In whose honor is it to be performed and how?"

Nanda replied — "Child, Indra is the Cloud-God. He will give us rains. The rains give life to all beings. Therefore people worship Indra by these sacrificial offerings. The enjoyment of that only which remains after sacrifice conduces to Dharma, Artha and Kāma."

Krishna replied: — "The birth and death of men are shaped by their own Karma. Happiness, misery, fear, well-being, these are all the effects of Karma. If there be any god who dispenses the fruits of Karma, he must also follow that Karma and not act independently of it. When people are governed by their own Karma, where does Indra come in? He can not undo what follows from Svabhāva (Svabhāva is Kārmic tendency). Karma is the Lord and Karma is to be worshipped. It is Rajas that works the clouds. What can Indra do? We do not live in towns or villages but we live in the forest. Therefore let us make Yajna offerings to our cows, our Brāhmanas and our hills. The preparations that you have already made will serve the purpose." Nanda and other Gopas approved of what Krishna said. They made offerings to the cows, the Brāhmanas and the Hill. They went round the Hill to shew respect. Krishna said "I am the Hill" and assumed some form which created faith in the Gopas. He then partook himself of the offerings to the Hill.

Indra became highly incensed. He sent forth his clouds and winds and there were rains and thunder-storms and hail-stones at Vrindāvana.

Krishna carelessly lifted up the Govardhana hill with one hand and the people of Vrindāvana with their cows took shelter in the cave.

For seven days it rained incessantly and for seven days Krishna held the hill aloft without moving an inch.

Baffled and surprised, Indra withdrew his clouds and winds. The people of Vrindāvana went to their own places and Krishna replaced the hill.

The Gopas struck with wonder approached Nanda. They related all the previous deeds of Krishna and then referring to the last incident said: — "Look here this boy only *seven years* old and there the holding aloft of this big hill. We wonder whether your son may not be the Ātmā of all beings." Nanda related to them what he had heard from Garga and they all ceased to wonder. Indra and Surabhi came down from the heavens. Indra fell at the feet of Krishna and glorified Him.

Krishna said to him: — "To favour you, Indra, I caused a break in your Yajna, that, maddened as you were by your position and powers, you might not forget me. It is only when one is blinded by powers, that one does not see me sceptre in hand. I take away the powers of him whom I want to favor. Therefore go now, Indra. You are to keep to your own station and do your duties as enjoined by me void of all pride." Surabhi, the divine mother of cows, thanked Krishna for the services done to her children.

She said: — "O Krishna, O thou great Yogin whose form is this Universe and who art the root of this Universe, we have found our Lord in Thee. Thou art our Supreme Deva O Lord of the Universe, thou shalt be our Indra, for the good of cows, Brāhmanas and Devas, and of all that are good. By the command of Brahmā, we shall install thee as our Indra."

So saying, Surabhi poured her milk over Krishna's head and Indra and other Devas, by the command of the Deva mothers, bathed Him with the waters of the Ākāsa Gangā. They all called him "GOVINDA." (He who attains (*Vinda*) as Indra the *Cows* or *Svarga* (Go) Śridhara.) The Rishis, Gandharvas, Vidyādharas, Siddhas and Chāranas all joined the Inauguration ceremony. The Deva girls danced and sang. The three Lokas became full of joy. The cows wet the earth with their milk. The rivers bore streams of milk and other drinks. The trees poured honey. The cereals bore grains without culture. The hills brought forth their precious stones. Even the wild animals became mild.

KRISHNA AND VARUNA, KRISHNA AND THE GOPAS.

SKANDHA X. CHAP. 28.

After observing the fast of the 11th Day of the Moon, Nanda went to bathe in the river Yamunā, on the twelfth day of the Moon. It was still dark. So the Asuras had possession of the hour. An Asura servant of Varuna carried Nanda to his master. The Gopas called out to Rāma and Krishna. Krishna entered the water and went to Varuna. The Lokapala worshipped him and gave back Nanda, excusing himself for the ignorance of his servant. Nanda on returning apprised the Gopas of what he had seen. Could Krishna be any other than Īshvara? The Gopas wished ardently that He might take them over to His supreme abode. The all-knowing Krishna knew this. He took the Gopas to that portion of the Yamunā called Bramha Hrada. Plunged in the waters, they saw Vaikuntha, the supreme abode of Krishna, far away from the limits of Prakriti.

THE FIVE CHAPTERS ON RĀSA

(AUTUMN AGAIN.)

SKANDHA X. CHAP. 29-33.

Suka said: —

"Seeing those autumnal nights, gay with Mallika flowers, Bhagavān wished to enjoy Himself by resort to Yogamāyā."

(It looks odd that there should be a show of conquering the God of love by enjoyment of others' wives. But it is really not so. For you have "By resort to Yoga Māyā." "Enjoyed though self enjoyer," "The subduer of the God of Love Himself," "With enjoyment all self contained," and such like passages, which show absolute self dependence. Therefore this show of Rāsa play is only meant to recite the conquest of Kāma Deva. This is the real truth. Moreover through this love topic, the five chapters on Rāsa are calculated to bring about a complete disinclination to worldly matters. *Śridhara*).

("Those nights" *Go back to Vraja. These nights you shall enjoy with me —* the nights promised by these words. *Śridhara.*')

At that time the moon had appeared on the horizon. As the lover reunited after long separation besmears the face of his beloved with orange coloured saffron, so he besmeared the face of the east with the most delightful orange rays which brushed away the sorrows of men (*charshani*). Krishna looked at the Moon, the lover of the Kumud flower, with unbroken disc, glowing like the face of Lakshmī, orange red like fresh saffron, and he looked at the forest illumined with the tender rays of the Moon and he indulged in song so sweet that it ravished the hearts of good-looking women.

Listening to that passion-exciting song, the women of Vraja, with minds absorbed in Krishna rushed forth to where their lover was without taking notice of each other, their ear-rings moving violently about.

Some left their houses while milking the cow. Some did not wait to see the boiling of the milk. Some did not take down boiled wheat from the oven. Some had been giving food to others, some had been giving milk to their own children. Some had been serving their husbands and some had been taking their own food. But they all left their work half finished. They gave up their household duties and, with clothes and ornaments all in disorder, they hurriedly went to Krishna, (Hearing the voice indicative of Sri Krishna, the Gopis became strongly inclined to Him, and they showed by their acts that then and there they had complete disinclination for works that had the three Vargas, Dharma, Artha and Kāma for their object. They left their half finished work and went over to Krishna straight. *Śridhara*.)

Their husbands could not keep them back nor their fathers, brothers and friends. Their hearts had been completely charmed by Govinda. They did not turn back. (Obstacles cannot overcome those whose hearts are attracted by Krishna. *Śridhara*.)

Some Gopis that had been inside their houses could not make their way out. Their thoughts had been already devoted to Krishna, and now with closed eyes, they held Him fast in their minds.

With sins all removed by the acute pain of unbearable separation from the dearest one, the Kārmic effects of good works taken away by the absolute pleasure caused by the embraces of Krishna in meditation, with their bonds completely severed at that very moment, those Gopis gave up their bodies composed of the Gunas, even though they united with Krishna as their paramour. (How could they give up their bodies composed of Gunas while they did not know Krishna as Parama Ātmā, but knew him only as their paramour, a relation caused by the Gunas? "Even though they &c." A thing is not dependent for its properties upon what another thinks of it. Drink nectar without knowing it is so. The effects are there. There is another difficulty. The Gopis had their Prārabdha Karma, or Karma that brought about the present birth and its surroundings, and Prārabdha is exhausted only after being worked out. So with the bonds of Prārabdha, how could they give up their body? "With their bonds completely severed at that very time." But Prārabdha cannot be exhausted without suffering and enjoyment. Where were the suffering and enjoyment in this case? "With sins all removed &c." The greatest suffering caused by separation removed all demerits and the greatest enjoyment caused by the embraces of Krishna removed the bonds of merits. Therefore when Parama Ātmā was attained by intense meditation, the suffering and enjoyment of the time completely eradicated Karma and the Gopis gave up their bodies composed of the Gunas. *Śridhara*.)

Asked Rājā Parikshit: —

"O Muni, they knew Krishna as only one enjoyable and not as Brahmā. The Gunas were mixed up in their understanding of Krishna. How could there then be a cessation of the flow of the Gunas?"

(Husbands, sons and others, even they themselves were Brahmā in essence.
But a devotion to them could not cause Moksha as they were not known as
Brahmā. How could union with Krishna cause Moksha, when he was not
known as Brahmā? Therefore this doubt. *Śridhara*.)

Suka replied: —

"O King, I have said before how Sisupāla attained Siddhi even by bearing
enmity to Hrishikesha (controller of the senses, Krishna.) What of those to
whom Krishna is dear? (The purport is that Brahmā-hood is eclipsed in the
Jiva. But Krishna is controller of the senses. Brahmā-hood is manifest in
him. He does not require to be known. *Śridhara*). Bhagavān manifests
himself for the Moksha of men though in reality, He is without end,
without measure, void of all Gunas and their controller." (Krishna being a
manifestation of Bhagavān, there is no comparison between Him and other
embodied men. *Śridhara*.)

"Bear any feeling *constantly* towards Hari, whether it be a feeling of love,
anger, fear, affection, kinship or devotion and you become full of Him. Do
not wonder at this. For Krishna is the Lord of all Lords of Yoga. All (even
the lowest life forms) attain Mukti from him. When the women of Vraja
drew near, Krishna addressed them thus: —

"'Welcome, ye great ones! What good can I do for you? Is it all safe in
Vraja? Tell me the object of your coming here. The night is fearful and
dangerous animals are treading round. Go back to Vraja. This is not a place
for women. You have got your mothers, fathers, sons, brothers, and
husbands. They are seeking you. Do not cause pain to your friends. What
more, you have now seen this forest adorned with flowers and illumined by
the tender rays of the full moon, where the trees and their tender branches,
gently moved by the breeze from the Yamunā, stand in all their beauty.
Now go back, O virtuous girls, speedily to your homes and look after your
husbands. The calves and your children are weeping. Go and let them have
their drink. Or if you have come here, forced by your love for me, it is only
meet and proper, for all people have their love for me. Devotion to
husband is the one great religion for women. They are to seek the well
being of their friends and to bring up their children. The husband may be
wicked, old, diseased or poor. But those who wish for higher Lokas should

not give up their husbands. The connection with one not the husband is disreputable and unbecoming. You may bear love to me in other ways than by such a near approach. Therefore go back to your houses.'"

"The Gopis were struck dumb for a time. They became overcome with sorrow. They had given up every thing for the sake of Krishna and they could ill bear to hear these unkind words. At last they broke forth: — 'O Lord, it is not for Thee to utter these unkind words. We have given up all objects and sought Thy feet. O Thou difficult to be reached, do not forsake us but please think of us, even as the First Purusha thinks of those that seek Moksha. Thou speakest, O love, of our duties to husbands, sons, and friends as if thou wert a religious teacher, but thou art thyself the goal of those religious injunctions. So let them rest in thee. Thou art the greatest friend of all beings, for thou art verily their own self. What do they care for husbands or sons, sources of misery as they are, who are attached to thee, the constant source of happiness?

"'Therefore do thou show favor to us and permit us to serve Thee.' Moved by their piteous appeal, Krishna gave his company to the Gopis. Proud of that company, the Gopis deemed themselves superior to all other women on the earth. To put down this loss of mental balance, caused by good fortune and this pride, Krishna suddenly disappeared from amongst them. The Gopis became disconsolate. Their hearts had been too much taken up by the gestures and movements of Krishna. So they imitated his deeds and even called themselves Krishna. They all sang loudly together and madly searched for Krishna from forest to forest. They asked the trees if they had seen their lover. They enquired of the creepers, the earth and the deer. Fatigued at last, they again took to reproducing the deeds of Krishna. Some played the part of Pūtanā or some other Asura, some played the part of Krishna in connection with some of his manifold deeds. They again made enquiries from the plants. They then found out the footsteps of Krishna marked by the divine symbols (flag, the lotus, the thunder-bolt and the goad). Tracing those steps a little further, they found they were mixed up with the footprints of a girl. The Gopis exclaimed: —

"'Surely this girl had made Ārādhanā (devout prayer for the Lord). Govinda left us that he might take her to a secret retreat. Sacred are the dust particles of Govinda's feet; even Brahmā, Śiva and Lakshmī hold them on their head for the extinction of sins. Look here we no longer see the foot marks of that girl. It seems Krishna carried her here on his back and his footprints are therefore deeply marked. Here He placed her down to pluck flowers and touched the earth with his toes only, for the steps are not fully marked. Surely he placed the girl on his lap here and adorned her hair with flowers.' And what of that girl? She deemed herself very fortunate that Krishna should shew particular attention to her. With this sense of superiority she spoke to Krishna. 'I can not walk. Take me to where I like on thy back.' Krishna said, 'Get up on my back.' But when she would do so, Krishna had already disappeared. The girl was loudly lamenting, when the other Gopis joined her. They heard her story and became very much surprised. (It is necessary to draw the special attention of the readers to the girl, who had made Ārādhanā of Hari. She is the Rādhikā of Nārada Pancharātra and of later day Vaishnavism. Rādhikā means literally one who makes Rādhanā or Ārādhanā. But I shall not touch upon her in a study of the Bhāgavata Purāna. The study of this Purāna is incomplete without a study of Chaitanya's teachings. And if I succeed in taking up those teachings, I shall consider the lofty ideal of Rādhikā).

"The Gopis all returned to the forest and searched for Krishna as long as there was moonlight. They gave up their search when it was dark. With thoughts all directed to Krishna, with conversations all about Him, with gestures and movements all after Him, with songs all about His deeds, the Gopis, all full of Krishna, they did not think of their homes. They went to the banks of the Yamunā, and all sang in a chorus about Krishna, ardently praying for his return. (I shall not touch with my profane hand the songs of the Gopis. They are far too sacred for any rendering into English and they baffle any attempt to do so. Sweet as nectar, the melody of those songs is inseparable from their very essence, and he would be murdering Bhāgavata who would attempt to translate those songs. For the continuity of our study it is only necessary to translate the fourth sloka.)

"'Thou art not surely the son of Yasodā. Thou art the inmost seer of all things. Implored by Brahmā thou hast appeared, O friend, in the line of the Sātvats, for the protection of the Universe.' While the Gopis were thus bewailing in melodious tunes, Krishna appeared with a smiling face. They formed a circle round Him and were so pleased to see Him that they reached the very limit of their joy. The Gopis spread out their outer garments as a seat for Sri Krishna, on the river bank. When Krishna sat down, they addressed him thus: —

"'Some seek those only that seek them; some do the contrary, (*i.e.* seek those even who do not seek them), others seek neither those that seek them nor those that do not seek them. Please tell us, what is all this.'

"Said Śrī Krishna: — 'Those that seek each other are guided in their efforts by selfishness. There is neither friendship nor virtue in that mutuality. It is all for a selfish end. (Even the beasts seek mutual good. *Śridhara.* And do not the Utilitarians and the evolutionists do so)? Those that seek the unseeking are either kind-hearted men or they are guided by affection like the parents. It is pure virtue in the former case and friendship in the latter.

"'Those that do not seek the people that seek them and far less those that do not seek them fall under one of the following four classes: —

"'(1) Those that seek pleasure in self (and not in the outside world), (2) those that are satiated, (3) the ungrateful and (4) the treacherous. But I do not belong to any of these classes, I do not seek those that seek me in order to make them seek me continually and constantly. For when a poor man gains wealth and then loses it, he becomes so full of that loss that no other thought can enter his mind (*i.e.* to help the continuity and constancy of the devotional feeling, I do not show open favor to a devotee. This is an act of supreme kindness and friendship). You have given up for my sake all worldly concerns, the Vedas and even your own relations. I seek you from behind, being out of sight. Therefore you ought rightly to be angry with me. Even with the life of a God, I cannot make any return for your devotion to me, for you have burst asunder the ever fresh chains of home life, in order to seek me. So let your own goodness be the only recompense for your devotion.'"

THE RĀSA.

Govinda commenced Rāsa with his devoted band. (Rāsa is a kind of dance in which many dancing girls take part.) The Gopis formed a circle, and

Krishna, the Lord of Yoga, was between every two of them and he pressed them all unto his shoulders, and each of them thought that Krishna was near to her. (How could one Krishna stand between every two of them and how could each Gopi think that he was near to her only, when he was near to them all? Therefore "the Lord of Yoga" *i.e.* of unimaginable powers. *Śridhara*.) The sky became filled with hundreds of chariots of Devas and Deva girls, eager to witness the scene. Drums beat and flowers rained. The Gandharva kings with their wives sang the pure glory of Krishna. Loud was the clash of the Gopis' ornaments. They danced and sang in great excitement. The moon lingered on with amazed look and the night became prolonged. So the dance continued till at last the Gopis became fatigued. Krishna wiped off their sweat and went with them to bathe in the Yamunā. After the bath they most reluctantly took leave of Krishna.

In these enjoyments Krishna was self-contained.

Asked Rājā Parikshit: —

"The Incarnation of Īshvara is for the spread of Dharma and the putting down of Adharma. What is this enjoyment of others' wives, contrary to all injunctions and hateful in itself, by one who is at once the originator and preserver of all Dharma?"

Suka said: — Even the great are seen to violate what we call Dharma and the gods become over bold. But this does not bespeak any evil of them, as they have got superior force, even as fire eats everything but is ever pure. But he who is not capable (*i.e.* who is a slave to his body and its attributes) is not to perform such acts even in mind. If he does such acts through ignorance, he is sure to be ruined. It is only Śiva that could drink the poison that appeared from the ocean of milk. The words of the Lords (Īshvara) are true. Their deeds are only sometimes true, (*i.e.* their exceptional life, which is governed by extraordinary consideration and unusual conditions, is not meant always as an example for ordinary beings. But what they say is always for the good of the universe and is to be followed as a teaching. What is given as their life is also sometimes allegorical and has to be understood in another sense). The wise man therefore follows such of their deeds as are consistent with the other words of the great ones. They have nothing to gain or lose by good or bad deeds.

For they have no Egoism in them. What is good and what is bad to him who is the Lord of all beings? By devotion to His feet and by power of Yoga, even Munis are freed from the bonds of good and evil. The Lord did only assume a body at will. Whence could there be any bondage in His case? (And was there really an enjoyment of others' wives? No for He dwells in all beings, even the Gopis and their husbands. He is the manifestor of all the senses. The assumption of the body is only a playful fancy. It is for the good of all beings that He became a man. His indulgences are such as are likely to make one devoted to Him, when heard of. Even the minds of those that are very much turned away from Īshvara are attracted towards Īshvara, by means of Sringāra Rāsa or love topics. Hence the love matter of Sri Krishna. This is the purport. *Śridhara*) The people of Vraja, deluded by the Māyā of Krishna, thought that their wives were by their side. They bore no ill-feeling towards Krishna. (It follows that those who perform such acts without such powers are sinners. *Śridhara*.)

When it was Brahmā Muhurta, (the part of the night immediately preceding the dawn), the Gopis, with the permission of Śri Krishna, reluctantly left Him and went home.

He who hears or recites this play of Vishnu with the women of Vraja acquires supreme devotion to Bhagavat and shakes off in no time that disease of the heart called Kāma or passion for women.

SUDARSANA.

SKANDHA X. CHAP. 34.

(The Rāsa is a teaching about conquering Kāma by treating of indulgence in Kāma itself. Similarly this chapter treats of the conquest of Vidyadhara. *Śridhara*.)

On the occasion of a sacred festival the Gopas went to the banks of the Sarasvati. (Students will mark the significance of the Sarasvati, which corresponds to Sushumnā in the human system at this stage of spiritual development). They adored Pasupati (Śiva) and Ambikā (Durgā). They passed the night on the river bank. A huge serpent swallowed Nanda. The

Gopas burnt the animal but it would not let go its hold; Krishna then touched it with his feet and out came a Vidyadhara from the serpent body. This Vidyadhara, by name Sudarsana, had been cursed by Rishi Angiras for having slighted him and became a serpent.

SANKHA CHŪDA.

SKANDHA X. CHAP. 34.

One day Rāma and Krishna came to the forest to have company with the Gopis. It was the first part of the night. They played upon the flute and the Gopis listened to the music with rapt attention. At this time Sankha Chūda, the well-known attendant of Kuvera, drove the Gopis away northward. The girls wept and called out to Krishna and Rāma for help. They ran after the Yaksha who in terror left the Gopis and fled away. Rāma remained in charge of the Gopa girls. Krishna overtook Sankha Chūda and severed his head with its jewel and presented the crest jewel to Balarāma.

THE SEPARATION SONG OF THE GOPIS.

SKANDHA X. CHAP. 35.

At night the Gopis enjoyed the company of Krishna. But the day was their time of separation and, when Krishna went to the forest, they passed the time any how in singing about him. For the separation song, please refer to the original.

ARISHTA.

SKANDHA X. CHAP. 36.

Arishta, an Asura in the form of a bull, attacked the quarters of the cows. The cows fled away and the Gopas cried out "Krishna, O Krishna save us," Krishna killed the Asura.

NĀRADA AND KANSA.

SKANDHA X. CHAP. 36.

Nārada told Kansa: — "The female child was the daughter of Yasodā; Krishna and Rāma are sons of Devaki. Vāsudeva kept them with his friend Nanda out of fear. Those two brothers have killed your spies." In rage the king of Bhoja took his sword to kill Vāsudeva. Nārada prevented him. But the King put Yasudeva and his wife in iron fetters. He then ordered Kesi to kill Rāma and Krishna. He called his ministers together in council. Addressing Chānur and Mushtika he said: — "Rāma and Krishna are to kill us. So Nārada told me." Those two Asuras came ready for Vraja. But Kansa said: "No, you need not go. I shall send for the two brothers and kill them in a wrestling match. So prepare the playground. Place the elephant Kubalayāpida at the entrance and let him kill my enemies. On the fourteenth day of the Moon, let us commence Dhanus Yajna, and let animals be killed in honor of Śiva."

Kansa then sent for Akrūra, one of the chiefs of the Yadu clan. "Akrūra," said he, "Thou art my friend and do the work of a friend. Please go to Vraja. Take this chariot and bring the two sons of Vāsudeva. Tell them, they are to see the Dhanus Yajna and have a sight of the town. Let Nanda and other Gopas come with presents. The elephant shall kill the two boys. Or if perchance they escape, the wrestlers shall do away with them. I will then make easy work of Vāsudeva, my old father Ugrasena, his brother Devaka, the Vrishnis, the Bhojas and the Dasārhas. Then, O friend, the earth will be left without a thorn. Jarāsandha is my guide. Dvivid is my friend. Samvara, Naraka, and Vāna have made alliance with me. With the help of these, I shall kill all kings that are on the side of the Devas. Know this to be my plan." Akrūra said: — "The design is all right. But it may or may not succeed. Even lofty desires are frustrated by unforeseen obstacles. Still man entertains them, to meet with either joy or sorrow. But I will do thy behests."

The council broke up.

KESI.

SKANDHA X. CHAP. 37.

In the meantime, Kesi, under the orders of Kansa, entered Vraja, in the form of a fiery steed, Krishna held him aloft by the feet and threw him away. The Asura regained consciousness and again ran after Krishna. He thrust his hand inside the mouth of the Asura and killed him at once. The Devas rained flowers over him and prayed. Rishi Nārada also appeared and adored him, making reference to his future deeds.

VYOMA.

SKANDHA X. CHAP. 37.

The Gopas were grazing cattle on the flat summit of a hill. Some played the part of thieves, some, that of cattle keepers and some the part of sheep. The Asura Vyoma, (the word meaning Ākāsa), son of Māyā, assumed the form of a Gopa, and playing the part of a thief carried away many Gopas, who became sheep and he confined them in a hill cave closed by stones. In the playground only four or five Gopas remained. Krishna found out the mischief, attacked the Asura and killed him.

AKRŪRA.

Akrūra was mightily pleased that he would see the lotus feet of Rāma and Krishna. His devotion to Krishna knew no bounds and he knew full well that, whatever his mission might be, the Lord would find out his inward devotion. At sunset he reached Gokula and, on seeing Rāma and Krishna, fell down at their feet. They duly honored him. Nanda also shewed every respect to Akrūra. At night Akrūra made a clean breast of everything to Rāma and Krishna, telling how Kansa oppressed the Yadus, how Nārada informed him of their presence in Vraja and who they were, how he planned their death, and the mission on which he sent him. Rāma and Krishna only laughed. The next morning they informed Nanda about the command of the king. Nanda asked the Gopas to prepare themselves with presents.

And the Gopa girls? Who could measure the depth of their sorrow? Their plaintive strains were most heart-rending. They wept. They followed the chariot carrying Rāma and Krishna. Krishna to console them sent word that he would come back. At last the chariot became invisible and the Gopis went back to their homes.

On reaching the banks of the Yamunā the brothers took their bath in the river and refreshed themselves with its water. They took their seat again in the chariot. Akrūra asked their permission and went to bathe. He plunged himself in the waters and duly performed the ablution ceremonies. He made a *japa* (repeated recital) of Veda Mantras. But lo! he found before him Rāma and Krishna. They were in the chariot. How could they appear then? He rose and saw the boys were really seated in the chariot. He plunged himself once more and saw in the waters the serpent king Ananta, with a thousand heads and a thousand crowns, dressed in blue clothes, white in body, adored by Siddhas, Chāranas, Gandhavas, and Asuras. Embraced by him was the dark Purusha, dressed in yellow clothes, with four hands, adored by the Rishis.

Akrūra made salutations and adored the Purusha with folded hands.

Krishna then withdrew his form, as a play is withdrawn from the stage. Akrūra got up and took his seat in the chariot.

Krishna said: — "Akrūra, you look as if you have seen something unusual." Akrūra replied: — "What is there in the universe that is not in thee. When I have seen thee, I have seen everything." They drove on again and at last reached Mathurā.

MATHURĀ.

SKANDHA X. CHAP. 41-42.

Akrūra asked Krishna and all the Gopas to come to his house. But Krishna would first kill Kansa before doing him this favor. So Akrūra sorrowfully left him and informed Kansa about the performance of his mission.

Krishna with Balarāma and the Gopas went out to see the town. The house tops became crowded with females who wanted to have a look at Krishna, whose fame had already preceded him. A washerman passed that way. Krishna begged him to give him some choice clothes. But he was the washerman of Kansa and he arrogantly refused to give any of the King's clothes. Krishna in anger cut off his head. The attendants left the clothes and fled away. Rāma and Krishna took as many as they liked and gave the rest to the Gopas.

A weaver came forward of his own accord and gladly dressed the brothers with choice clothes. Krishna rewarded him with great powers and provided for him Sārupya (a kind of Mukti) after death.

Then the brothers went to the house of a garland-maker named Sudāmā. Sudāmā fell down at their feet and adorned them and the Gopas with the best garlands. The garland-maker prayed for constant devotion, for friendship with the devotees and for love of all beings. Krishna gave him these boons as well as many other blessings.

A young girl went that way with fragrant paste in her hand. Though young and beautiful, she was hunch-backed.

Krishna said smilingly: — "Fine girl that thou art, tell me truly what this scented thing is for. Anoint us with this, and good shall be your lot." The girl said: — "My name is Trivakrā (with three bends). I am a servant of Kansa. He likes my paste very much. Who but you can deserve to have it?" The girl then anointed the brothers, with zeal and love. Krishna pressed her feet with the tips of his own feet and held up her chin with two fingers and with a little effort made her erect. The hunch on her back was gone and she became a beauty. She invited Krishna to her own house. Krishna knew her object and said "Let me first do my work and then I shall visit your house." He then passed through the traders' quarters. They made various presents. Krishna then enquired where the Yajna Dhanus (the bow to be used in the performance of the Yajna) was. Though warned by the citizens, he entered the place and easily broke the bow asunder. There was great noise. The warders ran to kill him. He killed the guardsmen with the two parts of the bow.

It was then sun-set. The boys returned with the Gopas to their quarters.

Kansa heard of the valour of the boys and passed the night in evil dreams. When the day broke, he made preparations for the wrestling match.

THE WRESTLING.

SKANDHA X. CHAP. 43-44.

Kansa took his seat on a raised platform with his ministers. There was beating of drums. The athletes appeared on the scene, headed by Chānur, Mushtika, Kūta, Sala and Tosala. Nanda and other Gopas made their presents and were shown over to another platform.

Hearing the noise, Rāma and Krishna also came to see the match. At the entrance they were obstructed by the elephant Kubalayāpida. Krishna asked the driver to remove the elephant, but he only set it upon him. There was a fight and Krishna at last succeeded in felling the elephant to the ground. He then plucked out its teeth and with their help, he killed both the animal and its driver. Blood-stained, the two brothers entered the wrestling ground with the ivory teeth in their hands. All were struck by their appearance. The account of the elephant's death struck terror into Kansa's heart. He began to tremble. The people of Mathurā were attracted by the divine form of the brothers and they began to talk about their deeds. Chānūra addressing the brothers said: — "You are known as good wrestlers. The King has therefore invited you to this match. Come and do the pleasure of the King, for the King is the embodiment of all Devas."

Krishna said: — "We dwell in the forest. But still we are subjects of the King of Bhoja. That we are ordered to please the King is a great favor to us. But we are boys. We shall play with those of equal might. There will then be a fair match and there will be no injustice attaching to those present here."

Chānūra replied: —

"You are neither a boy nor a youth below fifteen, Krishna. Nor is Balarāma so. You killed that elephant with the might of a thousand elephants as it were in sport. It is meet therefore you shall fight with the powerful. There is no injustice in this. You measure your strength with me and let Balarāma do so with Mushtika."

So it was. The fight was a drawn one. At last the brothers killed their rivals. Kūta then confronted Balarāma, who killed him with his fist. Sola and Tosala also fell dead before Krishna. The other wrestlers fled for their lives. Rāma and Krishna then called their Gopa companions and began to dance together on the wrestling ground. "Well done," "Well done," cried all, except Kansa.

THE DEATH OF KANSA.

SKANDHA X. CHAP. 44.

Kansa stopped the music. He exclaimed. "Let these two unruly sons of Vāsudeva be driven out from the town. Take away the wealth of the Gopas. Confine this wicked Nanda. Kill that vile Vāsudeva. My father Ugrasena is partial to my enemies. Kill him with all his attendants." While Kansa was thus bragging Krishna got angry and with one jump, he got upon the platform. Kansa stood up with his sword and shield. Krishna held him by his hair and threw him down from the platform. He then jumped over Kansa and his life departed. He then dragged the dead body of Kansa in the presence of all. Kansa through fear and anxiety had always thought of Krishna and now being killed by his hands, he attained the Rūpa of Krishna. The eight brothers of Kansa attacked Krishna but they were put to death by Balarāma. There was great rejoicing amongst the Devas.

The wives of Kansa loudly lamented the death of their husband. Bhagavān consoled them. He then liberated his father and mother and touched their feet. He then took leave of Nanda and the Gopas, promising a speedy return to them.

THE THREAD CEREMONY AND BRAHMACHARYA.

SKANDHA X. CHAP. 45.

Krishna placed Ugrasena on the throne. The Yadus, Vrishnis, Andhakas, Madhus, Dasarhas and Kukkuras, who had left Mathurā for fear of Kansa, now returned to that town. Vāsudeva called the Purohita (family priest) Garga and performed the Upanayana ceremony (investiture of the sacred thread) of his sons. They then became twice-born. (Dvija-Brāhmanas,

Kshatriyas and Vaisyas are the twice-born classes. Krishna was a Kshatriya by birth). After Upanayana, one has to practise Brahmācharya *i.e.* he has to reside at the house of his Guru, learn the Vedas from him and practise asceticism at the same time. According to practice, Rāma and Krishna went to reside at the house of Rishi Sandipani of Avanti of the line of Kasyapa. The brothers learned the Vedas, the Vedangas and all the branches of learning in sixty four days. Then they requested their Guru to name his Dakshinā. (When a disciple leaves his Guru after the completion of study, he has to give some Dakshinā or present according to his power to the Guru). Sandipani in consultation with his wife asked for the restoration to life of his son, who had been drowned in the sea at Prabhāsa Kshetra. "All right," said the brothers. They took their chariot and went to the sea-side. The sea brought presents. But Krishna asked for the restoration of his Guru's son. The sea replied: — "I did not carry him off, but one Asura named Panchajana, who lives in my waters in the form of a conch." Krishna entered the waters and killed Panchajana. But he did not find the boy within the Asura's body. Me took the conch and came back. He then went with Balarāma to the seat of Yāma called Sanyamani and blew the conch. Yāma adored the brothers and wanted to know their behests.

Bhagavān said: — "My Guru's son has certainly been brought here by his own Karma. But hear my command and bring him to me." "So be it" said Yāma, and brought back the Guru's son. The brothers took him to their father and said: "What more do you ask, O Guru?"

The Guru said: — "I have nothing more to ask. Now you may go home."

UDDHAVA AND VRAJA.

SKANDHA X. CHAP. 46.

Uddhava was the chief counsellor of the Vrishnis, the dear friend of Krishna and the direct disciple of Brihaspati. He was second to none in wisdom. His dress and decorations were those of Krishna.

Krishna called his friend aside and said: —

"Go, Uddhava, to Vraja. Bear my love to Nanda and Yasodā, Give my message to the Gopis, which will be a relief to them in their distress. Their desires are all centred in me. I am their life. They have given up all worldly connections for my sake. I am their dearest and nearest friend. I protect those that give up worldly duties for my sake. So painful is my separation to the Gopis that they are beside themselves. Any how they live and that with difficulty, only because I sent word of my speedy return."

Gladly Uddhava accepted the mission. He went to Vraja and stayed there for a few months, consoling the Gopas and Gopis.

To Nanda and Yasodā he said: —

"Rāma and Krishna are the efficient and the material cause of the Universe — Purusha and Pradhana. They pervade all beings and guide the workings of individual natures. Krishna would fulfil the promise he made to you on the wrestling ground and come back to Vraja ere long. Do not grieve O great ones. You shall see Krishna by your side: He is within the heart of all beings, as fire is inside all fuel, To him nothing is agreeable or disagreeable, nothing high or low. He has no father, no wife, no sons, no one near or distant, no body, no birth, no Karma. For the protection of Sādhus he manifests himself in different births at his own pleasure. Though void of all Gunas, he seeks them at pleasure for the purpose of creation. As a stationary body appears to be moving, so Ātmā appears to be working, though Chitta is the worker. Krishna is not your son only. But he is of all the sons, the self, father, mother and Īshvara. Nothing exists in reality but Krishna."

Excited were the effusions of the Gopis, on seeing Uddhava. (They may be interesting to the general reader but to the student the message delivered by Uddhava is the only necessary portion at this stage of the story. The reader is therefore referred to other translations for those highly poetical effusions.)

Uddhava informed the Gopis that he was the secret messenger of Krishna. He then delivered the following message from Bhagavān: — "You have no separation from me, for I am all-pervading. As the five elements earth, water, air, fire and ether enter into the composition of all beings, so I underlie Manas, Prana, the Bhūtas and the Indriyas, as also the Gunas themselves. I create, preserve and destroy self in self by self. By my Māyā, I become the Bhūtas, the Indriyas and the Gunas. But Ātmā is pure, it is all consciousness (Jnāna), separate, unconnected with the Gunas. It is only by the mental states of wakefulness, dream and dreamless sleep that egoistic perceptions are caused in Ātmā. (The objects of perception in one state appear to be unreal in another state.) The objects of dream perception appear to be unreal to the awakened man. The mind (being the common factor in all the three states) perceives these (unreal) objects of the senses and it underlies the senses themselves. Sleeplessly therefore control the mind. This is the final reach of the Vedas, of Yoga, and of Sānkhya, of relinquishment, of Tapas, of the control of senses, and of Truth itself. This is the ocean into which all rivers fall.

"That I, though pleasing to your eyes, remain away from you is because I want you constantly to meditate on me, for such meditation will attract your mind more towards me. The mind of women does not dwell so much upon the lover, near at hand, dearest though he be, as it dwells upon a distant lover, being full of him.

"By devoting your whole mind to me, free from all other thoughts, and by constantly meditating on me you shall forthwith attain me. Even those girls that remained at Vraja and could not join the Rāsa attained me by meditating on My powers." The words of Uddhava only reminded the Gopis of the doings of Krishna. They loudly took his name. They were full of Krishna and would not forget him. But they knew from His message that He was Ātmā and their pain of separation was gone.

Uddhava remained for several days at Vraja, reminding all of Sri Krishna. When he left Vraja he wished that he could be one of the creepers or herbs in Vrindāvana, that had been rendered sacred by the dust of the Gopis' feet. (With that wish let us take leave of the Vrindāvana Lilā of Bhagavān Sri Krishna.)

THOUGHTS ON THE VRINDĀVANA LILĀ.

Before making any remarks of my own, it will be necessary to draw upon the Upanishads.

Gopāla Tāpani is one of the chief Upanishads dealing with Krishna. The work is divided into two parts. The first part gives one yantra for the Upāsanā of Krishna. The second part gives a narration. The women of Vraja asked Krishna to name some Brāhmana to whom they could make offerings of food. Krishna named Durvasas. "But how can we approach him without crossing the Yamunā?" asked the Gopis.

"Take my name, that of Krishna, a Brahmācharin, and the Yamunā shall give you way" So it was. The Gopis crossed the Yamunā and went to the Āsrama of Durvasas, the incarnation of Rudra. They offered the sweet things to the Rishi and when he partook of these, he permitted the Gopis to retire. "But how can we cross the Yamunā?"

The Rishi replied: — "Remember me, the eater of Durvā (a kind of grass) and the river shall give way."

"Krishna a Brahmācharin! And thou an eater of Durvā only? How can that be?" asked the chief Gopi and she asked a number of other questions.

(According to the common exoteric notion Sri Krishna is the lord of many women and Durvasas is a voracious Rishi. This is the cause of the wonder.)

Durvasas first explained that Krishna was the all-pervading Purusha, underlying all. Then further on, there are seven *Sākāmya* Puris or places, on the top of Meru, as well as seven *nishkāmya* Puris.

(The commentator Visvesvara explains "Sākāmya," as regions where desires fructify. As on the Meru there are seven such Puris, so there are seven Nishkāmya or Moksha-producing Puri's). On the earth, these, are seven Sākāmya Puris (Ayodhyā, Mathurā and others.) Of these Gopāla Puri (Mathurā) is the direct abode of Brahmā.

As the lotus floats on the lake, Mathurā rears itself up on the earth, protected by Chakra, the disc of Vishnu. Hence it is called Gopāla Puri. This Puri is surrounded by twelve forests: —

Brihat Vana (from Brihat or great, large).

Madhu Vana (From Madhu, a daitya).

Tāla Vana (Tāla or palm tree).

Bahula Vana (From Bahula, a kind of tree).

Kumud Vana (From Kumud, flower).

Khadira Vana (From Khadira or the catechu plant).

Bhadra Vana (From Bhadra, a kind of tree).

Bhāndira Vana (From Bhāndira, the name of a religious fig tree).

Srī Vana (From Srī or Lakshmī).

Loha-vana (from Loha, the name of an Asura.)

And Vrindāvana (from Vrinda or Tulasi plant.)

These twelve forests are presided over by the 12 Ādityas, 11 Rudras, eight Vasus, seven Rishis, Brahmā, Nārada, the five Vināyakas (Moda, Pramoda, Āmoda, Sumukha and Durmukha), Viresvara, Rudresvara, Visvesvara, Gopalesvara, Bhadresvara, and 24 other Śiva Lingas.

There are two chief forests, Krishnavana and Bhadra vana. The 12 forests are included in these. They are all sacred, some of them most sacred.

There are four forms of Vishnu (Mūrtis) in these forests, Rāma (Sankarshana), Pradyumna, Aniruddha and Krishna (Vāsudeva).

There are twelve other Mūrtis in Mathurā:

Roudrī adored by the Rudras.

Brāhmi, by Brahmā.

Devī, by the sons of Brahmā.

Mānavī, by the Maruts.

Vighna nāsinī, by the Yinayakas.

Kāmyā, by the Vasus.

Ārshī, by the Rishis.

Gāndharvi, by the Gandharvas.

Gō, by the Apsarasas.

Antardhānasthā remains hidden.

Svapadangatā is at the supreme abode of Vishnu.

Bhūmisithā remains on the earth (Bhūmi).

Those who worship *Bhūmisthā* know no death, they become liberated.

Gopa is Jiva (Ego).

Gopāla = Gopa (Jiva) + āla (acceptor).

Gopāla is he who accepts the Jivas as his own.

He who realises "I am Gopāla" attains Moksha. Gopāla always remains at Mathurā. Mathurā is the place for devotion.

The Lotus of the heart is Mathurā with its eight petals. The two feet of Nārāyana are there marked with the divine Symbols (flag, umbrella &c.). The object of meditation there is either Krishna, with Srivatsa, with Kaustubha, with four hands, bearing Sankha, Chakra, Padma, and Gadā, with arms adorned by Keyūra, with the neck adorned by a garland, with a crown on the head and with Makara-shaped Kundalas on the ears; or it is Krishna with, two hands, bearing a flute and horn.

Mathurā is from *Math*, to put down, because materiality is put down there by divine wisdom. The eight Dikpālas (Indra, Agni, Vayu, Varuna and others) preside over the eight petals of the Lotus in the heart.

The "flags" have the glow of the Sun and the Moon.

The umbrella is Brahmā Loka.

The two feet are "above" and "below."

Kaustubha is that light which overpowers all other lights *viz.*, Surya, Agni, Vak and Chandra.

The "four hands" are Satva, Rajas, Tamas and Ahankāra.

"Sankha," consisting of the five Bhūtas, is held by the hand representing Rajas.

"Chakra," consisting of Manas, is held by the hand representing Satva.

"Padma" is the universe, the primal Māyā. It is held by the hand, representing Tamas.

"Gadā" is primal Vidya or wisdom. It is held by the hand, representing Ahankāra.

"Garland" round the neck consists of the Mānasa Putras of Brahmā. The crown is Sat, absolute existence. The different life forms and the underlying Jiva are the two "Kundalas" on the ear.

Then we come to MANTRA BHAGAVATA or Bhāgavata written in Vedic Mantras, a stiff work not quite intelligible without the excellent gloss of Nilkantha (published at the Venkatesvara Press, Bombay). This work is said to have been found out by Nilkantha. It is divided into four parts — Gokula Kānda, Vrindāvana Kānda, Akrūra Kānda and Mathurā Kānda. The chief events of Krishna's divine life (Lilā) are narrated in this book, but in the order of narration., it follows Hari Vansa more than the Bhāgavata Purāna. I refer only to those portions of the book, which to me appear important.

We take the following from the Gokula Kānda. The Gopas are re-incarnations of Devas. They are the messengers of Krishna. They are fond of *Gavya* or the products of Cows. The relation between Krishna and the Gopas is that between an object and its image. Krishna drove the cattle of Nanda, just as he drove the horses of Arjuna, the object of doing so being in both the cases the destruction of all the enemies (III). In commenting on the 5th Śloka, Nilkantha calls Krishna the white ray of the Sun, which becomes the blue ray, which is in reality the ray of Sat, Chit and Ananda. He refers in this connection to the word Bharga (ray) in the Gayatri. Krishna is the heart of the Sun.

The sixth sloka explains this: —

"It is Krishna who causes bliss. The Sun God (Savitri), being guided by Krishna, goes his way on the golden chariot (VI)."

In the 11th sloka, Krishna is called the Black ray.

Mother Aditi (Earth) asked her son Indra for relief (VII). At the request of Indra, Vishnu entered the womb of Devaki. He first ensouled seven Ardha-Garbhas. (*Ardha* is half and *Garbha* is a foetal child. The six sons of Kala-nemi — the name of a demon, literally, the rim of the wheel of time, known as Shat Garbhas, pleased Brahmā by worship and became immortal. They were the grandsons of Hiranyakasipu. He cursed them saying: —

"I am your own grandfather. But you disregard me for the sake of the Divine Grandfather Brahmā. Hence you shall be killed by the hands of your own father." They remained in their Linga Sarira in Pātāla.

They incarnated as the first six sons of Vāsudeva and were killed by Kansa, the incarnation of Kala-nemi. This is related in Harivansa. Therefore they are called Ardha Garbhas. The seventh Balarāma is also called Ardha-Garbha, as he was drawn away from Devakl to Rohini. *Nilkantha*) IX.

The Black ray (Sat, Chit and Ananda) incarnated in Devakt's womb.

Krishna is Antaryāmin or inside all beings.

Balarāma is Sutrātmā, the Ego. XIX.

The Cart Asura (*Sakata*) is a messenger of the death God from the South, XX.

Pūtanā is a weapon of death in the form of a bird. XXI.

Trināvarta is the disease, known as consumption.

The Gopas asked Krishna for the milk-products. As devas, they had never known such offerings in Yajnas. They informed Krishna, where the milk made things were to be found. (XXIII and XXIV.) For the gratification of the universe, the longings of Krishna are great and for this reason he did not spare any fresh butter of the Gopis. The Gopis learned from this that for the bare up-keep of their lives, they were to attend to their household duties (XXVI). (If the boys are to steal away all the butter, life itself will be extinguished. People should have enough left for their household requirement. If I taste only a little of the butter, all the three Lokas will be gratified, and the Gopis will acquire the merit thereof. Considering all this, Bhagavān tasted butter by stealth *Nilkantka*. This means, in so many words, that Krishna accepted the fruits of all the actions of the Gopis except such as sufficed to preserve their lives). The Gopis complained to Yasodā of the stealing acts of Krishna. XXVII.

Vrindāvana Kānda.

The dwellers of Gokula migrated with Krishna to Vrinddvana, for fear of Vrikas or wolves. (Kāma and other passions are the wolves, *Nitkantha*), I.

In treating of Pralamba Asura, mention is made of the nonperception of "I am Brahmā," VII.

Pralamba is said to be an aspect of the primal Daitya Madhu, IX.

There is some philosophical discussion about the concealment of calves by Brahmā, (X to XIV.)

The first six sons of Devaki are the Six Indriyas (including Manas) and the seventh is the Jivātma, the conscious Ego. XXXV.

In commenting upon this sloka, Nilkantha says, "Devaki and other names are merely allegorical, bearing an esoteric meaning. The narration is not the real point." He further supports his position while commenting on sloka XL, of Vrindāvana Kānda. He makes quotations from the Skanda Purāna, which speak of the twofold meanings of the narration texts, one Ādhyātmika and another Ādhi bhautika, the former being difficult to follow. Following up these quotations, Nilkantha says; "Those that are not prepared for the Ādhyātmika hindering of all modifications of the mind, must seek the Ādhibhautika Lilā of Bhagavān. And if they concentrate their minds on the *holy deeds of Bhagavān*, they acquire the result of Samādhi."

Krishna is Paramātmā. The intercourse of the Gopis was not therefore adulterous. (XXXVII and XXXVIII.)

Akrūra Kānda.

In this Kānda, Akrūra comes to Vraja and takes Rāma and Krishna to Mathurā.

Mathura Kānda.

This part treats of the killing of Kansa by Krishna.

Krishna is described as the knower of the hidden names of the cows. (It is to be understood that the cows have hidden names, *Nilkantha*.)

We now come to KRISHNA UPANISHAD, one of the Atharvana Upanishads.

The Gopas are Devas.

"Nanda" is Supreme bliss.

"Yasodā" is Mukti.

Māyā is three-fold Sātvika, Rājasika and Tāmasika.

Satvika Māyā is in Rudra, Rājasika in Brahmā and Tāmasika in the Daityas.

Devaki (*Deva+ki* or chanted by the Devas) is Brahmā Vidya.

"Vāsudeva" is Nigama.

The "Gopis" and the cows are Riks. (Vedic Mantras)

Brahmā is the stick of Krishna.

Rudra is His flute.

Indra is the horn,

"Gokula Vāna" is Vaikuntha.

The trees are the Rishis of Vaikuntha.

The Daityas (Trināvarta and others) are greed, anger and other passions. Krishna, in the form of Gopa, is Hari. Rāma is the Sesha serpent.

The eight principal wives and the sixteen thousand and one hundred minor wives of Krishna are the Riks and Upanishads.

"Chānūra" is Dvesha (Dislike).

"Mushtika" is Matsara (Egoism, Envy).

"Kubalaya pīda" is Darpa (pride).

"Vaka" is Garva (Arrogance).

"Rohini" is Dayā (Tenderness).

"Satya bhama" is Ahinsā, (Non-Injury).

"Agha" is some fatal disease, such as consumption &c.

"Kansa" is Kali(?) (The commentator Nārāyana says that by Kali we are here to understand Kalaha or quarrel, for Kansa is the incarnation of Kālanemi and Duryodhana is the incarnation of Kali.).

"Sudāman" is Sama (restraint of the mind).

"Akrūra" is Satya (Truth).

"Uddhava" is Dama (restraint of the senses).

"Sankha" is Vishnu himself in the form of Lakshmī.

The Milk products of the Gopis correspond to the ocean of milk in the universe.

Kasyapa is the Ulūkhala (wooden mortar used in cleansing rice), to which Krishna was tied by Yasodā.

The rope that was used in the tying of Sri Krishna is Aditi. Chakra is Veda.

The garland Vaijayanti is Dharma.

The umbrella is Ākasa.

Gadā is the Goddess Kalika.

The bow of horn (Sārnga) is the Māyā of Vishnu.

The Arrow is Kāla, the destroyer of all lives.

The Lotus is the seed of the universe. Garuda is the religious fig tree named Bhāndira.

The following is taken from GOPI CHANDANA UPANISHAD.

"What is Gopi?

"She who preserves.

"Preserves from what?

"Preserves people from Naraka, from death and from fear."

HARIVANSA says: —

"Kansa is Kālanemi,

"Kesin is Haya Grīva,

"Arishta is son of Bali, the Elephant is Rishta, son of Diti, Chānūra and Mushtika are the Asuras, Varaha and Kisora."

PADMA PURANA throws the greatest light on the Vrindāvana Lilā of Sri Krishna. The chapters refer to the Pātāla Khanda of that Purāna.

Ch. 38. Of innumerable Brahmāndas (solar systems), there is one supreme seat, that of Vishnu. Of this seat, Goloka is the highest aspect, and Vaikuntha, Śiva Loka and others are the lower aspects. Goloka is represented on the earth by Gokula, and Vaikuntha by Dvārakā. Vrindāvana is within the jurisdiction of Mathurā. Mathurā has the form of the thousand-petalled lotus, situated in the head.

Of the forests in Gokula, the twelve chief ones are: — Bhadra, Sri, Loha, Bhāndira, Mahāvana, Tāla, Khadir, Bakula, Kumud, Kāmya, Madhu and Vrindāvan. There are several sub-forests too, which witnessed some scene or other of Krishna Lilā.

Gokula is the thousand-petalled lotus and its disc is the seat of Govinda.

The petals are the seats of different performances of Sri Krishna and are different occult centres.

The southern petal contains a most occult seat, attainable with difficulty by the greatest of Yogins. The south-eastern petal contains two secret recesses. The eastern petal has the most purifying properties. The north-east petal is the seat of fruition. The Gopis attained Krishna on this petal, by worshipping Kātyāyani. Their clothes were also stolen on this petal.

The northern petal is the seat of the twelve Ādityas. It is as good as the disc itself.

The north-west petal is the seat of Kāliya. On the western petal, favor was shewn to the wives of the Vedic Rishis. Here the Asura Agha was killed. Here is also the Lake called Brahmā. On the south-western petal, the Asuras Vyoma and Sankha-chūda were killed.

These eight petals are situated in Vrindāvana. Outside Vrindāvana, there are sixteen petals. The first petal is the seat of Govardhana. Here Krishna was installed as Govinda. The first petal contains Madhuvana, the second Khadira, the fourth Kadamba, the fifth Nandisvara (residence of Nanda), the sixth Nanda, the seventh Bakula, the eighth Tāla (where the Asura Dhenuka was killed), the ninth Kumuda, the tenth Kāmya (where Brahmā knew Krishna as Vishnu), the eleventh many forests, the twelfth Bhāndīra, the thirteenth Bhadra, the fourteenth Sri, the fifteenth Loha, and the sixteenth Mahāvana. The deeds of Sri Krishna up to the age of five were all performed at Mahāvana.

Vrindāvana is the seed cavity of the thousand-petalled lotus. By all means place Vrindāvana in the heart cavity. Krishna is always a Kisora (between ten and fifteen) at Vrindāvana, (*i.e.* Vrindāvana proper, the particular forest of that name).

At the centre of Vrindāvana is the eight-cornered Yoga seat of Sri Krishna. Over that seat is a throne of jewels. The eight petalled lotus lies there. The disc of that lotus is the supreme abode of Govinda. He is the Lord of Vrindāvana. Brahmā, Vishnu and Śiva are all His parts. His primal Prakriti is Rādhikā.

CHAPTER 39.

Govinda with Rādhā is seated on the golden throne. Outside the throne, on the seat of Yoga, remain the chief favorites of Krishna, who are parts of Rādhikā.

Lalita stands on the west, Syāmalā on the north-west, Srimatī on the north, Haripriyā on the north-east, Visākha on the east, Saivyā on the south-east, Padmā on the south, and Bhadrā on the south-west.

Then there is another group of eight, Chandrāvali, Chitrarekhā, Chandrā, Madana Sundari, Sri, Madhumati, Chandra-rekhā, and Haripriyā.

Of this latter group, Chandrāvali holds almost equal position with Rādhikā.

These are the sixteen principal Prakritis. Then there are thousands of Gopis all devoted to Krishna.

On the right side of Sri Krishna are thousands of Sruti girls, who chant His divine mysteries. On the left side are the most beautiful-looking Deva girls, who turn towards Sri Krishna with the greatest eagerness.

Outside this inner temple are the Gopa boys, who look like Krishna. Sridāman is on the west, Sudāman on the north, Vasudāman on the east, and Kinkini on the south.

Outwards still more, inside a golden temple, seated upon a golden seat, adorned with ornaments of gold, there are thousands of Gopa boys, headed by Stoka Krishna, Ansu Bhadra and others, all devoutly singing the glory of Sri Krishna.

The whole of this is surrounded by a shining gold wall.

On the west of that wall, within a temple, situated under a Parijāta tree, is Vāsudeva, with his eight wives, Rukmini, Satyabhama, Jāmbavati, Nāgnajiti, Sulakshanā, Mitravindā, Anuvindā and Sunandā.

On the north, under a Harichandana tree, is Sankarshana with Revati. On the south, under a Santāna tree, is Pradyumna with Rati. On the east, under a Kalpataru, is Aniruddha.

Surrounding all this is a white stone wall, with four gates. White Vishnu preserves the western gate, Red Vishnu preserves the northern gate, yellow Vishnu preserves the eastern gate, Black Vishnu preserves the southern.

CHAP. 41. Rishi Ugra-tapas meditated on Sri Krishna for one hundred Kalpas. At the end of that period he became a Gopi, named Sunandā.

Rishi Satya-tapas meditated on Krishna for ten Kalpas, and he then became a Gopi named Bhadrā.

Rishi Hari-dhamā became a Gopi, named Raktavenī, at the end of three Kalpas.

Rishi Jāvāli became Chitra-gandhā after ten Kalpas.

Suchi-sravas and Suvarna became the daughters of the Gopa Suvira, at the end of one Kalpa.

Jatila, Janghapūta, Ghritāsin, and Karbu became Gopis after three Kalpas.

Suka, son of Dirgha-tapas, Vyāsa of the previous Kalpa, became daughter of Upananda.

One son of Svetaketu became the daughter of Bālāvani.

Chitra-dhvaja, son of Rājārshi Chandraprabha, became Chitrakalā, daughter of Gopa Viragupta, at the end of one Kalpa.

Rishi Punya-sravas practised meditation for thirty thousand Kalpas and he was born as the daughter of Nanda's brother, by name Labangā.

These are some of the favorite Gopis of Krishna.

CHAP. 42. The form of Sri Krishna, as seen at Vrindāvana, is constant. Mathurā, Vrindāvana, Yamunā, the Gopa girls, the Gopa boys, Sri Krishna as an Avatāra — are all constant.

The Gopis are the Srutis (forms invoked by Vedic Mantras), Deva girls and devoted Rishis, desirous of liberation.

The Gopa boys are Munis, full of the bliss of Vaikuntha.

The Kadamba tree is Kalpa Vriksha, (a divine tree that gives all that is desired).

The Siddhas, Sadhyas and Gandharvas are the Kokilas (cuckoos) of Vrindāvana.

Govardhana is the eternal servant of Hari.

CHAP. 43. Arjuna wanted to know the mysteries of Vrindāvana and of the Gopis.

Krishna said they were unknown to Brahmā even. He then advised Arjuna to worship the goddess Tripura-sundari, as through her favor only he could know all he asked about. The goddess asked Arjuna to bathe in a tank called Kulakunda. She then gave directions which were duly performed by Arjuna. The goddess then took Arjuna to the real, constant Vrindāvana, which is placed over Goloka. With the divine vision, given by the goddess, Arjuna saw the mysteries of Vrindāvana, and became full of devotional love. He then asked the goddess what to do next. She then asked him to bathe in another tank, and, when Arjuna did so, he became a female. A divine voice said, "Go back to the former tank. Touch its water and you will attain your object. There you will find your companions."

The Gopis gathered round Arjuna out of curiosity. One of them Priyamuda asked: — "Who art thou? How hast thou come here?" Arjuna related his story.

To satisfy the curiosity of Arjuna, Priyamuda said: — "We are all the dear companions of Krishna. Here are the girls of Vraja. Those are Srutis and these are Munis. We are Gopa girls. Some appeared here from the body of Krishna. They are constant, keeping constant company with Krishna and moving all over the universe. Of them, this is Purna-rasā, this is Rāsa Manthara (and so on). Then of the Srutis, this is Udgita, this is Sugita (and so on). Then of the Munis, this is Ugra-tapas, this is Priyavrata, this is Suvrata (and so on). Amongst us, the girls of Gopas, this is Chandravali, this is Chandrika, this is Chandra-rekha (and so on). You will have all these for your companions. Come bathe on the east side of the tank. I shall give thee the Mantra of Rādhikā". Arjuna worshipped Rādhikā with that Mantra and she appeared before him. She then gave him the Mantra of Krishna. With that Mantra, Arjuna succeeded in getting the favor of Krishna. He called Arjuna, in his female form, and gave him the privilege of his company. Arjuna was then made to bathe on the west side of the tank and he then regained his former form.

THE BRAHMA VAIVARTA PURANA follows the ideal of Padma Purāna. This ideal was further worked out and further revelations were made by Chaitanya, who is believed to be an Avatāra of Krishna Himself. A full discussion of these revelations will be made when we come to study the teachings of Chaitanya. No reference is therefore made in this book to the works which appeared and some of which preceded, but were connected with, the great movement of Chaitanya.

Such is the study of the Vrindāvana Lilā as authoritatively given in standard religious books. It gives us a clue to the mysteries, which should be worked out by each esoteric student for himself.

The mysteries are partly allegorical and partly historical. We shall first take the allegorical representation of the Lilā, which has reference to the spiritual development of every individual Bhakta and is therefore of the most abiding interest to all Bhaktas.

The Puri of Mathurā is in every man, the kingdom of his own mind, where the personal self is to be *put down*. Mathurā is from *math*, to put down. Lavana (Salt), the demon of materialism (for salt is an emblem of materialism; cf. the salt ocean) had hold of this Puri during the time of Rāma, and Satrughna killed the demon.

But materialism regained its lost ground and the forces of descent gathered strong round Kansa. Kansa was Kāla-nemi, or the mark left by the wheel of time. Each one of us has inherited through countless ages a strong element of materiality, which tries to reign over each one of us. This is the Kansa in each of us. There was also king Kansa of the period when Krishna appeared. He was brought down from his high platform and killed by Krishna, and the spiritual evolution of humanity became assured.

There are eight Prākritic principles in man, corresponding to eight senses. Earth or smell, water or taste, fire or form, air or touch, and akasa or sound, these enable Jivas to acquire experiences from the outside. Ahankāra, or the sense of egoism, enables man to assimilate those experiences to his personal self, and to make a small world of his own self.

Then there is Mahat and the universal sense corresponding to it. This sense takes man out of the limits of personality; it raises him to the level of spiritual life. It develops unselfishness and universal life.

Last of all is the eighth principle, Mula Prakritī. It gives the sense of perceiving Ātmā.

Krishna helps the evolution of the Jivas, by developing the outer senses first and then the inner senses.

When the first six senses are developed, the evolution of personality is complete. The powers that develop the senses do not come any more into requisition. Those powers were the first six brothers of Krishna, who lay slumbering in the ocean, and who were *ardhagarbha*, as Harivansa says. Their action was confined to the material stage of evolution and hence they are said to have descended from Hiranyakasipu. Kansa had no difficulty in slaying these half-dead powers.

The sixth brother was Balarāma. He was robed in blue, a highly spiritual color, the color of Mahat. He roused the spiritual sense of man. Jivas had wandered away from their spiritual home, where they were all united, and each had made a separate entity for himself. Balarāma tried to draw them together once more on the plane of Mahat. Hence he was called Sankarshana, and his instrument was called the plough. He was the first born, as men cannot come face to face with Īshvara, so long as they are not raised beyond the limits of personality. Jivas streamed forth from the plane of Mahat, presided over by Atlanta or Sankarshana, and they are drawn back to that plane so that they may set out on a higher spiritual journey.

Then came Sri Krishna and Yogamāyā, both together. Sri Krishna was the highest of the high, beyond the Māyā that enshrouded the Brahmānda. How could he come in contact with the Jivas of Brahmānda? The only plane of Prakriti with which He could come in direct contact was the plane of Mula Prakriti. But this plane was not developed in humanity as yet. Therefore He asked Yoga Māyā, the energy of Jivic evolution, who carries

Jiva from the lowest to the highest point, to serve as a medium between Him and the Jivas. Sri Krishna performed His mission with the help of Yoga Māyā. The Gopis met Sri Krishna because they worshipped Yoga Māyā (Kātyāyani). Sri Krishna had personal contact with the Gopis at Rāsa, because He invoked Yoga Māyā at the time and got her help. Yoga Māyā is the highest sense of which Jiva is capable, and, when Durga appeared in her third incarnation as Yoga Māyā, she was not to undergo further incarnation in this Kalpa. To the developing sense of Yoga Māyā, Śiva gave truth after truth, till the highest truths were revealed to her, which form the Agamas and Nigamas. The revelations to the developing sense of humanity are the Tantras.

Sri Krishna was born that men might come up to His ideal. He is the first Purusha. The limitations or Māyā of the solar system do not touch Him. He is the Lord of many solar systems. Even the materials that form the solar systems have their manifestation from him. Nothing that we know of, nothing that we are composed of, nothing that shapes our experiences, that causes our likes and dislikes, limits Krishna. Even Brahmā, Vishnu and Śiva, the triune aspect of the second Purusha, are limited by the universe they lord over. Śiva is also called an aspect of the first Purusha in Saiva Purānas.

Sri Krishna is Nirguna, for the Gunas we know of do not touch Him. He is the Absolute, for the relativities we know of, or which we may even think of, have no place in Him. The other Avatāras are said to be manifestations of the second Purusha. But Krishna is Bhagavān Himself, *i.e.*, the first Purusha (I-3-28).

There are three aspects of the Absolute, the non-transformable, which uphold creation. It is through these aspects that all beings come into existence, prosper and dissolve. It is through them that they are brought nearer and nearer in every Kalpa to Īshvara. In the perfected being, the aspects of sat (existence), chit (consciousness) and ānanda (bliss) are not restricted by the conditions of the universe in which those aspects are developed. When beings are perfected in this way, they reach the plane of Krishna, which is beyond the seven-fold plane of the Cosmic Egg. The Gopis are such perfected beings.

It will be out of place to enter here into a detailed study of these aspects. But it will be necessary to make a brief reference to them in order to understand the aspect of Bliss, as a factor in spiritual Evolution.

It is the *existence* aspect of the underlying ray of the Absolute Brahmān, in every individual, that gives a continuity to individual existence, through thousands of births and experiences, and makes individual evolution a possibility.

The *consciousness* aspect of the ray unfolds the blunt inanimate sense into the most highly developed mind. It gives the wisdom side of man's evolution, which leads to the path of Jnāna.

Then there is the *Bliss* aspect of the ray, which directly leads to the union of the human soul with the Over-soul, of Jiva with Īshvara, and it leads to the path of Bhakti. It is the sensation of pleasure that makes the lowest organic form, the primordial cell, break through the inertia of Tamas. The cell moves about, either for cell union or for the assimilation of food, because these give rise to some sensation, call it pleasurable, if you like. It is not so easy to form an idea of the sensation of pleasure in the vegetable kingdom, but the excitement caused by the union of the sperm cell with the germ cell cannot but strike any one with the existence of some such feeling, though in a most rudimentary state.

Animals feel pleasure in the company of their female partners. They also love their offspring. This gives rise to family connections, to the formation of society and of social virtues. With the evolution of body and mind, pleasures become many-sided, and the acquirement of pleasure becomes in itself the principal factor in the development of man. Man seeks his pleasure outside himself, and he does so either for himself or for others. A point is reached when self is lost sight of and self sacrifice for the good of others becomes a duty of pleasure. Self is estranged from the narrow groove of personality. It tries to identify itself with all beings. There is philanthropy, there is universal kindness. Still the differences cause unrest and disquiet. Self finds no rest, till it seeks its reality, till it makes a homeward journey, for even its own personality and the outside world lose all charm for it. Self finds bliss in self void of personality. This is spiritual bliss attained by those that are Antarmukh (facing inwards) and not by those that are Bahir Mukh (facing outwards). Self when seeking self becomes united to the universal self as its eternal friend and its real aspect. The universal self in Vrindāvana is Sri Krishna. And the bliss of the Gopis is self-attainment, attachment to self or Ātmā and not to non-self or worldly connections.

It is to those and those only that eagerly desire to make this inward journey that the Vrindāvana Lilā is addressed.

Nanda is bliss, he is spiritual Bliss the Bliss of an Antar Mukha. It is spiritual bliss that attracts spirit unto itself. It is the field for spiritual growth, the nursery ground of enthusiastic devotion and, what is more, of devotional love. The ideal spiritual bliss is that of Rādhikā and of her fellow Gopis. It is the Bliss aspect of Īshvara that in the Jiva causes mutual attractions and makes devotion a law, a necessity. Reflected in the Universe at large, it is the one bond that holds together all beings, and becomes a force of attraction on all planes. Man is guided by bliss in his relations to the Universe. He is guided by bliss in his relation to himself.

Nanda is located in the brain, in the thousand-petalled Lotus. The spiritual seat in the head is Gokul, the first abode of Nanda.

Krishna appears in Gokul. The devotee sets out on his devotional journey.

The first impediment of a devotee is Mala or impurity. In spite of himself, he cannot get the better of his passions, his personal desires. They have such a strong and apparent charm, there is such an hereditary and accumulated attraction toward them, that they easily overcome the devotional life in its infancy. The fascinating Pūtanā overtook all by her charms and she found an easy access to Krishna himself. She made an attempt to nurse Krishna with poisoned milk. She was killed and Mala was removed (X. 6.)

The next impediment is Vikshepa or distraction. The mind, with its load of outside experiences always responding to the outside world, is so much distracted, thinking now of this and now of that, that it has to be set right before further development is possible. The cart has to be upturned, with its load of food-articles, the cart of mind with its load of experiences. That is, the man has to become Antarmukha (X. 7.) When this is done, the Asura of distraction, Trināvarta or whirlwind, is easily killed (X. 7.). The Gopis were now void of impurities and void of distraction; yet more they were being attracted to Krishna. Krishna favored them by stealing the fruits of their karma or action and accepting them for himself. Sri Krishna said to Arjuna, "You have a right to the Karma only and not to the fruits thereof." The senses of the Gopis used to roam about in the performance of daily duties, and they brought back perceptions and conceptions for the day which were worked out by the Gopis as duty required. The perceptions and conceptions are the milk-products and milk. They were churned into the karma of the Gopis. The senses are the cows; the outside objects of perception, their grass. The Brahmā Vaivarta Purāna says: — "*Ghrita* is obtained from milk, *Yajna* is performed with *Ghrita*, and all happiness arises out of the performance of Yajna." *Prakriti Khanda*. The preparation of milk products is the karma or sacrifice of the Gopis. (X. 8.).

The husk-stand is the discriminating faculty, that which separates the husk from the grains. When Krishna becomes fastened to the discriminating faculty (not that any one can fasten him with any effort of his own), when right and wrong are centered in him, self becomes abnegated and offered up entirely to Krishna, Egoism and ignorance, the pair of Arjuna trees disappear, though deeply rooted in man (X. 10). When fruits are offered to Krishna, there is a rich return (X. 11.).

We have reached here a point in spiritual progress. Personality has been completely given up. Brain intellect is no longer congenial to spiritual progress. The head retards the spiritual man and does not carry him forward.

The elders of Gokula sat in council and they decided to leave Gokula for Vrindāvana.

Vrindāvana is the Heart. The eight-petalled lotus in the heart is the permanent abode of Sri Krishna. The twelve forests are twelve centres 4 x 3, the primary number being 4, the number of the sacred Tetraktys. Within the heart, the only Purusha is Sri Krishna. AH others have to make themselves passive to Him. The Gopis, the ideal devotees of the Purusha in the heart, left the world outside, their husbands and homes, and placed themselves entirely at the service of the Divine Lord. Let us approach the sublime truths of the Vrindāvana Upāsanā with the utmost solemnity possible. Those who cannot bring themselves to an exalted appreciation of the Vrindāvana Lilā had better not read the Bhāgavata at all.

The Gopas and Gopis went to Vrindāvana. Rāma and Krishna headed the Gopa boys and looked after the calves.

What are the cows and calves? Who are the Gopas, the Gopa boys and the Gopis?

Once more let us understand the triad — Adhyatma, Adhibhuta and Adhidaiva. Take sight.

The sense of sight comes in contact with the outside world and carries the perception of sight to the possessor of the eye, under the guidance of a conscious energy. The senses and the mind are Cows or Adhyatma. The outside world is grass or Adhibhūta. The possessor of the senses and the mind is the Gopi, the Ego or Jiva. In Vrindāvana, the Gopis are the highest Jivas or Rishis, as explained in the Upanishads. The conscious energy is the Gopa or Adhideva.

The Adhidevas are the Vedic Devas, as we have already seen.

The Gopas are reincarnations of the Devas, as explained in the Upanishads.

Ordinarily the Gopas lead the cows or the Adhi-Davas lead the senses, but in Vrindāvana the Devas surrender themselves entirely to Krishna.

The calves or the Vatsas are the modifications of the senses and the mind — the Vrittis.

In Vrindāvana, Rāma and Krishna first tended the calves. The Gopa boys were the attendants of Rāma and Krishna, the pārishads or companions who reached very near the state of divinity, the work-mates of Bhagavān in the preservation of the universe.

The Lord tended the Vrittis of the mind. Therefore they could not go astray.

Now let us follow up the working of the divine in the heart of the individual and the killing of all obstacles.

Vatsa, Baka, Agha and Brahmā. — The Vatsa Asura is a Vritti of the mind. If a non-spiritual Vritti becomes unconsciously mixed up with the spiritual Vrittis of the mind, it has instantly to be killed.

Baka or the crane, stands for religious hypocrisy. Spiritual life rejects all hypocrisy, all traces of untruth, in any form.

When these two Asuras are destroyed, a third Asura appears on the scene, the terrible Agha. Agha is sin, an evil deed. The sins of a man, his past evil deeds, stand up for a while and swallow up all that is divine in him. Even Gods can not overcome Agha. Those who know the struggles of a devotee know very well how hard it is when all that is evil in man the accumulated tendencies of innumerable births, rise up in rebellion as it were at a certain stage of his progress. Who else but Sri Krishna can save a devotee at such a crisis. The flesh itself has to be destroyed and the whole nature changed. The devotee undergoes a second birth as it were. His Vrittis are not the Vrittis of yore; even the energies that guide these vrittis undergo change.

Every Brāhmana knows the Mantra that is recited for the suppression of Agha (Agha-marshana). It goes back to the pre-manifesting period, when days and nights did not exist.

The serpent Agha swallowed up Krishna and his companions.

Krishna came out victorious and he revivified his companions.

The Vrittis underwent change by this process and also those that guided them. It was another creation altogether. The forms and varieties of Brahmā's creation had no meaning now in them.

What if the Vrittis were now removed from the Gopis or the Gopa boys kept out in a body? They all lost their distinctive features; their differences were gone. All was become divine — the Vrittis and the Gopa boys.

So when Brahmā concealed the calves and the Gopa boys, he only thought of his own creation. The Vrittis and the Gopa boys came out in divinity which was now their only reality. They were all parts of Sri Krishna himself. They were manifestly sparks or rays of Ātmā itself. The senses and the mind were now irresistibly drawn towards their calves. The Gopas were more than ever attached to their boys. Balarāma noticed this and spoke to Krishna. The query of Rājā Parikshit and the reply of Suka explain the whole position. This brings us to the end of the KUMARA LILĀ of Sri Krishna which prepares the way for the union of the human soul with the over-soul, of Jiva Ātmā with Parama Ātmā. We come next to the POUGANDA LILĀ when Krishna guided the mind itself and all were attached to Him.

Krishna, the tender of the cows.

Rāma and Krishna were now in charge of the cows themselves, the senses and the mind.

The Kāliya serpent.

Yāma is the Death-god. The river Yamunā is his sister. *Kāliya* is from kala or time. Kāliya with its one hundred hoods is the lifetime of one birth, represented by one hundred years. The serpent could not be killed but only sent away from Vrindāvana. The devotees got over the periodic death-transformation.

The conflagtation and Pralamba.

As the followers of Krishna were saved from death on the one hand, so they were saved from conflagration (annihilation of form) and loss of the Ego (Balarāma) on the other hand.

In the kingdom of Divine Bliss, everything now was divine. The purified mind did not go astray. It remained entirely attached to Sri Krishna. Personality was now thoroughly conquered. The Jiva had acquired matter congenial to the plane of the first Purusha, and he no longer ran the risk of death or annihilation. The Gopis completed their homeward journey and they knew nothing except their Lord Krishna. They gave up all for the sake of the Lord. The Lord was all in all to them. They were bound to Him by the most sacred ties of devotional love. We shall now see how they became united to the Divine Lord.

The Gopis and the stealing of their clothes.

The rains followed the summer and there was a flow of spirituality all around. The autumn followed and it was calm, clear and transparent.

When the water is pure, transparent and calm and the sun is over it can anything prevent the reflection of the sun's image on its bosom? The Gopis drew unto themselves the image of Sri Krishna. There was no muddiness in them as in ordinary mortals; they had not the calls of other desires.

It is not till the ear ceases to hear the outside world, that it is open to the music in the heart, the flute of Sri Krishna.

The Rupa of Krishna becomes manifest when all worldly Rupas lose their charm.

The Gopis even smelt the divine fragrance of Sri Krishna; they felt his divine touch and they tasted the honey of Sri Krishna's lips.

The charms of the world all dead and gone, there remains only one attraction, that of Sri Krishna, the only Purusha in Vrindāvana.

The Gopis now had a right to approach Sri Krishna as their lover. They became full of Him (*tanmaya*), and they worshipped Kātyāyani (Yoga Māyā) to gain their object. (X. 21.)

It was then that Sri Krishna stripped them of their clothes (X. 22.) No false shame, no false considerations should now deter the Gopis. They should lay themselves bare before Sri Krishna. No hiding, no half speaking. "Virtuous girls, I know your resolve. It is to worship me. I also approve of it and so it must succeed." This was the long and short of the whole affair. The Gopis saw they were found out. So it was to be a matter of open love now.

We shall pass over a few digressions before we come back to the Gopis and the consummation of their love (Rāsa Lilā).

Vedic Brahmāns and their wives.

Those that were under the influence of Vedic Yajnas could not easily accept the self-sacrificing path of compassion.

The students of Bhagavat Gitā know very well that Sri Krishna raised his voice against Vedic karma and preached the performance of unselfish karma in its stead. The Vedic Brāhmanas did not follow Him for a time. But the tide overtook their unselfish wives who were attached to the path of unselfishness and compassion blended as it was with the path of devotion to the Lord Sri Krishna. The wives brought their husbands round and the cause triumphed in all India.

The raising of Govardhana.

The raising of Govardhana is only a sequel to the suppression of Vedic Yajnas. Why are the gods, headed by Indra, worshipped? Because the Indriyas are their channels of communion with men and they can influence men through those channels. They are therefore called Adhi-Devas. They are also the hands of providence and through them we get all the things of the earth. But can they give us anything that is not allotted to us by our own karma? If a prolonged and unhindered connection with the manasic world or a prolonged Svarga experience is brought about by the performance of Vedic Yajnas it is on account of the superior force exerted over the Devas, acquired by such performances, and is therefore due to karma. The Devas cannot override karma.

But still men have to depend upon the gods in their everyday lives. They are the hands of the karmic dispenser. True they deal out things according to the karma of men. But they give to men the desired objects of life and in return they expect yajna-offerings to them. This is the old law of the existence of beings. The universe itself is the outcome of sacrifice and inter-dependence, the law of giving and taking.

If men broke that law, what wonder that the gods should resent it! But there was a higher law, governing men and Devas alike, the law of direct communion with the lord of all, the supreme karmic dispenser, the Adhiyajna of Bhagavat Gitā. If men placed themselves and their karma entirely at the service of the Lord, where was room left for the Devas? Against such men the gods themselves lost all power.

The Hill Govardhana is the accumulated karma of the Gopis, which gives the pasture ground for their cows. Krishna bears the burden of His Bhaktas' karma, and He lifted up the karmic hill of his devoted band with very little effort of his own. And when Sri Krishna bears the karma of His Bhaktas, the Devas are powerless against them. It is karma that nourishes the senses and hence the hill is called Govardhana (nourisher of the cows).

The Installation.

When the gods were displaced from their position of leadership, whom were the cows, the senses, to follow? Surabhi, the heavenly mother of the cows, said: — "Now that thou hast taken the place of Indra, we shall call thee our Indra, or GOVINDA." Śridhara says, *go* means a cow, as well as Svarga. Govinda is one who acquires supremacy over the cows or over Svarga. So the word means Indra as well. But the peculiar significance of the word Govinda has been elaborated in the Brahmā Sanhita and other works.

The plane of the first Purusha, which is the common plane of innumerable solar systems, with their sevenfold planes, has two broad aspects Vaikuntha and Goloka. Vaikuntha has reference to the solar systems as a whole. The energies that guide the Brahmāndas proceed from the plane of Vaikuntha. Both Śiva and Vishnu are aspects of the first Purusha, but not Brahmā. Śiva Loka or Kailāsa is therefore included in Vaikuntha. The plane of Brahmā is Satya Loka or Brahmā Loka, the highest plane of the Brahmānda. The worshippers of Brahmā or Hiranya-garbha reach the plane of Brahmā Loka. There they remain till the Brahmānda becomes dissolved at the end of the life period of Brahmān.

Vaikuntha is the plane of Vishnu as the first Purusha. He has four aspects on that plane — Vāsudeva, Sankarshana, Pradyumna and Aniruddha. His female aspect is Lakshmī. The worshippers of Vishnu, Preserver of the Universe, reach this plane.

Goloka is a higher aspect of the plane of the first Purusha. There Krishna is not the Lord of the Universe. He is the Lord of only His followers — those that give up everything for His sake. The highest spiritual life is on this plane. In Vaikuntha there is the majesty of power. In Goloka there is the sweetness of love. Love is a surrender which we all owe to Krishna, who makes the greatest sacrifices for us. Īshvara gives us existence, consciousness and bliss, so that we may develop new centres that approach the state of Īshvara, and when we do that we have no right to keep them to ourselves, but should give them back to Him from whom we owe them. Nothing can please the Lord so much as when we pay this willing homage to Him. He has full control over the senses and experiences of the Gopas and Gopis that dwell in Goloka. He can turn them to any use He likes. They are His own property, and the dwellers of Goloka form His own household. He is one with them as they are with Him. The highest spiritual life is in Goloka. Every kalpa adds to the number of the devoted band.

Vaikuntha is represented in the Dvārakā Lilā. The acts of Sri Krishna that constitute the Vrindāvana Lilā are constant (nitya).

They are reproduced in all Kalpas and on all the Dvipas or globes for the benefit of all Bhaktas. When there is the full manifestation of Krishna in any Kalpa, the Gopas and Gopis also appear with Him. But His relations with them are meant to serve as a guide only for the initiated Bhaktas, and not for the world at large. Sri Krishna as an Avatāra is different from Sri Krishna as the beloved and the lover. As an Avatāra, He forces allegiance, and expects it as of right. As a lover, He seeks His Bhaktas as they seek Him.

The Lord of Goloka is Govinda. When Sri Krishna was installed as Govinda, he had a right to the company of the Gopis, and not before. The Gopis became the property of Govinda, as soon as Krishna asserted himself as such. The Installation precedes the Rāsa Lilā. The significance of this Installation will never be lost sight of by those who want to make a critical study of the Rāsa Lilā, or to apply the ordinary canons of morality to this most sacred, most sublime, and most soul-enchanting act of Sri Krishna the RĀSA LILĀ.

THE RĀSA.

Who can presume to explain Rāsa! What mortal mind can approach, even in conception, the divinity, the sublimity of the five chapters on Rāsa! The Gopis were on the field of action. They had their husbands, their parents, their sons; they had their worldly duties to perform, some of them arduous enough to require constant attention. When the time came, however, for union with the Purusha of the Heart, when the signal music was heard, every Gopi threw aside all Karma, all actions, all attachments, all bonds and offered herself up completely to the Lord. Where is the glory of those that give up the world, that give up all duties in life, of those that force themselves out of all actions that they may be devoted to the Lord within and the Lord without? And when the Gopis approached the Lord, there was no trace of human passion in them, no love of human flesh, no idea of material gratification. They placed themselves entirely at the service of the Lord.

But there were those that had the yearning to do so, to free themselves from all material obstacles in their way, to offer their individuality to the Lord, but the Prārabdha Karma was too much for them. Their past Karma had woven a net round them which they could not break through. It was the yearning which the Lord looked to and not the overcoming of obstacles in the way. And though they died with that yearning only, the death completed what they yearned for, for then the Union was complete.

The Vrindāvana Lilā is Nitya or constant. The Rāsa Lilā is for all time, for all Bhaktas.

The night is the time for rest but it is the rest of bodily actions. For, towards the close of night, spiritual activity sets in. Men get spiritual teachings and spiritual advancement without knowing it. But it is only a few, who have a conscious union with the Lord who manifests Himself in the heart of man.

Purusha is one. Jiva Prakritis or Para Prakritis are many. To Purusha Jiva must be always negative, however positive it may be towards the forms of Apara Prakriti. Purusha is always Male. And to Him, Jiva Prakriti is always a female. As the Vaishnavas say, there is only one male in all Vrindāvana and that male is the Lord Sri Krishna. In devotional practice, one should consider himself a female, the male being the Lord of the universe, as reflected in the heart of every man.

The Gopis heard the music and went to Sri Krishna.

If you are of the world, go back to the world. But no, the Gopis were not of the world. They had every right to the union. And Sri Krishna could not deny them His companionship. Nay, it was a great thing to the Lord Himself that Jivas should return to Him with all their spiritual experiences that the Universe might be served and protected. The concession was natural, the joy was mutual. But in the midst of the union itself, there is a danger, a most subtle danger, that of Egoism, "I am in union with the Lord." The first and the last weakness of humanity, this I-ness is a drawback even in the highest spiritual life of man. The Gopis thought of *themselves* and there was an instant break in the union. The Lord disappeared. The Lord incarnated for the good of the Universe and not of individuals, and if individuals were dear to Him it was for the sake of the Universe. He was no special property of the Gopis; What did the Gopis do? They imitated his actions on the Earth. They followed His footsteps wherever found. They approached the Lord as much as they could in idea.

At last they broke out, "Thou art surely not the son of a Gopi. Thou art the inmost seer of all beings. Implored by Brahmā thou hast appeared, O friend in the line of the Sātvatas, for the protection of the Universe."

The Gopis now realised that the Lord they wanted to be united to was the Lord of the Universe. His mission was the protection of the universe. Could they share with Him? It was then and then only that they could expect a continuity of the union. It was not for themselves only that they had any further right. Hut the Gopis now cared not for themselves. They cared for their Lord, whom they now knew and realised to be the Lord of the Universe.

And lo! the Lord appeared again. This time there was union but not individual union. Hand in hand, the Gopis formed a circle with their Lord, not the individual Lord, but the universal Lord making Himself many. Every Gopi held the hands of the Lord and all the Gopis collectively formed one circle, and the circle went on dancing and dancing. The Devas looked with wonder and envied the lot of the Gopis. Let that wonder grow amongst us. Let us catch a glimpse of that divine dance, that Rāsa Lilā, that men may become gods on the Earth.

Sudarsana, Sankha Chuda, Arishta, Kesi and Vyoma.

The Vidyādharas and Yakshas were controlled and other obstacles overcome. Even the barrier of Akāsa, which forms the final limit of actions and wisdom in the universe, was pushed through. Work was now over at Vrindāvana. The Bhaktas were now fitted to pass across the limits of Brahmānda to Goloka.

Akrūra. With the advent of Akrūra, we move backwards from the heart to the head, from the world of Bhaktas to the world at large. When Kansa presided over Mathurā, men were guided by Self in their thoughts and actions. Jarāsandha, who represented the Brahmānism of self-seeking Yajnas, was the friend of Kansa.

Akrūra was the messenger selected by Kansa to fetch Rāma and Krishna from Vrindāvana. *Krūra* is cruel. Akrūra is one who is not cruel. It was not cruelty on the part of Akrūra to take Rāma and Krishna to Mathurā. He was no doubt seemingly cruel to the Gopis. But he was kind to the generality of mankind, who did not live in Vrindāvana.

The Gopis, followers of the path of Devotion, could not bear the sight of him and they called him a mock Rishi. But he was really a Bhakta himself, though he adhered to Vedic Karma. He performed the Vedic Sandhyā and recited Vedic Mantras; he was rewarded with the vision of Rāma and Krishna in meditation.

This votary of Karma Kānda was a fitting messenger from Kansa. He united in himself the spirituality of Karma Kānda and the unselfishness of the path of Devotion.

From Vrindāvana to Mathurā we proceed from the inner man to the outer man, from the everlasting companions of Sri Krishna to His surroundings as an Avatāra.

In the Vrindāvana Lilā, we find Krishna in his relations to the holy beings and to the Devas who incarnated with Him for the good of the universe. Whenever a great Avatāra appears on the Earth, his companions also appear with him. His relations to his own companions serve as a living example to others. They afford a lesson to all Bhaktas for all time. This part of the Lilā is based upon undying, eternal truths, upon the permanent relations between Jiva and Īshvara. The heart of man is the seat of this Lilā, which can be reproduced at all times, in the heart of every real Bhakta. The Gopis are the same now as they were when Krishna sanctified the Earth. They are the preservers of the universe, according to Gopi Chandana Upanishad. And their ranks may be increased by devoted Bhaktas who give up all for the sake of the universe and its Lord.

There is one point more in the relations of the Gopas and Gopis to Krishna. Love was the one bond which united them all to Him. They sought him in their inmost heart, they talked to him, they knew him as one of themselves. He was a son to them, a companion, a lover. Whatever pleased the Lord pleased them. Whatever was His work was their work too. They abnegated themselves. They merged themselves entirely in Krishna. There was no question of duty; no rules, no injunctions. The Vedas did not exist for the dwellers in Vrindāvana. The Smritis were not written for them. They did not tread the path of karma. Love-bound, they gave themselves entirely up to Krishna and they did not stop to ask the reason why, they did not stop to cast a glance at the world they left.

But the union was hardly complete; the Gopis had scarcely embraced their friend, their lover, than he disappeared into the regions of the Universe. The message came that He was to be sought in the Universe.

The Lord of the Universe was not the lover of the Gopis. He could not be the direct object of their love. But, when the Gopis knew that their own Krishna was the Lord of the Universe, they failed not to bear the same love to Him. But the majesty of the Universe was ill-adapted to the sweetness of their domestic love. They were out of harmony with the lordliness of their

Lord at Dvārakā. So when the Lord finally received them at Kurukshetra, the Gopis said that, home-bred as they were, they could not forget the lotus feet of Krishna in their heart. They were re-united to Krishna, as the all-pervading Purusha, the preserver of the Universe. The veil may be lifted a little further. We have already seen that life in the higher Lokas is purely unselfish, for, as the Bhāgavata says, the higher Lokas are transformations of Nishkāma Karma. We are to abnegate ourselves before we can go to Mahar Loka. This abnegation can be accomplished by merging ourselves in some one who stands across the Trilokī. Love alone breaks the barrier between man and man. If we can get an object of unselfish love, to whom we can give everything that we have, we may easily learn the lesson of self-surrender. By the bond of love, souls group together in Mahar Loka and they learn the first lessons of universal life. What better object of love can one have than one of the Avatāras himself? What union will be more glorious, more lasting, more spiritual? And Sri Krishna offered himself for such love to those that are devoted to him. And the most fortunate amongst humanity are those that complete the love-union with Sri Krishna. They form an inseparable group with Him, and the plane of their union is Goloka. The Vaishnavas place that Loka higher than Vaikuntha Itself. It is the plane proper of Sri Krishna, where he is always at home with his Bhaktas. There may be many centres round which souls might gather in the higher Lokas, many types of universal life, but there is none so high, so noble, so glorious, as the centre afforded by Lord Krishna. When Krishna incarnates, He cannot do so singly. The Gopis appear with Him. The Chaitanya Charitāmrita, which embodies the teachings of Chaitanya, says that the Lilā of Krishna is reproduced throughout the fourteen Manvantaras over all parts of the Brahmānda, just as days and nights are produced over all parts of the earth. The Lilā is constantly performed in Goloka, and it is reproduced over parts of Brahmānda, according to the will of Krishna. Vrindāvana is only a reflection of Goloka.

When we go to Mathurā, we find the Asura attendants of Kansa representing all the predominating vices of the time. Pride, arrogance, envy and malice, worldliness and anger, all that keep up the materiality in man were to be found among the best of his followers and advisers.

They were all subdued and Kansa himself brought down from his high platform.

When Krishna went to Mathurā and Dvārakā, we find him as an Avatāra, inaugurating a new era in the spiritual history of the Universe. We find him there in all His majesty, glory and divine lordship. Those who follow him there follow the path of Divine Lordship. Those who follow Him at Vrindāvana follow the path of Divine Love and sweetness.

END OF VRINDAVANA LILĀ

MATHURĀ LILĀ

THE HUNCH-BACKED GIRL AND THE PĀNDAVAS.

SKANDHA X. CHAP. 48-49.

To keep his word, Sri Krishna went with Uddhava to the house of the hunch-backed girl. He gratified her desire and gave her what she wanted.

Sri Krishna then went with Rāma and Uddhava to the house of Akrūra. Akrūra rose up to receive them. He adored Krishna saying: — "Thou hast come down for the good of the Universe. Whenever the olden path of the Vedas is crossed by the evil paths of unbelievers, Thou dost manifest Thyself, as now, by the attribute of Satva."

Sri Krishna said: —

"Good people like yourselves are to be always adored by men and the Devas. For while Devas are self-seeking, Sādhus are not so. The places of sanctity on the earth and idols and stones, that symbolise divinity, have the power to purify the mind after long service, while the very sight of Sādhus is purifying. Go thou to Hastināpura and make enquiries about the Pāndavas. They are still young and they have lost their father. We hear they are living with Dhritarāshra. But the blind king is too much in the hands of his evil sons and he may not be impartial to his nephews. So enquire whether his treatment of them is good or bad. When I know that, I shall do what is best for my friends."

Akrūra went to Hastināpura and learned from Vidura and Kunti the cruel treatment of the Pāndavas by Dhritarāshra and his sons. Dhritarāshra confessed that he could not hold the balance evenly between his sons and nephews, as his attachment for his sons was too great.

Akrūra returned to Mathurā and informed Rāma and Krishna of all that he had heard.

JARA SANDHA, YAVANA AND DVARAKA.

SKANDHA X. CHAP. 50.

Kansa had two wives, Asti and Prāpti. They were the daughters of Jarāsandha, king of Magadha (modern Bihar). The latter king learned from his daughters the fate of Kansa and became highly enraged. He collected an army of thirteen Akshauhinis, (one Akshauhini consisting of 21,870 chariots, as many elephants, 65,610 horses, and 109,350 foot), and he besieged Mathurā on all sides.

Krishna thought for a moment how he could best serve the object of his Avatarship. He found in the army before him a collection of the forces that oppressed the Earth. He thought of killing the army and of saving Jarāsandha, who might be instrumental in raising such large armies over and over again. "For it is to remove the weight now oppressing the Earth that I have incarnated. I have to protect the good people and kill those that are not so." Two chariots came from the Heavens fully equipped. Rāma and Krishna drove out on those chariots. They killed the whole army in no time. Rāma fell upon Jarāsandha and well-nigh killed him when Krishna caused him to be set free. Jarāsandha, in his disgrace, thought of practising asceticism but he was kept off by other kings who consoled him with words of worldly wisdom.

The king of Magadha was however not to be easily put down. Seventeen times he led his army to an attack on Mathurā, and each time he lost his entire army at the hands of Krishna and his followers. Before the fight commenced for the eighteenth time, Kala Yavana appeared on the field of battle with three crores of Mlechha troops. Krishna held counsel with Rāma as to the course to be adopted. The brothers might engage with Kala

Yavana in fight, but Jarāsandha would make havoc in the meantime amongst their clansmen at Mathurā. So Krishna planned the erection of a fort, within the seas, where he might harbour his clansmen in safety. So the fort was built extending over twelve Yajanas. It was laid out with a town of exquisite skill and workmanship. High buildings with golden towers, extensive roads, large gardens enhanced the beauty of the town. The Devas offered their best things and the Lokapālas surrendered their rulership to Sri Krishna. By Yogic powers Krishna removed his kinsmen to this town. He then left the town in charge of Balarām and himself went out to fight with Yavana. (Yavana, is one altogether outside the pale of Hinduism, a Mlechha.)

Kala Yavana recognized Krishna and pursued him. Krishna drew him inside a mountain cave. There Kala Yavana found a man lying asleep. He thought Krishna was pretending sleep. So he gave the man a kick. That man had been sleeping for a long time but he gradually opened his eyes and in anger looked at Yavana who became consumed by the fire proceeding from that look.

MUCHUKUNDA

SKANDHA X. CHAP. 51.

Rājā Parikshit asked — "Who was the man and why was he sleeping in the cave?"

Suka replied: —

"He was a descendant of the line of Ikshvāku, son of the great King Māndhātā, by name Muchukunda. He had helped the Devas in their fight with the Asuras. When the fight was over, the Devas showed him the cave and asked him to rest there. The Devas blessed him with a long sleep."

When Yavana was killed, Krishna appeared before Muchukunda.

"Who mayest thou be with such overpowering glory?" the latter asked.

Krishna replied: —

"My births and deeds are infinite. Even I cannot count them. At the request of Brahmā, I am at present born in the line of Yadu as the son of Vāsudeva, for the protection of religion and for the rooting out of the Asuras. I have killed Kansa who is no other than Kalanemi. I have killed Pralamba and others. This Yavana was also killed by me, by means of the fire from your eyes. I have now come here to favor thee, for I am bound by affection to my votaries. Ask what boon thou likest. Thou shalt have all thou desirest."

Muchu Kunda remembered the foresaying of Garga that there was to be a Divine Incarnation in the 28th Kali Yuga and he therefore knew Krishna to be the divine Lord. He asked for no boon but devotion to Krishna.

"Truly" said Krishna, "thy mind is pure and noble for it is not tempted by boons. Those that are wholly devoted to me do not yield to desires. Those that are not devoted may control their mind by Prānāyama and other practices but, as their desires are not overcome, they are found to go astray. Roam about the Earth, with mind fixed in me. Thy devotion shall never fail. Wash away the impurities of the present life with devoted concentration of the mind. In the next birth thou shalt be born as a Brāhmana and become the greatest friend of all beings, and thou shalt then fully attain me."

Muchu Kunda came out of the mountain cave. He found that the animals and trees were all short-sized and hence inferred it was Kali Yuga. He made his way to the north and engaged himself in devotional practices in the Badari Asram of Nara and Nārāyana.

(What has been the next birth of Muchu Kunda? How has he befriended the universe! Or is he still to come?)

Krishna came back to Mathurā. He killed the Mlechha troops. His men and cattle were carrying the booty to Dvārakā. When on the way, Rāma and Krishna were attacked by Jara Sandha with a large army. The brothers feigned a flight. Jara Sandha chased them with his army. They climbed up a mountain. Jara Sandha made a search, but could not find them. He then set fire to the mountain sides. The brothers jumped down eleven Yojanas and made their way to Dvārakā.

DVARAKA LILĀ.

RUKMINI.

SKANDHA X. CHAP. 52-54.

We have been already told of Balarāma's marriage with Revati.

Sri Krishna married Rukmini in the Rākshasa form. (The seizure of a maiden by force from her house, while she weeps and calls for assistance, after her kinsmen and friends have been slain in the battle or wounded and their houses broken open, is the marriage styled Rākshasa).

King Bhishmaka of Vidarbha had five sons, Rukmin, Rukmaratha, Rukma-vahu, Rukma-kesa, and Rukma-malin. He had also one daughter Rukmini. (*Rukma* means bright, radiant, also gold).

Krishna and Rukmini had heard of each other and they made a vow of marriage. Rukmin however betrothed his sister to Sisupāla, son of the king of Chedi. Rukmini secretly sent a Brāhmana messenger to Krishna and gave him a letter. The Brāhmana was received well by Krishna. He read out the following letter of Rukmini.

"O Achyuta, thou most lovely of all, my mind has forced through all false shame and has become attached to thee, for I have heard of thy excellences, which reach the ear only to remove all sufferings and I have heard of thy beauty, which gives all that is desired to the seer thereof.

"O Mukunda, O Nrisinha, where is the girl, however wellborn, modest and great she may be, that will not choose thee as her husband, unequalled as thou art in birth, grace, beauty, wisdom and riches, and the most pleasing to all mankind.

"Therefore thou art chosen by me as my husband. I offer myself up to thee. Come thou here and make me thy wife. Thou dost deserve to have me soon. Let not Sisupāla touch me, like a jackal touching the share of a lion.

"If I have done virtuous acts, if I have rightly served the great Lord Śiva, then come, O brother of Rāma, and hold my hand and let not others do so. The day after to-morrow is fixed for my marriage. Come thou unnoticed. Defeat Sisupāla and others and carry me away by force in the Rākshasa form of marriage.

"I shall tell you how it will not be necessary to kill my friends within the house. The day before the marriage there will be a large gathering outside the town to worship the goddess Durga, and I as bride shall be present there."

The message was thus delivered. Sri Krishna vowed to marry Rukmini by force. He ordered Daruka (His charioteer) to bring the chariot. Then he took the Brāhmana with him and reached Kundina, the town of Bhishmaka, in one day.

Kundina was gay with preparations for the marriage. Dama Ghosa, the father of Sisupāla, also made grand preparations. He came with a large retinue to Kundina. Bhishmaka went out to receive him, and led him to his quarters. Sālva, Jarāsandha, Dantavakra, Viduratha, Paundraka, and many other kings, friendly to Dama Ghosha joined him with large armies. They anticipated a fight with Krishna and Rāma and they came well prepared for the occasion. Rāma heard that Krishna went all alone and he heard of the preparations made by his enemies. So he lost no time in gathering a large army and marching for Kundina.

Bhishmaka heard of the approach of Krishna and Rāma. He gladly received them and gave them quarters. Rukmini, guarded by the army, went to the temple of Durga with her companions. She worshipped the Goddess and prayed for Krishna as her husband. She then left the temple and was about to get into the chariot when Sri Krishna carried her off by force in his own chariot.

Jara Sandha and other kings were defeated by the Yadu chiefs and they took to flight They consoled Sisupāla and then each went to his own place.

Rukmin vowed that he would not return to Kundina till he had killed Krishna and rescued his sister. He attacked Krishna but was defeated by him. Krishna was about to kill him when Rukmini interceded on his behalf. Krishna then partially shaved his head and chin and left him. Being thus disgraced, Rukmin made a town called Bhojukata and lived there.

Krishna brought Rukmini to Dvārakā and married her in due form.

PRADYUMNA.

SKANDHA X. CHAP. 55.

The god Kāma is an aspect of Vāsudeva. He had been burnt before by the fire of Rudra's anger. To get back his body, he was born as the son of Krishna by Rukmini and became known as Pradyumna. He was not unlike his father in any respect The Asura Samvara, who was Kāma (or passions) incarnate, (Kāma rūpin), knew the child to be his enemy and stole him away and threw him into the sea. A big fish swallowed him up. That fish with others was caught in a large net by the fishermen. They presented the fish to Samvara. The servant cut open the fish and the child came out. They made him over to Mayavati. She was frightened but Naroda told her all about the child. This Mayavati, named Rati, had been the wife of Kāma. She had been waiting for the reappearance of her husband in a body. She was employed by Samvara as a cook. Knowing the child to be Kāma Deva, she nursed him and became attached to him. In time, Kāmadeva grew tip and Māyāvati approached him with expressions of love. "What is this mother?" asked Kāmadeva, "Why this change in your feelings towards me!"

"Thou art Kāmadeva, O Lord, son of Krishna. Thou hadst been stolen away by Samvara. I am thy wife Rati. The Asura had thrown thee into the sea, when a fish devoured thee. I have got thee back from the stomach of that fish. Samvara is an adept in many forms of Māyā. Kill him by means of Delusion and other powers of Māyā known to thee."

Rati gave to Pradyumna the Vidya known as Mahamaya, the destroyer of all other Māyās.

Pradyumna fought with Samvara and killed him with the help of Mahamaya. Rati then carried her husband to Dvārakā. There the women mistook him for Krishna and bashfully moved aside. Even Rukmini could only half decide that he was her son. Krishna appeared with Vāsudeva, Devaki and Rāma. Nārada related the story of Pradyumna's adventures. There was great joy at Dvārakā and people welcomed Pradyumna and his wife. Pradyumna was an image of Krishna. What wonder if even his mother became attached to him!

THE JEWEL SYAMANTAKA, JAMBAVATI AND SATYABHAMA.

SKANDHA X. CHAP. 56.

King Satrajit was a votary of the Sun-God. He got a present from his deity of the Syamantaka jewel. He came to Dvārakā with the jewel on his neck. He shone with such a lustre that people took him for the sun. The jewel used to bring forth 16,000 palas of gold every day. Sri Krishna asked the jewel for the king of the Yadus, but Satrajit would not part with it. One day his brother Prasenajit rode on a hunting excursion into the forests, with the jewel on his neck. A lion killed him and his horse and carried away the jewel. The Bear-chief, Jāmbavat, killed the lion and took away the jewel into his cave and made it the plaything of his son. When Prasena did not return, Satrajit thought that he had been killed by Krishna. People also suspected him. To get rid of this unjust reproach, Sri Krishna went on a search himself with his men. He traced out the remains of Prasena, the horse and the lion. He then entered the cave of the Bear-chief, leaving his men outside. The infant son of Jāmbavat was playing with the jewel. Krishna appeared before the boy. The nurse screamed aloud. Jāmbavat rushed out in anger and attacked Krishna. The fight went on for twenty eight days and at last Jāmbavat was overpowered. He then knew Sri Krishna as Vishnu, the primal Purusha and prayed to Him. Sri Krishna said the object of his entering the cave was to recover the jewel, as he wanted to remove the suspicion that he himself had taken it. Jāmbavat gladly offered his daughter Jāmbavati with the jewel to Sri Krishna. He then returned to Dvārakā with his bride and the jewel. He called an assembly and, in the presence of all, made over the jewel to Satrajit. He also told him how he got it back. Satrajit felt deeply mortified. He came back to his kingdom and thought how he could best appease Sri Krishna whom he had offended by groundless suspicion. At last he offered his daughter Satyabhama to Krishna and also the jewel. Krishna said: — "We do not want the jewel, O King. Thou art the votary of the Sun-God. Let it remain with thee. We shall partake of its blessings."

SYAMANTAKA, AKRURA, KRITAVARMAN AND SATA DHANU:

SKANDHA X. CHAP. 57.

Hearing that the Pāndavas had been killed in the Lac-house, Rāma and Krishna went to Hastināpura to offer their condolences. Taking advantage of their absence, Akrūra and Kritavarman said to Satadhanu, — "Satrajit promised the Syamantaka jewel also when he made over his daughter to Sri Krishna. Why shall not the jewel be taken from him? Why shall he not share the fate of his brother?" The wicked Satadhanu under this evil inspiration killed Satrajit while he was asleep and carried away the jewel. Satyabhama went to Hastināpura and informed Krishna of the killing of her father. The brothers came back to Dvārakā. Krishna made preparations for killing Satadhanu and for recovering the jewel from him. Satadhanu sought the help of Kritavarman. But he knew too well the might of Sri Krishna and he declined to give any help. Satadhanu then turned to Akrūra. Akrūra knew Krishna as Ātmān and he would not do anything. Satadhanu however left the jewel with Akrūra and fled away on horse-back. Rāma and Krishna followed him to Mithila. He left the horse and ran away on foot. Sri Krishna overtook him soon and cut off his head with the Chakra.

He then searched for the jewel, but could not find it. Turning to his brother, he said, "For nothing have I killed Satadhanu. The jewel is not with him." Rāma replied — "Satadhanu must have left the jewel with some one. Try to find him out. Go back to Dvārakā. I shall in the meantime pass some time with my friend, the king of Mithila." Rāma remained at Mithila for a few years. Duryodhana also came there. He learned the art of fighting with the mall from Rāma.

Sri Krishna went back to Dvārakā and told Satyabhama how he had killed Satadhanu but could not find the jewel. Kritavarman and Akrūra heard all that took place and they fled for their lives from Dvārakā. In the absence of

Akrūra the people of Dvārakā suffered from bodily and mental pain as well as disturbances from the Devas and the elements. Those who forgot the glory of Sri Krishna attributed all this to the absence of Akrūra. But it was not possible that such things should happen where Sri Krishna resided (without His wish.)

"Once upon a time there were no rains at Kāsī (Benares). The king of Kāsī offered his daughter Gandivi to Svafalka and it rained at Kāsī. Akrūra is the son of that Svafalka. He has got the powers of his father. It rains wherever Akrūra lives and the land becomes free from epidemics and calamities."

The old people talked thus. Sri Krishna knew it was not so. He sent for Akrūra, shewed him every respect, and smilingly addressed him thus: — "O lord of giving (*Danapati*), Satadhanu must have left the Syamantaka jewel with thee. I knew this from before. Satrajit left no son. His daughter's son is therefore his true heir. But it is not so easy to keep the jewel. Thou dost keep the observances well. So let it be with thee. But in the matter of this jewel, even my brother does not believe me. Therefore shew it once and give peace to your friends." Akrūra made over the jewel to Sri Krishna. He shewed it to his clansmen, in order to remove the stain of suspicion against him. He then returned it to Akrūra.

THE OTHER WIVES OF SRI KRISHNA.

SKANDHA X. CHAP. 58-59.

Sri Krishna went to see the Pandava brothers at Hastināpura. They gave him a most devoted reception. One day Krishna and Arjuna went on a hunting excursion to the side of the Yamunā.

They saw there a most beautiful girl. Arjuna asked who she was. The girl replied: — "I am daughter of the Sun-god. Desiring Vishnu to be my husband, I have performed great Tapas. I shall have no other husband. Let that friend of the friendless be pleased with me. My name is KALINDI. I am to reside in the waters of the Yamunā in the abode built by my father till I see Achyuta." Krishna placed the girl on his chariot and took her to Yudisthira.

It was at this time that Krishna got a town built by Visvakarmān at the request of Arjuna and the Khāndava forest was burnt by the Fire-god.

The rains over, Krishna went to Dvārakā and there duly married Kalindi.

Vinda and Anuvinda, two princes of Avanti, were followers of Duryodhana. Their sister MITRA VINDA wanted to marry Krishna but they dissuaded her. So Krishna carried away the girl by force and married her. She was the daughter of his father's sister Rajadhi-devi.

In Ko-sala, there was a virtuous prince named Nagnajit. He had a daughter named SATYA, also called NAGNAJITI after her father. No one could marry her who had not overcome seven fierce bulls. Krishna went to Kosala with a large retinue and he was received well by the prince. The girl prayed to the Fire-god to have Krishna as her bridegroom. Krishna overcame the bulls and married the girl.

Krishna then married BHADRA of Kekaya, the daughter of her aunt (father's sister) Sruta-kirtī. He also carried away by force LAKSHANA, the daughter of the king of Madra.

Naraka, son of the Earth, deprived Aditi, mother of Indra, of her ear-rings, Varuna of his umbrella and Indra of his seat at Mani Parvat (Mountain of jewels). Indra complained to Krishna. He went with his wife Satyabhāma to Prākjyotisha, the town of Naraka. That town was well fortified and it was protected by the Daitya Mura and his meshes. Krishna forced his passage through all obstacles and had a fight with Mura whom he slew with his Chakra. The seven sons of Mura, — Tāmra, Antariksha, Sravana, Vibhāvasu, Vatu, Nabhasvat and Varuna, — under the lead of one Pithha also attacked Krishna, but they were all killed. Naraka then himself fought with Krishna and was killed by him. The Goddess Earth then approached Krishna and, after adoring him, said: — "This Bhagadatta, son of Naraka, takes Thy shelter. Please pass Thy hand round his head."

Krishna gave assurances of safety and he then entered the house of Naraka. Naraka had carried away 16 THOUSAND GIRLS by force. Krishna sent away these girls and much treasure to Dvārakā. He then went with Satyabhāma to the place of Indra and there restored the ear-rings to Aditi.

At the request of his wife, Krishna uprooted the Pārijāta tree and placed it on the back of Garuda. The Devas resisted, but Krishna defeated them all. The Pārijāta tree was planted in the quarters of Satyabhāma and it spread its fragrance all round. Krishna married the 16 thousand girls at one and the same moment by assuming as many forms.

KRISHNA AND RUKMINI.

SKANDHA X. CHAP. 60.

Krishna and Rukmini were once sitting together, when, turning to his wife with a smile, Krishna spoke the following words:

"Princess, thou wert coveted by great and powerful kings. Thy brother and thy own father offered thee to Sisupāla and others. How is it then thou didst accept me who am not thy equal? See how we have taken shelter in the sea being afraid of the kings. Having powerful enemies, we can hardly be said to occupy our kingly seats. O thou with beautiful eyebrows, woe to those women who follow such men as have unknown and uncommon ways of their own. Poor as we are, wealthy people hardly seek us. It is meet that they should marry or make friendship with each other, who are equals in wealth, birth, power and beauty. It is through ignorance and shortsightedness that thou hast married one who is void of all Gunas (good qualities) and who is praised only by Bhikshus (beggars). Therefore do thou seek some Kshatriya king who will be a match for thee. Sisupāla, Sālva, Jarāsandha, Danta Vakra and other kings and even thy own brother Rukmin, blindfolded by pride, shewed hostility to me. For the repression of their pride, I the punisher of evil men brought thee here. But we are indifferent to the body and the house, void of all desires, fixed in self, all full, the light within, without actions."

(Without anticipating our general study of the Dvārakā Lila, it is sufficient to mention here that Rukmini is the spiritual energy of Mula Prakriti, or rather the light of Purusha, as reflected on Prakriti. The gist of what Krishna says is that there is an essential difference between Prakriti and Purusha. Purusha is void of Gunas, while the Gunas form the essence of Prakriti. Coming from Prakriti, Rukmini must follow the Prākritic elements. And if Krishna wrested her away from the hands of the material energies of Prakriti and even from her own Prākritic basis (her brothers and father), it was because the material energies had asserted themselves too much. This was done in the Seventh Manvantara, when the spiritual ascent was a Kālpic necessity. Was Rukmini to remain wedded to Krishna for the remaining period of the Kalpa, or was she to go back to her brothers and their friends?).

Rukmini replied: —

"O Lotus eyed! even so it is as thou sayest. I am quite unlike thee, the Great Bhagavat. Lord of even Brahmā, Vishnu and Śiva, Thou art plunged in Thy own greatness. What am I to Thee, the Gunas forming my essence? It is only ignorant people who worship me. (For fear of kings, thou hast taken refuge in the sea.) But the kings are the Gunas, (Sound, Touch, Form, Taste, and Smell which compose the object world.) For fear of them, as it were, thou hast taken refuge in the inner ocean of the heart, and there thou dost manifest Thyself, as pure Chaitanya. The object-seeking Indriyas are no doubt thy constant enemies. But when thou speakest of giving up kingly seats, why even thy votaries give them up, as darkness itself. The ways of even Munis who worship Thy Lotus feet are unknown; what of thine own? When their ways are uncommon, what of thine? Thou art poor indeed, for there is nothing besides thee, (and so nothing can form Thy wealth.) But thou dost receive the offerings of others and they seek thee. It is not through ignorance, but knowing that thou art the Ātmā of the Universe, that I have sought Thee. The flow of Time that arises from Thy eyebrow swallows up the desires of even Brahmā and others. I did not even seek them for Thy sake. What speakest thou of others? As the lion carries away his share by force from other animals, so thou didst carry me away from amongst the kings. How can I believe that thou didst take shelter in the Sea from fear of such kings? Anga, Prithu, Bharata, Yayāti, Gaya and other jewels of kings gave up their kingdoms and sought thee in the forests. Did woe befall them that thou talkest of woe to me? The Gunas have their resting place in thee. Thou art the home of Lakshmī. Moksha is at Thy feet. What foolish woman shall follow others, neglecting Thee? I have accepted thee, the Lord and soul of the Universe, the giver of all blessings here and hereafter. Let thy Moksha-giving feet be my shelter. Let those women have the kings for their husbands, those asses, bullocks, dogs, cats, and servants who have not heard of Thee.

"(What is man without Ātmā?) Those that have not smelt the honey of Thy Lotus feet seek the dead body, though it seems to be alive, consisting of flesh, blood, bone, worms, excrement, phlegm, bile and gas, covered over with skin, hair and nails." (Mula Prakriti in the Universe, or Budhi in man, is wedded to Ātmā, represented by Sri Krishna. The kings represent here the followers of material elements in the Universe or in man.)

THE SONS OF KRISHNA.

SKANDHA X. CHAP. 61.

The wives of Krishna had each ten sons.

The Sons of Rukmini were. — Pradyumna, Charudeshna, Sudeshna, Chārudeha, Suchāru, Chāru Gupta, Bhadra Chāru, Chāru-Chandra, Vichāru and Chāru.

The ten sons of Satyabhāma were. — Bhānu, Subhānu, Svarbhānu, Prabhānu, Bhānumat, Chandra-bhānu, Vrihat-bhānu, Ati-bhānu, Sribhānu and Prati-bhānu.

Jāmbavati had ten sons. — Sāmva, Sumitra, Purujit, Satajit, Sahasrajit, Vijaya, Chitraketu, Vasumat, Dravida, and Kratu.

Nāgnajiti had ten sons. — Vira, Chandra, Asva-sen, Chitragu, Vegavat, Vrisha, Āma, Sanku, Vasu and Kunti.

Kalindī had ten sons. — Sruta, Kavi, Vrisha, Vira, Suvāhu, Bhadra, Sānti, Darsa, Pūrna Māsa and Somaka.

Mādrī had ten sons. — Praghosha, Gātravat, Sinha, Bala, Prabala, Urdhaga, Mahāsakti, Saha, Ojas and Aparājita.

Mitravindā had ten Sons. — Vrika, Harsha, Anila, Gridhra, Vardhana, Annāda, Mahānsa, Pāvana, Vahni and Kshudhi.

Bhadra had ten Sons. — Sangrāmajit, Brihat Sena, Sūra, Praharana, Arijit, Jaya, Subhadrā, Rāma, Āyu and Satya.

Rohini (illustrative of the 16 thousand wives) had Tāmra-taptā and other sons.

Pradyumna had, by Rukmavati, daughter of Rukmin, one son Aniruddha.

There were millions and millions in the line of Krishna. Though Rukmin vowed enmity to Krishna, he gave his daughter to Krishna's son, out of regard for his own sister Rukmini.

Balavat son of Kritavarman married Chārumati, daughter of Rukmini.

Rukmin also gave his grand-daughter Rochanā in marriage to Aniruddha.

THE DEATH OF RUKMIN.

SKANDHA X. CHAP. 61.

Rāma, Krishna, Pradyumna, Rukmini and others went to Bhoja Kata, the seat of Rukmin, on the occasion of Aniruddha's marriage. When the marriage was over, the assembled kings advised Rukmin to challenge Rāma to a game of dice. At first, the wager was laid by Rāma at one hundred, one thousand and ten thousand gold coins respectively. Rukmin won all the games. The king of Kalinga derided Rāma by shewing his teeth. Rāma did not like this.

Rukmin then laid the wager at one lakh of gold coins. Balarāma won the game. But Rukmin falsely declared that he had won it.

Rāma then laid the wager at ten krores. Rāma won the game this time also. But Rukmin falsely said: — "I have got it let the bystanders decide this." At this time, a voice from the heavens said that Balarāma had got the victory by fair means and Rukmin was telling a lie, But Rukmin under evil advice did not mind this. He and the kings derided Balarāma. "Keeper of cows, what know you of games? They are the province of kings."

Balarāma could bear it no longer. He took his club and killed Rukmin. He then broke the teeth of the king of Kalinga. The other kings fled in fear.

BANA.

SKANDHA X. CHAP. 62-63.

Bāna, the eldest son of Bali, had one thousand hands. He was a votary of Śiva. Śiva asked him to name a boon and he prayed to Śiva to be the keeper of his place. Once he told Śiva that there was too much fighting-inclination in his hands, but he found no match for him except Śiva himself. Even the elephants of space ran away in fear. Śiva said angrily: — "Fool that thou art, thou shalt fight with one equal to myself. Thy eminence shall then be lowered." The Asura chief gladly waited for the day.

Bāna had a daughter named Usha. She met Aniruddha in a dream. On getting up, she exclaimed, "Friend where art thou?" Her attendant Chitra-lekhā, daughter of the minister, named Kumbhanda, enquired whom she was looking for. Usha described the figure she had seen in her dream. Chitra-lekhā pointed out to her Devas, Gandhavas, and men, one after another. At last, when she pointed to the figure of Aniruddha, the princess indicated him as her lover. Chitra-lekhā by her Yogic powers went to Dvārakā and carried away Aniruddha, while he was asleep. The prince and the princess passed their days together in the privacy of Usha's apartment. The men of the guard found some significant change in Usha. They informed the King. Bāna came in unexpectedly and he found his daughter playing with a young man. The armed attendants of Bāna attacked Aniruddha but he killed many of them with his club and they ran away. Bāna then tied the prince with serpents' twinings.

Nārada gave the news to Krishna. Rāma and Krishna, with their followers and a large army, attacked Sonita-pura, the seat of Bāna. Śiva engaged in fight with Krishna, Kartikeya with Pradyumna, Bāna with Satyaki, Kumbhanda and Kūpakarna with Balarāma and Bāna's son with Sāmba. Krishna worsted Śiva and Pradyumna worsted Kartikeya. Bāna then attacked Krishna. After some fighting the king fled away. The Fever with three heads and three feet, known as Śiva's Fever, joined the battle. To meet him, Krishna created the Fever known as Vishnu's Fever. The two fevers fought with each other. Worsted in the fight, the Fever of Śiva sought the protection of Krishna. He got assurances that he need have no fear from Vishnu's Fever.

Bāna returned to the charge. Krishna began to cut off his hands with the Chakra. Śiva appeared at the time and asked Krishna to forgive Bāna as he had forgiven his father Bali. Krishna replied: — "O Lord, I cannot kill this son of Bali. I promised Prahlāda that I would not kill any of his line. His many hands caused grief to Earth and I have lopped them off. Now four hands shall only remain. With these hands, Bāna shall be thy constant companion, without fear of death or infirmity." Bāna bowed down his head. He made over his daughter and Aniruddha to Krishna.

NRIGA.

SKANDHA X. CHAP, 64.

The sons of Krishna went out to play in the forest. They saw a huge lizard in a certain well. They tried all means, but could not raise it up. They then informed Krishna. He raised it, without effort, with his left hand. The lizard assumed the form of a Deva. On inquiry from Krishna, he thus related his own story. "I am king Nriga of the line of Ikshvāku. My charities knew no bounds and they have become proverbial. One cow belonging to a Brāhmana got mixed with my herd and, without knowing that, I gave her to another Brāhmana. While he was taking away the cow, the owner found her out. The two Brāhmanas quarrelled and they came to me. They said: — 'You are a giver as well as taker.' I became surprised and, when the facts were known, I offered one lakh of cows for the return of the mistaken cow. One of them however said, 'I am not going to take a gift from the king.' The other said: — 'I do not wish for other cows even if they be ten lakhs.' They both went away. At this time the messengers of Yāma came and carried me away. Yāma said: — 'I see no end of your merits and the places acquired by them. Do you prefer to suffer for your demerit first or to enjoy those heavenly things?' I took the first choice and down I fell as a lizard into this well. Look how I have suffered for taking a Brāhmana's property." The king then thanked Krishna for his favor and ascended to the heavens. Krishna gave a discourse to those around him as to how iniquitous it was to take a Brāhmana's property, consciously or unconsciously.

BALARĀMA AND THE DRAWING OF THE YAMUNĀ.

SKANDHA X. CHAP. 65.

Balarāma went to Vrindāvana to see his old friends. The Gopas and Gopis gave him a warm reception and they complained of the hard-heartedness of Krishna. Balarāma remained there for the two months, Chaitra and Vaisakha. The Gopa girls used to join him at night. One day he went in their company to the side of the Yamunā. Fermented juice (Vāruni) fell from the trees, as directed by Varuna. Balarāma drank the juice with the Gopa girls and became intoxicated. He called the Yamunā to his side for a pleasure bath, but she did not came. Balarāma thought he was drunk and therefore the river goddess did not heed his words. He drew her by the ploughshare and said in anger: — "Wicked thou, I called thee. But thou didst not hear. I shall tear thee asunder with this plough." Terrified, the river goddess adored Balarāma and sought his pardon. Balarāma forgave her. He then had a pleasure bath with the girls. Lakshmī made presents to him of blue clothes, rich ornaments and an auspicious garland.

POUNDRAKA AND THE KING OF KĀSī (BENARES).

SKANDHA X. CHAP. 66.

Poundraka, king of Karusha, thought, "I am Vāsudeva." With this conviction, he sent a messenger to Krishna, calling him a pretender. He was staying with his friend, the king of Kāsī. Krishna attacked Kāsī, and both the princes came out with a large army. Krishna found Poundraka had the conch, the disc, the club, the bow made of horn and the Srivatsa, all his own symbols. He was adorned with the Kaustubha and a garland of wild flowers. He had yellow clothes and rich crest jewels. He had Makara-shaped ear-rings. He was seated on a false Garuda. Seeing Poundraka represent him in this way, as it were on the stage, Krishna began to laugh.

He killed both the princes in the fight. Poundraka had constantly meditated on Hari and he assumed his form and became all Hari himself.

Sudakshina, son of the Kāsī prince, vowed vengeance and worshipped Śiva. Śiva, being pleased with his worship, asked him to name a boon. He asked how he could kill the slayer of his father. Śiva told him to invoke Dakshinā Agni, with a Mantra of black magic (*Abhichāra*). Sudakshina did so with the aid of Brāhmanas. The fire went towards Dvārakā to consume Krishna. Krishna sent his Sudarsana disc which overpowered the fire. The fire fell back on Kāsī and consumed Sudakshina and the Brāhmanas. Sudarsana still followed the fire. The divine weapon burnt the whole of Kāsī and went back to Krishna.

DVI-VID (MONKEY).

SKANDHA X. CHAP. 67.

The Monkey-general Dvi-vid was a minister of Sugriva and brother of Mainda. He was a friend of Naraka, son of Earth. To take revenge for his friend's death, he began to do all sorts of mischief, especially in the regions of Dvārakā.

Balarāma was in the midst of some girls on the Raivataka hill. The monkey made all sorts of gestures to annoy and insult the girls and he provoked Balarāma again and again who then killed Dvi-vid, to the great joy of all.

SĀMBA, LAKSHANĀ AND BALARĀMA.

SKANDHA X. CHAP. 68.

Lakshanā, daughter of Duryodhana, was to select her own husband, and there was an assembly of princes. Sāmba, son of Jāmbavati, carried away the girl by force. The Kauravas could not brook this insult. Bhishma, Kāma, Salya, Bhūri, Yajna Ketu and Duryodhana united to defeat Sāmba and they brought him back as a prisoner. Nārada gave the information to the Vrishnis and their chief Ugrasena gave them permission to fight with the Kauravas. Balarama did not like that the Kurus and Yadus should fight with one another. So he went himself to Hastināpura. He remained outside the town and sent Uddhava to learn the views of Dhrita-Rāshtra. The Kurus came in a body to receive Balarama. When the formalities were over, Balarāma composedly asked the Kurus, in the name of king Ugrasena, to restore Sāmba. The Kurus proudly replied: "We have given the kingdom to the Vrishnis and Yadus. A wonder indeed, they want to become our equals and to dictate to us! Surely the lamb cannot take away the lion's game."

Balarāma thought how foolish the Kurus had become. They did not know the powers of Ugrasena and of Krishna. In anger he exclaimed, "I will make the earth to be stripped of all Kauravas" He took his plough and gave a pull to Hastināpura. The town became topsy-turvy. The Kurus came and adored him. They brought back Sāmba and Lakshanā. Duryodhana made large presents and Balarāma became appeased. He went back with Sāmba and his bride to Hastināpura and related what had happened to the Yadus.

NARADA AND THE WIVES OF SRI KRISHNA.

SKANDHA X. CHAP. 69.

"What a wonder that Sri Krishna married 16 thousand girls, all at one and the same time, with but one body!" So thought Nārada and he came to see things with his own eyes at Dvārakā. He entered one of the rooms and found Krishna seated with one of the girls. Krishna washed the feet of Nārada and sprinkled the water over his body.

The Rishi entered another room. Krishna was playing at dice with one of his wives and with Uddhava. He entered another room and found Krishna was taking care of his children.

So he entered room after room. Krishna was either bathing or making preparations for the sacrifice, or feeding Brāhmanas, or making recitals of Gāyatrī, or riding, or driving, or taking counsel of ministers, or making gifts, or hearing recitals of sacred books. He was in one place following Dharma, in one Artha and in another Kāma.

Nārada smiled and said: — "O Lord of Yoga, I know the Yogic Māyā, by service at Thy feet, as it is manifest in me, though hard of perception by those that are themselves under the influence of Māyā. Now permit me to roam about the Lokas, filled with Thy glory, singing Thy deeds, which purify all the worlds."

Sri Krishna said: —

"O Brāhmana, I am the teacher, the maker and the recogniser of Dharma. It is to teach people that I have resorted to all this. O Son, do not be deluded."

THE RAJA SUYA AND JARASANDHA.

SKANDHA X. CHAP. 70-73.

Krishna was holding council in the Assembly Room called Sudharmā. A Brāhmana came as a messenger from the Rajas who had been imprisoned by Jarāsandha and confined in a hill fort. The Rajas sought their delivery from Krishna, who had defeated Jarāsandha seven times and had been defeated by him only once.

Nārada appeared at the time. Krishna enquired from him about the Pāndavas. The Rishi said: —

"Rājā Yudhisthira intends to perform the great Yajna Rājā Sūya in Thy honor. Please give thy consent". Krishna turned towards Uddhava and asked for advice.

Uddhava gauged the feelings of Nārada, of Krishna and the assembly and said: —

"It is meet thou shouldst help thy cousin in the performance of Rājā Sūya Yajna and also that thou shouldst protect the Rajas that seek relief from thee. Kings all round will have to be conquered at the Rājā Sūya sacrifice. The defeat of Jarāsandha will follow as a matter of course. Thus shall we see the fulfilment of our great desire and the liberation of the Rajas shall redound to Thy glory. Both ends will be served in this way. But Jarāsandha is very powerful. He should not be fought with while at the head of his large army. Bhima is equal to him in strength. Let him fight singly with Jarāsandha. That king does not refuse any prayer of Brāhmanas. Let Bhima ask for single combat in the disguise of a Brāhmana. Surely that son of Pāndu will kill him in thy presence."

Krishna gave kind assurances to the messenger of the captive kings and left for Hastināpura.

The Pāndavas vied with one another in shewing respectful love to Krishna and Arjuna delivered up the Khāndava forest to Agni and liberated Māyā. In return for this kindness, Māyā made the magical assembly ground for the Yajna.

All the kings were brought under submission by Bhima, Arjuna, Nakula, Sahadeva and the allied kings, except Jarāsandha.

Bhima, Arjuna and Krishna went to the seat of Jarāsandha in the disguise of Brāhmanas.

They begged hospitality from the king. King Jarāsandha concluded from their voice, their shape and from the arrow marks on their hands that they were Kshatriyas. He also thought they were his acquaintances. "These are Kshatriyas, though they wear the marks of brahmanas. I will give them what they ask even though it be my own self, so difficult to part with. Is not the pure glory of Bali spread in all directions, though he was deprived of his lordly powers by Vishnu in the disguise of a Brāhmana? Vishnu wanted to restore the lordship of the Trilokī to India. Bali knew the Brāhmana in disguise to be Vishnu. He still made over the Trilokī to him, even against the protests of his Guru Sukra. This body of a Kshatriya, frail as it is, what purpose will it serve if wide fame is not acquired by means of it for the sake of a Brāhmana?" Turning to Krishna, Arjuna and Bhima, Jarāsandha said: — "O Brāhmanas, ask what you wish for. Even if it be my own head, I shall give it to you."

Krishna replied: "Give us a single combat, if you please, O King. We are Kshatriyas and have come for fight. We desire nothing else. This is Bhima. This is his brother Arjuna. Know me to be their cousin Krishna, thy enemy." The king of Magadha broke out in loud laughter. In anger he then exclaimed: — "O fools, I will give you a fight then. But thou art a coward. Thou didst run away from Mathurā and didst take shelter in the sea. This

Arjuna is not my equal in age. He is not very strong. He is unlike me in his body. So he cannot be my rival. This Bhima is my match in strength." So saying he gave one club to Bhima and took one himself. The two heroes fought outside the town. The fight was a drawn one. Krishna knew about the birth, death and life of Jarāsandha. He thought in his mind about the joining together by the Rākshasa woman Jara. (The legend is that Jarāsandha was born, divided in two halves, which were put together by the Rākshasa woman Jara.) Krishna took a branch in his hand and tore it asunder. Bhima took the hint. He put his foot on one of the legs of Jarāsandha and took the other in his hand and tore asunder the body in two equal parts.

Krishna placed Sahadeva, the son of Jarāsandha, on the throne of Magadha, He then liberated the kings who had been imprisoned by Jarāsandha. They were twenty thousand and eight hundred in number. They saw Krishna with four hands and with all the divine attributes. Their eyes, tongues and noses all fed upon him, as it were, and their hands were stretched forth to receive him. They all fell at the feet of Krishna and began to adore him.

"We do not blame the king of Magadha. O Lord, it is by Thy favor, that kings are deprived of their thrones. Humbled, we remember Thy feet. We do not long for any kingdom in this life, nor do we care for the fruits of good works after death. Tell us that which will keep the recollection of Thy feet ever fresh in this life."

Sri Krishna replied: —

"From this day forward let your devotion towards me, the Lord of all, be made firm and fixed. Your resolve is commendable. It is true as you say that riches and power turn the heads of princes. Look at Haihaya, Nahusha Vena, Rāvana, Naraka and others. Though kings of Devas, Daityas and men, they came down from their lofty position through pride. Knowing as you do that the body and all other things that have a beginning have also an end, you should worship me, perform sacrifices and duly protect your subjects. Indifferent to good and bad things alike, fix your minds completely on me and you shall attain me in the end."

Krishna made arrangements for their comfort. At his bidding, Sahadeva
supplied them with kingly dresses and valuable ornaments and gave them
princely treatment. Krishna sent them to their respective kingdoms.
Krishna, Bhima and Arjuna then returned to Hastināpura.

SISUPĀLA.

SKANDHA X. CHAP. 74.

Yudhisthira commenced the performance of the Yajna. He asked
permission of Krishna to make a respectful call on the priests that were to
officiate at the ceremonies. Vyāsa, Bharadvāja, Sumanta, Gotama, Asita,
Vasishtha, Chyavana, Kanva, Maitreya and other Rishis, Drona, Bhishma,
Kripa and others, Dhritarāshra with his sons, Vidura, Brāhmanas, Vaisyas
and Sudras: all the kings and their subjects came to witness the Yajna. The
Brāhmanas prepared the sacrificial ground with golden ploughs. They then
initiated king Yudhisthira according to the Vedic rites. The Ritvik
Brāhmanas duly assisted at the performance of the Rajasūya. On the day of
extracting Sōma Juice, the king duly worshipped the priests and their
assistants. Then the time came for worshipping those that were present at
the assembly. Now who was to be worshipped first? There were many
head-men present and the members consulted with one another as to who
deserved to get the first offering but they could not come to a decision.
Sahadeva then addressed the meeting thus: —

"Sri Krishna, the Lord of the Sātvats, deserves the first place. All the
Devas, Time, Space, wealth and all else are but himself. He is the soul of
the Universe. He is the essence of all sacrifices, the sacrificial fire, the
sacrificial offerings and Mantras, Sānkhya and Yoga; all relate to him. He
is the one without a second. Alone, He creates, preserves and destroys. By
His favor men make various performances and from Him they attain the
fruits of those performances. Give the first welcome-offering of respect to
that Great Krishna. All beings and even Self shall be honored by this.
Krishna is the soul of all beings. All differences vanish before him."

All good people approved of the proposal of Sahadeva.

Rājā Yudhisthira washed the feet of Krishna and sprinkled the water over his own head and that of his relatives. He then made valuable offerings to him. All people saluted Krishna, saying "Namas" (salutation) and "Jaya" (Victory), and flowers rained over his head.

Sisupāla could not bear all this. He stood up in the midst of the assembly and thus gave vent to his feelings.

"True is the saying that time is hard to overcome. Or how could even old men be led away by the words of a boy? You leaders of the assembly know best what are the relative merits of all. Do not endorse the words of a boy that Krishna deserves to get the first welcome-offering of respect Here are great Rishis, fixed on Brahmā, great in asceticism, wisdom and religious practices, adored even by the Lokapālas, their impurities all completely removed by divine perception. Overstepping them all, how could this cowherd (*Gopāla*) boy, the disgrace (*pansana*) of his family (*Kūla*), deserve to be worshipped, as if the crow (*Kāka*) deserves to get the sacrificial oblation (*purodāsa*)? (Śridhara explains this Śloka and the following ones as a veiled adoration of Sri Krishna. *Gopāla* is the protector of Vedas, of the Earth and of others. The word *go* means the Vedas and the Earth, besides "cow." *Kula pānsana* = Kulapa+ansana. *Kulapas* are sinners. He who destroys (*Ansa*) them is *Kula pānsana*. *Kāka* may be read as compounded with another word in the Śloka, in the form of *akāka*. *Kāka* is ka + aka. *Ka* is happiness, *aka* is misery. He who has neither happiness nor misery is *akāka i.e.,* one who has got all his desires. One who has got all his desires does not only deserve to get the *purodāsa* offering of the Devas but all other offerings. I do not think it necessary to reproduce the double interpretation by Śridhara of the other Ślokas, which is continued in the same strain.) He has gone away from his Varna, Āsrama and Kula. He is outside all injunctions and duties. He follows his own will. He is void of attributes (*Gunas*). How can he deserve to be worshipped? King Yayāti cursed his line and it is not honored by good people. His clansmen are addicted to unnecessary drinking. How can he deserve to be worshipped? They left the the lands where the Rishis dwell, and made their fort on the Sea; moreover they oppress their subjects like robbers."

Sisupāla went on in this way and Krishna did not say a word. The lion heeds not the jackal's cry. The members of the Assembly closed their ears and went away, cursing Sisupāla in anger. They could not hear the calumny of Bhagavat. For he who hears the calumny of Bhagavat and of those that are devoted to him and does not leave the place goes downwards, deprived of all merits. The sons of Pāndu and their allies of Matsya, Kaikaya and Srinjaya, took up arms to kill Sisupāla. Sisupāla also took his shield and sword and reproved the kings on the side of Krishna. Krishna then rose up and asked his followers to desist. He cut off the head of Sisupāla with the Chakra. A flame like a glowing meteor rose from the body of Sisupāla and entered Sri Krishna. For three births, Sisupāla had constantly followed Vishnu in enmity. By this constant though hostile meditation, he attained the state of that he meditated upon. (The readers are reminded here of the story of Jaya and Vijaya, the gatekeepers of Vishnu in Vaikuntha).

The Rajasūya sacrifice came to a close. Rājā Yudhisthira performed the bathing ceremony, enjoined at the close of a sacrifice (*avabhritha*).

THE SLIGHT OF DURYODHANA.

SKANDHA X. CHAP. 75.

The fame of Yudhisthira went abroad. All sang the glory of the Rajasūya sacrifice. Duryodhana became filled with jealousy. One day king Yudhisthira was seated on a golden throne in the assembly hall, prepared by Māyā, with Krishna and others around him. The proud Duryodhana, surrounded by his brothers, entered the place with crown on his head and sword in his hand, showering abuse on the gate-keepers and others. He took land to be water and drew up his clothes. He also took water to be land and wet himself. The Māyā (Magic), displayed by Māyā, in the preparation of the assembly ground, caused this delusion. Bhima laughed, and the females and other kings laughed too, though forbidden by Yudhisthira. Krishna however approved their laughter.

Overpowered with shame, with his head cast down, Duryodhana silently left the place and went to Hastināpura.

Krishna kept quiet. He wished to relieve the Earth of the weight of the Daityas who were oppressing her. It was only His will that Duryodhana should thus be deluded (and the disastrous results would follow).

SĀLVA.

SKANDHA X. CHAP. 76-77.

When Krishna carried away Rukmini, he defeated the kings in battle and, amongst others, he defeated Sālva, king of Soubha, the friend of Sisupāla. Sālva vowed at the time to kill all Yādavas. He ate only a handful of dust and worshipped Śiva. After a year Śiva became pleased with his worship and asked the king to name a boon. He prayed for an invulnerable chariot that would carry terror to the Yādavas. At the bidding of Śiva, Māyā prepared an iron chariot, called Soubha, which could move at will to any place. Mounted on this chariot, Sālva attacked Dvārakā, with his large army. He threw weapons, stones, trees and serpents from above and demolished walls and gardens. The people of Dvārakā became very much oppressed. Pradyumna and other Yādavas engaged in fight with Sālva and his army. Sālva's chariot was sometimes visible and sometimes not. It now rose high and now came low. With difficulty, Pradyumna killed Dyumat, the general of Sālva. But still the fight went on for seven days and seven nights. Krishna had been at Hastināpura. He felt misgivings and hurried to Dvārakā with Rāma. The fight was then going on. Krishna placed Rāma in charge of the town and himself went to fight with Sālva. Sālva tauntingly addressed Krishna who gave the king a heavy blow with his club. Sālva disappeared. Instantly a man came and informed Krishna that he was a messenger from Devaki. Sālva had carried away his father Vāsudeva.

Krishna asked: — "How could Sālva conquer Rāma so as to carry away my father?" But he had scarcely finished when Sālva appeared with somebody like Vāsudeva, saying "O fool, here is your father. I will kill him in your presence. Save him, if you can." He then cut off the head of Vāsudeva, and entered the chariot. Krishna found this was all the Māyā of Sālva and in reality his father was neither carried off nor killed. He broke the chariot Soubha with his club. Sālva left the chariot and stood upon earth, club in hand. Krishna cut off his hands and then cut off his head with the Chakra.

DANTA VAKRA AND VIDURATHA.

SKANDHA X. CHAP. 78.

Danta-Vakra was the friend of Sisupāla, Sālva and Paundraka. He came to attack Sri Krishna with club in hand and, seeing him, exclaimed: "It is good fortune, that I see you. You are our cousin. But still you have killed our friends and you now want to kill me. I will therefore kill you with this club." (Śridhara gives a second meaning to this Śloka. At the end of his third birth Danta Vakra was to regain his place in Vaikuntha. Sisupāla and Danta Vakra, as explained before, were Jaya and Vijaya, gate-keepers of Vaikuntha. By the curse of the Kumāras, they incarnated as Asuras. The third and last cycle of material ascendancy was to be ended. Jaya and Vijaya were not to incarnate any more. Therefore Danta-Vakra exclaimed that it was his good fortune to meet Krishna and so on). Krishna struck him with his club and killed him. A flame arose from the body of Danta-Vakra, as from that of Sisupāla, and it entered Sri Krishna.

Vidūratha, the brother of Danta-Vakra was afflicted with grief at the death of his brother. He now attacked Krishna. Krishna cut off his head with the Chakra.

BALARĀMA AND THE DEATH OF ROMAHARSHANA.

SKANDHA X. CHAP. 78-79.

Balarāma heard that the Kurus and Pāndavas were making preparations for a mutual fight. He belonged to neither side. So he went out on pretext of a pilgrimage. He went to Prabhāsa and performed the ablution ceremonies. He went to several other places and at last reached the Naimisha forest. The Rishis all rose up to receive him. Romaharshana, the disciple of Vyāsa, did not leave his seat. He belonged to the Sūta community, — a mixed class, born of Kshatriya father and Brāhmana mother, — but he took his seat higher than that of the Brāhmanas. Balarāma thought that the Sūta had learned the Itihasas, Purānas and all Dharma Sāstras from Vyāsa but he had not learned humility and self-control and that he had become proud of his wisdom. Balarāma cut off his head with the tip of a Kusa grass. The Rishis broke forth into loud cries of lamentation. Addressing Balarāma, they said: "O lord! thou hast done a wrong. We gave him this seat of a Brāhmana. We gave him age and freedom from fatigue, till the Yajna was completed. Not knowing this, thou hast killed one who was, while on his seat, a Brāhmana. Thou art not regulated by the Vedas. But of thy own accord, do thou perform some Prāyaschitta, and thereby shew an example to other people." Balarāma enquired what he was to do. The Rishi asked him to do that by which their words as well as the act of Balarāma both might prove true. Balarāma said: "One's son is one's own self. So say the Vedas. Therefore the son of Romaharshana, Ugrasravas, shall be your reciter of Purānas. He shall have long life and freedom from fatigue. What am I to do, O Rishis, by which I may atone for my deed?"

The Rishis asked Balarāma to kill Valvala, son of the Dānava Ilvala, who used to pollute the sacrificial ground on certain days of the moon. They also asked Rāma to travel all over Bhārata Varsha for twelve months, and take his bath at the sacred places.

Rāma killed Valvala and went out on pilgrimage. On his return to Prabhāsa he heard about the death of the Kshatriya kings in the war between the Kurus and the Pāndavas. He went to Kurukshetra. Bhima and Duryodhana were then fighting with each other with their clubs. Balarāma tried to bring about peace. But they did not heed his words. He then returned to Dvārakā.

Balarāma once more went to Naimisha and he was adored by the Rishis.

SRĪDĀMAN.

SKANDHA X. CHAP. 80-81.

Krishna had a Brāhmana fellow-student, by name Srīdāman. He was well-read in the Vedas, self controlled and contented. He had a wife. He lived on whatever was freely given to him by others. His wife was ill-clad and ill-fed, like himself. One day she approached her husband and said: —

"Husband, your friend is the Lord of Lakshmī (the goddess of wealth) herself. Go to him and he will give you wealth. He gives even his own self to those that meditate on his lotus feet. What can not that Lord of the Universe give to those that worship him with some desire?" Being repeatedly pressed by his wife, he at last resolved to go to Krishna, thinking that the sight of his friend would be his greatest gain. He asked his wife for some offering for his friend, She begged four handfuls of flattened rice (*Chipītaka*) from the Brāhmanas and tied that up in one corner of her husband's rag. The Brāhmana went to Dvārakā, thinking all the way how he could meet Krishna. He passed through certain apartments and went into one of the rooms. Krishna was seated with one of his wives. He saw the Brāhmana from a distance and rose up to receive him. He came down and embraced his former companion with both his hands. Krishna gave him a respectful welcome and a seat by his own side. He then talked with him about the old reminiscences of student life, how they passed their days at the residence of Sandipani, how faithfully they carried out the behests of the Guru and his wife, how necessary it was to respect the Guru and such other topics. He then smilingly looked at the Brāhmana and said: —

"What have you brought for me from your house? Even the smallest thing brought by my Bhaktas becomes great by their love, while the largest offerings of those that are not devoted to me cannot please me." The Brāhmana, though asked, was ashamed to offer the flattened rice to the Lord of Lakshmī and he cast down his head. The all-seeing Sri Krishna knew the object of the Brāhmana's coming. He found that the Brāhmana had not at first worshipped him with the object of attaining wealth. It was only to please his devoted wife that he now had that desire. The Lord therefore thought he would give him such wealth as was difficult to acquire. He then snatched away the flattened rice from the rags of the Brāhmana saying, "What is this! O friend you have brought this highly gratifying offering for me. These rice grains please me, the Universal Ātmā." So saying he partook of one handful. When he was going to take the second handful, Lakshmī held his hand, saying, "O Lord of the Universe, this much will quite suffice to give all such wealth as can be needed for this world as well as for the next, such that it will even please thee to see that thy votary has got so much wealth."

The Brāhmana passed the night with Krishna. The next morning, he went home. Krishna went a certain distance with him to see him off. Krishna did not give him wealth nor did he ask for any. He thought within himself "What am I, a poor Brāhmana and a sinner and this Krishna, whose breast is the abode of Lakshmī, gave me a reception as if I were a god. The worship of His feet is the root of all Siddhis, all enjoyments, of Svarga and even of Mukti. Kind as he is, he did not give me any the least wealth, lest a poor man should forget Him by the pride of wealth."

When he reached home, he found palatial buildings, gardens and lots of well-dressed male and female attendants. They received him with valuable presents. His wife also came out to receive him, with a number of female attendants. The Brāhmana was surprised. He saw this was all the outcome of his visiting Sri Krishna. He controlled himself while enjoying this immense wealth and, meditating on Sri Krishna, he at last attained His supreme abode.

THE MEETING AT KURUKSHETRA.

SKANDHA X. CHAP. 82-84

There was a total eclipse of the sun. Krishna and all the Yādavas went to Kurukshetra to bathe on the occasion. Nanda, the Gopas and Gopis, all came there. Kunti and her sons, Bhishma, Drona and all the kings also went. They all went together. (The Bhāgavata Purāna carefully avoids the battle at Kurukshetra. It barely mentions the duel between Bhima and Duryodhana. According to the Mahābhārata, Bhishma, Drona and all the brothers of Duryodhana had been killed before the fight took place between Bhima and Duryodhana. But we find here that they were all present at the Kurukshetra meeting. A slight explanation will be necessary to put the readers on the right line of thought. The ideal of the Mahābhārata was Tatva-masi, the unity of Jiva and Īshvara. Krishna and Arjuna looked alike. They were close companions. This Advaita view struck at the root of Upāsanā excepting as a means to an end; it put into the shade altogether the Path of compassion, the Path of service of which Nārada is the guide for this Kalpa. So we find even Bhishma being killed. Bhishma died at Uttarayana and necessarily passed through the Devayāna Mārga, as an

Upāsaka. Whatever might be the goal of Upāsanā, the Bhāgavata Purāna
treats of Upāsanā as an end and not as a means. The Bhāgavatas, the
Sātvatas, the Vaishnavas do not ask for Nirvana Mukti they ask for
devotion to the Lord of the Universe. They work in the Universe as
servants of the Lord, taking the whole Universe to be their own selves. The
Kurukshetra battle is therefore out of place in the Bhāgavata Purāna. This
explains the great meeting at Kurukshetra instead of the Great
Annihilation.)

Kunti complained to Vāsudeva that he did not make any enquiries about
her and her sons, in her many afflictions. Vāsudeva said, for fear of Kansa
the Yādavas had scattered themselves, and they could not make enquiries
about one another. The Kurus, Pāndavas and the kings were all glad to see
Krishna and his wives. Rāma and Krishna duly honoured them all and
made valuable presents. They all admired the good fortune of the Yādavas,
in having Krishna always in their midst.

Nanda and Yasodā were duly respected by Vāsudeva and his wives.

Krishna met the Gopis in privacy. He embraced them all, and, after enquiry
about their safety, said smilingly: — "Do you remember us, O friends? For
the good of those whom we call our own, we have been long in putting
down the adverse party. Or do you think little of us, feeling that we have
been ungrateful to you? Know for certain, it is the Lord who unites and
separates all beings. As the wind unites masses of clouds, grass, cotton and
dust particles, and again disunites them, so the creator does with all beings.
Devotion to me serves to make beings immortal. How glad I am that you
have this love to me, for by that love you gain me back. I am the beginning
and end of all beings, I am both inside and outside. As the material objects
resolve themselves into the primal elements, (Akāsa, air, fire, water and
earth), so (the material parts in) all beings resolve themselves into the
primal elements. Ātmā pervades all beings as the conscious Perceiver
(Ātmā). Know both (the Perceiver and the Perceived) to be reflected in me,
the Supreme and the Immutable."

The Gopis were taught this Adhyātma teaching by Sri Krishna. Bearing
this teaching constantly in mind, they cast off the Jiva sheath (Jiva Kosa)
and they attained Krishna. And they said: — "O Krishna let thy lotus feet

be ever present in our minds, home-seeking though we may have been. The lords of Yoga by their profound wisdom meditate on thy feet in their hearts. It is by thy feet that those that have fallen into the well of Sansara are raised."

(Here we take a final leave of the Gopis. They had known Krishna as the Purusha of the Heart. They now knew him as the all-pervading Purusha. They were drawn back into the bosom of that Purusha, their Linga (Sūkshma) Sarira destroyed. They now entered the divine state, but even there they did not forget the lotus feet of Krishna. They became centres of devotional love in the bosom of the Universal Lord.)

Yudisthira and other friends of Krishna addressed him as all-incarnating Purusha. The wives of Krishna related to Draupadi how they came to be married to him. The Rishis addressed Sri Krishna as Īshvara. They then took leave of him. Vāsudeva however detained them, saying they should instruct him as to how he could exhaust his Karma. Nārada said it was no wonder that he should ask this question of them and not of Krishna. For proximity is the cause of disregard.

The Rishis, addressing Vāsudeva, said: —

"Karma is exhausted by Karma. Worship Vishnu by Yajna. He is the lord of all Yajnas. Wise men do not wish for riches by the performance of Yajna, nor do they wish for men or enjoyments. They give up all desires and then go to the forest for Tapas. The twice-born are indebted to the Devas, Rishis and Pitris, by their birth. You have paid up your debts to the Rishis and to the Pitris. Now pay up your debts to the Devas, by the performance of Yajna and then give up your home." Vāsudeva then performed Yajna, and the Rishis officiated. The Yajna over, the Rishis went away. Dhritarāshra, Vidura, the Pāndavas, Bhishma, Drona, Kunti, Nārada, Vyāsa, his friends and relatives, parted with a heavy heart. Nārada and his followers were detained for three months by the Yādavas, such was their love for them. They then received many presents and left for Mathurā. Seeing the approach of the rainy season, the Yādavas also went back to Dvārakā.

VASUDEVA, DEVAKI, AND THEIR DEAD SONS.

SKANDHA X. CHAP. 85.

Vāsudeva now believed his sons to be lords of the Universe. He once asked them whether they had not incarnated for relieving the pressure on the Earth. Krishna replied: — "I, yourselves, this Rāma, the people of Dvārakā, nay the whole universe are to be known as Brahmā. Ātmā, though one and self-manifest, becomes manifold, according to the nature of the beings in which its manifestation takes place. Compare the variety in the manifestation of the Bhūtas in the Bhoutic objects."

Hearing these words of wisdom, Vāsudeva learned to see unity in diversity.

Devaki had heard of the powers of Rāma and Krishna in bringing back to life the deceased son of their Guru. She asked them to shew her the sons that had been killed by Kansa.

Rāma and Krishna entered by Yogic power the regions of Sutala. Bali shewed them every respect and worshipped them.

Krishna said: "In the Svayambhava Manvantara, Marīchi had six sons by Urna. These sons of the Rishi laughed at Brahmā, because he grew passionate towards his daughter. For this they became Asuras and sons of Hiranyakasipu. Yoga Māyā carried them to the womb of Devaki and they became her sons. They were killed by Kansa. Devaki takes them to be her own sons and laments over their death. They are now with you; I shall take them over to my mother to remove her grief. They shall then go to Devaloka, free from the effects of their curse. Smara, Udgitha, Parishvanga, Patanga, Kshudra-bhuka and Ghrini — these shall by my favor again attain a good state." (Smara is called Kirtimat.)

Krishna took the boys to Devaki and she embraced them all. They were then taken to Devaloka.

ARJUNA AND SUBHADRĀ

SKANDHA X. CHAP. 86.

Rājā Parikshit enquired how Arjuna had married his grandmother Subhadrā, the sister of Rāma and Krishna.

Suka replied: —

"Arjuna heard that Rāma was going to give Subhadrā (the cousin of Arjuna) in marriage to Duryodhana. He disguised himself as a Sanyāsīn and went to Dvārakā. The people of Dvārakā and even Rāma could not recognise him. Arjuna lived there for a year and received due hospitality. Once Arjuna was invited by Balarāma and he was taking his food when Subhadrā passed by him. They looked at each other and felt mutual love. One day, Subhadrā, with the permission of her parents and of Sri Krishna, came out on a chariot to worship an idol outside the fort and a strong guard accompanied her. Arjuna availed himself of this opportunity and carried away the girl by force. Balarāma became greatly enraged. But Sri Krishna and other friends appeased him."

SRUTADEVA AND BAHULĀSVA.

SKANDHA X. CHAP. 86.

Srutadeva, a Brāhmana of Mithila, was much devoted to Sri Krishna. The prince of Mithila, Bahulāsva, was also a favorite of Sri Krishna. To favor them, Sri Krishna went with Nārada and other Rishis to Mithila. Srutadeva and Bahulāsva each asked him to go to his own house. Krishna to please them both went to the houses of both at the same time, being unnoticed by each in respect of his going to the other's house. Both Bahulāsva and Srutadeva received Sri Krishna and the Rishis with due respect. Sri Krishna taught Srutadeva to respect the Brāhmana Rishis as much as he respected him. After giving proper instructions to the prince and the Brāhmana for sometime, Sri Krishna returned to Dvārakā.

THE PRAYER TO BRAHMAN BY THE SRUTIS.

SKANDHA X. CHAP. 87.

Rājā Parikshit asked: —

"O Great Sage, Brahmān is undefinable, void of Gunas, beyond both causes and effects. How can the Srutis, which have the Gunas for their Vritti (*i.e.* which treat of Devas and sacrifices which are full of attributes), directly cognise Brahmān?"

Suka replied: —

"The Lord created Buddhi, Indriya, Manas and Prana in Jivas that they might obtain their objects (Mātrā), their birth-producing Karma (Bhava), their transmigration to different Lokas (Ātmā), and also their Mukti (Akalpana)." (These four words respectively mean Artha, Dharma, Kāma and Moksha. The Srutis treat of Bhagavat, of Sat-Chit-Ananda the all-knowing, the all-powerful, the lord of all, the guide of all, the all-object of Upāsanā, the Dispenser of all fruits of Karma, the Resort of all that is good, as one with attributes. The Srutis begin with attributes, but at last drop these attributes saying "Not this", "Not this" and end in Brahmān. The sayings about Upasan and Karma treat of things with attributes, as a means to attain wisdom and thereby indirectly lead to Brahmān. This is the purport. *Śridhara.*)

"The Upanishad speaks of Brahmān. She was accepted as such by even those that were older than those whom we call old. He who accepts her with faith attains well-being." (The Bhāgavata tries to refute the idea that the Vedas treat of the Devas only and not of Īshvara and Brahmā).

"I shall relate to thee here a conversation between Nārada and Nārāyana.

"Once upon a time Nārada went to see the great Rishi Nārāyana. For the well-being of Bhāratavarsha, for the good of all men, he remains in his Āsrama, fixed in Tapas, since the beginning of this Kalpa. The Rishis of Kalāpa sat round him. Nārada saluted him and asked this very question.

"Nārāyana said: —

"In Jana Loka, the Manas, born Rishis of that place performed Brahmā Yajna (Yajna, in which 'What is Brahmān' is ascertained, some one becoming the speaker and others forming the audience). You had gone to Sveta Dvipa at the time. This very question was raised in the assembly. Sanandan became the speaker. He said: —

"The Supreme drank up his own creation and lay asleep with His Śaktis. At the end of Pralaya, the Srutis (which were the first breath of the Supreme. *Śridhara*) roused Him up by words denotive of Him.

"The Srutis said: —

"Glory be to Thee! Destroy the Avidyā of all moveable and immoveable beings. She has got attributes for the sake of deluding others. All Thy powers are completely confined in Thee. Thou art the Manifester of all Śaktis in Jivas. Thou art (sometimes — *Śridhara*) with Māyā and (always — *Śridhara*) by Thyself. (But wherever thou art) the Vedas follow Thee. (The Vedas treat both of Saguna and Nirguna Brahmān).

"All that are perceived, (Indra and other gods), know Thee to be the Big, and themselves to be only parts. For their rise and setting are from Thee. (Then is the Big transformable? Hence the next words. *Śridhara*). But thou art untransformed. Even as the (transformed) earth pots have their rise and setting in the (untransformed) mother earth. Therefore the Rishis — (the Mantras or their perceivers. *Śridhara*. Every Vedic Mantra has its Rishi, who first perceived that Mantra) — set their minds, their words and actions in Thee (or had their purport and meaning in Thee. *Śridhara*). For wherever people may roam, their footsteps always touch the earth.

"O Thou Lord of the Three Gunas, the wise plunged into the nectar ocean formed of words about Thee, — an Ocean which removes the impurities of all people — and they got rid of all miseries. What of those then who, by the perception of Self in them, free themselves from the attributes of mind (likes or dislikes) and of time (the transformations of age) and worship Thy real self which gives rise to perpetual happiness?

"Those that are animated by life breathe truly if they follow Thee, otherwise their breath is the breath of bellows. Inspired by Thee, Mahat, Ahankāra and others lay their eggs (create collective and individual bodies). Thou dost permeate the five sheaths (Annamaya and others) in man and become those sheaths, as it were, by this permeation. But thou art the last in the sheaths, as taught in the Upanishads.

"Thou art beyond the gross and subtle sheaths, the Indestructible and Real.

"Among the Rishis, the Śārkarakshas (or those that have an imperfect vision) meditate on Brahmā in the navel. The Ārunis, however, meditate on Brahmā in the cavity of the Heart, which is the seat of the nerves. Ananta, from the Heart, the Sushumnā (the nerve which causes Thy perception) leads to Thy supreme place in the Head. He who once attains that place does not fall into the mouth of Death again. (The Upanishads speak of one hundred and one nerves of the heart. Of these, one goes to the head).

"Thou hast Thyself created various life kingdoms and various forms. Though Thou pervadest them all from of old, having brought them all about, yet Thy special manifestation in them is relatively greater or smaller, according to the nature of the things created by Thee even as fire, though one and the same, burns differently according to the character of the fuel. Those that are of pure intellect follow the one Real amidst the many unreal forms. The (perceiving) Purusha in all beings is said to be Thy part only. Knowing this to be the truth about Jivas, wise men worship Thy feet.

"Brahmā and other Jivas did not know Thy end. Even Thou dost not know Thy own end. For Thou art endless. Drawn by the wheel of time, the Brahmāndas, with their Avaranas, (outer circles) roll on together in Thy middle, even as if they were dust particles in the air. The Srutis fructify in Thee (have Thee, for their end and goal.) (Though they cannot directly speak of Thee) their words are directed towards Thee, by discarding every thing else." (Though the Vedas treat of Indra and other Devas, they ultimately lead to Brahmā, by saying "Brahmā is not this, not this," in the Upanishads.)

THE RESTORATION OF BRAHMAN BOYS TO LIFE.

SKANDHA X. CHAP. 89.

At Dvārakā a Brahmān lost his son at birth. He took the dead child to the palace and placed it at the gate, blaming the king for his misfortune. For the sins of kings visit themselves upon their subjects. In this way nine sons died one after another and the Brahmān did the same with all of them and, when the ninth son died, Arjuna was sitting with Krishna and he heard the reproaches of the Brāhmana. Arjuna promised the Brāhmana that he would protect his son this time, or would otherwise enter the fire for breach of his promise. The son was born again. And Arjuna was there with his famous bow. But lo! the child wept and it rose up high and disappeared, The Brāhmana taunted Arjuna for making promises he had not the power to keep. Stung by these words, the Pāndava went to Yāma Loka. He went to Indra Loka. He went to the regions of Agni, Nirriti, Chandra, Vāyu and Varuna. He went to Rasātala. He went to Svarga. But the Brāhmana boy was no where to be found. He then made preparations for entering the fire. Sri Krishna made him desist. He said: — "I shall show you the Brāhmana's sons. Do not disregard yourself. Those that blame us now shall sing our glory hereafter."

Krishna and Arjuna went towards the west. They crossed the seven oceans and the seven Dvipas. They crossed the Loka-aloka and entered the regions of chaotic darkness. The horses could not proceed further. So by Krishna's order the glowing Chakra, Sudarshana, pierced through the darkness and the horses followed the track. Infinite, endless, divine light then spread out. Arjuna re-opened his eyes. They then entered the regions of primal water. They found one house glittering with gems and stones. The thousand-headed Ananta was sitting in that house. Seated upon Ananta was the Supreme Purusha, the Lord of the Lords. Krishna and Arjuna saluted Him. The Purusha then smiled and said: — "I brought the Brāhmana boys that I might see you both. For the protection of Dharma on the Earth, you have incarnated as my parts (Kalā.) Kill the Asuras that oppress the Earth and come back soon to me. Filled are your own desires, O you Rishis, Nara and Nārāyana. But for the preservation of the Universe, do that which others may follow."

Krishna and Arjuna said "Om". They brought back the Brāhmana boys and restored them to their father.

THE LINE OF KRISHNA.

SKANDHA X. CHAP. 90.

Vajra was the son of Aniruddha.

Prati-bāhu was the son of Vajra.

Su-bāhu was the son of Prati-bāhu.

Upasena was the son of Su-bāhu.

Bhadra-sena was the son of Upasena.

END OF THE TENTH BRANCH.

THOUGHTS ON THE MATHURĀ LILĀ.

Kansa was killed and all good men that had fled from Mathurā returned to it. Krishna fast developed Himself as Īshvara. He restored his Guru's son to life.

Uddhava, the embodiment of Bhakti Yoga mixed with wisdom, was the messenger of Krishna to the Gopis. It was through him that Sri Krishna sent words of wisdom, which He himself could not have spoken to them at Vrindāvana. For the Gopis would have spurned such words from Him, so great was their personal love for Him. Krishna now placed another ideal before them for meditation. They were now to seek Him, not as the lovely Krishna, playing upon the flute, but as the all-pervading Ātmā to be known by discriminating wisdom. He asked the Gopis to meditate on this ideal, and He now returned to them as the all-pervading immutable principle in the Universe.

In the stories of Jarāsandha, Yavana and Muchukunda we find the historical Krishna.

Jarāsandha was an incongruous combination of materiality and spirituality, (the two parts which Jiva put together). He was the performer of Vedic Yajnas, the supporter of Brāhmanas, the representative of the old state of things. Naturally therefore he was the most powerful king of his time and the most powerful enemy of Krishna. Vaishnavism had to fight hard with orthodox Brahmānism. Vaishnava kings were put to death in large numbers. Krishna could not kill him on account of his connection with Brāhmanas and with Vedic Yajnas. He even feigned a retreat and fled away to Dvārakā. Dvārakā was a spiritual centre on earth, created by Krishna, for the performance of His mission as Avatāra. The town was washed away as soon as Krishna disappeared.

It will be interesting to know the future mission of Muchukunda. But the Bhāgavata is silent about it.

THOUGHTS ON THE DVĀRAKĀ

At Dvārakā, we find Sri Krishna as the Lord of the Universe, a Kālpic Avatāra, and as such something more than the historical Krishna.

Sri Krishna as an Avatāra.

It is time that we should know something definitely of Sri Krishna as an Avatāra.

To restore the Brāhmana boys, Sri Krishna went with Arjuna to the abode of Purusha. Purusha smiled and said: — "I brought the Brāhmana boys, that I might see you both. For the protection of Dharma on the Earth, you have incarnated as my parts (Kalā). Kill the Asuras that oppress the Earth and come back soon to Me. Sātiated are your own desires, O you Rishis, Nara and Nārāyana, but for the preservation of the universe do that which others may follow."

The Purusha is the Virāt Purusha of our universe, the Second Purusha or the Second Logos.

When the first Purusha woke up, the process of transformation went on and the material creation was completed. The materials could not however unite to form individual bodies. Purusha infused the material creation and became known as the Second Purusha or Virāt Purusha, As regards this Virāt Purusha, the Bhāgavata Purāna says as follows: —

"He is the resting place and eternal seed of all Avatāras. Brahmā is His part, Marichi and other Rishis are parts of His part. Devas, animals and men are brought into manifestation by parts of His part." Bhāgavata I. 3-5.

"He is the primal, unborn Purusha, who in every Kalpa creates, preserves and destroys self (objective) as self (nominative), in self (locative), by self (instrumental)." II. 6 XXXVII.

"He is the primal Purusha Avatāra of the Supreme." II. 6 XL.

He is also called the Thousand-Limbed and the Egg-born. II. 5, XXXV., III. 6, VI.

This Virāt Purusha upholds the manifested universe. All materials are in Him and all individuals take their rise from Him and end in Him. He is the one ocean of endless bubbles which have their beginning and end in Him. The Avatāras also all rest on the bosom of Virāt Purusha.

We have looked at Virāt Purusha from the standpoint of the First Purusha. Now let us proceed upwards from below.

The Brihat Aranayaka Upanishad thus speaks of Virāt Purusha, at the beginning of the Fourth Brāhmana of the first chapter: —

"This was before soul, bearing the shape of a man. Looking round he beheld nothing but himself. He said first: — 'This am I.' Hence the name of I was produced. And, because he as the first of all of them consumed by fire all the sins, therefore he is called Purusha. He verily consumes him who, before this, strives to obtain the state of Prajāpati, he, namely who, thus knows."

The following is the commentary of Sankarāchārya.

"This was before the soul." The soul is here defined as Prajāpati, the first born from the Egg, the embodied soul, as resulting from his knowledge and works in accordance with the Vedas. He was what? "This," produced by the division of the body, "was the soul" not separated from the body of Prajāpati, "before" the production of other bodies. He was "also bearing the shape of man", which means that he was endowed with head, hands and other members, he was the Viraj, the first born. "Looking round reflecting who am I, and of what nature, he beheld nothing but himself", the fulness of life, the organism of causes and effects. He beheld only himself as the Universal soul. Then, endowed with the recollection of his Vedic knowledge in a former birth, "he said first: This am I" *viz.*, Prajāpati, the universal soul. "Hence," because from the recollection of his knowledge in a former world he called himself I, therefore his name was I "And because he" — Prajāpati in a former birth, which is the cause, as the first of those who were desirous of obtaining the state of Prajāpati by the exercise of reflection on works and knowledge *viz.* "as the first of all of them," of all that were desirous of obtaining the state of Prajāpati, consumed by the perfect exercise of reflection on works and knowledge of all the sins of contact which are obstacles to the acquirement of the state of Prajāpati, — because such was the case, therefore he is called Purusha, because he is *Purvam Aushad,* (first burnt). As that Prajāpati, by consuming all opposite sins, became this Purusha Prajāpati, so also any other consumes, reduces all to ashes by the fire of the practice of reflection on knowledge and works, or only by the force of his knowledge, and He verily "consumes" Whom? "Him who before this sage strives to obtain the state of Prajāpati." The sage is pointed out as he who thus knows, who according to his power manifests his reflection on knowledge. "But is it not useless for any one to strive for the state of Prajāpati, if he is consumed by one who thus knows? There is no fault in this; for consuming means here only that the highest state, that of Prajāpati, is not obtained, because the eminence of reflection on knowledge is wanting. Therefore by the words, "He consumes him" is meant, that the perfect performer obtains the highest state of Prajāpati; he who is less perfect does not obtain it, and by no means that the less perfect performer is actually consumed by the perfect; thus it is said in common life, that a warrior who first rushes into battle, consumes his combatants, which means that he exceeds them in prowess.

In order to understand this better, let us consider the scheme of human evolution.

Ātmā is the same in all beings and, when free from the limitations of individual life, it becomes all pervading.

Sympathy and compassion open the door to the liberation of Ātmā.

The Upadhi, or vehicle of Ātmā, or the body of its manifestation, becomes less and less gross, as Ātmā proceeds in its course of liberation, the body becomes better able to do good to all mankind and it does not act as a barrier to communion with the real self.

The most highly evolved beings become universal and not individual, and they live normally on the spiritual plane.

They at last reach the state of divinity. Then they may become Avatāras. When these Avatāras have to work on the physical and intellectual planes, they assume a body and become born, like ordinary beings. They have then to *come down* from their normal state, but their vision and power remain undestroyed. When their mission is over, they reach again their normal state. The Avatāras have not to work out their own Karma. They are liberated Ātmās, staying back for the liberation of other individuals in the universe. Karma-less themselves, they bear the Karma of the universe upon their shoulders. The thin veil that separates their state from the state of the absolute Brahmā is Māyā, which is the highest manifestation of Prakriti which enables them to assume cosmic responsibility out of their unbounded compassion for all beings.

The Avatāras may cast off their veil at will, but as long as they choose to keep that veil, the whole universe is at their command and they guide the whole course of universal evolution.

Now of all Avatāras one takes upon himself to hold all individuals in His bosom, to sustain them all and to make Him the field of their Involution and Evolution, in the Kalpa.

He is called Virāt Purusha. He is practically the Īshvara of our universe.

The body of this Purusha, called the First Avatāra, the Second or Virāt Purusha, and the Egg-born, is formed by the Tatvas, numbered twenty-four in the Sānkhya philosophy. These Tatvas collect together to form an Egg and the Second Purusha breaks forth from that Egg and becomes the Thousand-headed Purusha of the Upanishads. For the sake of meditation, He is imagined to be seated on the Serpent Ananta. The lotus stalk grew out of his navel.

The Tatvas themselves are brought into manifestation by the awaking of the First Purusha.

The Second Purusha enters into all beings as their Ātmā, becoming three-fold in his aspect *viz.* Adhi-Ātmā, Adhi-bhuta and Adhi-deva. Then He is called the Third Purusha. Says the Sātvata Tantra, as quoted by Śridhara: —

"There are three forms of Vishnu known as Purusha — the first is the creator of Mahat, the Second is the permeator of the cosmic Egg, and the third is the permeator of all beings." Virāt Purusha is the seat af all Avatāras. Therefore all Avatāras are called parts of the Virāt Purusha.

Speaking of other Lilā Avatāras, Bhāgavata calls them parts and aspects of the Second Purusha; "but Krishna is Bhagavat Himself."

Bhagavat is here the First Purusha. I. 3 XXVIII.

In the Tenth Skandha, Rājā Parikshit says: "Tell us the mighty deeds of Vishnu, incarnated as a *part* in the line of Yadu." X. 1 II. Later on again: —

"The supreme Purusha, Bhagavat Himself, shall be born in the house of Vāsudeva." X. 1 XXIII.

The Devas said, addressing Devaki: — "Rejoice mother, the Supreme Purusha, Bhagavat Himself, is in thy womb *by His part*" X. 2 XII.

The Purusha, seated on Ananta, addressed Arjuna and Krishna as Nara and Nārāyana.

The Mahābhārata also calls them Incarnations of Nara and Nārāyana. These Rishis are invoked all throughout the Mahābhārata. They were the sons of Dharma by Mūrti, daughter of Daksha.

Nara and Nārāyana are looked upon as two in one and they were adored by the Devas, as manifestations of Purusha Himself. (IV. 1 XLVI).

They went after their birth to Gandha Madana. (IV. 1 XLVIII.) It is these Rishis, parts of Bhagavat Hari, who have now appeared for the removal of her load from the Goddess Earth, as Krishnas, in the lines of Yadu and Kuru. (IV. 1 XLIX.)

Krishna in the line of Kuru is Arjuna.

In explaining this Śloka, Śridhara quotes the following from a Vaishnava Tantra: —

"In Arjuna, there is only the Āvesa (suffusing) of Nara. Krishna is Nārāyana Himself."

Sri Krishna said to Arjuna: — "I have passed through many births as well as thou. I know them all. Not so thou."

This shows that Arjuna was not Nara himself, the supplement of Nārāyana, for in that case he would have remembered his previous births. But, as the Tantra says, "Arjuna was possessed by the Nara aspect of the dual Rishi."

Sri Krishna said to Devaki: —

"At my first birth, in the Svāyam-bhuva Manvantara, thou wert born as Prisni and this Vāsudeva was named Prajāpati Sutapas I was born as your son, Prisni-garbha. I was also born of you, when you were Aditi and Vāsudeva was Kasyapa, as Upendra, also called the Vāmana or Dwarf Avatāra. At this third birth, I am your son again, with the same body." X. 3 XXXII. to XLIII.

These are the three Incarnations of Nara Nārāyana, mentioned in the Bhāgavata. They are certainly not the many births to which Sri Krishna alludes in the Gitā. Those many births took place in previous Kalpas of which we know nothing. In this Kalpa, however, he appeared at the turning points in the Evolution of our universe. He appeared in the First Manvantara, the Manvantara of manifestation, as Prisni-garbha. We do not know the good done by Him in His first birth.

As Vāmana, however, he restored the Trilokī to the Devas and asserted the supremacy of the spiritual forces.

The Earth was again overpowered by the Asuras. The Kalpa was about to be half over. The last struggle was to be made. Satva had to be infused into all beings, even into the materials composing them. Every thing in the universe was to be wedded to the Lord of Preservation. An upward trend was to be given to the whole course of evolution. Materialism could not be stamped out all at once. But henceforth there was to be a steady fall of Materiality and rise of Spirituality, subject to such variations as minor Cycles might cause.

Sri Krishna is therefore the greatest Avatāra of our Kalpa. "For the good of those that seek Ātmā, Nara Nārāyana shall perform Tapas in Bharata Varsha, unknown to others, till the end of the Kalpa." V. 19-9

Sri Krishna as Bhagavat is greater than the Second Purusha.

To the devotees, he is greater than the Purusha manifestation.

He now appeared as the preserver of the Universe, the embodiment of Satva, the force of ascent. And the Tatvas had to be wedded to him, so that they might acquire the energy of higher evolution in them.

Unless there was change in the innate downward tendency of the Tatvas, the spiritual ascent of the universe was not possible.

The Lord brought about this change by permeating the whole universe with His Satva body, or becoming something like the spiritual soul in every being. Therefore Lord Krishna is in the hearts of all beings and can be perceived by all in meditation. He is everywhere, in every atom. Whether Sri Krishna is Bhagavat Himself or some manifestation of Bhagavat makes no difference whatever. By His works, He is Bhagavat. His worshippers are bound for the abode of Bhagavat. They have not to wait in Brahmā or Satya Loka, till the end of Brahmā's life. Those who worship. Hiranya garbha or Brahmā cannot pass beyond the limits of Brahmā Loka.

In answer to Rājā Parikshit, Suka Deva delineated the Paths to be followed after death.

I. The Prompt Path of Liberation (Sadyo Mukti). Those who meditate on the abstract Absolute, called Brahmā, attain prompt liberation. The All-pervading principle is abstracted from the phenomenal universe, there is no thought of man, no thought of fellow beings, no thought of the universe, there is the pure abstraction by the process of "Not this." "Not this" liberates one from all phenomenal connections. This is Sadyo Mukti. (II. 2 XV. to XXI.)

II. The Deferred Path of Liberation (Krama Mukti), when one wishes to go to Brahmā Loka or to the abode of the Siddhas. Where the eight siddhis are acquired, he retains the Manas and the Indriyas and goes all over the universe of Seven Lokas. II. 2 XXII.

With their Linga Sarira, these Lords of Yoga go inside and outside Trilokī. II. 2 XXIII.

On their way to Brahmā Loka, they are carried by Sushumna first to Agni Loka. Then they go to the farthest limit of Trilokī, the Sisumara Chakra, extending over to Dhruva or the Polar star. II. 2 XXIV.

When at the end of a Kalpa, the Trilokī becomes consumed by fire from the mouth of Sankarshana, they go to Brahmā Loka, which lasts for two Parārddhas, and which is adorned by the chariots of great Siddhas. II. 2 XXVI.

There is no sorrow, no infirmity no death, no pain, no anxiety in Brahmā Loka. But those who go there are, out of their compassion, afflicted by the endless miseries of those that do not know the path. II. 2 XXVII.

Then they pass through the seven Avaranas or covers of the Universe and, having the Vehicle of Mula Prakriti only, become full of Bliss and, when that Upadhi is destroyed, they obtain absolute bliss and do not return again. This is the attainment of the state. II. 2. XXVIII to XXXI.

Those who go to Brahmā Loka pass through three different paths.

1. Those, who come with great merits acquired in life, get posts of duty according to their merits in the next Kalpa (*i.e.* they become Prajāpatis, Lokapālas. Indras and so on.)

2. Those who go to Brahmā Loka merely by force of their Upāsanā of Hiranya-Garbha become liberated, when Brahmā becomes liberated at the end of his life ('extending over two Parārddhas.)

3. Those that worship Bhagavat pierce the Brahmānda at will, and rise to the abode of Vishnu. The Ślokas XXVIII to XXXI refer to the piercing of Brahmānda by the Bhāgavatas. *Śridhara.*

The worshippers of Sri Krishna attain the last state. The deferred path of Liberation is the path of all Bhaktas. It is the path of compassion, of service. The Bhaktas spurn all sorts of Mukti, even if they be offered to them. They become servants of the Lord in the preservation of the Universe.

In the Dvārakā Lila, we shall find Sri Krishna, as the greatest Avatāra of the Kalpa, carrying out His work of Preservation.

The Purāna does not speak of the Nara aspect of Sri Krishna as manifested in Arjuna. That is the subject matter of the Mahābhārata. The study of the one is complementary to the study of the other, as the study of the Bhagavat is complementary to the study of the Gitā. In one, we see the Evolution of Man, in the other we see the work of Bhagavat. We see in both together the whole of our Lord Sri Krishna.

THE WIVES.

As Lord of the Universe, Sri Krishna became wedded to the eightfold energies of Prakriti, His eight principal wives, so that he might influence, through them, individuals formed by these divisions of Prakritis. These energies are: —

1. *Rukmini* or Mula Prakritī, Buddhi.

2. *Jāmba-vati* or Mahat, Universal mind.

3. *Satya-bhāmā* or Ahankāra.

4. *Kālindi* or Akāsa-Tanmāttra, sound, Akāsa.

5. *Mitra Vinda* or Vāyu-Tanmatra, Touch, Air.

6. *Satya* or *Nagnajiti*, Agni-Tanmatra, Form, Fire.

7. *Bhadrā*, Ap-Tanmātra, Taste, Water.

8. *Lakshanā*, Kshiti-Tanmātra, smell, Earth.

The Energies of Prakriti have a double tendency, one of lower transformation, of materialisation, of descent and another of higher transformation, of spiritualisation, of ascent. Sri Krishna, by His Avatārship, attracted to Himself the higher tendency of all the energies of Prakriti. This is how he was wedded to all the aspects of Prakriti.

Rukmini is the spiritual energy of Mula Prakriti. Read the talk between Krishna and Rukmini (X. 80).

The legend of the Syamantaka jewel is a mysterious one. It was the gift of the Sun-God. It used to produce gold every day.

The Hiranya-Garbha Purusha of Vedic Upāsanā has its seat inside the Sun-God. "The Purusha inside Āditya." This Purusha is the Adhi-daiva of Bhagavat Gitā, as explained by Sankarāchārya. All the Devas proceed from *Him*. He is the one Deva, also called Prāna. (Vide Yajnavalkya's answer to Sakala Brihat Aranyaka Upanishad III. 9.) Hiranya is gold. Hiranya-garbha is that which has gold in its womb. The Syamantaka jewel gave protection against diseases, accidents, and other dangers. These are all the results of Hiranya-garbha Upāsanā. Syamantaka represents Hiranyagarbha Upāsanā.

Sri Krishna wanted that this Upāsanā should be replaced by the Upāsanā of Īshvara.

The jewel was lost. It was carried away by some religious movement, represented as a lion.

Jāmba-vat snatched it from the Lion. Jāmbavat, the bear king, was one of the chief allies of Sugriva. He was the oldest in years and the wisest in counsel.

"When Vāmana stepped over the three Lokas, I made a respectful circuit round Him." Rāmayana Kishkindha Kānda. Chap. 64-15.

"When Vāmana became an Avatāra I moved round the earth twenty one times. I threw plants into the Sea which yielded Amrita by churning. Now I am old." Rāmayana Kishkindha Kānda Chap. 65-32.

While Rāma was about to ascend to heaven he addressed the old Jāmbavat, as a son of Brahmā, and asked him to stay behind till the approach of Kali — Uttarā Kānda. Chap. 121-34.

Jāmbavat represents a very old religious movement, which was out of date even in Rāma's time.

Hiranyagarbha Upāsanā became old and a thing of the past. But however hoary it might be with years, it was holy with the traditions of the Vedas and though Krishna had no direct hand in its disappearance, people thought the disappearance was the outcome of His Avatarship. To save His reputation, Krishna restored the jewel from Jāmbavat, but it could not long remain in the hands of Satrajit. Vedic Upāsanā did survive. But it survived only in Vedic Sandhyā and Gāyatri, which were represented by Akrūra.

Krishna was wedded to Jāmbavatī, the spiritual energy of Mahat.

Satya-bhāmā is the spiritual energy of Ahankāra. She holds the Vinā, with the seven notes of differentiation. The Vedas proceed from these notes and also all departments of knowledge, Satyabhāmā is the goddess of learning.

There is not much to say about the five other principal wives.

The last of these wives, Lakshanā, represents the spiritual energy of earth. Coming down to earth, we proceed to Naraka, son of Earth. The word Naraka literally means Hell, hence gross materiality. We have found that the Purāna writers place Naraka below the Pātālas. Sixteen thousand girls representing all earthly and material energies had been snatched away by Naraka. They all became wedded to Sri Krishna.

Vāsudeva, Sankarshana, Pradyumna, Aniruddha.

The following correspondences were given by Kapila to his mother Devahūti. (III. 26).

Upāsya	Adhibhūta	Adhyatma	Adhideva
Vāsudeva	Mahat	Chitta	Kshetrajna
Sankarsana	Ahankāra	Ahankāra	Rudra
Aniruddha	Manas	Manas	The Moon god
Pradyumna	Buddhi	Buddhi	Brahmā

Chitta is transparent, without transformation, and calm, even as the first state of water. III. 26. XXI.

"Transparent" — capable of of receiving the image Bhagavat.

"Without transformation" — without indolence and distraction. *Śridhara*

Chitta is the abode of Bhagavat, *i.e.* Bhagavat is perceived by Chitta. III. 26. XX.

Differences cause many-sidedness and distraction.

Ahankāra Tatva brings differences into manifestation.

Beyond the plane of Ahankāra Tatva, is the plane of Mahat.

Mahat literally means big, great, universal.

It is the plane of universal manifestation.

The mind is universal on this plane. As soon as the One Purusha wished to be many, Prakriti gave rise to the Mahat transformation and Mahat took up the wish to be many. It was one, but it had the potency of becoming many. The whole universe that was to manifest itself was mirrored in Mahat, and was the subject matter of one thought, the thought of one who had the universe for his body. During the period of creation, Mahat soon transformed itself into Ahankāra, the Tatva of differences. Ahankāra gave rise to different bodies, different minds and different faculties; individuals appeared and they started on separate lines of manifestation and of evolution.

On their homeward journey, individuals again reach the plane of Mahat, when they rise above all differences, lose all sense of personality and carry their experiences to the plane of the Universe. Their thoughts then become thoughts of the Universe, guided by one feeling, that of compassion for those that remain behind. There is no thought of self, no distraction, no impurity, it is all calm and tranquil; such a mind is called *Chitta* by Kapila. This Chitta is the abode of peace, the abode of Bhagavat.

Bhagavat, when reflected on Chitta, is VASUDEVA. He is the Purusha seated on Ananta.

SANKARSANA is Bhagavat as reflected on Ahankāra. He is called Ananta or endless, as there is no end of individuals. He is Bhagavat as manifested in every individual and may be called, in one sense, the Purusha of Individual souls. Balarāma is said to be an incarnation of Sankarshana. As individuals proceed in their course of life journeys, they become crystallised into separate entities, with a strong sense of personality. The inner self, the real self, runs the risk of becoming swallowed up by the outer self, the Upadhi of individuality. The point is reached, when individuals are to be drawn back to their homes, their real selves. Therefore Balarāma used the plough to draw in others. This is a process of destruction. The material nature is gradually destroyed in us. Therefore Balarāma is also called an incarnation of Rudra or Śiva according to Vaishnava texts. He is Rudra Himself. The fire from the mouth of Sankarshana burns the Trilokī at Pralaya. Sankarshana literally means "he who draws in completely." The process of Pralaya has already set in. The whole process of spiritual ascent is a process of material Pralaya. According to some therefore, Vishnu and Śiva united to form Harihara, at the time of the Great Churning, when this process first set in. When individuals throw off their material garb, or when, by Pralayic force, their material cover is forcibly removed, they become fit to be gathered together and to become merged at Pralaya in the One.

PRADYUMNA is the wish of Bhagavat, as imprinted on the course of universal evolution. He is the wish of God. When the one wished to be many, He represented that wish and gave the entire turn to the course of evolution, that it might adopt itself to that wish. Individuals multiplied. Desires became many and all actions became Sakama. Pradyumna was then called Kāmadeva, the God of Love, or desire.

When the course of descent was arrested, Kāmadeva was destroyed by fire from the forehead of Śiva. He appeared again, but this time he appeared as the son of Krishna. The wish of his father now was to be one again, for He had already become many, as many as the Karma of the previous Kalpa would allow. And Pradyumna had to impress this wish upon individuals generally, so that the ascent of matter to spirit might be universal.

According to Kapila, Pradyumna is reflected on Buddhi. Buddhi is defined by him as that faculty by which objects are perceived. Doubt, false understanding, true understanding, memory and sleep, these are the indications of that faculty. (III. 26. XXVIII, XXIX).

ANIRUDDHA is the son of Pradyumna. According to Kapila, he is reflected on Manas, the faculty of Sankalpa and Vikalpa. Sankalpa in Sānkhya terminology is the first or general idea of a thing.

Vikalpa is the idea of the peculiarity of a thing. Thus when I cast a passing glance at a man, I know nothing of him except that he is a man. But when I look at him carefully, I know his peculiarities and can differentiate him from others.

The first idea is the idea of a thing in its primity or dawn.

The second idea is the idea of its peculiarities. It is the second idea which gives rise to likes and dislikes.

In the course of ascent, we must carry general ideas. We must rise from particulars to generals. The mind will thus be freed from the burden of personal and material thoughts.

Aniruddha became wedded to Usha or Dawn. He is Bhagavat as perceived by Manas.

END OF THE TENTH SKANDHA.

THE ELEVENTH SKANDHA

THE MUSHALA. XI. I.

Sri Krishna, with the help of Rāma, the Yādavas and the Pāndavas, killed the Daityas, born as Kings. He made the Pāndavas his instruments in the great war. When the Kings on both sides and their armies were killed, Sri Krishna thought within himself: — "The pressure is not yet all removed from the earth. For these powerful Yādavas, backed by me, have become mad with power. I shall bring on disunion among them, which will be the cause of their death. Then I can have rest and may go to my own abode."

Visvā-mitra, Asita, Kanva, Durvāsas, Bhrigu, Angiras, Kasyapa, Vāmadeva, Atri, Vasistha, Nārada and other Rishis went to a sacred place called Pindaraka near Dvārāka. The Yadava boys were playing among themselves. They dressed Sāmba, son of Jāmbavati, as a girl and took him to the Rishis, saying she was pregnant and inquiring whether she would have a son or a daughter. The Rishis could not bear this impertinence and they said: — "O you fools, she will bring forth a *Mushala* (a pestle) that will be the ruin of your line." The boys were terrified. Sāmba did produce an iron pestle. They took the pestle and went home. The boys related the story to all the Yādavas. Āhuka, the chief of the clan, ordered the pestle to be ground down to powder and the powder to be thrown into the Sea. This was done, but a portion remained. That portion was also thrown into the

Sea. A fish swallowed the iron piece. The fish was caught by a fisherman. He made two spears of the iron found in the fish. The powdered iron grains were carried by the waves to the coast and there they grew into reeds.

THE BHĀGAVATĀ PATH.

SKANDHA XI. CHAP. 2-5.

Vāsudeva asked Nārada about the Path of Bhagavat which leads to Moksha. Nārada said: —

Of the sons of Rishabha, nine became well-versed in Ātmā Vidya. They were Kavi, Hari, Antariksha, Prabuddha, Pippalayana Avirhotra, Drumila, Chamasa, and Kara-bhājana.

The Rishis of Bharata Varsha were performing Yajna at the place of Nimi and these nine Rishis went there.

1. Nimi asked the Rishis about the *path of Bhagavat.*

Kavi said: —

The path of Bhagavat consists of such expedients as the Lord mentioned Himself (for those that are not wise) for the speedy acquisition of self knowledge. In following this Path, man is not overcome by obstacles (as in the path of Yoga). He may run along this path even with closed eyes without fear of losing his steps (with closed eyes *i.e.* even without knowing where he goes and what he does).

(What is the path then?)

Whatever a man does, whether it be the body or speech or mind or the senses or intellect or the sense of I-ness that acts, let him offer that all up to the Supreme Nārāyana.

He who is removed from Īshvara, (first) forgets (Īshvara), (*Asmriti*), then there is wrong perception such as "I am the body" (*Viparyaya*). This is caused by the Māyā of Bhagavat. Fear arises from devotion to the Second.

Therefore wise men worship the Lord only, with unfailing Bhakti, knowing his Guru to be one with Īshvara and Ātmā.

(The Bhāgavata School classifies Jivas under two heads — Antar Mukha and Bahir Mukha. Antar Mukha is literally one with his face turned inwards *i.e.*, one who withdraws himself from the outside world and looks to self within, which is only an aspect of Īshvara.

Bahir Mukha Jiva is one with his face turned outwards *i.e.* one who withdraws himself from the self-within and therefore from Īshvara. He first loses sight of Īshvara, forgets that he (the Jiva) is an aspect of Īshvara and that he is not the same as the body. He then considers the body as one with himself and concerns himself only with its relations to the outside world. This is called forgetting and wrong perception. "Fear arises from devotion to the Second." The Second is that which is not self. In meditation, the Guru stands between Īshvara and self, and is Īshvara for all practical purposes to the devotee).

The Dvaita (Mayic manifestation), though not existing, appears to exist, through the mind of man, like dreams and desires. Therefore wise men should control the mind, which gives rise to desires and doubts about actions. Then there shall be no fear.

The existence of the outside world and of the body is like the existence of dreams and desires. The dream exists for the time being and then disappears altogether, The dream has its existence because the mind brings it into existence. It is a creation of the mind, not permanently attached to the Jiva. So desires are also creations of the mind, not permanently attached to the Jiva, But they have got a temporary existence. That existence, however, is an existence in the mind of the man entertaining the dreams and desires and not outside the mind. Therefore the existence is not a real one.

So the body of the Jiva and its surroundings are temporarily attached to the Jiva. As the dream vanishes in the wakeful state, so the body and its surroundings disappear with the transformation called Death. Body after body, surroundings after surroundings, are dreams, as it were, in the mind that bears all through the bubbles arising in the ocean of Jivic existence.

The realisation of this temporary connection of the body and its surroundings is a training for the Antarmukha Jiva, for it enables him to turn towards Ishvara and the permanent aspect of Jiva.

The non-existence of Dvaita has always to be understood with reference to Jiva or Ishvara, and not *independently*, for the flow of Prakriti is eternal. The disregard of this primary idea has given rise to many misconceptions. (Then as to Antarmukha practices.) Hear about the Incarnations of Vishnu and His blessed deeds, hear about his names full of import as to those deeds and Incarnations, hear and sing the songs about Him, without any sense of uneasiness as to what others will say. Then roam over the earth free from all worldly attachments.

By such practices, and by the recital of His dear names, love for Bhagavat grows up. The heart then melts away. The devotee laughs loudly, he weeps, he cries aloud, he sings and he dances like a mad man. He loses all control over himself.

He salutes Akāsa, Vayu, Agni, Water, Earth, the planets, the trees, the Seas and all beings as forming the body of his Hari. For he knows nothing else.

He, who worships Bhagavat in this way, has Devotion (Bhakti), perception of Ishvara (Anubhava) and dispassion (Virakti) — all three growing at one and the same time, as, by eating, one gets pleasure, nutrition and satisfaction of hunger all at one and the same time.

The Bhāgavata then attains supreme peace.

2. Nimi then asked: "What are the *Characteristics of a Bhāgavata* and what are the *Signs by which a Bhāgavata is known?*"

Hari replied: —

"He who sees in all beings the existence of Bhagavat as in his own self, and sees all beings in the Bhagavat within himself is the highest Bhāgavata.

"He who bears love towards Īshvara friendship towards his dependents, kindness toward the ignorant, and indifference towards his enemies belongs to the next class of Bhāgavatas.

"He who worships an image as Hari with faith, but has no regard for Bhaktas and for other beings is only a beginner as a Bhakta.

"The highest Bhāgavata perceives the objects with his senses, but does not feel either aversion or pleasure. He looks upon the universe as the Māyā of Vishnu.

"By constant meditation on Hari, he is not affected by the changes of life. Desires have no place in his mind, so devoted is he to Vāsudeva.

He is the favourite of Hari, who does not take pride in his birth, Karma, caste or Āsrama.

"The highest Bhāgavata does not know "Mine" and "Thine," either in wealth or in body. He looks upon all beings with equal eyes, His mind is always at peace.

"Even for the sake of all the three Lokas, the Vaishnava will not for a moment forget the lotus feet of Bhagavat.

"And more, he is the greatest of all Bhāgavatas, to whose heart Hari is bound down by the tie of Love."

3. Nimi asked: — "What is then this Māyā of the Supreme Lord?"

Antariksha replied: —

"Māyā of Bhagavat is that which causes the creation, preservation and dissolution of this universe."

4. Nimi asked: — "How can one whose mind is not controlled and who is of dull understanding easily cross over this Māyā?

Prabuddha replied: —

"Have recourse to a Guru, who knows the Truth and is fixed in the supreme. Learn the duties of Bhāgavatas from him. Practise non-attachment, keep company with Sādhus. Be kind to your inferiors, friendly to your equals and respectful to your superiors. Keep your body and mind pure. Regulate your life by fixed rules. Have forgiveness. Do not talk idly. Read the sacred books. Be upright. Be temperate. Be harmless to all beings. Bear good and evil, pleasure and pain with equanimity. Find out Ātmā and Īshvara everywhere. Free yourself from all connections. Do not bind yourself down to your house. Have that which is easily got for your clothing. Be content with anything and everything. Have faith in the Bhāgavata Sāstra, but do not blame any other Sastra. Control your mind, speech and actions. Speak the truth. Control your inner and outer senses. Hear, recite and meditate on the deeds and Avatāras of Hari. Let all your exertions be for Him. Offer up all, even your wife, children and your own life, to Him. In the company of Bhāgavatas, interchange devotion and love, remind each other and speak to each other of the glory of Bhagavat, till your hair stands on end, and you will sometimes dance and sometimes sing, maddened by your devotional thoughts about Achyuta.

"These are the duties of a Bhāgavata and by practising these, he may easily cross over Māyā."

5. Nimi asked: — "How can one be fixed in devotion to Nārāyana?"

Pippalāyana replied: —

"When through the desire of attaining the feet of Vishnu, one has strong devotion, the impurities of one's mind are destroyed. When the mind is purified, it becomes fixed in Ātmā."

6. Nimi asked: — "Tell me about Karma Yoga, by the performance of which Karma is speedily destroyed."

Āvirhotra replied: —

"Vedic Karma does not directly lead to Moksha. Offer up your Vedic Karma to Īshvara, and perform it, without any worldly attachment, however.

"He who wants speedily to cut asunder the tie of Ahankāra shall worship Vishnu in the way prescribed in the Tantras or Āgama. (Vedic Karma at first consisted of Vedic Yajna. The Gitā gave a death blow to the performance of Vedic Yajnas. *Nishkāma* Karma took the place of *Kāmya* Karma, The Vedic Karma however survived in the Sandhyā Mantras, which conform themselves to the Path of Upāsanā.

"The Vedic Sandhyā is however meant only for Brāhmanas.

"The Tāntric Sandhyā is an imitation of the Vedic Sandhyā, adapted to all classes of men, and it supplements the Vedic Sandhyā by laying down a method of worshipping the Lord in the heart and of worshipping His image. Mantras are also prescribed. Devotion is the chief element in Tāntric Upāsanā and this Upāsanā is enjoined for all Bhāgavatas or Vaishnavas. There are Śiva Tantras, Śakti Tantras, Ganapati Tantras, Sūrya Tantras as well as Vaishnava Tantras. There are black rites prescribed in some of the Śakti Tantras and the Tantras have therefore got a bad name with many. But the Tantras as a whole form the only science of practical occultism in Sanskrit, and the Vaishnava Upāsanā is strictly a Tāntric Upāsanā."

(I do not enter here into the details of that Upāsanā, though some details are given in the text.)

7. Nimi said: — "Tell me about the *Avatāras* and Their deeds O Rishis." Drumila gave a short account of the Avatāras, commencing from the First Purusha. As this is nearly a repetition of what has been said before, no attempt is made to reproduce it.

8. Nimi asked what is the *destiny of those that do not worship Bhagavat, those that have no control over their mind and their senses.*

Chamasa replied: — "They enter the regions of darkness (Tamas)."

9. Nimi asked:

"What is the Color of the manifestation of Bhagavat at each period, how does he manifest Himself, by what name is He known and in what way is He worshipped?"

Karabhājana replied: —

"In Satya Yuga, Bhagavat becomes white, with four hands, with tufts of braided hair, with bark round His waist. He bears a black deer-skin, the sacred thread and beads, and has Danda (the rod of an ascetic) and Kāmandalu (the water-pot of an ascetic) in his hands. (*i.e.* He looks like a Brahmācharin).

"Men are then peaceful and friendly towards one another. There are no differences amongst them. They worship the Lord by means of Tapas, by control of the senses and of the mind.

"Bhagavat is then known by the following names: — Hansa, Suparna, Vaikuntha, Dharma, Yogesvara, Amala, Īshvara, Purusha, Avyakta, and Paramātmān.

"In Tretā, Bhagavat becomes Red. He has four hands and golden hair. His form is that of Yajna. Men are pious at the time. They worship Bhagavat by Vedic Yajna.

"Bhagavat is known by the following names: —

"Vishnu, Yajna, Prism-garbha, Sarvadeva, Uru-krama, Vrishā Kapi, Jayanta and Urugāya.

"In Dvāpara, Bhagavat is *Syama*. (The word Syāma ordinarily means dark-blue. But Śridhara explains the word here as the color of an Atasi flower, which is generally yellow. This is because the Bhagavat speaks before of white, red, yellow and black as the colors of Yuga Avatāras.) His cloth is yellow.

"Men worship Him both by Vedic and Tāntric methods.

"Vāsudeva, Sankarshana, Pradyumna, Aniruddha, Nārāyana, Visvesvara and Visva are his names.

"In Kali, worship is made according to the Tantras, which are various.

"Bhagavat is black (Krishna). Men worship Him, His Symbols and attendants mostly by loud recitals of names and prayers (Sankirtana). Wise men praise Kali because worship is so easily made by mere Sankirtana. Even men in Satya Yuga wish to be born in Kali Yuga."

Nimi respected the nine Rishis and they disappeared in the presence of all men.

Vāsudeva and Devaki heard this story from Nārada. They realised Krishna as Īshvara and they acquired wisdom.

KRISHNA AND UDDHAVA.

SKANDHA XI. CHAP. 6.

Brahmā and other Devas went to Dvārakā. Addressing Krishna; Brahmā said: — "All that we prayed for has been done. One hundred and twenty-five years have passed away since thou didst appear in the line of Yadus. That line is also well nigh extinguished. Now go back to thy own abode, if it pleases thee."

Sri Krishna replied: — "The extinction of the Yādavas has been set on foot by the curse of the Rishis. I shall remain on Earth, till it is completely brought about." There were unusual phenomena at Dvārakā. The elders came to Krishna. He proposed a pilgrimage to Prabhāsa. So the Yādavas made preparations for going to Prabhāsa. Uddhava saw the evil portents and he heard what Sri Krishna said. "I see, O Lord," said he to Sri Krishna, "thou shalt leave this earth, as soon as the Yadus are destroyed. I can not miss thy feet even for half a moment. So take me to thy own abode."

Sri Krishna replied: — "It is true as you say. My mission is fulfilled. The Devas ask me to go back. The Yādavas shall be killed by mutual quarrel. On the seventh day from this, the sea shall swallow up this seat of Dvārakā. As soon as I leave this earth, Kali shall overtake it and men shall grow unrighteous. It will not then be meet for you to remain here. Give up all and free yourself from all attachments and roam about over this earth, with your mind fixed on me, looking on all beings with equal eyes. Whatever is perceived by the senses and the mind, know all that to be of the mind, and so Māyic and transitory. "This is this" and "this is that" this conception of difference is only a delusion of him whose mind is distracted (*i.e.* not united to Me). It is this delusion which causes experiences of right and wrong. It is for those that have got notions of right and wrong that (the Vedas speak) differently of the performance of prescribed work (Karma), the non-performance of prescribed work (Akarma), and the performance of prohibited work (Vikarma). (This has reference to Varna and Āsrama duties. As long as a man identifies himself with some Varna or Āsrama he looks upon others also as belonging to some Varna or Āsrama. He therefore makes a distinction between men and men. The Varnāsrama duties are prescribed by the Vedas for a man, so long as he entertains ideas of difference. When he looks equally upon a Brāhmana and a Chandāla, when he finds his Lord every where and finds all beings in the Lord within himself, he becomes a man of the Universe, a Bhāgavata. For him the Vedas do not make any rule. He is above all rules and restrictions. But the Varnāsrama duties are to be respected, so long as one makes any difference between man and man.) Control thy senses and control thy mind. See the wide-spread Universe in thyself and see thyself in Me, the Lord. Learn and digest all that is given in the scriptures. Contented with self perception, the very self of all other beings, you shall have no danger from others. You will do no wrong but not because it is prohibited by the Scriptures, and you will do what is prescribed but not because it is so prescribed (*i.e.* the sense of right and wrong will be natural in you, independently of Sastric teachings.) You will exceed the limits of both right and wrong and do things just like a child. The friend of all beings, calm and quiet at heart, fixed in wisdom and direct knowledge, you will see the Universe full of Me and you will not be drawn back to births."

Uddhava said: —

"Lord of Yoga, what thou sayest for my final bliss is a complete renunciation of all worldly attachments. It seems to me however that the giving up of desires is not possible for those that have their mind filled with the object world, unless they are completely devoted to Thee.

"I have not yet got over the sense of 'I' and 'Mine.' Tell me how I can easily follow out Thy teachings."

Sri Krishna replied: —

"Generally those men that are skilful in discrimination rescue self from worldly desires by means of self, (*i.e.* they may do so, even without the help of a Guru, by means of self discrimination.) Self is the instructor of self, specially in man (Purusha.)" (Even in animals, preserving instincts proceed from self. So self is the instructor. *Śridhara*) "For it is self that finds out final bliss by direct perception and by inference. Wise men, well versed in Sānkhya and Yoga, look upon Me as Purusha pervading all beings, and possessing all powers. (This is according to Śridhara, the direct perception by which final bliss is attained. The word Purusha here has something like the sense of a Monad in Theosophical literature. The passage quoted by Śridhara from the Upanishads to illustrate the idea of Purusha also shews this.) There are many habitations created for life manifestation, some, with one, two, three or four feet, some with many feet and some with no foot. Of these, however, that of man (Pourushi) is dear to me. For in this form of Man those that are fixed in meditation truly find me out, the Lord, though beyond all objects of perception, by the indications of perceived attributes as well as by inferences from the same." (*Indications*. Buddhi, Manas and others, the perceived attributes, are in their nature manifestless. The manifestation is not possible except through one that is self manifest. Therefore Buddhi and others point to Him.

Inferences. Whenever there is an instrument, there is some one to use it. Buddhi and others are instruments. There is therefore one who guides these. *Śridhara*.) In this matter of self instruction, hear the story of an Ava-dhuta (an ascetic who renounces all worldly attachments and connections.)

SELF-INSTRUCTION.

SKANDHA XI. CHAP. 7-9.

Yadu asked an Ava-dhūta how he could get that clear spiritual vision, by which he was able to give up all attachments, and roam like a child in perfect bliss.

The Ava-dhūta replied: —

I have many Gurus, O king — Earth, Air, Ākāsa, Water, Fire, the Moon, the Sun, the pigeon, the huge serpents, the ocean, the insect, the bee, the elephant, the collector of honey, the deer, the fish, Pingalā, the osprey, the child, the maid, the maker of arrows, the serpent, the spider and the wasp. These are my twenty four Gurus.

Though oppressed by the elements, the Earth does not deviate from her path, as she knows that they are only guided by the divine law. This forbearance I have learned from the Earth. I have learned from the mountain (which is a part of the Earth) that all our desires should be for the good of others and that our very existence is for others and not for self. I have learned entire subordination to other's interests from the trees (also part of the Earth).

I have learned from the vital air, that one should be content only with such things as keep up the life and should not care about the objects of the senses. (The sage should keep up his life so that his mind be not put out of order and his mental acquisitions lost; but at the same time he should not be attached to the objects of the senses, so that his speech and mind be not disturbed.)

Though placed in the midst of the objects with different attributes, the Yogi should not be attached to them. This I have learned from the outside air. The soul enters the body and the bodily attributes seem its own, but it is not so. The air is charged with smell, but the smell is no attribute of air.

Ātmā is all pervading and it is not affected by the body and bodily attributes. This I have learned from Akāsa which, though all pervading, seems to be conditioned by clouds and other objects.

Transparency, agreeability and sweetness, I have learned from water. The sage purifies others like water.

Powerful in knowledge and glowing with asceticism, the sage receiving all things does not take their impurities even as fire.

Fire eats the sacrificial ghee when offered to it and consumes the sins of the offerer. The sage eats the food offered to him by others but he burns up their past and future impurities.

Fire is one though it enters fuels of various sorts.

One Ātmā pervades all beings, however different they may appear by the action of Avidyā.

Birth, death, and other affections are states of the body, not of Ātmā. The moon looks full, diminished and gone, though it is the same in all these states.

The sun draws water by its rays and gives it all away in time. The sage takes in order to give, and not in order to add to his own possessions.

The sun reflected on different surfaces appears to the ignorant as many and various. The Ātmā in different bodies, even appears as such.

Too much attachment is bad. This I have learned from a pair of pigeons. They lived in a forest. One day they left their young ones in the nest and went about in search of food for them. When they returned they found the young ones netted by a hunter. The mother had too much affection for the young ones. She fell into the net of her own accord. The father also followed suit and the hunter was pleased to have them all without any exertion of his own.

The huge Ajagara serpent remains where he is and is content with whatever food comes to him.

The sage is calm and deep, not to be fathomed or measured. He is limitless (as the unconditioned self is manifested in him). He is not to be disturbed even like the tranquil ocean. The ocean may receive volumes of water from the rivers at times or may receive no water at other times. But it remains the same, even as the sage at all times.

He who is tempted by woman is destroyed like an insect falling into fire.

447

The bee takes a little from every flower. The Sanyāsī should take only a little from each Grihasthā, so that the Grihasthā may not suffer.

The bee extracts honey from all flowers big or small. The Sage should extract wisdom from all Sāstras big or small. Do not store anything for the evening or for the morrow. Have only so much for your *bhikshā* (alms given to a Sanyāsī) as may suffice for one meal. The bee is killed for his storing.

The Bhikshu shall not touch a woman though made of wood, even with his feet. The elephant is shewn a female and is drawn into a trap. The woman is the death of the sage. He should never approach her. The elephant seeking a female is killed by stronger elephants.

The miser neither gives nor enjoys his riches. What ever he collects with difficulty is carried away by some one else. The collector of honey carries away the honey collected by others. He does not make it by his own effort. The Sanyāsī without any effort of his own gets food from the Grihasthās, as it is their duty to feed him.

Do not hear vulgar songs. The deer is attracted by songs and is entrapped.

The love of taste is to be conquered above all, for it is most difficult to conquer. When the sense of taste is controlled, all other senses are controlled. The fish is killed when tempted by the bait.

Pinglā, a courtesan of Videha waited the whole day for some lover who might come and make presents to her, with breathless expectation. The night approached and she grew restless She then thought within herself: — "For what a trifle, am I so uneasy. Why not seek Īshvara, the eternal giver of all pleasures and all desires." She gave up all hopes and expectations that troubled her ere long and became happy. She had good sleep in the night. It is hope that gives us trouble. Without hope we are happy.

When the bird kurara (osprey) gets some flesh to eat, the stronger birds kill him. He is happy when he renounces the flesh. Renunciation of dear objects is good for the sage.

The child has no sense of honor or dis-honor. It has not the thoughts of a man of the world. It is self content and it plays with self. I roam about like the child. The child is however ignorant, but the sage crosses the limits of the Gunas.

Some people came to select a bride. The maid was alone in the house. She received the men who came. She went to a solilary place to beat off the impurities of the rice for their meal. She had shell-made bracelets on her wrists. These made a great noise. She felt disgust and broke the bracelets one by one, till only one remained on each hand. When there are two or more at one place, they cause a jarring sound, and they quarrel. I have therefore earned solitariness from the maid.

I have learned concentration of mind from the maker of arrows.

The serpent has no home. It roams in solitude. So do I.

Nārāyana draws in the whole creation at the end of the Kalpa and becomes one, the resort of all.

By Kāla Śakti, the thread, Mahat, first comes out and the universe is again brought into manifestation. The spider brings the thread out of himself, spreads out the web and devours it himself.

(There is a kind of wasp, which catches a particular insect and carries it into a hole. It is supposed that the insect assumes the form of the wasp through fear.) When either through affection, hatred, or fear, a man throws his whole heart upon some object and the mind holds it fast, he attains the form of that object. I have learned this from the wasp.

Thus I have learned from my Gurus, My own body is also my Guru. I have learned from it dispassion and discrimination. The body is born only to die. Constant misery is its lot. I know the truths, by a discriminative study of the body. Still I regard it as not mine and so I feel no attachment for it (The body belongs to the dogs and jackals who devour it after death. *Sridhara.*)

What does not a man do for the enjoyment of the body — but it comes to an end after all, having created the germs of another body.

The possessor of the body is now drawn away by this sense, now by that sense, now by this action now by that action. The senses suck his very life blood, even as the many wives of one husband.

The Lord created vegetable and animal bodies. But he was not satisfied with them. For the human body only has the power to perceive Brahmān.

Therefore after many births, when the human body is once attained, one should strive promptly for his supreme bliss.

Yadu heard these words of wisdom, and he gave up all attachments.

ĀTMĀ A REFUTATION OF THE SCHOOL OF JAIMINI.

SKANDHA XI. CHAP. 10.

Sri Krishna continued: —

(Self-study is the first stage. It leads to the power of discrimination. Without self study no progress is possible. Therefore Sri Krishna speaks of it as an essential condition. He then goes on to the next stage of preparation.)

"Subject to what I have said as to one's own duties (in Pancha Rātra and other Vaishnava works; *Sridhara*) and knowing me to be the final resort, you should dispassionately follow the Varna-Āsrama and family duties. (But how is dispassion possible?) With the mind purified by the performance of duties, reflect on this that worldly men take up things, thinking them to be real but the end shews that they are not so.

"Objects of desire are unreal, as their perception as separate entities is caused by the senses and they are altogether sense-made. Even they are as unreal as dreams and fancy, both caused by the mind."

(Actions are fourfold, (1) those that have the fulfilment of selfish desires for their object or Kāmya Karma, (2) those that are prohibited by the Scriptures or Nishiddha Karma, (3) those that are required to be daily performed or Nityā Karma, (4) those that are required to be performed on certain occasions or Naimittika.

The first two are Pravritta or selfish Karma. The last two are Nivritta or unselfish Karma. The Smritis say that those who want Moksha or liberation must not perform Pravritta Karma. But they should perform Nitya and Naimittika Karma, as their non-performance might give rise to obstacles.) Perform Nivritta Karma and being devoted to Me, give up all Pravritta Karma. But when you fully enter the path of wisdom, then you need not care much even for Nivritta Karma. Constantly practise Yāma. Being fixed on Me, you may sometimes practise Niyama (Yāma and Niyama are detailed in the 19th chapter.)

"Devotedly follow one Guru, who knows Me and is full of Me, being calm and quiet at heart.

"Be humble and unenvious, active, free from the sense of "Mineness", strong in friendship (towards the Guru. *Śridhara*) not over-zealous, eager to know the truths and free from malice. Do not indulge in idle talk. Be indifferent to wife, son, house, land, relations, riches and all other things, for Ātmā is the same every where and its working is the same in all bodies.

"This Ātmā is neither the gross body nor the subtle body. It is the self illumined seer. Fire that illuminates and burns is separate from the fuel that is illuminated and burnt.

"The fuel has beginning and end. It is big and small. It is of various kinds. The fire that pervades it is limited by the nature of the fuel. So Ātmā which is separate from the body bears the attributes of the body.

"The birth and re-birth of the Jiva have their origin in the gross and the subtle body, which are the outcome of the Gunas, subordinated by Īshvara. The knowledge of Ātmā (as separate from the body) cuts off the course of rebirths.

"Therefore by seeking after knowledge fully realise that Ātmā in self is separate and is beyond the body. Then by degrees do away with a sense of reality in respect of the gross and the subtle body.

"The preceptor is the lower piece of wood used for kindling the sacred fire. The pupil is the upper piece of wood. The teachings form the middle portion of the wood where the stroke is made. Vidyā is the pleasing fire that comes out. (The pupil by constant questioning should extract the fire of wisdom from the Guru *i.e.* one should learn Ātmā Vidyā from his Guru.)

"The pure wisdom that is thus acquired from the Guru shakes off the Māyā that is begotten of the Gunas. It burns up the Gunas themselves, which constitute this universe of re-incarnation and then it ceases of itself. The fire consumes the fuel first and then it is extinguished of itself.

"Or if you think that the doers of actions, their pleasures and pains, the enjoyers and sufferers (Jivātmas or Egos) are many and that the place and time of enjoyment and suffering, and the scriptures relating thereto and to the enjoyer or sufferer are all alike not constant."

(We have found in the former slokas that Ātmā is one and constant. It is self manifest and it is conciousness itself. When we speak of Ātmā as the Doer, the Enjoyer and so on these attributes really relate to the body which forms the phenomenal basis of Ātmā. Every thing else besides Ātmā is transitory and formed of Māyā. It has been therefore said that one should free himself from all attachments and should attain liberation by the knowledge of Ātmā. This is the conclusion arrived at by a reconciliation of all the Srutis. But there is another school, that of Jaimini, which arrives at a different conclusion. To remove all doubts whatsoever, the author refers to it for the sake of refutation. The followers of Jaimini deem Jivātmas — the doers and enjoyers in all beings to be essentially separate and many. According to them, Ātmā is known by the feeling of "I-ness." Now this feeling is different in different bodies. "I am the doer" "I am the enjoyer" every one feels this separately for himself. There is no one Parmātmā, which is the essence of all these Jivātmas and which is above all transformations. Therefore freedom from attachments or dispassion is not possible. You may think, that the enjoyments are transitory, and so also that the time and place of enjoyment, the scriptures that enjoin them, and the *enjoying* Ātmā itself are not constant. Hence you may justify dispassion. But all this is not a fact. This is the argument of the followers of Jaimini. *Śridhara.*)

"And if you consider that all substances are constant by the eternal flow of their existence and that consciousness grows and is separate according to the difference in every particular form." (According to the followers of Jaimini there is no break in the objects of enjoyment nor are they formed of Māyā. All substances perpetually exist by the constancy of their flow. They say that there was no time, when the Universe was not what it is. Therefore there is no maker of the Universe, no Īshvara. And the Universe is not a delusion — Māyā. It is what it appears to be. There is no one and constant consciousness of which the essence is Ātmā. "This pot" "this cloth" — Our consciousness grows by the process of perceiving these differences. Therefore consciousness is not constant and it has separate forms. The hidden purport is this. Ātmā is not absolute consciousness itself, but it is transformed into consciousness. But you can not say, because it is subject to transformation, therefore it is transient. For it has been said authoritatively that its transformation into consciousness does not interfere with its eternity. Therefore for the purpose of liberation (Mukti), Ātmā can not transform itself without the help of the senses &c. And if Ātmā attains liberation, in the state of jada (or unconsciousness) nothing is gained. Therefore the best path to follow is that of Pravritti or Inclination and not that of Nivritti or Disinclination. *Sridhara*. The above commentaries of Śridhara form one of the best expositions of the philosophy of Jaimini. Only the last passage requires a little elucidation. Ātmā in itself is not consciousness. Its transformation into consciousness is its highest evolution or Mukti. Now this transformation is caused by the perception of objects, it is made complete by the perception of all objects and it is made constant by a constant desire for all objects. This object, or that object may vanish, this man or that woman may die, this flower or that flower may perish, but there is no time when the objects as a class do not exist, when there is no enjoyer, no object to be enjoyed. So there is a constancy in the desires. Therefore one must form attachments, have desires, that Ātmā be made fully conscious. But if Ātmā be left to itself, it will remain Jada or unconscious. There is nothing to be gained by this. Therefore one should persistently follow the path of desires as laid down in the Karma Kānda of the Vedas, analysed by Jaimini in his Pūrva Mimānsā. One should not give up Vedic Karma and selfish desires as he is taught to do in the Jnāna Kānda of the Vedas, the Upanishads, as analysed by Vyāsa in his Uttara Mimānsā, and as expounded by Sri Krishna in the Bhagavat

Gītā. It must be remembered that this philosophy of Karma, so effectually refuted by Sri Krishna, was suited to the materialistic cycle of evolution, when Rajas had to be sought rather than put down. The minerals and vegetables were unconscious. The animals shewed a slight development in consciousness. But the full development was in Man. And this was due to the pursuit of the Path of Inclination or Pravritti Mārga up to a late period in the past history of the Universe. Notwithstanding the attacks of Sri Krishna, the school of Jaimini had its followers till the time of Srī Sankarāchārya, when Mandana Misra the most learned Pandit of the time, was its chief exponent. After his memorable defeat by Srī Sankarāchārya the Mimānsākas fell into disrepute and Vedic Karma became a thing of the past.)

"Granting all that, O dear Uddhava, all Ātmās have constantly their births and other states, by connection with the body and by reason of the divisions of time." (*i.e.* though you may say that Ātmā itself is transformed, still you can not deny that the transformations take place by its connection with the body and that they are brought about by time.)

"It follows then that the doer of actions, the enjoyer of joys and the sufferer of sorrows is dependent on other things." (For Ātmā is dependent upon the body and upon time for its highest transformation. Śridhara says if Ātmā is the doer and enjoyer, why should it do wrong acts and suffer sorrows if it were independent. Therefore Ātmā must be dependent according to the Mimānsākas). Now who in seeking his greatest good would worship one that is dependent on others?

"(Do not say that those who know Vedic karma thoroughly are always happy and only those that do not know that are unhappy. For it is found that — *Śridhara*) even wise men sometimes have no happiness and the ignorant have no misery. Therefore it is mere vanity (to speak about Karma). Even if (the followers of the path of Pravritti) know how to gain happiness and destroy misery, they certainly do not know the means by which they can get over death. And when death is near at hand, what objects of desire can give joy? What can please the victim that is carried to the place of sacrifice? (This is so far as this life is concerned. Then as to life after death). What you hear about Svarga life, even that is as bad as the

454

life we lead on this earth. For in Svarga, there is jealousy, there is fault finding, there are inequalities and consequent uneasiness, and there is a finality in the enjoyments and the desires are full of obstacles, even as agriculture is and so after all even Svarga is of no good. When the Vedic Karma is properly performed without any obstacle whatsoever, hear how the performer of Karma loses the place acquired by his Karma. He makes offerings to Indra and other Devas by the performance of Yajna and he goes after death to Svarga. There he enjoys heavenly objects like the Devas, objects acquired by his own Karma. He moves in white chariots the acquisitions of his own merits, among Deva girls and is adored; by the Gandharvas. The chariot moves at his will. It is adorned by small bells. He whiles away his time with the Deva girls in the gardens of Svarga and he does not know his own fall. But he remains in Svarga only so long as his merit is not exhausted. And when the merit is run out, down falls the man by the force of time, even against his will. (The above is the course after death of those who perform Kāmya Karma, according to Vedic rules. This is one way of following Pravritti Mārga. There is another way — the following up of one's own inclinations, in disregard of the Vedic rules. The next Śloka refers to the performers of prohibited Karma). And if again a man indulges in the prohibited acts, through evil company, if his senses are not controlled, and if in consequence, he is passionate indiscriminate, greedy, excessively fond of women, and unkind to other beings, if the man kills animals wantonly and worships Pretas and Bhūtas, he goes, driven by the law, to the Narakas and finds there intense Tamas.

"Therefore karma (selfish actions) ends in unhappiness. By performing karma with the body, men seek the body again. What happiness is there in the possession of this transitory body? The Lokas and Lokapālas have to fear me, they who live for one full day of Brahmā. Even Brahmā who lives for 2 Parardhas has fear of me."

(Therefore Pravritti Mārga leads to evil. It should be shunned and Nivritti Mārga should be adopted. This is the purport. *Śridhara*).

(Now Sri Krishna goes on to refute the first two assumptions (1) that Ātmā is the doer and (2) that Ātmā is the enjoyer). The Gunas create actions and the Gunas lead the Gunas. (The Gunas are Satva, Rajas and Tamas. These primal attributes of Prakriti give rise to all her manifestations. The Indriyas, the senses, and the mind are Sātvic and Rājasic transformations of the Ahankāra manifestation of Prakriti. So they are the Gunas first referred to. The senses and the mind create actions. Our actions are all prompted by them and not by Ātmā. So Ātmā is not the doer. It may be said however that the senses and the mind are guided by Ātmā. But it is not so. The primal attributes (Gunas) lead the senses and the mind (Gunas). If Satva prevails in a man his actions are Sātvic and so on. It is the nature of the Prākritic transformations of a man that determines his actions. This is only an elaboration of Śridhara's notes.)

The Jiva enjoys the fruits of Karma, being connected with the Gunas (The enjoyment by Jiva is also due to its phenomenal basis. "Connected with the Gunas" *i.e.* connected with the senses and other Prākritic elements. Jivātma dwells in the body. When the house falls down, he occupies another house. When the houses are merely halting stations in his long journey, he does not care much for the house itself, he does not identify himself with the house. So when Jivātma becomes indifferent to the body, it is not affected by the changes of the body. When a house burns, the dweller in the house feels pain. When the house is comfortable, the dweller in the house feels pleasure. His connection with the house is however temporary.)

As long as there is difference in the Gunas (i. e, Guna transformations, Ahankāra &c.), so long there is plurality in Ātmā. As long as there is plurality so long is it dependent on others. (The difference in Jivātmas or individuals, is not due to any difference in Ātmā, but to differences in the Guna transformations which give rise to the body. Dependence is also an accompaniment of those transformations),

So long as Jiva is dependent on others it has fear from Īshvara. Those that worship the Guna transformations are given up to sorrow and they become deluded.

BONDAGE AND LIBERATION.

SKANDHA XI. CHAP. 11.

Uddhava asked: —

"Ātmā dwells in the transformations of the Gunas forming the body. Why should it not be bound down by the Gunas. Or if Ātmā is free (like Akāsa) why should it be at all in bondage? What are the indications of Ātmā in bondage and of liberated Ātmā? Is Ātmā ever in bondage? (for connection with the Gunas is eternal. *Sridhara*) or ever in liberation (for if liberation is a state to be acquired, Ātmā can not be permanent. *Sridhara*)"

Sri Krishna replied: —

"Bondage and liberation are terms applied to Me not with reference to my real self, but with reference to My Gunas (the Guna limitations, Satva, Rajas and Tamas that are subordinate to me. *Sridhara*). The Gunas have their origin in Māyā. Therefore I have neither liberation nor bondage.

"Sorrow and delusion, joy and grief, even the attainment of body — these are all due to Māyā. The dream is only an illusory form of the mind, even so the course of births is not real. Vidya and Avidyā both proceed from My Māyā, O Uddhava. I am one and the Jiva is only my part (as the ray is of the sun). The bondage of Jiva is caused by Avidyā and its liberation by Vidya. This is eternally so. Now I shall tell you the different indications of the imprisoned and the liberated Jiva. (The difference is twofold: that between Jiva and Īshvara and that amongst the Jivas themselves. The author first speaks of the former. *Sridhara*.) Jiva and Īshvara though of different attributes dwell in the same body. They are two birds like each other (for both are manifestations of conciousness), companions that have made a nest for themselves (the heart), in the tree of body, of their own free will.

"Of these one (the Jiva) eats the fruits of the tree. The other (Īshvara) though not a partaker of the fruits is the mightier of the two. For He who does not partake of the fruits is the knower of self as of others. But the partaker of fruits is not so. He (Jiva) who is joined with Avidyā is always imprisoned. He (Īshvara) who is joined with Vidya is always liberated. (Māyā of Īshvara or Vidya does not throw a veil round and does not delude). The "conscious" are two in every individual. The consciousness of Īshvara is universal. Jivātma however takes upon himself the limitations of individuality and becomes the conscious centre in every man. "I perceive" "I conceive" "I do," that "I" is Ātmā limited by the sense of individuality.

The perception and conceptions are of Jivātma and he is the partaker of the fruits. This "Jiva" element in an individual is in bondage. But the Īshvara element in him is always liberated. And Jiva becomes liberated, when the individual limitation is withdrawn).

"(Now the difference amongst Jivas liberated and imprisoned).

"The liberated (Jiva) though dwelling in the body does not dwell in it as it were, even like one aroused from dream. (The awakened man remembers his dream body, but realises it as unreal, So the liberated Jiva looks upon his body as unreal or a temporary halting station, not a part of his own self). The ignorant identifies himself with the body, like the man in dream.

"The senses perceive the objects of the senses. The Gunas perceive the Gunas. The wise (Jiva) does not identify self with these. He is therefore not distracted.

"The ignorant, however, while dwelling in this body brought about by prior Karma, in which the senses act, thinks that he is the doer and becomes thus bound down.

"The wise one sees with disgust that the actions of others bind him. Sleeping, sitting, walking or bathing, seeing, touching, smelling, eating or hearing, the wise (Jiva) does not bind himself like the ignorant, for in those acts, he realises that the Gunas (senses) perceive (and not his self). He dwells in the body, but is not attached to it, like the Akāsa, the sun and the air. (Space is in all things, but the things form no part of space. The sun becomes reflected in water, but is not attached to water. The air moves about all around, but does not become attached to any thing). By the force of dispassion, the vision becomes clear. All doubts are removed. And the wise (Jiva) rises as it were from sleep, and withdraws himself from the diversities (of body and other material objects).

"The Jiva whose Prānas, Indriyas, Manas and Buddhi function without the promptings of self-centred desires is freed from the attributes of the body though dwelling in the body.

"Whether injured by others or adored the liberated Jiva is not affected in the least. He neither praises nor blames others for their good or bad deeds or words. He knows no merits nor demerits. He looks on all with an equal eye. He does not do anything, he does not say anything, he does not think on any thing, good or bad. He is self-entranced and moves like a sense-less being (Jada).

"If a man well-versed in the Vedas is not fixed in the Supreme, his labour becomes fruitless like that of a man who keeps a breeding cow that bears no calf. A cow that does not give milk, an unchaste wife, a body that is under the control of others, an undutiful son, wealth that is not given to the deserving and words that do not relate to me: he only keeps these whose lot is misery.

"With discrimination such as this do away with the notion of diversity in self. Then fix your purified mind in Me, who am all pervading, and desist from everything else.

"If you can not fix your mind in Me, then offer up all your actions unconditionally to Me. Hear with faith the words that relate to Me. Sing of Me, meditate on my deeds and Incarnations. Imitate these. Whatever you do, do that for Me. Then will be gained, O Uddhava, fixed devotion to Me. That devotion (Bhakti) is to be acquired in the company of Sādhus."

SĀDHU AND BHAKTI.

SKANDHA XI. CHAP. 11-12.

Uddhava asked: —

"Who according to Thee is a Sādhu? What sort of Bhakti (devotion) may be offered to Thee?"

Sri Krishna replied: —

"Compassionate, harmless, forgiving, firm in truth, faultless, impartial, doing good to all, undisturbed by desires, self restrained, mild, pure, not asking for anything, indifferent, temperate in eating with controlled mind, steady in the performance of duties, seeking refuge in me, given to meditation, careful, profound, patient, having control over the six-fold waves (hunger, thirst, sorrow and delusion, infirmity and death), not seeking respect from others, but respecting others, able, friendly, tender-hearted, wise, such is a Sādhu. He who knowing my injunctions and prohibitions in the performance of one's own Dharma or duties of life, even gives them all up for my sake is the best of all Sādhus. Those who seek me and nothing else, whether they know or not what I am, are the best of My Bhaktas.

"To see, touch and worship My symbols and my votaries, to serve and adore them, the humble recital of My glory and of My deeds, Faith in hearing words about Me, constant meditation on Me, the offering up of all gains to Me, even the offering up of self in a spirit of service, the observance of the sacred days, rejoicings in the houses set apart for Me (all good Hindus have a house or room set apart for divine worship), initiation according to the Vedic and the Tāntric System (one who is initiated is to recite the Mantras a certain number of times, every morning and evening and he can not take his meals without doing so in the morning) to observe fasts, enthusiasm in founding My image for worship, and in founding gardens, buildings and towns (in connection with My worship) humility and silence about one's own good deeds, — these are the indications of Bhakti.

"Sun, Fire, the Brāhmana, the Cow, the Vaishnava, Akāsa, Air, Water, Earth, Ātmā, and all beings — these are the eleven places of my worship.

"I am to be worshipped in the Sun, by Vedic Mantras, in the fire by sacrificial Ghee, in the Brāhmana by hospitality, in the cows by the offer of grass, in the Vaishnava by friendly treatment, in the Akāsa of the heart cavity by meditation, in the air by the contemplation of Prana, in the water by offerings of libation and so forth, in the Earth by secret Mantras, in Ātmā by experiencing (Bhōga) and in all beings by equality.

"In all these places of worship I am to be meditated on as with four hands, bearing conch, disc, club and lotus.

"He who worships Me as above and serves the Sādhus acquires Devotion. Except by devotion that is acquired in the company of Sādhus, there is hardly any other way of liberation. I am not so easily attainable by Yoga, Sānkhya, Dharma, the reading of Scriptures, Tapas, gifts, charitable acts, fasts, Yajnas, the Vedas, resort to pilgrimage, Niyamas or Yāmas as by the company of Sādhus. Even those that are the lowest by birth, those that have Rajas and Tamas predominant in them, the Daityas, Asuras, and Rākshasas attain me easily by the company of Sādhus. The Gopis in Vraja, the wives of the Vedic Brāhmanas did not read the Vedas, they did not observe fasts, they did not perform Tapas, but they attained Me, through the company of Sādhus. Therefore O Uddhava care not for Srutis or Smritis, for biddings and for forbiddings. Have recourse to Me, the Ātmā of all beings, with all devotion, and thou shall have no fear from any quarter."

(The following stages are to be marked: —

1. Study of Nature and self instruction.

2. Self discrimination, resuting in the separation of the conscious Ātmā and the unconscious Non-Ātmā.

3. The understanding of what is bondage and liberation, and the relation between Jiva Ātmā and Parama Ātmā (Īshvara.)

4. The liberating process during which the rules are to be observed, sacrifices to be made, the duties of life to be performed and active good done to all beings. During this process, the whole nature of the man becomes one of universal compassion and friendliness. Differences vanish. Good and bad become all alike.

5. The Jiva rests in his own Ātmā, which is the Ātmā of all beings, and then all is calm and quiet.

6. The company of Sādhus.

7. Devotion acquired in that company.

8. When Devotion (Bhakti) becomes a part of one's nature then the giving up of all rules, all karma, whether pertaining to the Srutis or the Smritis.)

WHY GIVE UP ALL KARMA

SKANDHA XI. CHAP. 12.

This Jiva-Īshvara becomes manifest in the cavities (nerve-plexuses). He enters the cavity (called Ādhāra or prostatic plexus) with the Prana (energy) of sound (called Para). He passed through subtle mind-made forms (Pasyanti and Madhyamā) in the plexuses called Manipura or Solar and Visuddhi or laryngeal and at last comes out as) very gross (Sound forms, called Vaikhari, consisting of) Mātrā (Measures, such as long, short &c), Svara (accents known as Udātta or high, Anudātta or low and Svarita or mixed; and Varna the (letters of the alphabet, *ka, kha* &c.)

(The ruling idea is that the teachings of the Vedas and the Smritis are conveyed in articulate expressions and are adapted to planes corresponding to articulation. But articulation is the last and grossest expression of Divine Sound energy. In man the highest manifestation of sound energy, the primal voice, the divine voice, the first Logos, is Para. It is the Light which manifests the whole Universe. In that highest plane of manifestation there is no difference between Light and Sound. The seat of this Light is Mūla-Ādhāra Chakra.

Coming down the line of material manifestation, this Divine Light, this Parā Voice, become Pasyanti in the plane of causes, of germ thoughts, of root ideas, the Karana plane. The germs are transmitted in Man from birth to birth and in the Universe from kalpa to kalpa. They are the *causes* of the subsequent manifestations, whether individual or universal. The Parā voice passing through the causal plane, becomes the root-ideas or germ thoughts.

In the next plane, the Sūkshma plane, the voice becomes the thoughts themselves or Madhyamā.

The last expression of the Voice is the articulate expression, Vaikhari.

The Srutis and Smritis as written or spoken belong to the plane of lowest manifestation. They are governed by the root-ideas and ideas of the present universe, the root-ideas and ideas of the Rishis through whom they are manifested.

When you seek the *unmanifested* light of the Logos, the Divine Voice, or only the first manifestation of that Voice, what care you about the lower manifestations, the Srutis or Smritis, what care you about karma that pertains to the lower planes?)

In Akāsa, fire is only unmanifested heat (Ushman). It is manifested further down in the fuel. By friction in the fuel, it becomes a spark. Kindled by *Ghee*, it becomes a flame. Such is my manifestation also in this articulate Voice.

So also the senses of action (Karmendriyas) and of perception (Gnanendriyas), the faculties of Desire, Discrimination, and Egoistic perception, the thread-giving Pradhāna, the transformations of Satva, Rajas and Tamas are all my manifestations. (*i.e.* I am manifested through all of them).

Primally, this Jiva Īshvara is unmanifested and one. But being the resort of the three Gunas, being the generator (Yoni) of the lotus (of the Universe), He becomes in time of divided energy, and appears as many, even like seeds that have found the soil.

This Universe exists in Me, even as a piece of cloth exists in threads.

The essence of this eternal tree of the Universe is Inclination. It begets flowers (Karma) and fruits (the fruits of Karma). Two are its seeds (Merit and de merit). Hundreds are its roots (the desires). Three are its stems (the Three Gunas). Five are its trunks (the five Bhūtas, Akāsa &c). The branches produce 5 sorts of juice (Sound, Touch, Sight, Taste and Smell); the Ten senses and the mind are the branches of the tree. Two birds (Jivātma and Paramātmā) make their nest on it. Wind, bile and phlegm are its dermal layers. Joy and sorrow are the two fruits of this tree. It extends up to the solar regions (for beyond the Solar system, the Trilokī, there are no rebirths.) The country loving Gridhras (in the first sense, vultures and in the second sense, home loving men of desires) partake of one fruit (sorrow). And the forest frequenting Hansas (in one sense swans and in the other sense discriminating men who give up desires) partake of the other fruit (joy).

He who, through the favor of his Guru knows the One as becoming Many through Māyā, knows the Truth.

Thus with the axe of wisdom, sharpened by whole-minded devotion acquired by the worship of the Guru, do thou calmly and steadily cut asunder the sheaths of Jiva and on attaining Paramātmā, do thou let go of the instrument itself.

THE GUNAS.

SKANDHA XI. CHAP. 13.

Satva, Rajas and Tamas — they are the Gunas of Buddhi (Prakriti), not of Ātmā — control Rajas and Tamas by means of Satva and control Satva by Satva itself. When Satva grows in Man, he acquires Dharma, which is Devotion to Me. By worshipping Sātvic objects Satva increases and Dharma is the outcome. That Dharma kills Rajas and Tamas and it increases Satva. When Rajas and Tamas are killed, Adharma which is an outcome of Rajas and Tamas is also killed. The scriptures, water, men, land, time, karma, regeneration, meditation, mantra and purification these ten are accessaries to the Gunas. Of these what the Sages praise are Sātvic, what they blame are Tāmasic, what they neither praise nor blame are Rājasic. Have resort to only those of them that are Sātvic, for then Satva will increase. Dharma follows that increase and wisdom follows Dharma. But wisdom has its field only so long as memory lasts and the (Gunas) are not exhausted. Fire that is produced by the friction of bamboo pieces, burns up the forest and is then extinguished of itself even so the body caused by disturbance of the Gunas is extinguished of itself, (at that final stage).

(Of the scriptures, there are some that speak of inclination, others that speak of disinclination. The latter only are to be followed. Water which has a purifying effect, as that of a sacred place is to be used, not pointed water and wine. Bad men are to be shunned and good men are to be mixed with.

Quiet solitary places are to be sought, not highways and gambling places. The time before sun rise is preferable for meditation not night fall or night. Nitya Karma is to be performed, not Kāmya Karma. Initiation causes a second birth. Vaishnava or Saiva initiation is Sātvic and not Sakta initiation. Meditation upon Vishnu is Sātvic and not the meditation upon women or upon those that are hostile to Vishnu. The Pranava Mantra is Sātvic and not the lower Kāmya Mantras. The cleansing must be purification of self, not the mere cleansing of Deva houses. *Śridhara.* By these Sātvic pursuits, Satva Guna prevails in man. When Satva prevails the whole nature becomes Sātvic. The tendencies are all such as to lead to calmness, which is the essence of Satva. This is Dharma Adharma is the opposite of this. It is identified with such a nature as leads to distractions. Dharma is followed by wisdom. For when the mind is calm and tranquil, truths are reflected on it in their entirety and they are fully perceived. That wisdom lasts as long as memory lasts *i.e.* as long as Dvaita perception exists. But when the Gunas themselves die out, wisdom vanishes of itself, for when there is direct perception of Brahmā as self, the knower, the known and knowledge become one and the same.)

HOW TO WITHDRAW FROM THE OBJECTS OF THE SENSES.

SKANDHA XI. CHAP. 13.

Uddhava asked: —

"Generally people know that the objects of the senses lead them to misery. How is it, O Krishna, they still follow them, like dogs, donkeys and goats?"

Sri Krishna replied: —

"When in the heart of the undiscriminating man, the false perception of 'I' arises (with regard to body &c.), the terrible Rajas takes possession of the Manas, which by its origin is Sātvic. Doubts and desires arise in the mind. The mind then dwells upon attributes (oh! how beautiful, what a nice thing!) and acquires a strong liking for it. Guided by the passions, with the senses uncontrolled, deluded by the strong current of Rajas, the helpless man knowingly does things that bear evil fruits. The mind of the wise man is also distracted by Rajas and Tamas. But he sleeplessly controls his mind and he finds fault (with his own actions). He is not attached to them. Gradually and steadfastly offer up your mind to Me, being wide awake, at all times, controlling your breath and regulating your seat and you will then be able to control your mind.

"This is the Yoga, as taught by My disciples Sanaka and others."

Uddhava asked: —

"When and in what form did you teach Sanaka and others?"

Sri Krishna replied: —

"Sanaka and other Manas-born sons of Brahmā asked their father as follows: — The mind enters the Gunas (objects *i.e.* the mind naturally becomes attached to objects) and the Gunas (*i.e.* the objects when experienced) enter the mind (as desires). How can those that want to cross over (the objects) and to become liberated cause a separation between the two?

"Brahmā could not gauge the question in his own mind. So he meditated on me. I appeared before him as a Hansa. (The Swan can discriminate between milk and water. So the bird symbolises a discriminating sage.) The Brāhmanas and Brahmā asked: 'Who art thou?' I said as follows: —

"O Brāhmanas does your question relate to Ātmā — If so, Ātmā is not many. So the question does not arise. And who will reply to whom?

"If your question relates to the body, then also the elements composing the body being the same in all beings, and Atmā being the same in all, your question is meaningless.

"Whatever is perceived by the senses and the mind, I am that — There is nothing besides Me. Rightly know this to be so.

"True the mind enters the Gunas and the Gunas enter the mind. The Gunas and mind thus mutually blended are but the body of the Jiva, its reality being My own self. (If mind wedded to objects, be the essence of Jiva, then their separation is not possible. But the essence of Jiva is Brahmā. Mind is only attributed to Jiva. And Jiva's connection with the objects is through the properties of the mind. Therefore Jiva by realising that it is Brahmā will find out that the objects have no existence as far as its own self is concerned. Therefore by devotion to Bhagavat, Jiva completely rests in its own self. *Śridhara*. This is not a separation of Manas and objects, but the withdrawal of self from both.)

"By constant pursuit of the Gunas, the mind enters the Gunas. The Gunas also (being turned into desires) take a firm hold of the mind. Knowing Me to be thy own self give up both (the objects and the mind wedded to them.)

"Wakefulness (Jāgrat), Dream (Svapna) and Dreamless sleep (Sushupti) are states of mind, caused by the Gunas, Jiva is beyond all these states. For it is the witness of all these states. The bondage caused by mind imparts the actions of the Gunas to Ātmā. Therefore being fixed in Me, the Fourth (*i.e.* beyond the three states of consciousness), get over the bondage of mind. That will be the (mutual) giving up of the mind and the Gunas. This bondage of Ātmā is caused by Ahankāra (the sense of 'I-ness') Know this to be the cause of all evils. Knowing this, be fixed in the Fourth, and give up all thoughts of *Sansāra* (*i.e.* of mind and of the connections caused by mind.)

"So long as the idea of manifoldness is not destroyed by reasoning, man dreams in ignorance even in the wakeful state, just as in dream, the ignorant man thinks he is wakeful.

"All things, other than Ātmā are unreal. The differences made amongst them (such as, this is Brāhmana, this is Sudra, this is Grihasthā, this is Sanyāsīn), the different destinations (Svarga and other Kārmic fruits) and even Karma (action) itself are unreal, so far as Ātmā is concerned.

"He who throughout the constantly following stages of life (childhood, youth, age etc.) perceives the objects in the wakeful state, with the help of all the senses, he who perceives the likes of those objects in dream in the heart, and he who brings those perceptions to an end in dreamless sleep are all one and the same. For the same memory runs through all these states. The Lord of the senses is one and the same. (The outward senses perceive the wakeful state. Mind, perceives the dream. Buddhi perceives dreamless sleep. Ātmā, is the Lord of all these senses).

"Ponder well over this that the three states of mind are caused in Me by the Gunas, through My Māyā. Knowing this definitely, cut asunder the source of all doubts (Ahankāra) by the sword of wisdom sharpened by reasoning, the teachings of Sādhus, and the Srutis. And worship Me, that dwell in the heart.

"Look upon this Universe as a delusion, a play of the mind. Now seen, now destroyed. So rapid is the succession, that it is like a whirling fire brand that looks circular (on account of the rapid motion, though it is not circular). One consciousness appears as many. The phenomenal existence (*Vikalpa*) caused by the threefold Guna transformations is but Māyā, a dream.

"Turn away your sight from this object world. Give up all desires. Be calm and find bliss in the perception of self. At times you will have experience of the objects in your daily life (for getting the necessaries of life). But what you have once thrown aside as unreal shall not be able to cause delusion in you. Till the fall of your body, the objects will haunt you like things of the past, stored as it were in memory alone. This frail body, through which he has known his real self, may rise or sit, may move away from its place or come back, just as chance will have it, but the Siddha sees it not, even as an inebriate person does not see the cloth he puts on.

"The body waits with the Prānas and Indriyas till the *Commenced* Karma exhausts itself. But being fixed in Samādhi, the knower of the truth does not care for the body and the object world, which are all visionary to him.

"I said all this to the Brāhmanas and came back to my own abode."

BHAKTI YOGA.

SKANDHA XI. CHAP. 14.

"O Krishna, thou speakest of Bhakti Yoga. Others speak of other expedients. Are they all same or is any one of them superior to others?"

Sri-Krishna replied: —

"The tendencies of men are different, according to the differences in their nature. So different paths have been spoken of. But the regions (or fruits) acquired by the votaries of the other paths, and as created by their actions have a beginning and an end, a miserable future and an end in Tamas. The pleasures there are small and they are not unmixed with sorrow. Where is that bliss to be found in objects that is to be found in Me.

"Fixed in Me, and finding bliss in Me, all is blissful to My votaries. They do not wish for universal supremacy, they do not ask for supremacy over Svarga, Bhūr or Pātāla, they do not long for Siddhis, they do not even ask for Mukti. Surrendering Self to Me they wish for nothing else but Myself. Brahmā, Śiva, Sankarshana, Lakshmī and My own form are not so dear to Me, O Uddhava, as thou art to Me. I always seek my Bhaktas. It is they only that know what bliss they enjoy, Bhakti consumes all impurities, even as fire consumes the fuel. Yoga, Sānkhya, Dharma, study of the scriptures, asceticism, or relinquishment nothing wins me so much as powerful Bhakti does. I am attained only by faithful Devotion. Bhakti purifies the Bhaktas, even though they be Chandālas by birth.

"Dharma, though combined with truth and compassion, wisdom though wedded to asceticism, do not completely purify self, if devotion to Me is wanting. How can mind be purified without Bhakti. For by Bhakti the hairs stand on end, the heart melts away and tears of bliss run down the cheek. Words become choked with devotional feelings. The Bhakta weeps, and smiles, and sings and dances forgetting himself. Such a Bhakta (not only purifies self, but) he purifies the whole world.

"Gold loses its impurities under fire and regains its own form. Ātmā (Jiva Ātmā) shakes off its impurities under Bhakti Yoga and regains its own form. As Ātmā becomes more and more purified, by hearing and meditating on the sacred sayings about Me, it sees more and more of subtle objects, as the eye touched with collyrium does.

"Think of objects and your mind will be attached to objects. Think of Me and your mind will be attached to Me. Therefore fix your mind on Me, giving up all other thoughts.

"Shun from a distance the company of women and of those that keep the company of women. Be self controlled. Go to a solitary place, free from dangers and then sleeplessly meditate on Me.

"There is not so much misery, so much bondage from other quarters as from the company of women and of those that associate with them."

MEDITATION.

SKANDHA XI. CHAP. 14.

Uddhava asked: —

"O Lotus-eyed! how to meditate on Thee! Tell me what is the nature of that meditation and what it is?"

Sri Krishna replied: —

"Be seated on an Asana (Seat), that is neither high nor low (say, a blanket), with your body erect and in an easy posture. Place your hands on the lap. Fix your gaze on the tip of the nose (in order to fix the mind). Purify the tracks of Prāna by Puraka, Kumbhaka and Rechaka, and then again in the reverse way (*i.e.* first breathe in by the left nostril with the right nostril closed by the tip of the thumb, then close the left nostril by the tips of the ring finger and the little finger and retain the breath in both the nostrils. Then remove the tip of the thumb, and breathe out through the right nostril. Reverse the process by breathing in through the right nostril then retaining the breath in both the nostrils and then letting out the breath through the left nostril). Practise this Prānāyama gradually with your senses controlled.

"'Aum' with the sound of a bell, extends all over, from Mūlādhāra upwards. Raise the 'Aum' in the heart, by means of Prāna (twelve fingers upwards) as if it were the thread of a lotus-stalk. There let Bindu (the fifteenth vowel sound) be added to it. Thus practise Prānāyama accompanied by the

Pranava reciting the latter ten times. Continue the practice, three times a day and within a month you shall be able to control the vital air. The lotus of the heart, has its stalk upwards and the flower downwards, facing below (and it is also closed, like the inflorescence with bracts of the banana. *Śridhara*). Meditate on it however as facing upwards and full-blown, with eight petals and with the pericarp. On the pericarp, think of the Sun, the Moon, and Fire one after another. Meditate on My form (as given in the text) within the Fire. First Meditate on all the limbs. Then let the mind withdraw the senses from their objects. Then draw the concentrated mind completely towards Me, by means of Buddhi. Then give up all other limbs and concentrate your mind on one thing only My smiling face. Do not meditate on anything else. Then with draw the concentrated mind from that and fix it on Akāsa. Give up that also and being fixed in Me, (as Brahmā) think of nothing at all. You shall see Me in Ātmā, as identical with all Ātmās, even as light is identical with another light. The delusions about object, knowledge and action shall then completely disappear."

THE SIDDHIS

SKANDHA XI. CHAP. 15.

When the senses and the breath are controlled and the mind is fixed on Me, Siddhis or powers overtake the Yogi. There are eighteen Siddhis and eighteen Dhāranas. Of these, eight belong to me (eight of them are normally the powers of Ishvara and they exist in a some what lesser degree in those that approach the state of Ishvara. *Śridhara*. The remaining ten cause the appearance of Guna *i.e.* they cause an excellence of Satva. *Śridhara*.)

1. *Animā*, the power of becoming as small as an atom.

2. *Mahimā*, the power of increasing size.

3. *Laghimā,* the power of becoming light. These three Siddhis relate to the body.

4. *Prāpti*, to be in the relation of presiding Devas to the corresponding senses of all beings.

5. *Prākāmya*, power of enjoying and perceiving all objects seen or unseen.

6. *īsitā*, control over the energies of Māyā in Īshvara, over the lower energies in other beings.

7. *Vasitā*, Non-attachment to objects.

8. *Kāmāvasāyitā*, the power of attaining all desires.

These are My eight Siddhis and they normally exist in Me.

1. The cessation of hunger and thirst.

2. The hearing from a distance.

3. Seeing from a distance.

4. Motion of the body with the velocity of the mind.

5. Assumption of any form at will.

6. The entering into another's body.

7. Death at one's own will.

8. Play with Deva girls.

9. The attainment of desired for objects.

10.Irresistible command.

These are the ten Siddhis that relate to the Gunas. There are also five smaller Siddhis.

1. Knowledge of the present, past and future.

2. Control over the Pairs, such as heat and cold &c.

3. Knowledge of other's minds.

4. Suspending the actions of fire, sun, water, poison &c.

5. Invincibility.

These are only illustrative of the Siddhis.

Now about Dhārāna or the modes of concentration of the mind.

Those that fix their mind on Me as pervading the Tanmatras acquire the power of becoming an atom.

Those that concentrate their mind on Me as pervading Mahat Tatva acquire *Mahima*.

The object of Dhārāna	... ...	The power acquired
The Lord pervading the atoms	...	Laghima.
Do. Do. Sātvic Ahankāra	...	Prāpti.
Do. Do. Sūtra or Mahat	...	Prakamya.
Vishnu the Lord of the three Gunas	...	īsita.
Nārāyana, the Fourth, Bhagavat	...	Vasita.
Nirguna Brahmā (Brahmā without attribute)	... ...	Kāmavasayita.
Lord of Sveta Dvipa (White Island) ...		Cessation of hunger and thirst.
Akāsa	... ...	Distant hearing.
Sun	... ...	Distant vision.

&c.   &c.   &c.

THE VIBHŪTIS OR POWERS OF THE LORD.

SKANDHA XI. CHAP. 16.

The Sixteenth Chapter deals with the Vibhūtis of the Lord, much in the same way as the tenth chapter of the Bhagavad Gitā.

VARNA AND ASRAMA RULES.

SKANDHA XI. CHAP. 17-18.

The seventeenth and eighteenth chapters deal with Varna and Āsrama rules.

WHAT ONE IS TO DO FOR MOKSHA.

SKANDHA XI. CHAP. 19.

Jnāna (knowledge), Vairāgya (dispassion), Vijnāna (direct knowledge), Sraddhā (faith) Bhakti (Devotion), these are the requisites of Moksha. The nine (Prakriti, Purusha, Mahat. Ahankāra and the five Tanmatras), the eleven (five Jnānendriyas, five Karmendriyas and Manas), the five Bhūtas, the three (Gunas), that knowledge by which one knows that these constitute all beings and that the One underlies all these is *Jnāna*.

(The first training of the mind is to break up the objects into their component elements. Thus we can mentally resolve any object into its chemical elements and this Universe into a mass of homogeneous nebula. The process is to be carried further, till we get the Tatvas or the ultimate principles of the Sānkhya philosophy. Then the next step is to realise the one Purusha as underlying all the Prākritic principles.)

Vijnāna is the direct knowledge of the One by itself and not as pervading all Prākritic forms. (Jnāna is indirect knowledge and Vijnāna is direct knowledge of Brahmā).

All the existing things being formed of the three Gunas have their growth, existence and end. What follows the transformation from one form into another, at all the three stages of beginning, middle and end, and what remains behind after the destruction of all forms — that is the existing (Sat).

The Vedas, direct perception, the sayings of great men and logical inference are the four Pramanas or evidences. The world of transformations does not stand the test of any of them (*i.e.* there is only one real existence, the existence of the transformable and transformed world being only relative and unreal. This is the conclusion arrived at from all sources. Therefore the wise man becomes dispassionate to all things.

Transformation is the end of all actions. Therefore the wise man sees all the regions that may be attained by actions from that of Brahmā downwards, as miserable and transitory even like the worlds that are seen. This is Vairagya or Dispassion.

I have told you already of Bhakti yoga. Hear again what I say. *Sraddhā* or faith in the nectar like sayings about Me, constant recitals about myself, steadiness in worshipping Me, the chanting of devotional hymns, the hearty performance of divine service, adoration by means of the body, worship of my votaries, the realisation of my existence in all beings, the directing of the daily actions and of the daily talks towards Me, the offering up of the mind to Me, the giving up of all desires, of all objects, of all enjoyments and of all joys for my Sake, the performance of Vedic karma all for Me — by all these, Bhakti grows up towards Me.

THE SADHANAS OR EXPEDIENTS.

SKANDHA XI. CHAP. 19.

Yāma consists of —

1. *Ahinsā* — the non-infliction of pain.

2. *Satya* — the practice of truth.

3. *Asteya* — Not even the mental stealing of other's properties.

4. *Asanga* — Non-attachment.

5. *Hri* — Modesty.

6. *Asanchaya* — Want of storing for the future.

7. *Astikya* — faith in religion.

8. *Brahmacharya* — Abstinence.

9. *Mauna* — Silence.

10. *Sthairya* — Steadiness.

11. *Kshamā* — forgiveness.

12. *Abhaya* — fearlessness.

Niyama Consists of

1. *Saucha* — bodily purity.

2. *Do.* — Mental purity.

3. *Japa* — Mental repetition of Mantras or Names of deities.

4. *Tapas* — Asceticism.

5. *Homa* — Sacrificial offering.

6. *Sraddhā* — faith.

7. *Atithya* — hospitality.

8. *Archanā* — daily worship.

9. *Tīrthātana* — Wandering on pilgrimage.

10. *Pararthehā* — desire for the Supreme object.

11. *Tushti* — Contentment.

12. *Achārya Sevana* — Service of the spiritual teacher.

Yāma and Niyama are practised by men, either for furtherance in life or for Moksha.

Sama — is fixing the mind on Me (and not mental quietness only).

Titikshā — is forbearance.

Dhriti — is the restraint of the senses of taste and generation.

The best *Dāna* (gift) is not to oppress any creature.

Tapas — is really the giving up of desires.

Saurya — or power is the control of one's own nature.

Satya or Truth is the practice of equality.

Rita — is truth speaking that does not cause pain.

Saucha — is only non-attachment to karma, but *Tyāga* is its complete renunciation.

The wealth to be coveted for is *Dharma*. I Myself am *Yajna*, Spiritual teaching is the *Sacrificial gift*, *Prānāyama* is the greatest strength.

Bhaga is my Lordly state.

The best attainment is devotion to Me.

Vidyā is the removal of the idea of separateness from self.

Hrī is the abhorrence of all unrighteous acts (and not merely modesty.)

Srī is (not merely riches but) virtues. Happiness is that which seeks neither happiness nor misery.

Misery is nothing but longings for enjoyment.

The Sage is he who knows about liberation from bondage.

He is ignorant who knows the body to be self.

The Path is that which leads to Me.

The evil path is that which distracts the mind.

The increase of Satva is Svarga (and not merely Indra Loka.)

The increase of Tamas is Naraka.

Guru is the friend and I am that Guru.

This human body is the house.

He is rich who is virtuous.

He is poor who is not contented.

He who has not conquered the senses is the helpless man.

The Lord is he who is not attached to the objects.

He is a slave who is attached to them.

THE THREE PATHS: KARMA, JNĀNA AND BHAKTI.

SKANDHA XI. CHAP. 20.

Uddhava said: —

"Karma is to be performed and Karma is not to be performed — both are Thy injunctions in the Vedas. The Vedas speak of merits and demerits in connection with Karma. They speak of Varna and Āsrama, of differences in time, space, age and objects, of Svarga and Naraka.

"The sense of right and wrong is not innate but it is acquired from the scriptures, and the same scriptures undermine all ideas of difference. All this is confounding to me."

Shri Krishna replied: —

"I have spoken of three paths leading to the attainment of Moksha by men — Jnāna, Karma and Bhakti Yogas. There is no other means what so ever of attaining Moksha. Jnāna Yoga is for those that are disgusted with the performance of Karma and so give it up.

"Karma Yoga is for those that are not disgusted with the performance of Karma but are attached to it.

"He who perchance becomes fond of what is said or spoken of Me, but has no aversion for Karma nor has any undue attachment to it is fit for Bhakti Yoga.

"Perform Karma so long as you do not feel disgust for it or as long as you are not drawn by love for me. True to your duties, perform Yajnas but without any selfish desires. Do not perform prohibited Karma. Then you shall cross the limits of both Svarga and Naraka.

"By the performance of one's own duties, the purified man may acquire pure wisdom (Jnāna) and Bhakti.

"The dwellers of Svarga wish for the human body and so the dwellers of Naraka. For that body is a means to the attainment of of Jnāna and Bhakti both, not so the Svarga body or Naraka body.

"The far-sighted man does not wish for Svarga or Naraka. He does not even wish for human existence. For connection with the body causes selfish distractions.

"The sage knows the body as leading to desired for ends. But he realises at the same time its transitory character. He therefore loses no time in striving for Moksha before the approach of death. Even so the bird loses all attachment for its nest and flies away free and happy before the man who strikes at the tree succeeds in felling it.

"The human body which is the primal source of all attainments is a well built boat, so hard to secure and so cheap when once attained. The Guru is at the helm of this boat, and I am the favorable wind that drives it. The man that does not cross the ocean of births with such a boat is a killer of self.

"*Jnāna*: — When a man feels disgust for karma and becomes dispassionate and when his senses are controlled, he should practise concentration of mind.

"When in the act of concentration, the mind suddenly goes astray and becomes unsettled, you should bring it back under the control of self, with unremitting efforts, after allowing it to go in its wandering course a little.

"Never neglect however to check the course of the mind with your Prānas and senses all controlled. With the help of Sātvic Buddhi bring the mind under the control of self.

"This control of the mind is the highest yoga. The horseman slackens the reins at first but never lets go the reins. Reflect on the creative manifestation of all objects and then the contrary process of their dissolution, according to the Sānkhya method. Do this till the mind attains calm.

"By cultivating a sense of disgust, by the growth of dispassion, by constant pondering over the teachings of the Guru, the mind gives up its delusion.

"By practising Yāma and other ways of Yoga, by discrimination of self and by worshipping Me, the mind is able to think of the Supreme.

"If by loss of mental balance, the Yogi does some improper act he should burn up the impurity by Yoga alone, but not by any other means (not by expiatory rites. *Śridhara*)

"Adherence to the particular path of one's own following is the right thing. People have been taught to distinguish between right and wrong, not because the acts are not all impure by their very nature but because the distinction is necessary to regulate the acts themselves with a view to cause a final abandonment of all attachments to them". (It may be said that according to the scriptures, Nitya Karma (acts ordained to be daily performed) and Naimittika Karma (acts ordained to be occasionally performed) purify the mind. Hence they are *right* (*guna*). The killing of animals and such other acts make the mind impure. Hence they are *wrong* (*dosha*). Expiatory acts (Prāyaschitta) are required to be performed in order to remove the consequences of wrong acts. Therefore Prāyaschitta is a right thing (*guna*). How can impurities be destroyed by means of Yoga then and not by means of Prāyaschitta: therefore it is said that what is called Guna (right) and Dosha (wrong) by injunctions and prohibitions, is only a regulation of acts. The purport is this. The impurities of a man are not the outcome of his own inclinations. Man is impure through his natural tendencies. It is not possible for him all on a sudden to have disinclination for all actions. Therefore "Do this," "Do not do this," these injunctions and prohibitions only put a restriction upon the inclinations of a man and by this means, they lead to disinclination. The Yogis have no inclinations. The rules of Prāyaschitta are therefore not meant for them. *Śridhara.*)

Bhakti: — "He who has reverential faith in all that is said about Me, and who feels disgust for all actions, who knows that desires are identical with misery, but is yet in-capable of renouncing them, such a man should worship Me, with sincere devotion and firm faith. Though gratifying his desires, he should not have any attachment for them, knowing that they lead to misery in the end. Those that constantly worship Me according to Bhakti yoga as already expounded by Me, have all the desires of their heart destroyed as I myself dwell in their heart. The bondage is broken asunder, doubts all cease to exist, the accumulated actions fade away, when I, the Ātmā of all, am seen. My Bhakta speedily attains every thing that is attained by other means, Svarga, Moksha or even My own abode, if he has any desire for any of these. But My Bhaktas who are solely devoted to Me do not desire any thing even if it be offered by Me, not even final liberation. They are beyond the limits of Guna and Dosha."

GUNA AND DOSHA OR RIGHT AND WRONG

SKANDHA XI. CHAP. 21.

Those who do not follow the Paths of Bhakti, Jnāna and Karma, but who only seek paltry desires become subject to rebirths [For those that are matured in Jnāna and Bhakti, there is neither Guna (right) nor Dosha (wrong). For those that practise Disinclination, the performance of Nitya and Naimittika Karma is Guna, for it leads to the purification of the mind. The non-performance of such Karma and the performance of prohibited Karma are Dosha, for they give rise to impurities of the mind. Prāyaschitta counteracts such Dosha, and therefore it is Guna. For those pure men that are fixed in the Path of Jnāna, the practice of Jnāna is Guna; Bhakti is Guna to them that are fixed in the path of Bhakti. What is opposed to Jnāna and Bhakti is Dosha to the followers of those two Paths. All this has been said before. Now Guna and Dosha are detailed for those that do not follow the Paths, but seek their selfish ends. *Śridhara*]. Devotion to the path of one's following is Guna. The reverse is Dōsha. This is the proper definition of Guna and Dosha (Guna and Dosha are relative terms. They do not appertain to the thing itself. *Śridhara*).

Purity (Sūddhi) or Impurity (Asūddhi), Right (Guna) or Wrong (Dōsha), Auspicious (Sūbha) or Inauspicious (Asūbha) are terms applied to the same objects, in relation to religion (Dharma), Society (Vyavahara) and living (Yātrā), respectively.

I have explained Āchāra (rules of life) for those that want to be guided by Dharma (Sanctional religion). (Shri Krishna refers here to the works of Manu and other Smriti writers).

The body of all beings is composed of the five elements (earth, water &c). They are all ensouled by Ātmā. Though men are all equal, the Vedas give different names and forms to their bodies (saying this is Brāhmana, this is Sudra, this is Grihasthā, this is Sanyāsī) with a view to do good to them. (The object is to put a limit to the natural inclinations and thereby to secure Dharma, Artha, Kāma and Moksha. *Śridhara*). Similarly classification is made of time, space and other things, solely with the object of regulating actions (Karma.) Thus those lands are impure where the black deer do not roam (Details are not given for which read the original).

"Those that perform Yajna attain Svarga." Sayings like these do not speak of final bliss. They are only tempting words really meant for the attainment of Moksha, just like words said to a child to induce him to take medicine (The father says; "Eat this Nimba — a bitter drug. I shall give you this sweet meat." The child takes the medicine. But the sweet meat is not what he really gets, for his real gain is recovery from disease).

From their very birth, mortals are attached to some objects of desire, to their lives and powers and to their own people. But these are only sources of misery in the future. Why should the Vedas then teach attachment to such things? Some wrong-minded people say so without knowing the purport of the Vedas. They are deluded by the performance of fire sacrifices, and they resort to Pitri Yāna (*i.e.* they are drawn to rebirths on the Earth after temporary enjoyment of Svarga). They do not know their own abode, which am I as seated in their heart, from whom the universe proceeds. Not knowing the real meaning of the Vedas, they worship Indra and other Devas and perform Yajnas at which animals are sacrificed. Parā, Pasyanti and Madhyamā remain deep and unfathomable like the ocean and only Vaikhari becomes manifest in the Vedas originating in Pranava and appearing through the letters of the alphabet and the Metres. Even that Vaikhari is not properly understood by men. (The Vedas form the sound manifestation of Īshvara. That sound has four divisions. *Parā*, which finds manifestation only in Prāna, *Pasyanti*, which finds manifestation in the mind, *Madhyamā* which finds manifestation in the Indriyas, and Vaikhari which finds manifestation in articulate expression. Those who have mental vision can only find out the first three. But the Vedas as expressed in language are also difficult to understand.) Further details are given, which are not reproduced.

THE TATVAS.

SKANDHA XI. CHAP. 22.

Uddhava asked: — "How many Tatvas (elemental principles) are there? The Rishis give the number differently."

Sri Krishna replied: —

"The discussion about the number is useless. The principles are interpenetrating. Their order and their number are therefore differently understood."

Uddhava asked: —

"Prakriti and Purusha though different by themselves are interdependent. They are never seen separately. Ātmā is seen in Prakriti (body) and Prakriti is seen in Ātmā (Where is then the difference between body and Ātmā?)

"This is my doubt."

Sri Krishna replied: —

"Prakriti and Purusha are essentially different."

PRAKRITI AND PURUSHA.

SKANDHA XI. CHAP. 22.

(1). *Prakriti* is subject to manifestation.

(2). It is subject to transformation.

(3). It consists of the transformations of the Gunas.

(4). It is various, — broadly speaking threefold, Adhyātma, Adhi-bhūta and Adhi-daiva.

(5). It is not self manifest.

Ātmā is one, immutable and self manifest.

Ahankāra is at the root of all doubt and delusion. They last as long as the mind is turned away from me.

RE-INCARNATION.

SKANDHA XI. CHAP. 22.

Uddhava asked: —

"Those that are turned away from Thee take on and give up bodies. Tell me something about rebirth."

Sri Krishna replied: —

"The mind of men imprinted with karma moves with the five senses from body to body. Ātmā (under the denomination of 'I') accompanies the mind.

"The mind (after death) thinks of such seen and unseen objects as the karma of men places before it. It awakes (unto those objects, it thinks of) and fades away (in respect of previous objects). The memory (connecting the present with the past) dies away in consequence.

"When one loses all thoughts of one's body on account of close application to another object (body), through some cause or other, that utter forgetfulness is his death." (By karma, man gets after his so-called death either a deva body, or a body of inflictions. In the former case, it is through pleasure and desire and in the latter case, through fear and sorrow, that the Jiva utterly forgets his former body. That is the death of the Jiva who used to identify himself with the former body and not the destruction of Jiva as of the body.*Śridhara*.

The Deva-body is the phenomenal basis of the Jiva in Svarga Loka. The body of inflications is the astral or Kāmic body, in Bhūta, Preta and Pisācha Loka, where the Jiva undergoes inflictions. The Jiva identifies itself with these new bodies or new states in such a way as to forget completely its former physical body. The connection with the former body is thus completely cut off in the mind. This is the death of the Jiva in relation to its previous body.)

"The birth of a Jiva is the acceptance of a body as one's own self. It is even like dream or fancy. In dream or fancy, a man does not know his present self as the former self. The mind by its application to a new body causes a birth into that body, and the ideas of good, bad and indifferent crop up in self.

"Though a father may have neither friend nor enemy, he is affected by the connections formed by his vicious son, even so it is with Ātmā. Growth and decay are happening every moment in the body. But they are hardly perceptible owing to the extreme subtlely of time.

"The burning lamp, the flowing current, the ripening fruit, pass through stages, as all beings also pass through the stages of childhood, youth and age. We say it is the same fire, it is the same water (though the particles of fire and water are continually changing.) So we say, it is the same man. The understanding and the words of ignorant men are all confounding (for they speak and think assuming that the same body continues). But even the ignorant man does not acquire birth or death, by Karma engendered by self, for the self is immortal and the notion of birth and death is itself a delusion with reference to self. Fire, as an element lasts through out the Kalpa. But it seems to come into existence or to become extinguished. Fecundation, foetal state, birth, childhood, grown up childhod, youth, ripeness, age and death are the nine states of the body. These states of the body which is other than self are only fancies of the mind (so far as self is concerned). Some accept them as their own, by contact with Gunas and some reject them to some extent (by discriminating knowledge). From the death of the body inherited from the father and the birth of another child body, one can infer the birth and death of his body only, he the knower not being affected by either birth or death. The seer of the growth and decay of the tree is different from the tree itself, so the seer of the different states of the body is different from the body itself. One is bound down to the wheel of rebirths, by want of discrimination. One becomes Deva or Rishi by the action of Satva, Asura or man by the action of Rajas and Bhūta or animal by the action of Tamas. As a man seeing the performance of singers and dancers involuntarily imitates them (in the mind) even so Ātmā follows the actions of Buddhi. The tree seems to move when the water is moving. The earth seems to roll when the eyes are rolling. Births and rebirths are as unreal to Ātmā as are dreams but they have an existence even as objects in dream have an existence so long as the mind thinks of those objects.

"Whatever others may say or do unto you, do not care the least about that, but with single minded devotion restore self by self."

Uddhava said: —

"Human nature is human nature, O Lord. Hew can one bear all that is said or done by the impious?"

FORBEARANCE.

SKANDHA XI. CHAP, 23.

Sri Krishna said: —

"In days of yore, there was a wealthy Brāhmana in the Malava regions. He earned money by the evil ways of the world, but did not spend any thing on charity. In time the wealth was all gone. He repented and felt disgust for wealth. He renounced the world and became a wandering Bhikshu. He went to villages for alms. People called him all sorts of names — thief, hypocrite and so on. Some pelted him, others abused him, others put him to chains and confined him.

"He bore all this with perfect calm. This is how he used to reason within himself: —

"These men, the Devas, self, the planets, Karma and Kāla (periodicity) none of them is the cause of my happiness or misery. Mind is the one cause, which causes the wheel of births to move. They make friends and enemies, who do not conquer the mind. The connection with the body is only an act of the mind. Deluded men however think, this is my body and they go astray.

"One man can not be the cause of grief and joy to another. Ātmā in all men is not the doer. All acts proceed from the gross and the subtle body. If the tooth bites the tongue, who should you be angry at?

"If the Devas (the Adhidevas) be the cause of sorrow, it is not their Ātmā that is so but their bodily transformations. And the Devas (who guide the senses) are the same in all beings. If one limb causes pain to another limb, who should be the object of anger?

"If self is the cause of joy and sorrow, then you have not to look to the outside world. But every thing else besides Ātmā is only a seeming existence. Therefore there is no real existence of any cause of joy or grief and there is no joy or grief.

"If the planets by their position at birth bring about joys and sorrows, then no body is to blame for that. And the planetary Purusha is separate from the bodies of the planets. There is none to be angry at. Karma can not be the cause of Joy and sorrow. Karma has its sphere in which there is both a conscious and an unconscious element. The unconscious element undergoes transformation and the conscious element in search for the desired object leads to action. But the body is absolutely unconscious. And Purusha (or Self) in man is absolutely conscious. There is no root of Karma either in body or in Purusha.

"*Kāla* is part of Ātmā, for Kāla is an aspect of Īshvara. Fire does not destroy its spark, snow does not destroy its flakes.

"One who is awakened to his real self has fear from no one else. Purusha has no connection with the pairs of opposites." (Cold and heat, happiness and misery &c.)

SANKHYA.

SKANDHA XI. CHAP. 24.

"There is only one perception and one undivided object of perception, when there are no Yugas (i.e. in Pralaya), in Satya Yuga, as well as for men skilful in discrimination, that object of perception is Brahmān, the absolute Truth, beyond the reach of worlds and of mind. I became two fold, by means of Māyā. Of the two one is Prakriti consisting of causes and effects. And the other is Purusha.

"Following the Kārmic record of Jivas, I disturbed Prakriti, and Satva, Rajas and Tamas became manifest. The Gunas gave rise to Sutra or Thread (which represents Kriyā Śakti). Mahat (Jnāna Śakti) is not separate from Sutra (Sutra and Mahat form one Tatva. It is two-fold, on account of its double aspect of Jnāna and Kriyā or knowledge and action).

"Ahankāra is the transformation of Mahat. It is three-fold, Sātvic or Vaikāric, Rājasic or Taijasa and Tāmasic.

"The Adhi-daivas and Manas came from Sātvic Ahankāra, and the 5 Tanmātras from Tāmasic Ahankāra.. The five Mahā bhutas came from the five Tanmātras.

"Prompted by Me, all these principles united together to form the Egg which was My own abode. I incarnated in that Egg which was immersed in the (Pralayic) water (as Sri Nārāyana or Virāt Purusha).

"Out of my navel grew the Lotus called the Universe. Brahmā was manifested in that Lotus.

"He brought into manifestation the Lokas (Bhūr, Bhuvar &c.,) and the Lokapālas.

"Svar was the abode of the Devas, Bhuvar of the Bhūtas, Bhūr of men, the higher Lokas of the Siddhas and the Lower Lokas of the Asuras and Nāgas.

"All actions (Karma) bear fruits in the Trilokī. Mahar, Jana and Tapas are attained by Yoga, Tapas and Renunciation. My abode (Vaikuntha, which is beyond the Seven Lokas) is attained by Bhakti Yoga.

"All beings in this Universe wedded to karma are made by Me, who as Kāla am the Dispenser of all karma, to merge out of or to dive down in the flow of Gunas (*i.e.* they are made to go up to the higher Lokas or to come down to the lower Lokas).

"All things big or small, thick or thin are pervaded by Prakriti and Purusha.

"That which is at the beginning and at the end of a thing is also at the middle, as in the case of ornaments and earth-pots, the intervening transformations having a separate existence only for the sake of conventional use (thus the ornaments of gold are called by different names only for temporary uses. But they are gold when the forms are made and destroyed. The forms are all transitory and the ornaments are essentially gold).

"That is only Real which gives rise to the original transformation, which is at the beginning and at the end. Prakriti the material cause, Purusha — that pervades Prakriti and Kāla or periodicity which causes disturbance in the Gunas — these are three in one and I am that three-fold Brahmā. The creative process flows on in order of succession without a break. The multifarious creation unfolds itself to serve the purposes of the jivas and it lasts so long as the period of Preservation continues and so long as Īshvara looks at it.

"The order is reversed in Pralaya, and transformations are merged in the principles from which they proceeded. The body merges in to the food grains. The food grains merge in to the roots of plants. The roots merge into the earth, The earth merges into smell, smell into water, water into Taste, Taste into fire, fire into Form, Form in to Air, Air into Touch, touch into Akāsa and Akāsa into sound.

"The Indriyas merge into the Adhi-daivas. The Adhi-daivas merge into the Manas. Manas merges into Ahankāra.

"Ahankāra merges into Mahat (*i.e.* gives up the unconscious portion and becomes Jiva Śakti and Kriyā Śakti itself. *Śridhara*.)

"Mahat merges into the Gunas.

"The Gunas merge into unmanifested Prakriti. Prakriti merges into Kāla. Kāla merges into Jiva. Jiva merges into Ātmā. Ātmā rests in self.

"When these processes are meditated on, there is no delusion."

SATVA RAJAS AND TAMAS.

SKANDHA XI. CHAP. 25.

"*Sama* or Control of the mind, *Dama* or Control of the Senses, forbearance, discrimination, tapas, truthfulness, compassion, memory, renunciation, contentment, faith, shame and charitableness are the attributes proper of *Satva*. Selfish desire, Selfish exertion, pride, discontent, variety, selfish-invocation of the Devas, idea of separateness, material enjoyment, love of excitement, love of fame, derision, power and violence, are the attributes proper of *Rajas*.

"Anger, greed, untruthfulness, cruelty, begging, parading of religion, languor, quarrel, repentance, delusion, grief, dejection, sleep, helplessness, fear and indolence are the attributes proper of *Tamas*.

"The sense of I-ness and My-ness is produced by the mixture of the three Gunas (I have Sama, selfish desire and anger. My Sama, selfish desire and anger. Thus *I* and *My* are common to all the three Gunas. *Śridhara*) All our dealings having the elements of Manas (Sātvic), the Tanmātras (Tāmasic), the Indriyas and the Prānas (Rājasic) in them, proceed from a mixture of the three Gunas. Devotion to Dharma (Sātvic), Kāma (Rājasic) and Artha (Tāmasic), that bears the fruits of faith (Sātvic), attachment (Rājasic) and wealth (Tāmasic) is also based on a mixture of the Gunas.

"The performance of religion for the gratification of desires (Kāmya Dharma which is Rājasic), the performance of the duties of married life (Grihasta Dharma which is Tāmasic) and the performance of the daily and occasional duties assigned to one's position in life (Svadharma which is Sātvic) are based on a union of the three Gunas. Man is Sātvic, when he has got the Sātvic attributes. He is Rājasic when he has got the Rājasic attributes. He is Tāmasic when he has got the Tāmasic attributes.

"When a man or woman worships Me with unselfish devotion and by the performance of duties, he or she is Sātvic.

"The person who worships Me, for the attainment of desires is Rājasic.

"The person who worships Me with a view to do injury to others is Tāmasic.

"Satva, Rajas and Tamas are attributes that grow in the minds of jivas, they are not My attributes.

"When Satva prevails over the other two Gunas, man acquires religiousness, wisdom, and other attributes, as also happiness. When Rajas prevails, it causes distraction, attachment and a sense of separateness. Man acquires karma, fame and wealth. But he becomes miserable.

"When Tamas prevails, delusion, inaction and ignorance follow.

"When the Mind attains calm, the senses become abstemious, the body free from fear and the mind free from attachments, Satva grows up and makes it easy to perceive Me.

"When the mind becomes distracted by actions, and desires multiply, when the senses of action become disordered and the mind always wanders away, Rajas has its hold over man.

"When the mind can not grasp, when it languishes, when even desires do not crop up, and there is indolence, melancholy and ignorance, they all proceed from Tamas.

"With Satva, the Deva element prevails, with Rajas, the Asura element prevails and with Tamas, the Rākshas element prevails.

"The waking is from Satva, dream from Rajas and deep sleep from Tamas.

"By Satva, people go higher and higher up, by Rajas they move about in the middle, and by Tamas they move lower down.

"Satva takes one to Svarga Loka, Rajas to human Loka and Tamas to Naraka. Those who are void of Gunas attain Me.

"Action that is offered up to Me or that is unselfish is Sātvic. Selfish action is Rajasa. Heartless action is Tamasa.

"Sātvic wisdom is that which relates to Ātmā, as separate from the body.

"Rājasic is half perceived wisdom. Tāmasic is wisdom relating to the material universe.

"Wisdom centred in Me is Nirguna or without Gunas.

"Sātvics like to reside in the forest. Rājasics in human habitations and Tāmasics in gambling houses. Houses where I am worshipped are beyond all the Gunas. Births are caused by Guna and Karma. Those who conquer these become devoted to Me and attain my state."

COMPANY.

SKANDHA XI. CHAP. 26.

"King Pururavas was forsaken by Urvasi. He then thought within himself what the body of a woman was composed of, where its beauty lay, and the origin and the end of that body. 'Therefore' said he 'wise men should not associate with women or those that are addicted to women. By contact of the senses with their objects, mind gets disturbed, not otherwise. What you have not seen or heard of before can not disturb your mind. Let not the senses indulge in objects and mind will attain calm.' Keep company with Sādhus.

"Give up bad company. Acquire from the Sādhus devotion to Me and you shall ultimately attain Moksha."

KRIYA YOGA AND IDOL WORSHIP.

SKANDHA XI. CHAP. 27.

(The details will not be interesting to the general reader).

JNĀNA YOGA.

SKANDHA XI. CHAP. 28.

"Do not either praise or blame other men and their actions. Look upon all as one, pervaded by the same Prakriti and the same Purusha. By criticising others, the mind is directed to a false channel and it deviates from the right path. What is good or what is bad of Dvaita? By direct perception, reasoning, self intuition, and scriptural teachings, know every thing in this manifested Universe to have a beginning and an end and to be thus unreal. Therefore free yourself from all attachments. (The ways of acquiring discriminative knowledge are then given in eloquent terms for which read the original).

"Clearing up all doubts by discrimination, the sage should be fixed in the bliss of self, having abstained from every thing else.

"The body of gross matter is not Ātmā. The Indriyas, their guiding Devas, Manas, Buddhi, Chitta and Ahankāra are not Ātmā. The Bhūtas, the Tanmatras and Prakriti are not Ātmā. These do not affect the seer. Whether the clouds gather or disperse, what is that to the Sun.

"Akāsa is not affected by the attributes of air, fire, water and earth nor by the changes of seasons.

"The immutable is not affected by the impurities of Satva, Rajas and Tamas, however often they may cause the birth and rebirth of the Ahan principle.

"But still (the unliberated sage) should avoid contact with the Gunas. He should by firm devotion to Me, cast off all attachments and all passions. When the disease is not properly treated, it gives trouble again and again.

So when attachments are not completely removed and Karma is not counteracted they trouble the imperfect Yogi.

"The yogis that deviate from the path on account of obstacles that are spread out for them by the Devas through men (For the Sruti says: — "The Devas do not like that men should know all this." *Sridhara*) are re-united to the path of Yoga in a better birth through the practices of their former birth.

"The immature Yogi may be overpowered by diseases and other grievances of the body. He should overcome some of them by Yoga concentration (by concentration on the Moon, the Sun and others he should overcome heat cold &c., *Sridhara*), others by prescribed postures accompanied by retention of breath (diseases caused by gaseous derangement are to be overcome by postures, accompanied by retention of breath), and some others by Tapas, Mantra and medicine. He should overcome some evils by meditating on Me, by taking My name, and by making rehearsals about Me. He should overcome other evils by following the lords of Yoga.

"Some practise these to keep themselves young and free from diseases, solely with the object of attaining some Siddhis. This is not approved of by good people. The effort is fruitless. The body has an end. True in following the path of Yoga, the body sometimes becomes free from diseases and infirmities. But the Yogi should put no faith on these Siddhis.

"When the Yogi gives up all desires, becomes fixed in self-bliss, and makes Me his all in all, he is not overcome by obstacles."

BHAKTI YOGA.

SKANDHA XI. CHAP. 29.

Uddhava said: —

"This path of Yoga seems to Me to be difficult of pursuit. Tell me O Achyuta, some means by which man may attain perfection without such exertion. Generally those that try to concentrate their mind become tired at last, being unsuccessful in their attempts. The discriminating sage has

495

recourse to Thy lotus-feet, the fountain of all bliss. Tell me the path that leads to Thee."

Shri Krishna replied: —

"Do all actions for Me and bear me in mind as much as you can. Offer up the mind and all thoughts to Me. Be attached to the duties of Bhāgavatas. Live in sacred lands, where my Bhaktas dwell. Follow what they do — see Me in all beings as well as in self, pure as Akāsa. With the eye of pure wisdom, look upon all beings as my existence and respect them as such. Brāhmana or Chandāla, stealer or giver, big as the sun or small as his ray, tender hearted or cruel, the sage must look upon all alike. Then he shall have neither rivalry, nor jealousy nor reproach for others. His egoism shall also be gone. Mind not the ridicule of friends, mind not the bodily differences that may cause a feeling of shame, but salute even horses, Chandālas, cows and asses. As long as you do not learn to see Me in all beings, do not give up this practice in speech, body and mind. There is not the least chance of failure in the Bhāgavata Path. Even what is otherwise fruitless becomes a Dharma, when it is unselfishly offered up to Me. There is no higher wisdom, no higher cleverness than this that the Real is attained by the Unreal, the Immortal is attained by what is mortal. This is the essence of Brahmā Vidyā.

"Now that you have learned all this give it unto those that are deserving.

"Go Uddhava now to Badari Āsrama and follow what I have said."

THE END.

SKANDHA XI. CHAP. 30.

Uddhava went to Badari. Sri Krishna advised the Yadus to leave Dvāraka. "Let the females, children, and the aged go to Sankha-Uddhara and let us go to Prabhāsa." The Yadu chiefs went to Prabhāsa. They drank the wine called Maireya and got intoxicated. They quarreled and fought with one another. They snatched the fatal reeds and killed one another. Rāma went to the Sea-side and by practicing Samādhi, left this world. All was now over. Sri Krishna sat under an Asvatha tree (religious fig). A huntsman named Jara took Him for a deer and pierced him with a spear, formed of the fatal pestle.

The huntsman then saw Krishna bearing four hands and became terrified. "Fear not" said Sri Krishna "you shall go to heaven." The chariot came down from the heaven and took up the huntsman.

Daruka, the charioteer of Sri Krishna traced Him to the spot.

Sri Krishna asked him to inform all friends at Dvārakā of the death of the Yadu chiefs, the disappearance of Rāma and of His own state. "Do not remain any more at Dvārakā, for the Sea shall swallow it up. Let our parents and all others go to Indraprastha under the protection of Arjuna."

Daruka saluted Krishna and went away.

The Garuda marked chariot of Sri Krishna came from high above. Brahmā and all other Devas gathered to witness the scene.

The Lord disappeared from the earth and truth, Dharma, forbearance, glory and Lakshmī all followed Him.

There was great rejoicing in the heavens. The Devas sang and flowers rained.

Daruka gave the information to Vāsudeva and Ugrasena. All came to see the place of the occurrence. Vāsudeva died of grief. Some of the ladies followed their husbands to death. Those that remained were escorted by Arjuna to Indraprastha. He installed Vajra as the successor of the Yadu chiefs. The Pāndavas made Parikshit their successor and left Indraprastha for the Final Journey.

END OF THE ELEVENTH SKANDHA.

THE TWELFTH SKANDHA.

SKANDHA XII. CHAP. 2.

When the present Kali Yuga will be about to end, Bhagavān will incarnate as KALKI. He will take birth at Sambhal as the son of Vishnu-Yasas.

On His advent, Satya Yuga will make its appearance. The Sun, the Moon and the Jupiter will then enter together the constellation of Pushyā. (Jupiter enters the constellation of Pushyā in Cancer every twelve years, and there may be a conjunction of that planet with the Sun and the Moon on new Moon nights, but the text here means the *entering together* of the three. *Śridhara*.)

One thousand one hundred and fifteen years will expire from the birth of Rājā Parikshit to the beginning of King Nanda's reign. (But in the detailed account given in the Bhāgavata Purāna, the period comes up to 1448 years, as shewn by Śridhara.)

Of the Seven Rishis (forming the constellation of the Great Bear), the two that are first seen to rise above the horizon have through their middle point

498

a correspondence with some constellation (in the Zodiac). The Rishis remain united to that constellation for one hundred mortal years.

At present (*i.e.* when Sukadeva was reciting Bhāgavata to Rājā Parikshit), the Rishis are united to Maghā.

The form of the Great Bear or the constellation of the Seven Rishis is given below.

```
6      5            ×
×      ×            1

×      ×      ×     ×
7      4      3     2
```

Sridhara gives the following names :—
  No. 1 is Marichi.
  No. 2 is Vasishtha with Arundhati.
  No. 3 is Angiras.
  No. 4 is Atri.
  No. 5 is Pulastya.
  No. 6 is Pulaha.
  No. 7 is Kratu.

"Such being the configuration of the Rishis, the two that are first seen to rise above the horizon are Pulaha and Kratu. The longitudinal line passing through the middle point of the line joining them crosses some one of the 27 constellations, Asvini, Bharani and others. The Rishis have their position in that constellation for one hundred years." *Śridhara.*

So soon as the Krishna named divine body of Vishnu ascended the heavens, Kali entered this Loka. As long as the Lord of Lakshmī touched this Earth with His lotus feet, Kali could not overtake the planet. (While Sri Krishna was still on this Earth, Kali appeared in its Sandhyā or Dawn. When Sri Krishna disappeared, the Sandhyā period was over, and the period proper of Kali set in. *Śridhara*).

The Yuga shall become darker and darker, as the Seven Rishis will pass on from Maghā to Pūrva-Āshādhā, *i.e.*, till the period of king Nanda. (The darkness will go on increasing till the reign of king Pradyotana. It will still go on increasing very much till the reign of king Nanda. *Śridhara.*

This gives us a cycle of 1,000 years. The line of the Ecliptic is divided into 27 constellations, which form the 12 signs of the Zodiac. Each sign of the Zodiac contains 9 parts of these constellations, if each constellation be divided into four parts.

Thus Aries contains Asvini, Bharani and 1/4 Krittika;

Taurus contains 3/4 Krittika, Rohini and 1/2 Mrigasiras;

Gemini contains 1/2 Mrigasiras, Ārdrā and 3/4 Punarvasu;

Cancer contains 1/4 Punarvasu, Pushyā and Ashlesha;

Leo contains Magha, Pūrva Falguni and 1/4 Uttar Falguni;

Virgo contains 3/4 Uttara Falguni, Hastā, and 1/2 Chitra;

Libra contains Chitra, Svāti and 3/4 Visākhā;

Scorpio contains 1/4 Visākhā, Anurādhā and Jyeshthā;

Sagittarius contains Mūla, Pūrva Āshādha and 1/4 Uttara Āshādhā;

Capricornus contains 3/4 Uttara Āshādhā, Sravanā, and 1/2 Dhanishtha;

Aquarius contains 1/2 Dhanishthā, Sata-bhishā, and 3/4 Pūrva Bhādrapada;

Pisces contains 1/4 Pūrva Bhādrapada, Uttara Bhādrapada and Revati.

Abhijit is included in Uttarāshādhā and Sravana. From Maghā to Pūrva Āshādhā there are eleven constellations. This gives a cycle of 1,000 years.

The reference to king Nanda's reign leaves no doubt as to the cycle being one of 1,000 years, for the period is given in this very chapter as 1,115 years.

The lines of Kshatriya kings have been given in the Purāma, The lines of Brāhmanas, Vaisyas and Sudras are to be similarly known.

Devāpi, brother of Santanu and Maru of the line of Ikshvāku are now waiting at Kalapa. They will appear towards the end of Kali Yuga and will again teach Varna and Āsrama Dharma. (They will start again the lines of divine kings which came to an end in the Kali Yuga. *Śridhara.*)

PRALAYA.

SKANDHA XII. CHAP. 4.

Four thousand Yugas form one day of Brahmā. This is also the period of one Kalpa, during which fourteen Manus appear. The night of Brahmā follows for an equally long period. The three worlds — Bhūr, Bhuvar and Svar then come to an end. This is called *Naimittika* Pralaya. Drawing the universe within self, Nārāyana sleeps at the time over Ananta and Brahmā sleeps too. (*Nimitta* is cause. Naimittika is proceeding frome some cause. This Pralaya procedes from the sleep of Brahmā as a *cause*).

When two Parārddhas of years expire, the seven subdivisions of Prakriti (Mahat, Ahankāra, and the five Tanmatras) become subject to dissolution. (The life period of Brahmā is two Parārddhas). This is called *Prākritika* Pralaya. When this dissolving factor comes in, the whole combination known as the Cosmic Egg breaks up. (As the subdivisions of Prakriti as well as the Cosmic Egg which is formed by their combination become all dissolved, this Pralaya is called Prākritika Pralaya). With the advent of this Pralaya, there will be no rains for one hundred years. Food will disappear. People will devour one another. The Sun will draw in moisture from the seas, from the body, and from the earth, but will not give it back. The fire called Samvartaka, arising from the mouth of Shankarshana, will consume the Pātālas. Winds will blow for one hundred years, followed by rain for another hundred years. The universe will be covered by one sheet of water. Water will draw in earth, fire will draw in water, and so on till Pradhāna in due time will devour all the Gunas. Pradhāna is not measured by time, and it does not undergo transformation. Beginningless, endless, unmanifested, eternal, the cause of all causes, without diminution, it is beyond the reach of Gunas, the rootless root, that passes comprehension, like the void.

Jnāna is the ultimate resort of Buddhi (the perceiver or knower), the Indriyas or senses (perception, knowledge or the instruments of perception and knowledge) and the objects (things perceived and known). It is Jnāna alone that appears in this threefold form. That which is subject to perception, which in its nature is not separate from its cause, and which has both beginning and end is no real substance. The lamp, the eye and the object seen are not different from light itself. So Buddhi, the senses and the objects are not separate from the one Truth (Brahmān, for they all proceed from Brahmān), but Brahmān is quite separate from all others. Wakefulness, dream and dreamless sleep are all states of Buddhi. They are all transitory, O king. The diversity appears in Pratyagātma (the separate self). The clouds appear and disappear in space, even as the universes appear and disappear in Brahmān. Of all forms, the common element is the only reality. But the forms seem to have an existence of their own independently of the primal element. The threads that form the cloth look separate from the cloth itself. All that appears as cause and effect is unreal, for there is interdependence, and there is both beginning and end.

The transformations can not exist without the light of Ātmā. If they are self-manifest however, they are not in any way different from Ātmā itself.

Do not think Ātmā is many, (as there is Ātmā in every being). It is ignorance to think so. The space confined in a pot and the limitless space are one and the same, even so the sun and its image in water, the air inside and outside.

Men call gold by different names, according to the different ornaments it forms. So the language of the Vedas and the language of ordinary men give different names to Bhagavān.

The cloud that is generated by the sun, that appears by the light of the sun, that is in fact rays of the sun so transformed stands between the eye and the sun. Even so Ahankāra, proceeding from Brahmān, manifested by

Brahmān, even a part of Brahmān, eclipses the perception of Brahmān by Jiva.

When the cloud disappears, the eye perceives the sun. When Ahankāra, the *upādhi* of Ātmā, disappears by discrimination, then the Jiva perceives "I am Brahmān."

When by discrimination, such as this, the tie of unreal Ahankāra is cut as under, and the unfailing perception of Ātmā becomes fixed, it is called *Ātyantika* Pralaya.

(Ātyantika is from Atyanta = ati+anta, the very last. After this Pralaya, which is individual and not general, one does not return to life in the universe. It is the final liberation of a man from the limitations of life in Brahmānda).

Every day all beings, from Brahmā downwards, undergo according to some seers of subtleties states of beginning and end.

These beginnings and ends are caused by the changes in states of all beings subject to transformation, changes that follow the flow of time. (One does not grow adult or old in one day. The change must be going on constantly. The fruit does not ripen in one day. But the process of ripening day by day is not perceptible. Water flows in a continued stream but the water particles constantly change at a given space. So the lamp burns and the flame looks one and the same though the particles that ignite do constantly change. Even so our body is not the same from day to day. There is a change going on every moment of our life. Particles of the body are rejected every day and they are replaced by new particles. There is the beginning with our new particles, and an end or Pralaya with the old particles.) This is called NITYA Pralaya. (Nitya means constant).

Pralaya is thus fourfold — Nitya, Naimittika, Prakritika and Atyantika.

Such are the stories of Bhagavat as related in the Bhāgavata Purāna.

Rishi Nārāyana first related the Purāna to Nārada, Nārada related it to Vyāsa and Vyāsa to Suka. Suta heard the Purāna from Sukadeva, when he related it to Rājā Parikshit, and he expounded it to the assembly of Rishis at Naimisha, headed by Sounaka.

THOUGHTS ON PRALAYA.

Prakriti changes its forms and states. The body disintegrates into particles, particles into molecules, and molecules into atoms. Solid becomes liquid, liquid becomes gaseous and gaseous becomes ultra-gaseous. Life manifests itself through the endless varieties of Prakriti and becomes manifold in its manifestations. The hard mineral matter does not admit the mineral life to be expressed in any other way than by a fixed form. The more plastic vegetable matter shews vegetable life in all the activities of life and growth. Subtler matter appears in the animals and makes the sensing of the object world possible. Even sublter matter becomes the basis of brain activities. The Prākritic basis of the mind is two-fold in its character Ahankāra and Mahat. When the mind is capable of thinking only from the standpoint of one life and one birth only, it is limited by Ahankāra matter. When that limit is overcome, mind is on the plane of Mahat. Individuality is not lost, but the individual has consciousness of all births, *i.e.* consciousness on the plane of the universe. Such consciousness does not normally exist in Trilokī. When a man becomes normally conscious on the plane of Mahat, he is carried to Mahar Loka and becomes a Rishi. Bhrigu is such a Rishi. The acquirement of such consciousness is the object of life evolution in our solar system. When the solar system is destroyed, it is the Manasic consciousness that alone survives. The three Lokas — Bhūr, Bhuvar and Svar are destroyed, The Prākritic forms and states of these three Lokas become destroyed and the different states of consciousness corresponding to those forms and states finally disappear. The harvest of Manasic evolution, which is the only harvest reaped by means of one solar system is stored in Mahar Loka. But when the three lower Lokas are destroyed, the flames of dissolution reach even Mahar Loka and all the gains of a Kalpa's evolution are transferred to the higher plane of Jana Loka. This is therefore the highest plane of our consciousness. The highest evolved beings of the previous solar system could not after Pralaya go beyond Jana Loka, and their consciousness was the consciousness of Jana Loka. When our earth was formed and when they came down in time for further evolution, they brought down their highest consciousness with them as a possibility, for it was obscured in their entrance to Trilokī. As the soul gathers spiritual strength in Svarga Loka after death, so the disembodied soul after Prayala gathers spiritual strength in Jana Loka or the Loka of Kumāras. "When the three Lokas are consumed by fire from the mouth of Sankarshana, afflicted by the heat, Bhrigu and others go to Jana Loka" III-II-XXX. The Lord of Yoga goes by means of Sushumna through the radiant path in his subtle body and at last reaches Mahar Loka, where Bhrigu and other Rishis who live for one Kalpa remain. "Then seeing the Trilokī consumed by fire from the mouth of Ananta he goes towards that supreme abode, which is adorned by the chariots of great Siddhas, and which lasts for the whole life period of Brahmā." (II-2-XXVI).

Those who did not reach the Manasic state, in the last Kalpa were no acquisitions to the higher planes of Brahmānda, which stand over the three mortal planes, where all experience is to be gathered. Those who developed the Manasic state were gathered to the third of the higher planes, Jana Loka, because further development was possible, nay it was a necessity, in the Trilokī that was to come. But there were others, who did not quite reach the Manasic state, but they were still on the way to acquire such state, and in fact they acquired the human form. They were also preserved to carry out a certain purpose in the life evolution of the coming Kalpa which will be shortly mentioned. How they were preserved, the Purānas do not speak of. They became the Pitris of the present Kalpa. The Pitris reached different states of development and were therefore classed under seven heads. Some of them had developed the fire in them and some were without the fire. "Agnishvatta, Barhishad, Sōmapa, and Ajyapa are Pitris with fire; the others are without fire. They were all wedded to Svadha, the daughter of Daksha." IV-1-III.

The mention of the word "fire" requires a little explanation. The Upanishads say that the three mortal Lokas of form Bhūr, Bhuvar and Svar are the transformations of "Tejobanna" *i.e.* of fire, water and earth. The other two elements do not enter into the constitution of forms. The element earth predominates on the plane of Bhūr or the material plane. Water is supreme on Bhuvar or the Astral plane. Our Kamic tendencies proceed from the presence of water in us. Fire is the element of Svarga or the Mental plane. Fire devas are therefore the highest devas of Trilokī. The forty-nine forms of fire are therefore so many forms of consciousness. Some of the Pitris developed fire in them, *i.e.* they developed the principle of mind in them, in however rudimental a form it might be.

Devas and Rishis were also preserved. Jana Loka is the Loka of Kumāras. We shall therefore call the souls preserved in Jana Loka as Kumāras, or Kumaric souls.

Commenting on the fourth sloka, twelfth chapter, Third Skandha, Śridhara says: — "Sanaka and others are not created in every Kalpa. The mention of their creation has reference to the Brahmā Kalpa, *i.e.* the first Kalpa. In fact the objects of Mukhya creation and others are brought into existence in every Kalpa. Sanaka and others are only created in the Brahmā Kalpa and they follow the other Kalpas." The Mukhya creation has reference to chapter 10, Skandha III. It is the same as Urdha Srotas (p. 25). Śridhara means to say that plants, animals and men are only created in every Kalpa.

The Kumaric souls of the last Kalpa that went to Jana Loka have to play the most prominent part in the present Kalpa and they are the heroes of our solar system. Their stay at Jana Loka was only a fitting preparation for the most responsible work of the present Kalpa. The Īshvara of our system, addressing Puranjana, said: — "Wishing to have an abode, drawn to earthly enjoyments, thou didst leave me. But, o great one, both I and thou were swans (Hansa) and friends in the Manas Lake. We dwelt there without any abode, for one thousand years." IV. 28 LIV. "One thousand years" is indicative of Pralaya, which lasts for one thousand yuga cycles. In Pralaya, the kumaric soul had no body *i.e.* no abode. The body separates Jiva from Īshvara. Without the impediment, the obstacle of the body, without any obscuring agency, the Jiva meets Īshvara face to face in Jana Loka, and being both essentially alike become friends. Nārada says, esoterically the Mānasa Laka is the heart and Hansa means the pure. But in Pralaya, the heart of the Jiva is in Jana Loka, which is the Mānasa or mental Lake. This friendly union of Jiva and Īshvara gives all the promise of the future for the Jiva.

What is not preserved in Naimittika Pralaya, the forms of the past kalpa, are all borne in the mind of Brahmā as images. It is the mind of Brahmā that reproduces the forms of the previous creation. The image of all that was remains in the mind of Brahmā. Creation in Brahmā Kalpa is not the same as creation in the succeeding Kalpas. In Brahmā Kalpa, all the seven Lokas, and the dwellers of all the planes are created. In the succeeding Kalpas, the three Lokas and their dwellers only are created.

The Naimittika Pralaya comes on, as Brahmā sleeps.

This Pralaya corresponds to our physical death. When we die, the body is destroyed. Just as when the universe bodied Brahmā goes to sleep, His Trilokī body is destroyed. Men go after death first to Bhuvar Loka, and then to Svarga Loka. At Pralaya, the Mānasika Jivas first go to Mahar Loka and then to Jana Loka.

The Naimittika Pralaya affords the greatest relief to Jivas. It makes up for all the ups and downs of manifested life, for all miseries, all sorrows, all sufferings and all disappointments. Īshvara can do more for Jivas in Pralaya, than in manifestation. He gives company to those, who by their advancement reach Jana Loka, There is the Īshvara of our system or Brahmānda and there is the Īshvara of many systems.

The Īshvara of many systems, "Bhagavān Himself" is the First Purusha. He is the manifestor of the Tatvas, the first Principles, the Karan or causal creation, which enter into the constitution of all the solar systems or Brahmāndas. When He wishes to become many, to appear through many manifestations, to bring up all unto Himself and His own state, through œons and œons of cosmic manifestation, though it might be, the Tatvas start forth into activity and form an ocean by themselves. Many solar systems are evolved out of this Karan Samudra or the ocean of the causes and each system gets its Īshvara, the Second Purusha. That Second Purusha becomes three fold — Brahmā, Vishnu and Śiva, for the Creation, Preservation and Dissolution of His own Universe. He is Virāt Purusha or the universe bodied, Nārāyana seated on the waters of Karana Samudra, and Sahasra Sirsha Purusha or the thousand headed Purusha of the Upanishads. "All this, the past, present and future is this Purusha. The universe is pervaded by Him As Prana (*i.e.* the sun, for Prana is the solar deity according to the Sruti. *Śridhara*) by illumining his own circle illumines the outside as well, so Purusha by illumining his Virāt body illumines the inside and outside of this Brahmānda as well. I (Brahmā) create by His direction, Śiva destroys, under His control, as Vishnu, He preserves this universe He is the primal Avatāra." II. 6.

"First of all, Bhagavān took form as Purusha for the creation of the Lokas form made by Mahat and others, having 16 parts. (*Mahat and others* — Mahat, Ahankāra, and the Tanmatras. 16 parts the eleven Indriyas and the 5 elements. Though this is not the form of Bhagavān meaning the First Purusha still for the Upāsanā in Virāt form of the Virāt Purusha who indwells all Jivas, this is given. *Śridhara*). (In the Padma Kalpa), Brahmā, the Lord of Prajāpatis, appeared in the lotus that rose out of the navel of (this Purusha), who while lying down on the ocean, spread the sleep of Samādhi all round. The Lokas are but parts of His body. His form is pure and intensified Satva. The Yogins perceive Him by their vision of wisdom, as one looking wonderful with a thousand feet, thighs, hands and mouths, with a thousand heads, ears, eyes and noses, glittering with a thousand crowns, and ornaments. This (Virāt Purusha) is the immutable seed and final resort of the many Avatāras. Brahmā is His part. Marichi and other Prajāpatis are parts of Brahmā. So through parts of His part, Devas, animals and men are created. (He does not appear and disappear like other Avatāras. He is the end not only of the Avatāras, but of all beings.*Śridhara*.)" I-3.

Brahmā appeared in the lotus, it is said, in the last Kalpa, which from this event is named Pādma Kalpa. How Brahmā appeared out of Nārāyana in the previous Kalpas is not given. That he appeared in our Kalpa in the same way as in the last Kalpa is evident, as no difference is noted. Brahmā took up the creation, which was two-fold — direct or Mānasa and indirect or through Prajāpatis and Manu. The creation or bringing into manifestation of those that had been preserved at Pralaya is direct or Mānasa. The mind born sons of Brahmā took up positions in the universe of duty and responsibility and in this Kalpa they have not to look to themselves, but to others. Their own evolution is not a matter of their concern. The innumerable Monads were created through Manu and the real history of the Kalpa is the history of their evolution.

First there was the process of involution. There was no form and forms had to be first brought forth. Limitation after limitation had to the imposed, to chain life in forms. For when set forms were arrived at with set organs, Jivas could be trusted with independent action.

No energy is spent in vain in the economy of the universe. Each monadic flow as it appeared in the universe could be carried on to a certain stage, by one common guiding influence. This requires a little explanation.

Each particle of each Tatva is alive. The Tatvic life is the life of the first Purusha. But the particles combine, and the power of combination proceeds from the life of the second Purusha, the Ishvara of our system. Every combination however large has the life of Ishvara in it and it is that life which keeps up the combination. Each combination for the time being has its ruler, who is the viceroy of Ishvara, and who is called the Monad of that combination. Monad is Jivātma or Jiva Ātmā or Ātmā as limited by every Jiva.

The combination transforms, but the Monad remains constant. The vegetable becomes animal, and the animal becomes man, but one Monad runs through all these transformations.

By rulership over higher and higher combinations the Monad or Jivātma, ultimately approaches the state of Ishvara Himself and that is the goal of evolution in this universe.

Whenever a combination is formed, there is one life governing that combination — the life of the ruler of that combination. Ail other lives have to surrender themselves completely and entirely to that one life. This is the law and we have to bow down our heads to the inevitable. There is life in every cell that composes the human body. But the cell lives are all subordinated to the life of the man, the Jivātma ruling the combination that forms the man. So long as the cell is attached to the human combination, it has no independence whatsoever. And this is to the immense benefit of the cells themselves. They receive the impress of souls much more evolved than their own and are able to evolve themselves at a much more rapid rate, than if they had been left to themselves. This is the law of giving and taking, the law of sacrifice, the Yajna which is the essence of creation. And even as men approach the state of Ishvara, they have to surrender themselves completely to Him and to merge themselves in His existence.

The Jivic or Monadic flow first appears on the plane of Svarga, it comes down to Bhūvar and then to Bhūr, to appear finally in the mineral Kingdom of our Earth. This process of coming down does not require separate guidance for separate combinations. The downward flow is homogeneous. It is carried on under the guidance of the Prajāpatis. It is all involution during this process taking in grosser and grosser matter and not rejecting anything. Rudra had no work to do during the earliest stages of monadic life. The mineral Kingdom appeared and the Himalayan chain reared up its head. The legend says the sons of Himalaya had wings on and they could move about but the Devas cut down their wings and they became fixed. No doubt the mineral Kingdom hardened and became immobile in time. The immobility of the mineral Kingdom, the final reach of matter in its downward course was the turning point in the life history of Jivas. Their foetal stage was over and they were now born into the Kalpa, as it were.

There was need for separation now, for the rejection of particles and the drawing in of new ones, and Durga appeared as the daughter of Himalaya.

She became wedded to Śiva once more and since then there was change continually going on in all forms of life, that evolved out of the mineral Kingdom. There was continual adjustment of external and internal conditions, called life. The vegetable appeared, the animal appeared and the man appeared. The life process means continual transformation. Forms changed and dissolved. Change is continually going on all round and is called Nitya Pralaya.

During the transformation that goes on, combinations are guided by rulers, who are the Pitris. They lead the combinations on till the human form is reached. When the human form is reached each combination is a man. The highest of the Pitris can give only germinal Manas. When the Pitris give to the combination, all that they could give, their work is over, for this Kalpa.

Then come the Kumaric souls, the Puranjanas from the Mānasa Laka (P. 89). They find the abode ready made and leaving their friend and companion they enter their chosen abodes. There are nine gate ways in that abode, and every enjoyment reaches Puranjana through those gate ways. He becomes mad in the pursuit of enjoyments. He forgets himself. He

forgets his friend the eternal companion of Jiva. He identifies himself with
the abode. He thinks that he is inseparable from that abode. So he goes on
and on hopelessly in his course of riotous joy and the Friend whom he
forgets gives him rebuff for every joy that he meets. The rebuffs at last
make him a little attentive. The friend then speaks through the Vedas, the
Smritis through sages and at last He comes down Himself as an Avatāra.

The Eternal Friend first allows Puranjana to run on in the midst of
enjoyments, just as he likes. If he goes beyond the limits of temperance
and moderation he gets some unpleasant experience. If he does something
wrong, he feels the painful consequence. The sting of pain makes
Puranjana ponder over what he does. He registers the pleasurable and
painful experiences and reasons about the causes and effects. He tries to
know what is right and what is wrong.

With the power of discrimination in its infancy, with the "enjoyment"
nature or the self-seeking Asuric element too strong in him, Puranjana, the
Kumaric soul, is helpless. He is drifted away, though sometimes much
against his will.

The Friend comes to the rescue. The Devas and Asuras combine and with
their joint efforts, the ocean of Milk is churned, and the Goddess of
Evolution, the Energy of Vishnu, makes Her divine appearance in our
universe. The Devas become more than a match for the Asuras. The
Vaivasvata Manvantara steps in, the Manvantara teeming with the fate of
man and of the universe. Īshvara, the eternal friend of Puranjana, is most
busy in the Vaivasvata Manvantara. Every effort is made to raise humanity
to a higher level and to open out all the possibilities of man.

First, the enjoyments of Svarga are held out before the rising vision of men
as an allurement. Man admires those enjoyments and makes every effort to
attain them. The Vedic sacrifice is revealed to Pururavas, who becomes
mad after Urvasi, the nymph of Svarga. Later on, the heavenly cow,
Surabhi, attracts Visvāmitra. And he becomes the chief actor in the
promulgation of Vedic sacrifice. In the firmness of resolve, in the bold and
determined pursuit of objects, and in the intolerance of inferiority,
Visvāmitra stands prominently out as an example to humanity, for all ages

to come and it is meet and proper that in the next Manvantara, he will act as one of the seven sages guiding the affairs of the universe.

The Karma Kānda of the Vedas is a monument of Visvamitara's gigantic efforts for the good of humanity. Īshvara made revelations. He prompted the sages.

If the Karma Kānda holds out the allurements of Svarga life, it lays down rules and restrictions at the same time, that regulate life and beget temperance and moderation. Meritorious acts are enjoined and acts that retard evolution are prohibited. Men do what is good and avoid what is evil, that they may attain heavenly things. They do what is right and shun what is wrong, not because that is the Law, the divine will, but because it gives them some reward. All the same, the mind is trained, the man curbed and regulated. The bitter pill is taken and if the child thinks that it is for the sweetmeat he is only mistaken. When the child grows he knows, that he takes the bitter pill as it is the law of nature that he should do so. Do what is right, because that is the law. Shun what is wrong, because it is against the law. We are all carried forward by the law, and we must willingly give ourselves up to that law. When we do that, we partake ourselves of divine life. The ground had to be prepared for further teachings.

Events in Svarga foreshadow and forestall events that are to transpire on the earth. The Devas and Asuras by their mutual fight in Svarga bring about a state of things which casts its shadow on the earth below.

Two great events happened in Svarga the killing of Vritra, and the deposition of Bali.

Vritra, though an Asura was a votary of Sankarshana, the Shankara aspect of Vishnu. Vritra was great in all respects and his wisdom extracted the admiration of Indra. But he represented the idea of personal self in Jiva, which is so strong-rooted, and which is the hardest thing to over come. Vritra was killed by a weapon, which is no other than the most willing and ready sacrifice of personal self by Dadhīchi.

Bali, the Asura king, ungrudgingly gave all that he had to Vāmana. The Asura had become so great both in intellect and in spirituality, that there was no question of killing him or of his being overpowered by the Devas. The Asuras and Devas both combined to make Svarga, the store-house of spiritual life. The Asuras by their willing surrender permitted the Devas to have entire hold of Svarga. By this sacrifice, they established their indisputable right to Svarga, in the broad dispensation of providence and in the succeeding Manvantara, Bali is to become the Indra of the Devas.

Vāmana was the same as Lord Sri Krishna on our earth. If diplomacy had succeeded so easily below as above, if the Asura chiefs on earth had behaved as splendidly as Bali in Svarga, the horrors and heartrending scenes of Kurukshetra could have been avoided. The same result was however brought about in Svarga as it was subsequently brought about on the Earth. The actor was the same, the diplomacy was the same, only the result of diplomacy was different on the different planes. The deposition of Bali was bloodless while the deposition of Duryodhana was a bloody one.

Coming down to Earth let us see how events in Svarga were followed up on the terrestrial plane.

Two great human Avatāras came, one the ideal and the other the apostle of unselfishness. But we must take a running survey of the Avatāras as a whole.

Vishnu appeared on Earth Himself, through His direct manifestations called Avatāras. Ten of them have been specially picked out as Great Avatāras, though no specification has been made in the Bhāgavata Purāna.

There were three great Asuric movements in this Kalpa, caused by the three successive incarnations of Jaya and Vijaya. And these gave our four great Avatāras.

Hiranyāksha was killed by Varaha, Hiranyakasipu was killed by Nrisinha. Rāvana and Kumbhakarna were killed by Rāma. Sisupāla and Dantavakra were killed by Sri Krishna. Kūrma was a great Avatāra as He prepared the way for the spiritual regeneration of the universe, by the Churning of the ocean of Milk.

Vāmana was a great Avatāra as He reclaimed the Trilokī from the Asuras.

Parasurāma and Buddha did work, which revolutionised the whole humanity

Kalki will give the final blow to the Asuric element in us.

Matsya is important with reference to our own Manvantara. Every Manvantara is followed by a deluge, which destroys the existing continents and swallows up all living beings. When the last Manvantara was over, our Manu saved the germs of creation with the help of Matsya. Opinion is divided as to whether there is Pralaya after every Manvantara. The Bhāgavata Purāna says when there was deluge (sanplava) following the Chakshusha Manvantara, Vishnu assumed the form of Matsya. Commenting on this, Śridhara says there is no Pralaya at the end of a Manvantara. There may not be such a Pralaya at the end of a Manvantara as happens at the end of a Kalpa. But other Purānas speak of some sort of Pralaya on the expiry of every Manvantara. Sūrya Siddhanta, the renowned work on Astronomy, also says: — "There is a period called Sandhi (the meet between two Manvantaras) measured by the period of one Satya Yuga, followed by another Manvantara. There is deluge by water then."

The Avatāras of Vishnu infuse more and more of Satva into men, that they may become Satvika. Increasing Satva put down Rajas and Tamas in man and makes him divine.

But of all these Avatāras two stand out most prominently one the ideal and the other the apostle of unselfishness. The brightest luminary of the solar line held out in His life, an example of unselfishness, of purity of character and of scrupulous regard to duty, an example that is the admiration of all people in all ages, as perfect as the limits of humanity will allow and as elevated as the loftiest ideal of human character may be, unsurpassed in its pathetic grandeur, unrivalled in the straight forward pursuit of duty along a most thorny and uneven path. The divine founder of Dvārakā of the Lunar line asserted Himself as the supreme Īshvara, He took up the reins of Trilokī in His own hands, the Devas installed Him as the king of Svarga or Govinda, and men on earth had now to look up to Him only and not to the Devas for their guidance. For men had now to pass the limits of Trilokī, and the friend of Puranjana came down Himself to hold out the torch of divine light. Sri Krishna laid down the triple path of Karma, Bhakti and

Jnāna, and shewed the relative importance of each. His teachings are perfect, thorough and exhaustive. Ever since His manifestation, those teachings have been re-iterated in a thousand forms, they have been adapted to different powers of understanding and all the modern scriptures of Hinduism have grown up, round the central point of those teachings. Men had no longer to complain of teachings. They had to follow those teachings now and to live up to them. They had to begin with unselfishness, and end with liberation. New vistas opened out before the growing spiritual vision of men, vistas of new worlds, new planes, of masters of Yoga and wisdom, forming every link between man and Ishvara. Possibilities became realities. Liberation was no longer a word of the lips.

Now liberation is a relative term. First there may be liberation from the bonds of Trilokī only. Or it may be from the limitations of Janaloka which was the highest possibility with which the Jiva started. Or it may be liberation from the bonds of the Brahmānda itself. The last liberation is again two fold in its character. There may be liberation from all concrete things and all ideas, including the idea of Ishvara Himself or the liberation may lead to the great Ishvara from whom many solar systems proceed. Mukti is not only liberation from bondage. It is also something more. It is an acquisition, Starting from the plane of Jana Loka, the Kumaric soul acquires higher and higher possibilities. He may transcend Jana Loka. He may transcend even the Satya Loka. But passage across Satya Loka is not easy in this Kalpa. Mukti in its fullest and highest sense means freedom from all limitations caused by Prakriti, caused by Time and Space and identification with Brahmān, who is absolute bliss, absolute consciousness and absolute existence beyond the limits of Time and Space. This is called Atyantika Pralaya or absolute dissolution. But this Mukti lean never be obtained till all the duties of a man are performed. These duties are nothing else but sacrifices or Yajna. Man must perform each one of his duties he must perform all that he owes to himself, to all other beings, and last of all the highest duty he owes to the Ishvara of the Universe the Lord of Sacrifice, Yajnesvara Himself, "Adhiyajna am I, here in the body, best of living beings."

The Bhāgavatas do not care to go beyond the Yajna Purusha, They do not care to leave the life of sacrifice, as long as their Īshvara stands out as the embodiment of all sacrifice.

"Salutation to Thee, Bhagavān, let me meditate on Vāsudeva. Salutations to Pradyumna, Aniruddha and to Sankarshana. He who, by knowing these *mūrtis* in the *mūrtiless*, whose only *mūtrti* is mantra makes offerings to Yajna Purusha, is the complete seer." I. 5. 37 "When the Indriyas," said Kapila, "that manifest the objects of external and internal perception, become trained by the performance of Vedic Karma, their spontaneous Vritti (or function) in a man of concentrated mind is in Satva which is the same as Vishnu. This Vritti which is void of all selfishness is Bhakti in Bhagavāna. It is superior to Mukti. It instantly destroys the Kosha, as the digestive fire consumes food. The devoted have no yearning for that Mukti which makes the Jiva one with Me. But they prefer ever to talk with each other about Me, to exert themselves for My sake and ever to meditate on me. Mukti comes to them unasked. My Vibhutis, the eight Siddhis, and all the glory of the highest Lokas are theirs though they want them not. I am their Teacher, their Friend, their companion, their all. So even Kala can not destroy them."

Again, "The devoted spurn Salokya, Sarshti, Samipya, Sarupya and Sayujya, even when offered to them and they prefer to serve Bhagavān ever and ever. Compassion and friendliness to all beings are the essential qualifications of the devoted. They must be humble respectful and self controlled. They must pass their days in hearing and reciting the glory of Bhagavān." Kapila makes the following classification as to the final destiny of men (p. 46):

1. Those who selfishly perform their Dharma and worship Devas and Pitris go to Sōma Loka, and after partaking of Sōma, they are again re-born. Their Lokas are destroyed with the daily Pralaya of Brahmā.

2. The worshippers of Hiranya-garbha (Brahmā) reach Brahmā Loka or Satya Loka and there wait for two Parārddhas *i.e.* for the life time of Brahmā and upon the final dissolution of the Brahmānda, they enter with Hiranya-garbha, the Eternal Supreme Purusha, who is supreme Bliss and their sense of individuality becomes then lost.

3. "Brahmā with Marichi and other Rishis, with Kumāras and other lords of Yoga, and with Siddhas who are leaders of Yoga, do by their unselfish action, and at the same time the retention of their individuality, and their vision of separateness reach Saguna Brahmā or the Second Purusha, who is the Īshvara of our system. And when Kala, as an aspect of Īshvara, causes a disturbance in the Gunas on the approach of the creative period they are born again just as they had been before. (They are born because of their individuality and their vision of separateness. They are born in the same state on account of their non-attachment and their unselfishness. *Śridhara*). As long as the Trilokī lasts, they enjoy all the divine things of Satya Loka, according to their Karma. (And when the Trilokī is destroyed, they attain the Saguna Purusha, who is First Avatāra. *Śridhara*). When the Gunas are disturbed again they come back (i.e. they revert to their former posts respectively. *Śridhara*)" III 32 xii-xv.

4. Those who unselfishly perform their duties and give themselves up entirely to the Supreme Purusha void of all attachment and all egoism, calm, tranquil and pure in the mind go through the gateway of the Sun to the all pervading Purusha, the Lord of all, the material and efficient cause of all this.

Commenting on II 2 xxviii, Śridhara says: — "There are three courses for those that go to Brahmā Loka. Those who go by the excellence of their merits, become holders of responsible positions in the next Kalpa, according to their respective merits. Those who go there by worshipping Hiranya-garbha and others, become liberated along with Brahmā. Those who are worshippers of Bhagavān, pierce the Brahmānda at will and reach the State of Vishnu."

The classification is the same as made by Kapila.

Hiranya-garbha Upāsanā, which was prevalent at one time is now out of use. It was the worship of the Life aspect of Īshvara, as manifested in the Solar system. There is a higher duty, the highest duty of a Jiva manifested in this universe, to realise that this universe itself is a part of a big universe, and there is Īshvara of that big universe Bhagavān Himself and to surrender one self completely up to Him in pure love and devotion. He will not then be of this universe, but he will be of many universes, he will transcend the limits of all the seven planes of our system at will. What his work then will be, it is for Bhagavān to say not for him. The work of Bhagavān is his work, the life of Bhagavān is his life. He becomes a Bhāgavata. The Gopis are ideal Bhāgavatas and the Vrindāvana Lilā is the consummation on this earth of the relation of a Bhāgavata with Bhagavān. This to all Bhaktas is the highest form of Mukti.

To the Bhakta, there is no Mukti, without the universe and the lord of universe.

Forget the universe, forget every thing, only meditate on the eternal unchanging element in you, be fixed in that and that only and you attain Atyantika Pralaya.

PEACE BE TO ALL.

Index

A

T

Made in United States
Orlando, FL
29 November 2021

10860867R00332